Cultures of Insecurity

BORDERLINES

A BOOK SERIES CONCERNED WITH REVISIONING GLOBAL POLITICS
Edited by David Campbell and Michael J. Shapiro

Cultures of Insecurity

*States, Communities,
and the Production of Danger*

**JUTTA WELDES, MARK LAFFEY, HUGH GUSTERSON,
AND RAYMOND DUVALL, EDITORS**

FOREWORD BY GEORGE MARCUS

BORDERLINES, VOLUME 14

 University of Minnesota Press

Minneapolis

London

An earlier version of chapter 6 appeared as "The UN Security Council, Indifference, and Genocide in Rwanda," by Michael N. Barnett, in *Cultural Anthropology* 12, no. 4 (November 1997): 551–78; reproduced by permission of the American Anthropological Association. Not for further reproduction.

Published by the University of Minnesota Press
111 Third Avenue South, Suite 290
Minneapolis, MN 55401-2520
http://www.upress.umn.edu

Library of Congress Cataloging-in-Publication Data

Cultures of Insecurity : states, communities, and the production of
    danger / Jutta Weldes . . . [et al.], editors.
        p.   cm. — (Borderlines ; v. 14)
    Includes bibliographical references and index.
    ISBN 978-0-8166-3307-4 (hc : acid-free paper).— ISBN 978-0-8166-3308-1
(pbk : acid-free paper)
        1. International relations—Social aspects.   2. Security, International—
Social aspects.   3. Ethnology.   I. Weldes, Jutta.   II. Series: Borderlines
(Minneapolis, Minn.) ; v. 14.
JZ1251.C854   1999
327.1'01—dc21   99-22491

Printed in the United States of America on acid-free paper

The University of Minnesota is an equal-opportunity educator and employer.

14 13 12 11 10 09 08   10 9 8 7 6 5 4 3 2

Contents

Foreword

GEORGE MARCUS

It was a privilege for me to participate in the final conference of the project that has led to the publication of this book. The energy and acuity of the analyses present in the papers and discussions of the conference have been rarely matched in other projects of the same sort. These projects of the self-critique of disciplines in the humanities and social sciences, conducted from within by their own members and constituencies, taken together mark the effects of a broad-based interdisciplinary critical movement that has had diffuse effects in both the academy and the professions over the past decade and more. As a kind of traveling ethnographic witness and chronicler of this movement and the particular projects of critique that it has inspired within disciplinary sites (Marcus, 1992), beginning with my own early involvement in the critique of anthropology through challenging its authoritative forms of representation (Marcus and Cushman, 1982; Clifford and Marcus, 1986; Marcus and Fischer, 1986; Marcus, 1994a, 1994b), I have been particularly interested in the effects and transformative potential of these various projects of critique in the arenas where they might be thought to have the most difficult opposition and reception. I especially have in mind those projects that seek to alter mainstream habits of thought and practices of work in paradigms of knowledge production, such as science, law, economics, and for this volume, those in the political science specialty of international relations (IR), all of which derive prestige

as the intellectual engines of modern rationality with embedded institutional functions related to governance and social order.

Quite frankly, is there any hope of productive exchange between
practitioners and scholars working within the mainstreams of such
culturally prestigious formations of knowledge production and their
"distaff" or self-consciously critical wings, as represented for IR in
the contributions of this volume? If so, then by what strategies of critique? The relevant frame here for asking these questions is of course
the community of international relations scholarship, but it could
just as well be that of science—of particular sciences, rather—of law,
of business, of diplomacy, of economics, or of any other discipline/
profession deemed essential to the discourse of reason and whose
self-confidence has historically been guaranteed by this prestige.

I have been an interested observer of and sometime participant in
at least three other projects of critique within extremely rationalist
arenas—the challenge of the Critical Legal Studies movement to
legal education and discourse in the early 1980s (and which has since
dissipated); the recent formation of a *Journal of Feminist Economics*
(begun in 1995) as a broad forum for various cultural critiques of
economics as a discipline; and the entry of a strongly cultural critical
element into the existing field of the social studies of science (about
which I have recently edited a volume [Marcus, 1995b]). Here, I
want to offer to the project represented in this volume merely the
raising of some issues about the politics of positioning of such critical movements in relationship to relatively indifferent, uncompre-
hending, or even hostile disciplinary mainstreams and about what
they hope for their critiques to achieve. In a sense, I want to lay out
the space of possible ambitions and options for the self-presentation
of the project of critique exemplified in this volume and in other projects like it.

Constructionist arguments about the social constitution of the
real in any domain, combined with attention to the rhetorical dimensions by which any discourse establishes its authority, have been the
basic and widespread techniques by which the critical movement has
been diffused and developed in different disciplines. While varying in
the degree of radical claims as well as in intellectual weight or theoretical backing, these techniques have proved to be so powerful because they are accessible, simple, and provocative. The issue is whether
social constructionism is a kind of critical truth for the already con-

verted, so to speak, or whether it is an opening for dialogue with those who might be most threatened or provoked by it, not necessarily so as to convert or win them over, but to have some sort of effect on the mainstream and its extended channels of influence and prestige.

To examine this issue further, I want to consider schematically the range of self-presentations and ambitions for the self-identified constructionist project, for example, in the field of IR (or in any of the other noted projects like it). As a baseline position, one could claim a very limited purpose for the constructionist project—not so much to have an impact on the mainstream by having it "take in" the critique in some transforming way, but merely to secure a domain for alternative work on its own merits. By this option, engaged dialogue with the mainstream is not sought as much as, at most, a legitimate if marginal space to operate alternatively within the discipline. There indeed has always been, from the mainstream perspective, a legitimate "reservation" for work critical of its assumptions, and such spaces have even found important patrons among revered figures of the discipline who in their seniority have had the license to cultivate a certain maverick position against the mainstream that reveres them. In the past, such marginal domains might have operated under the label "Marxist," for example; at present, the designation "feminist" or "postmodern" or "cultural studies" labels this "reserved" space.

The real constituency for such vibrant alternative work in international relations that does not necessarily seek to engage with the mainstream (indeed, this might be viewed as debilitating to the development of a clear alternative to international security studies) is located within the contemporary interdisciplinary realm of critical literary/cultural studies, broadly conceived, from which it has importantly derived its intellectual capital (as, for example, a channel for French poststructuralist theories); that is, the work of alternative IR scholarship (among other varieties of critical social science) is the kind of congenial and complementary social science that the broad realm of cultural studies, which inspires it, *needs*. Often applied in text-based disciplinary styles of inquiry, critical cultural theories fueling specific projects of critique need empirical partners, so to speak, to keep in touch with a sense of contemporary reality that further validates in the form of the data of social science their insights about, say, gender, structural inequalities, and relations of power.

Satisfying by its own standards and supported by its interdisciplinary alliances, an alternative international relations scholarship can thus thrive in structural opposition to mainstream IR without any effort to engage it on its own terms, and perhaps transform it. It is thus satisfied to be another "tribe" within IR as long as it has viable institutional space and support.

Although the contributions to this volume represent a number of positions along the continuum of the constructivist critique of conventional security studies, overall the volume seems distinct from a more radical poststructuralist critique. This latter critique, as represented by the writings of Richard Ashley, David Campbell, James Der Derian, and Michael Shapiro, for example, has been largely ignored by most practitioners in the field. The poststructuralist writers seem positioned on the borders between an admiring cultural studies constituency, as described above, and a much more limited sympathetic constructionist constituency tolerated and positioned somewhat more securely in the community of IR scholars. Strongly allied *intellectually* with the poststructuralist critics, the participants in the critical project that this volume represents clearly do not want to be ignored by the mainstream to the same extent. To what extent they want to engage with it, or just guarantee an alternative space for themselves within this community, remains unclear.

For me, having worked with the signature ethnographic method of cultural anthropology and having attempted to practice cultural critique derived from it, the limited purpose of a mere space for alternative work is insufficient. However difficult, to find an engaged constituency within the mainstream that might even be "convinced" is for me irresistible and the most important index of the power of a particular project of critique. Engaged debate (dialogue? confrontation?) with the mainstream could be, and often is, discussed in terms of metaphors of missionizing, warfare, or political struggle. And indeed, a certain will to power always figures in projects of critique, such that images of wanting to overcome and replace dominant forms with something better are irresistible in characterizing the confrontational setting of critique. Critique is often powered by either the desire to convert (or merely convince) or the desire to subvert (calling up images of revolutionary action). Still, in trying to suggest here a somewhat hopeful strategy for a practice of critique that seeks engaged response from a glacial mainstream—at worst unlikely to listen to it, or at best, likely to marginalize it—I prefer to give it an anthropological expression, even though I am keenly aware of how anthropology itself has historically wrestled with missionizing and subverting both as metaphoric and literal aspects of its own endeavors.

The strategy I have in mind rests on finding and intellectually probing effective oppositional space within mainstream discourses. This means finding where the "cracks" are—that is, finding those concepts, methods, ideas, practices, and life experiences within the culture of the mainstream about which there is self-doubt and uncertainty among mainstream IR scholars themselves. This in turn means understanding these potentially self-critical cultural formations within IR scholarship, *ethnographically,* in their own terms and expressions. What are the anxiety and rationalization structures supporting the maintenance of conservative modes of thought in IR research? How are such anxieties and rationalizations expressed?— in what cultural idioms? To whom are such expressions directed? (Perhaps, for example, not to the overt critics of mainstream IR, but rather to those who expect most from it in government and bureaucracy.) What sorts of arguments could be developed to establish a connection of sustained argument with embedded self-critical tendencies in mainstream IR? What are the perhaps buried intellectual affinities between these discovered and elicited self-critical tendencies within the mainstream and the manifest forms of critique that oppose it?

According to this strategy, the measure of the power of critique is involved response from within the mainstream. This strategy does not argue against the mainstream with a counterdiscourse more powerful than its own, because it does not have one that is more powerful. Rather, this strategy depends on mapping the cracks, inconsistencies, and hesitations of mainstream discourse such that if the critic pointed these out, the mainstream would become upset and moved to respond because it would recognize the critique in its own internal idiom. The test of such critique is that the mainstream would neither be indifferent nor dismissive to what the critic says, but would at least partially recognize itself in such critique.

But who is to say that such self-critical spaces exist at all in such unquestionably prestigious, and apparently self-confident, domains of work as mainstream IR. Well, one response is that the mere fact of the development of a constructionist IR itself among highly talented scholars on the margins of the mainstream suggests that such spaces probably exist in other locations within the IR community. Further, if there is any empirical truth or value to the idea that postmodernity, in its complex theorizations, cogently describes actual conditions of structural change in the world—as I think serious cultural critics must believe—rather than being merely an artifact of an academic fashion, then one must suppose that these changes are registered in quite different and perhaps less acknowledged ways in terms of dominant discourses, mainstream practices, and so on, protected by institutional sources of prestige. The task of engaged critique is to make these translations between its own truths and posited affinities with them in the realm of its "other," that is, power/knowledge, like IR scholarship, which it, as critique, explicitly opposes.

Now, what I am proposing may seem like "psyching out" mainstream IR scholarship in order to convert (or convince) it, but, as I indicated, I prefer to understand this strategy specifically in terms analogous to the practice of cross-cultural ethnographic research in anthropology. Based on recent critical discussions of this enterprise, the creation of ethnographic knowledge is inseparable from its contexts of collaborative productions with specific others as informants (in the older terminology), consultants, associates, or simply interlocutors in the field. Although ethnographic knowledge can be got up in a highly objectified discursive form to suit what has evolved as standard social science discourse, not only its form and substance, but its very purposes are entwined within the self–other negotiations so central to the formulation of translations and interpretations in anthropology.

I am suggesting analogously that any critique of mainstream IR seeking engaged response from those to whom the critique is directed would proceed approximately in terms of the same conditions of ethnographic practice. This requires working in an analytic space that might be less attractive and supportive to the critic of IR, because it requires working dialogically within the mainstream. It means being oppositional, but without a clear "outside" bounded space of opposition. Certainly, the open-ended possibilities of the pursuit of ethnographic knowledge through dialogically working on the "inside" of another culture make the idea of "converting" or "convincing" the other side far too simple and inappropriate a metaphor to describe this sort of critique, because, to be effective, one must put one's own position at risk in opposing and critiquing that of an "other." There is no other way to be effectively oppositional from within.

The ideal measure of the success of such a strategy of critique—that those critiqued be motivated to respond and engage with the critique—derives from a parallel "ethos" of success or achievement in ethnographic practice, relating to central issues of cultural translation. Even though anthropologists have always produced interpretations and descriptions primarily for their own academic, largely Western community, they have always had a deep sense that the knowledge that they produce should be accountable to the "natives" (anthropological knowledge has rarely been tested in this way away from sites of fieldwork, but it is increasingly the case that as objects of study and world conditions change, the nature of the realms of reception of anthropological scholarship are both broadening and diversifying). The simplest and ethically least implicated form of this concern is often expressed as wondering, not whether the "native" would judge the anthropologist right or wrong as to a particular interpretation or detail of fact, but whether the discourse itself that the anthropologist has produced would be meaningful at all to natives, whether the latter would even be able to comment at all on what the anthropologist says (writes?) about them. The worry of the anthropologist is less that the native would be dismissive than that she would be indifferent to what the former produces as "knowledge." "Getting it right," about which ethnographers argue endlessly, is more about being meaningful to an "other" than about being correct or accurate. The imaginary of such successful ethnographic engagement has been a very strong guide and self-critical measure in anthropological work, and would operate likewise in the strategy of engaged critique "from within" that I am proposing. At the level even of an imaginary, the requirement of accountable engagement serves to keep ethnography—and presumably would keep the critique of IR scholarship—honest in not hardening the lines of its own inevitable self-promotions and morale-building endeavors.

However, practical rather than imaginary success certainly matters in projects of critique, because more is perhaps explicitly at stake normatively than in the pursuit of ethnography. Are there not some mainstreams, dominant discourses, and so on, for which the strategy of engaged critique will just not succeed in any way that satisfies the critic? Even if such connection is made, exchange might be endlessly frustrating or contentious. Or, pure acts of institutional power, prerogative, and arrogance might summarily end overtures to engaged critique, even when such critique skillfully strikes the right nerve, so to speak.

Indeed, there may be some discourse domains in which, however good the strategy of engaged critique may sound, there is simply no "talking to it"—its defenses (as well as those on the side of critique) may be too great; sufficient, minimal good faith does not exist. For example, during the 1980s, the Critical Legal Studies movement had successes in terms of the strategy of engaged critique, especially in challenging and changing models of legal education, but it was diminished to some degree by its success—the growth in numbers of those in the legal profession attracted to it led to a consequent loss in rigor and focus while it was still very much an oppositional movement—and to a large degree by the reassertion of authority of centrist and conservative wings of the profession. Indeed, then, politics and power moves may preemptively determine the outcomes of projects of critique in certain fields. Even to get that far, however, the critic must have created an effective provocation—one that could not be dismissed, easily marginalized, or not understood by those to whom critique is directed.

I do not think such pessimism about the possibility of engaged critique with disciplinary mainstreams applies to IR scholarship given the vitality, analytic acuity, and shrewdness about the positioning of their arguments evidenced in the contributions to this volume. The volume itself, as noted, positions itself within the discipline, wanting to be heard, through its "constructionist" identity tolerated by the mainstream, rather than be considered "beyond the pale" like the more radical poststructuralist scholars to which it is nonetheless very sympathetic intellectually. Still, what remains is a certain ambiguity about whether the project that this volume represents wants to remain a recognized reserve within the discipline for its own self-identified constituency, dedicated to critical commentary and alternative analyses in relation to mainstreams, or whether it wants to have a transformative effect through some sort of complex response from and engagement with the mainstream of security studies in IR. Indeed, all constructionist arguments incorporate such a dynamic tension within themselves, because, while critically provocative to some mainstream, dominant scholars who are less self-consciously reflexive about their own practices, the constructionist tendency is always already embedded in some form and expression among such mainstream subjects, just as it is made explicit, analytic, and theoretical among the critical scholars who work to provoke them. The movement into engagement with the existing but submerged constructionist tendency in the mainstream requires a complex translation and negotiation initiated by the critical scholar on the margins of a discipline with scholars identified with the same potential tendency in the mainstream. The results of such engagement may not be satisfying, or even pleasurable, but they would extend the reach of constructionist arguments beyond their often closed circles of reception. What is so fascinating and, for me, most exciting about the essays in this volume is that, through variously expressed dynamic tensions in most of them, they are on the verge of pushing their pointed critiques of security studies in this more activist direction that addresses the mainstream in terms that will require complicated responses from it.

Acknowledgments

This volume emerged out of a series of three workshops held in 1994 and 1995. The impetus for those workshops was provided by Peter Katzenstein's project on the topic "Norms and Security." Each of the editors acted as a discussant at a meeting of the "Norms" group at the University of Minnesota in January 1994. It was out of this engagement that we first considered bringing together a group of anthropologists and political scientists to discuss the relationship between culture and the construction of insecurity. We thus thank Peter and the other members of the "Norms" project for stimulating our effort.

Our first workshop, funded by the Committee on International Peace and Cooperation of the Social Science Research Council (SSRC), was held at the University of Minnesota in October 1994. We would like to thank Tarak Barkawi, Shampa Biswas, Simona Goi, Prabhakara Jha, John Mowitt, Jennifer Pierce, Nilgun Uygun, and Asha Varadharajan, who acted as discussants of the paper proposals and as interlocutors for the project as a whole, and Carlos Cordero-Cancio, who had the unenviable task of driving the participants to and from the airport. The second workshop was funded by the Department of Political Science and the University Research Council, Kent State University, and held at Kent in April 1995. We are grateful to Anjuman Ali, Mike Barnett, Robin Chapin, Tom Davis, Rick Feinberg, Elaine Hall, Jonathan Hill, Gilbert Khadiagala, Frank

Klink, Greg Sanders, and Alex Wendt, all of whom gave their time and energy to discuss the revised and expanded papers presented at this meeting. The third workshop, funded by the Midwest Consortium for International Security Studies (MCISS) as well as the Department of Political Science, the College of Liberal Arts, and the Institute of International Studies at the University of Minnesota, was held at the University of Minnesota in October 1995. Thanks are due to John Collins, Lisa Disch, James Fernandez, Edward Kolodziej, George Marcus, John Mowitt (again), Richard Price, and Michael Shapiro, who provided valuable feedback on the individual papers and on the project as a whole. Subsequently, George and John agreed to contribute a Foreword and a concluding essay, respectively, to this volume, for which we are also grateful.

Several of these papers were presented on two panels at the 1995 Annual Meeting of the American Political Science Association, held in Chicago August 30–September 2, 1995. Ann Tickner, as organizer of the "International Security" section, arranged for the panels to be on the program; Lynn Eden and Thomas Risse acted as chairs and discussants of the two panels: thank you. Small grants from the SSRC and the MCISS enabled the editors to present drafts of the Introduction to audiences at the Center for International Security and Arms Control (CISAC) at Stanford University in March 1996, and at the Program on International Politics, Economics and Security (PIPES) at the University of Chicago in October 1996. Thanks again to Lynn Eden and to David Holloway at CISAC, and to Charles Lipson and Duncan Snidal at PIPES.

Not all of the papers that appear in this volume were presented at the workshops we organized, and not all of the papers presented there appear in this volume. Patty Gray, Karen Brown Thompson, and Naeem Inayatullah and David Blaney also presented papers at some or all of the workshops. For a variety of reasons, they were unable to contribute essays to this volume. Nonetheless, each added a distinct and significant voice to our collective conversation and we gratefully acknowledge them here. Ralph Litzinger, Jennifer Milliken, and Michael Barnett joined the project in mid-1995. Joseph Masco was added to the project after we had completed the workshops. Finally, John Borneman also presented a paper at the third workshop. Although he too was eventually unable to contribute to this book, we would like to thank him for participating in the workshop and for his continuing support.

As editors of the Borderlines series at the University of Minnesota Press, David Campbell and Michael Shapiro must be acknowledged for their support of this project. We are also grateful to Carrie Mullen—not least for her continuing enthusiasm—and Robin A. Moir at the Press, and to Charles Hale and an anonymous reviewer for their suggestions for revising the manuscript. We are also grateful to David Thorstad for his thorough copyediting. The volume is better for his help. This book was also reviewed for publication by Duke University Press. Thanks to Valerie Millholland and to Hayward Alker and the other, anonymous, reviewer.

Finally, the daughter of Jutta Weldes and Mark Laffey, Sadie Weldes, has been present—in one form or another—at all of the workshops and at the American Political Science Association presentations. Although she was unable to join in the discussions, her presence has served as a welcome antidote to pomposity and as a constant reminder of the wholly artificial boundaries presumed to exist between scholarship and the other spaces of social life. We dedicate this volume to her.

Introduction: Constructing Insecurity

JUTTA WELDES, MARK LAFFEY,
HUGH GUSTERSON, AND RAYMOND DUVALL

One of the defining features of contemporary world politics has been the alleged "return of culture" as both a source of insecurity and an object of analysis.[1] That "return"—manifested in concerns about ethnic, nationalist, and other forms of cultural conflict, for example—provides the point of departure for the essays in this book. Assertions about the return of culture might be taken to imply that other insecurities, such as those associated with the Cold War or with nuclear weapons, were not or are not cultural phenomena. Such claims are, of course, simply false.[2] For us, in contrast, the end of the Cold War and the collapse of the Soviet Union, which are frequently cited as emblematic, if not causal, of a new era of cultural insecurities, do not signal culture's return but only make it easier to see what has been the case all along: *all* social insecurities are culturally produced.[3]

"Culture," an increasingly central term in the vocabulary of international relations, is a highly contested concept. Indeed, Raymond Williams argued that it is "one of the two or three most complicated terms in the English language" (1983: 160). We do not intend to provide a definitive conceptualization of culture here, a fruitless task in any case. For the authors in this volume, insecurities are cultural in the sense that they are produced in and out of "the context within which people give meanings to their actions and experiences and make sense of their lives" (Tomlinson, 1991: 7). Culture can thus be thought of as encompassing the multiplicity of discourses or "codes of intelligibility" (Hall, 1985: 105) through which meaning is produced—including discourses about "culture" itself. This multiplicity in turn implies (as we will discuss in more detail) that meanings can be contested. We thus understand culture to be composed of potentially contested codes and representations, as designating a field on which are fought battles over meaning. Building on this understanding, the chapters in this volume individually and together offer accounts of cultural processes through which insecurities of states and communities—and the identities of the subjects through which insecurities have meaning—are produced, reproduced, and transformed.

Drawing on this understanding of culture, we have set out to stimulate a conversation across disciplinary boundaries among scholars in sociocultural anthropology and international relations.[4] As anthropology "discovers" the state and the international system, and international relations seeks to integrate cultural variables into models of interstate behavior, we find a new basis for an interdisciplinary conversation organized, for us, around the insecurities of states and communities, and the discourses through which they are effected. We hope that such a conversation, and the empirical studies it has provoked, will contribute to ongoing efforts to rethink security and insecurity, while stimulating more exchange between international relations and anthropology.[5] The chapters collected here begin to map the contours of a conceptual and theoretical space in which anthropologists, international relations scholars, and others hopefully can engage in new conversations around shared concerns about the production of insecurity.

This Introduction lays out the bases and justification for such a conversation. It begins, in the next section, with an account of the disciplinary contexts in which our project emerged. We then proceed to outline the shared object of analysis and the analytic commitments that structure the contributions to this volume. In the penultimate section, we discuss the politics of disciplinarity as it is manifested in competing models of cross-disciplinary scholarship. The Introduction concludes with a brief outline of the rest of the book.

CULTURE: SEE ANTHROPOLOGY; STATES: SEE SECURITY STUDIES

This project stems from its contributors' shared commitment to a critical constructivist engagement with the production of insecurity.

Out of the interpretive and linguistic turns there developed within the human sciences a common metatheoretical language that, in the context of apparently ongoing changes outside the academy associated with globalization and the end of the Cold War, provides the grounds for a growing convergence between the fields of anthropology and international relations. This convergence is most clearly visible in reinvigorated debates organized around "culture" and "the state." The field of international relations is now abuzz with discussions of strategic culture, ethnic conflict, and the clash of civilizations. At the same time, anthropologists, until recently so unconcerned with the state and the interstate system, are increasingly interested in genocide, violence, and interstate processes.

A New Variable? Security Studies and Culture

The end of the Cold War, almost overnight, dissolved the structure around which security studies had crystallized in the latter years of the 1980s and promptly precipitated a paradigmatic crisis (e.g., Gaddis, 1992–93). Writing from a distinctively American point of view just before the disintegration of the Soviet Union, Nye and Lynn-Jones (1988) argued that security studies had come of age during the 1980s, as neorealism acquired mature hegemonic status within the field and security studies programs secured unprecedented funding as well as institutional and academic recognition. From the vantage point of 1988, they saw the field as centered on the U.S.-Soviet relationship and on discussions of the military balance between the superpower blocs. Although they thought this gave security studies coherence, they also worried that its potential for growth might be stifled by this narrow focus. The sudden and unexpected collapse of the Soviet Union changed all that. The issue—at least for policymakers, to whom scholars in the field had long aspired to speak— was no longer how to manage an arms race and superpower competition, but how to manage the implosion of a superpower and the disintegration of a global power structure until recently presumed highly impervious to change, and how to organize not an arms race but graceful disarmament. Meanwhile, with the end of the Cold War there suddenly reemerged ethnic, nationalist, and other forms of conflict that, at least in recent years, had been regarded as secondary or marginal phenomena within the universe of security studies (e.g., Posen, 1993; cf. Lapid and Kratochwil, 1996). How applicable, then, would the accumulated wisdom of the field be to the new era? More fundamentally, the failure of scholars to foresee, predict, or explain the sudden end of what was allegedly the central fact of world politics in the second half of the twentieth century—the superpower conflict itself—suggested an empirical anomaly of gross proportions and raised questions about the adequacy of the basic theoretical presumptions of neorealism, arguably the dominant approach to international relations and security studies (see Gusterson, this volume). As Friedrich Kratochwil put it, neorealism had been "embarrassed" by the changes (1993: 63). This failure led directly to the appearance of an increasingly large body of work designed more or less self-consciously to refurbish the field after the Cold War (e.g., Lebow and Risse-Kappen, 1995).

It is in this context, of a series of both empirical and, as we will show, theoretical challenges to its previously taken-for-granted assumptions about international security, that security studies has rediscovered the significance of cultural phenomena for understanding and explaining international politics. Besides the obligatory Geertz reading (e.g., 1973) on international relations syllabi, and considerable works on the subject earlier in the century (e.g., Lasswell, 1953 [1935]; Wright, 1942; Deutsch, 1953), security studies specialists have more or less ignored culture. However, driven by the limited explanatory power of existing neorealist models of international relations (cf. Keohane, 1988), scholars have turned increasingly to "cultural" variables such as ideas (e.g., Goldstein and Keohane, 1993), epistemic communities (e.g., Haas, 1992), strategic culture (e.g., Johnston, 1995), and norms (e.g., Katzenstein, 1996) to account for anomalous phenomena. Mainstream work such as this proceeded from a recognition that neorealist models—however elegant or parsimonious—oversimplified their objects of analysis. Cultural variables were marshaled to fill the inevitable gaps.

Meanwhile, at the same time as mainstream international relations was absorbing cultural variables into its traditional models, a broader critique of positivism as a plausible model for the human sciences was also beginning to register within security studies. During the 1980s, work in what Keith Krause and Michael Williams (1997) have dubbed "critical security studies" became an increasingly prominent, if still marginal, component of the field. This scholarship sets out to refashion security studies in two distinct ways. On the one hand, there has been a concerted effort to rethink the very foundations of the field, through the reengagement with conceptual, epistemological, and ontological questions that the mainstream of the discipline had ignored or regarded as settled. Examples include postpositivist philosophy of science and the linguistic turn (e.g., George, 1994), the critique of structuralism (e.g., Ashley, 1984), questioning of the ontological status of the state (e.g., Ringmar, 1996), and the rethinking of anarchy (e.g., Wendt, 1992). On the other hand, a growing body of empirical and theoretical work has emerged that both engages with traditional topics and issues within the field—such as the nature of sovereignty (e.g., Biersteker and Weber, 1996), imperialism and international hierarchy (e.g., Doty, 1996b), the logic of deterrence (e.g., Williams, 1992), crises and the concept of the national interest (e.g., Weldes, 1996, 1999), and foreign policy more generally (e.g., Campbell, 1992, 1993)—and pushes into new or seldom studied terrain, such as gender (e.g., Sylvester, 1994), race (e.g., Doty, 1996a), migration and refugees (e.g., Soguk, 1996), and postcoloniality (e.g., Darby and Paolini, 1994).

Ironically, international relations and security studies specialists are developing an interest in "culture" just at the moment when some anthropologists—concerned that it connotes a static, reified, or overly holistic model of collective consciousness—are becoming ambivalent about the continuing use of the term, at least as a noun.[6] In the words of Sylvia Yanagisako and Carol Delaney, "perhaps no other concept in the social sciences and humanities has been subjected to as unrelenting a critique over the past decade as that of culture" (1995: 15). Despite these reservations within anthropology, the rejection of positivism and a reengagement with culture within international relations and security studies has opened a space for conversations between anthropologists and (critical) security scholars that would have been inconceivable little more than a decade ago.[7] At the same time that security studies has been rediscovering culture, anthropology has been rediscovering the state and the international system.

A New Anthropology? Violence and the International System

Anthropologists have paid relatively little attention to the state or the interstate system. Thus, while the end of the Cold War precipitated considerable intellectual ferment in international relations and security studies, it barely registered in anthropology. In 1990, for example, one year after the fall of the Berlin Wall, the American Anthropological Association at its annual meeting scheduled an invited session on the topic "The End of the Cold War and the Peace Dividend" in a large ballroom. The panel was attended by about ten people.[8] For anthropologists, the Cold War between the superpowers had simply not been a major point of reference.[9] Instead, their interest in security issues has emerged in recent years in response to ethnic conflict, the increasing use of torture and genocide as forms of social discipline, especially in Latin America, the realization that the kinds of small-scale communities anthropologists had traditionally studied were among the main victims of systematic violence in the world, and an increasing interest in the state and in global processes.

Orin Starn's (1992) essay "Missing the Revolution" serves as a useful starting point for a discussion of anthropology's historical indifference to the kinds of issues central to security studies. Starn points out that anthropologists working in Peru were almost completely taken by surprise by the Shining Path guerillas' attempted revolution in the 1980s and by the ensuing orgy of state-sponsored and revolutionary violence. Anthropologists failed to discern the emergent insurrection, Starn argues, because their orienting intellectual framework—which he labels "Andeanism"—had positioned the highland peasants outside history and in a more or less unbroken lineage with a folkloric past of self-contained peasant communities. Preoccupied with adaptation, ritual, and cosmology, these anthropologists had scarcely noticed the increasing integration of their subjects into the global system and the increasing intrusion of a repressive state apparatus into their lives. Such a frame made it difficult for anthropologists engaged in ethnographic research in the villages of the region to conceive of the possibility of a violent peasant uprising.

Anthropology has spent much of its institutional life skirting the edges of the state system in one way or another. The first generation of anthropologists at the beginning of the twentieth century, especially British social anthropologists, established its reputation in part by describing and valorizing "stateless societies"—communities with social and political organizations based on kinship rather than formal state apparatuses (e.g., Evans-Pritchard, 1940; Evans-Pritchard and Fortes, 1958)—or by describing societies that made their home on the edges of the state system (e.g., Boas, 1925; Malinowski, 1961). An implicit division of labor developed within the social sciences according to which anthropologists wrote about the political systems of kingdoms and stateless societies in the "underdeveloped" world, while political scientists wrote about the political systems of modern bureaucratic states.[10] Most of the societies studied by anthropologists under this division of labor were, until the 1960s, under the control of colonial state bureaucracies. As Talal Asad (1973) and others have observed, quite apart from the force of the Durkheimian convention inherited by anthropology that the communities they studied were organic, self-contained wholes, it was more or less a taboo in the field explicitly to explore the relationship of domination and subordination between "traditional" peoples and colonial states—a relationship in which anthropologists themselves were implicated in complex and contradictory ways.[11]

Anthropologists have, until recently at least, been further inhibited from studying the state and the interstate system by their own traditional research methodology: in-depth participant observation at a single field site. If anthropology's conventional insistence on participant observation as a defining research methodology once served to mark the discipline's distinctive identity among the social sciences, it now threatens to become a straitjacket that obstructs anthropologists from addressing new problems in new ways. Akhil Gupta points out that anthropology's privileging of "face-to-face contact and spatial proximity—what one may call a 'physics of presence'" makes it very difficult for anthropologists to study what he calls "nonlocalizable institutions" such as the state (1995: 375).

Since the late 1980s, anthropology has opened up new modes of investigation and new zones of inquiry in an effort to remake its relevance to a world undergoing rapid and intense reconfiguration on a global scale. A number of anthropologists are advocating what George Marcus (1995a) calls "multi-sited ethnography" and more heterogenous research methodologies that de-emphasize participant observation, thus opening up the possibility of studying translocal and transnational processes and institutions without losing one's anthropological union card (e.g., Gupta and Ferguson, 1997a, 1997b; Visweswaran, 1994). There is, however, a danger that the new translocal anthropology will reproduce an older anthropology's disinterest in the state and the interstate system, skipping straight from stateless societies to what Arjun Appadurai (1996: chapter 8) calls "post-national" forms of identity and organization. Anthropologists who are currently theorizing translocal and transnational processes tend to emphasize global flows of capital and media images, the emergence of global migration patterns and diaspora that undermine the coherence of nation-states, and development institutions and discourses that operate orthogonally to the state; they show less interest in the grid of state bureaucracies and foreign policy relationships that these global processes traverse (e.g., Escobar, 1994; Hannerz, 1989). Thus, Appadurai argues that "deterritorialization . . . is one of the central forces of the modern world," and that "the relationship between states and nations is everywhere an embattled one. . . . state and nation are at each other's throats, and the hyphen that links them is now less an icon of conjuncture than an index of disjuncture" (1996: 37, 39). He argues that we should understand global society in terms of the interaction between what he calls "finance-scapes," "ethnoscapes," "technoscapes," "mediascapes," and "ideo-scapes" (ibid., chapter 2). We would add to this list "securityscapes," pointing out that organized violence and the elaboration of security cultures are also important facts of translocal life, and that, depending on local circumstance, they often work in ways that entrench the state rather than "deterritorialize" it or disarticulate it from the imagined community of the nation.

In recent years, a body of anthropological scholarship on intra-state and interstate violence and militarism has begun to emerge.[12] It includes work on torture and genocide in Latin America (e.g., Coronil and Skurski, 1991); on terrorism in Northern Ireland (e.g., Feldman, 1991); on civil wars in Africa (e.g., Besteman, 1997), in Sri Lanka (e.g., Daniel, 1996), in Yugoslavia (e.g., Denich, 1994), in the Middle East (e.g., Peteet, 1994), and in Nicaragua (e.g., Hale, 1994); and on the culture of the nuclear state (e.g., Gusterson, 1996). There is also a small but growing literature that explicitly seeks to integrate anthropological and political science models in the study of war and ethnonationalism (e.g., Comaroff and Stern, 1995). This interest in the state, and in violence and its relationship both to individual states and to a broader global state system, opens up a bridge between the traditional subject matters of anthropology and security studies; and the turn to culture in the latter field creates a meeting point for such a bridge.

CONSTRUCTING INSECURITY

The chapters that follow are efforts to traverse that bridge. They are in certain respects heterogeneous. In part this reflects the different disciplinary backgrounds of the authors; in part it reflects differences of emphasis, method, and the specific question being asked. For these reasons, this volume is more an entry into an emergent conversation than the articulation of a single, coherent theoretical framework exemplified or tested by empirical case studies. The following remarks, therefore, should be read as indicating shared reference points within that conversation rather than an agreed-upon conceptualization of or argument about the cultural production of insecurity. At the same time, our recognition that a variety of analyses are consistent with a critical constructivist approach to the cultural production of insecurity should not be understood to imply that anything goes in constructivist analyses. A critical social constructivist analysis of the cultural production of insecurity entails at least one substantive assumption about insecurity, as well as a number of analytic assumptions about the nature of a critical social constructivism. In this section, we lay out in broad strokes the shared substantive and analytic commitments that structure the various contributions to this project.

Insecurity as the Object of Analysis

The structure of knowledge in security studies stereotypically takes the form of positing the existence of certain entities—often but not always states—within an environment in which they experience threat(s). The nature of those entities is assumed to be both given and fixed, at least for all practical purposes, and security is thus understood to mean securing these fixed entities against objective and external threats. These foundational assumptions naturalize those actors and their insecurities, while rendering contingent and problematic their actions and strategies for coping with the insecurities. Actors and their insecurities are naturalized in the sense that they are treated as facts that, because they are given by the nature of the interstate system, can be taken for granted. Taken as natural facts, states and other organized actors become the foundational objects the taken-for-granted existence of which serves to ground security studies. Threats to these foundational objects are taken to be relatively self-evident, or at least discernible by the acute states-person or analyst, and, at the limit, are understood to issue from the ubiquitous "security dilemma" (Herz, 1951)—the inevitable, perpetual, and inherently unstable competition for power and security—that states and other actors face in an anarchic international system. Security studies, then, treats insecurities as unavoidable facts while problematizing, and consequently focusing its attention on, the acquisition of security for pregiven entities—usually the state. Invoking security in this conventional sense thus invokes the discourse of organized political actors, particularly the state.

If conventional analyses in security studies begin with a set of pre-given entities and asks "how can they be secured?" the papers in this volume flip this strategy on its head. We take discourses of insecurity, or what David Campbell (1992) has called "representations of danger," as our objects of analysis and examine how they work. Analysis begins with a set of discourses and asks "what do they do?" Because we seek to challenge conventional understandings of actors and their security problematics, the focus of all of the analyses presented in this volume is always and expressly on *in*security and its cultural production. In one way or another, each of these studies takes as its object of analysis the organized political actors and their insecurities taken for granted by security studies and calls them into question. In doing so, they seek to denaturalize the state, other communities, and their insecurities, in particular by demonstrating how both insecurities *and* actors such as states and communities are culturally produced. Most important, the chapters that follow attempt to show how the cultural production of insecurities implicates and is implicated in the cultural production of the identities of actors.

The basic substantive assumption unifying the analyses presented in this volume is thus that insecurities, rather than being natural facts, are social and cultural productions. One way to get at the constructed nature of insecurities is to examine the fundamental ways in which insecurities and the objects that suffer from insecurity are mutually constituted; that is, in contrast to the received view, which treats the objects of insecurity and insecurities themselves as pregiven or natural, and as ontologically separate things, we treat them as mutually constituted cultural and social constructions: insecurity is itself the product of processes of identity construction in which the self and the other, or multiple others, are constituted.[13] Although not all of the following analyses use the same language or concepts, they can all be seen as resting on the assumption that identity and insecurity are produced in a mutually constitutive process.

William Connolly provides a useful gloss on these issues. Any identity, whether of an individual, a state, or some other social group, is always "established in relation to a series of differences that have become socially recognized. These differences are essential to its being. If they did not coexist as differences, it would not exist in its distinctness and solidity" (1991: 64). Identity, that is, can only be established in relation to what it is not—to difference. Difference, in turn, is constituted in relation to identity. Identities, then, are always contingent and relational, and they are "performatively constituted" (Campbell, 1992: 8). Moreover, as Connolly continues,

> Entrenched in this indispensable relation is a second set of tendencies, themselves in need of exploration, to congeal established identities into fixed forms, thought and lived as if their structure expressed the true order of things. When these pressures prevail, the maintenance of one identity (or field of identities) involves the conversion of some differences into otherness, into evil, or into one of its numerous surrogates. Identity requires difference in order to be, and it converts difference into otherness in order to secure its own self-certainty (1991: 64).

Furthermore, these "differences" that define identity also have a tendency "to counter, resist, overthrow, or subvert definitions that apply to them" (ibid.), thereby undermining the identity they supposedly define. Thus, there is always a politics of identity and difference through which difference can, but need not, be transformed into otherness. When it is, it becomes a source of insecurity. An identity is then insecure or threatened "not merely by actions that the other might take to injure or defeat the true identity but by the very visibility of its mode of being as other" (ibid., 66). Difference and otherness thus stand in a "double relation" to self-identity: "they constitute it and they threaten it" (ibid., 67).

Connolly's argument nicely captures the substantive assumption underlying this project—namely, that insecurity, rather than being external to the object to which it presents a threat, is both implicated in and an effect of the very process of establishing and reestablishing the object's identity.[14] This assumption—that insecurity emerges in various ways out of cultural processes of identity construction and that insecurities are thus cultural productions—provides the substantive theme that unifies the following analyses, that opens a space for further conversation, and that provides the basis for additional research.

At this point it is important to clarify what we mean in referring to insecurities as social constructions, in order to preempt objections that some readers may have. Critics of constructivism sometimes understand a phrase such as, for example, "the social construction of the Soviet threat" (e.g., Nathanson, 1988) to mean that the Soviet threat did not in fact exist, that it was purely a fabrication. However, to refer to something as socially constructed is not at all the same as saying that it does not exist. A brief discussion of the example of nuclear insecurity may help define the distinctive nature of a constructivist perspective in security studies. Our constructivism would not deny that nuclear weapons exist, that their use could maim and kill millions of people, and that a number of states possess a nuclear capability (including the United States, Russia, Britain, France, China, Israel, India, and Pakistan, at least). On this a constructivist and the most empiricist of arms-control experts can agree. However, our constructivism is interested in how one gets from here to such widely shared propositions as these: that the United States is threatened by Russian, but not British, nuclear weapons; that Third World states are more likely to use their nuclear weapons than Western countries; that Iraq's nuclear potential is more threatening than the United States' nuclear arsenal; and that the United States is safer with nuclear weapons than it would be without them. In the face of the heterogeneous dangers represented by nuclear weapons, there is nonetheless an established common sense, made real in collective discourse, that foregrounds some dangers while repressing or ignoring others so that, for example, Americans are likely to be more afraid of Pakistani than of British nuclear weapons, although neither have ever been used. It is this discursive constitution of the *threat* represented by nuclear weapons that we refer to as "construction," and it means not that the weapons have been made up but that their meaning has been molded in discourse.

As the nuclear example immediately makes clear, these are not simply academic issues without significance in the "real world." It matters deeply for a host of social relations whether one is more afraid of, say, an Iraqi or a Swedish bomb, of carcinogens produced at the Rocky Flats plutonium plant or of a Russian first strike. Although conventional approaches in security studies might produce claims of a clear answer to such questions, a critical constructivist analysis works more deconstructively, producing not simple answers but forms of analysis that show how such answers can become, in Roland Barthes's phrase, "falsely obvious" (1972: 11).

Analytic Commitments

The papers in this volume share a set of basic analytic commitments. Although not every study addresses each commitment overtly, critical social constructivist analysis implies a commitment to the following three interrelated analytic principles or, more loosely, reference points on the map we are sketching out:

1. What is understood as reality is socially constructed.
2. Constructions of reality reflect, enact, and reify relations of power. In turn, certain agents or groups of agents play a privileged role in the production and reproduction of these realities.
3. A critical constructivist approach denaturalizes dominant constructions, offers guidelines for the transformation of common sense, and facilitates the imagining of alternative life-worlds. It also problematizes the conditions of its own claims; that is, a critical constructivism is also reflexive.

Reality Is Socially Constructed

Our claim that insecurities are social productions derives from the recognition of a deceptively simple fact: that people "act towards objects, including other actors, on the basis of the *meanings* that the objects have for them" (Wendt, 1992: 396–97, emphasis added). Constructivism assumes that the world is constituted in part through the meaningful practices of social subjects, and that people act on the basis of the meanings that things have for them.[15] These meanings are fundamentally cultural: they are made possible by particular discourses or codes of intelligibility that provide the categories through which the world is understood. Meaning is thus a social rather than an individual or collective phenomenon: it is not that everyone has the same "ideas" inside their heads, but rather that meaning inheres in the practices and categories through which people engage with each other and with the natural world. Such codes of intelligibility constitute the world as we know it and function in it: they tell us "what the world is and how it works, for all practical purposes" (Hall, 1988: 44).

On this view, identities (both of self and of others) and insecurities, rather than being given, emerge out of a process of representation through which individuals—whether state officials, leaders or members of nationalist movements, journal editors, or users of the Internet, for example—describe to themselves and others the world in which they live. These representations—narratives, collective memories, and the imaginaries that make them possible—define, and so constitute, the world. They populate it with objects and subjects, endow those subjects with interests, and define the relations among those objects and subjects. In so doing, they create insecurities, which, as we have argued, are threats to the identities, and thus to the interests, of these socially constructed subjects.

A constructed object that lies at the center of much contemporary discourse in security studies is the state. In conventional studies of security, the state is treated as a natural fact, but any particular "state" is in fact a cultural production; it is an effect of a set of statist discourses. Statist discourses, that is, produce the state, and produce it as a particular kind of subject. As some of the following chapters (e.g., Weldes and Muppidi) indicate, states are produced and reproduced as actors with particular kinds of interests in representations of their insecurity. Within U.S. statist discourse, for example, it is "the United States" that occupies the central subject-position.[16] Most fundamentally, such representations establish the existence of "the United States" *as* a subject. Out of a polyglot citizenry and a political and legal abstraction is created an anthropomorphization, an apparently acting subject. Moreover, these representations establish that the United States is a particular *kind* of subject, with a specific identity and with the interests attendant on that identity. As a result of the discursive constitution and "interpellation" (Althusser, 1971) of this subject-position, "the United States" becomes the central object of discussion, the interests articulated in those discussions are the interests of the subject "the United States," and the insecurities of importance are the insecurities of "the U.S." state. At the same time, "the United States" becomes the central subject of discussion; it is not only the object facing insecurities but the subject charged with providing security. Of course, statist discourses also produce citizens as particular kinds of subjects, often as consumers of statist representations of insecurity and danger and as a unified population with shared interests. On this basis, statist discourse is then deployed to mobilize state subjects in support of its definition of state interest and, concomitantly, its conception of insecurity (Weldes, 1996; Litzinger and Masco, this volume).

Although the state is an important subject produced through discourses of insecurity and the representations of danger they enable, it is by no means the only one. A plethora of other subjects are constituted as well. Nationalist discourses, for instance, produce "imagined communities" (Anderson, 1991) ostensibly unified by blood, language, or culture. These imagined national communities are not always well synchronized with state boundaries—as in the case of the contemporary Kurds or Basques, for example. The interests imputed to such nations or ethnic groups are, in fact, often antithetical to those of the state(s) in which they live and in such cases it is the state that is constituted as a danger threatening the identity of the nation; instead of being the source or locus of security, the state becomes a major source of insecurity. Transnational or trans-state subjects are also produced in codes of intelligibility. As Milliken argues in her contribution to this volume, "the West" as a subject has been constituted through a number of "representations of danger." In representations of the Korean War, this collective subject has been produced and reproduced as a particular form of security community, with the attendant interests and insecurities. As these examples suggest, each of these discursively constituted subjects has specific characteristics, is endowed with particular interests, and is thus vulnerable to those insecurities that might threaten its (socially constructed) identity and interests.

The constitution of identities is often a reciprocal process. As each subject seeks to perform its identity, it threatens others, whose identities are consolidated in response. This is so, as Saco argues in her chapter, in the case of the U.S. state in its conflict with both the loose community of Internet users and the tighter community of "cypherpunks" over the policing of the Internet and the use of the "Clipper chip." As the U.S. state seeks to protect its "national security" and so to reaffirm its identity by exerting regulatory control over the Internet, these Internet users constitute themselves discursively as a community that is rendered insecure by these state actions. The two identities are thus in significant respects mutually constitutive through a relation of insecurity.

The fact that cultures are composed of multiple discourses or codes of intelligibility, and that the world therefore can be and is represented in different, and often competing, ways, has significant implications. In particular, it means that any representation can potentially be contested and so must actively be reproduced. Meanings are not given, static, or final; rather, they are always in process and always provisional. The production of insecurities thus requires considerable social work—of production, of reproduction, and, possibly, of transformation. Dominant discourses must constantly reproduce themselves to answer challenges to their constructions of the world and their identification of those insecurities worthy of a response. Defining security and insecurity requires considerable ideological labor. Contesting discourses, in turn, attempt to rearticulate insecurities in ways that challenge the dominant representations (see, for example, Ballinger, this volume). In addition, discourses are themselves not perfectly coherent but always entail internal contradictions and lacunae. These contradictions make possible both resistance to a dominant discourse and the transformation of discourses. It is in this sense, then, that culture can be viewed as a field on which processes of discursive contestation are set.

It should be noted that, in analyzing such constructive processes, we are not examining mere rhetoric. It is in any case misleading to associate the notions of culture, of discourse, or of codes of intelligibility with the "merely linguistic." As Laclau and Mouffe have argued (1987: 82–84), discourses are composed of linguistic and nonlinguistic (that is to say, material) practices, both of which are indispensable to the production of worlds and of insecurity.[17] After all, discursive articulations, including the construction of insecurities, are always "materialized in concrete practices and rituals and operate through specific state [and other] apparatuses" (Hall, 1988: 46). Discourses and their codes of intelligibility have concrete, and significant, material effects. They allocate social capacities and resources and make practices possible. We use the terms *construction* and *production* loosely to maintain the distinction between linguistic and nonlinguistic practices. Linguistically, discourses are the vehicle for the *construction* of categories (of difference, of identity, of threat, etc.). Through both linguistic and nonlinguistic practices, they are the vehicle for the *production* of social facts (such as insecurities).

Exposing Relations of Power and Locating Agency

Constructions of reality and the codes of intelligibility out of which they are produced provide both conditions of possibility and limits on possibility; that is, they make it possible to act in the world while simultaneously defining the "horizon of the taken-for-granted" (Hall, 1988: 44) that marks the boundaries of common sense and accepted knowledge. Such codes and the constructions they generate become common sense or accepted knowledge when they have successfully defined the relationship of particular constructions to reality as one of correspondence; that is, they are successful to the extent that they are treated as if they naturally or transparently reflect reality. In this way, social constructions are reified or naturalized, and both their constructed nature and their particular social origins are obscured. The creation of common sense and accepted knowledge is thus what Stuart Hall has called "the moment of extreme ideological closure" (1985: 105). In essence, the creation of common sense and accepted knowledge depends on the explicit invocation of an empiricist epistemology—such as underpins conventional security studies and "rationalist" (Keohane, 1988) international relations theory in general. It depends on the implicit or explicit invocation of a correspondence theory of language and meaning in which words and concepts are thought to point to their ostensible empirical referents. By authoritatively defining "the real," dominant representations of insecurity remove from critical analysis and political debate what are in fact particular, interested constructions, thus endowing those particular representations with "common sense" and "reality." Conversely, anything outside of the discourse—statements expressing other possible worlds or forms of life, for example—is represented as implausible, ideological, or spurious and so often consigned to the realms of fiction, fantasy, or nonsense.

A corollary of this argument is that discourses are sites of social power in at least two important ways. First, some discourses are more powerful than others because they are located in and partake of institutional power. Statist discourses are a prominent example. All things being equal, the representations of state officials have immediate prima facie plausibility to the extent that these officials can be constructed as representatives who speak for "us." Such representations are likely to be so regarded not because they tell us what the world "really" is like but because they issue from the institutional power matrix that is the state. In their representations of insecurity, for example, state officials can claim access to information produced by the state and denied to most outsiders. They also have privileged access to the media (Herman and Chomsky, 1989). And, an important point not to be overlooked, their representations have constitutional legitimacy, especially in the construction of insecurity. After all, "national security" is generally understood to be quintessentially the business of the state and the identification of insecurities is thus a task thought rightly to belong to its officials. Dominant discourses, especially those of the state, thus become and remain dominant in part because of the power relations sustaining them. In extreme cases, when there is little or no challenge to the legitimacy of such dominant discourses, their representations of insecurity become hegemonic—that is, they receive assent from most, if not all, of their publics and competing representations are easily dismissed as at best naive, and at worst treasonous.

Discourses are implicated in power relations in another important way as well. Because discourses bring with them the power to define and thus to constitute the world, these representations of insecurity are themselves important sources of power. As Foucault argued, "power and knowledge directly imply one another; . . . there is no power relation without the correlative constitution of a field of knowledge, nor any knowledge that does not presuppose and constitute at the same time power relations" (1979: 27). As a result, they themselves become sites of contestation.

An issue we have so far neglected but that is obviously raised by any discussion of the social construction of insecurity is the question of agency: just who is it that defines or constructs insecurities? Who actually articulates these "discourses of danger" and produces particular insecurities? In statist societies, the primary site for the production of insecurity is the institution or bundle of practices that we know as the state. Because identifying danger and providing security is, in modern politics, considered fundamentally to be the business of the state, those individuals who inhabit offices in the state play a central role in constructing insecurities. As Hans Morgenthau argued, statesmen are the representatives of the state who "speak for it, . . .

define its objectives, choose the means for achieving them, and try to maintain, increase, and demonstrate power" (1978: 1080). It is state officials who are granted the right, who have the authority, to define security and insecurity—to identify threats and dangers and to determine the best solution to them, although they are often assisted by what have been called "intellectuals of statecraft" (Ó Tuathail and Agnew, 1992: 193), including the "defense intellectuals" (Cohn, 1987) associated with weapons contractors and university research centers and the "security intellectuals" of think tanks such as RAND (Dalby, 1990). Beyond the state narrowly defined, discourses of insecurity are also produced and circulate through what Gramsci called the extended state (1971: 257–64 and *passim*)—schools, churches, the media, and other institutions of civil society that regulate populations.

Although the state has primary authority for identifying certain forms of insecurity, insecurities are defined by others as well. As Saco argues, the community of cypherpunks and other Internet users have defined the U.S. state and its attempts to (re)assert control over the Internet as a major threat to their identity and security. Similarly, Masco's chapter shows how the U.S. nuclear weapons complex has been differently experienced—often as a source of insecurity—by local and ethnic communities in New Mexico. Insecurities, it turns out, are constructed by many different communities—including scholarly ones (see Gusterson, this volume)—as they seek to assert, maintain, or reproduce their identities. It is in the clash between those different identities that the politics of difference and otherness, and hence the cultural production of insecurity, is to be found.

Denaturalizing the Taken-for-Granted

It is, of course, possible and indeed perfectly reasonable for some purposes to take the commonsense interpretive categories of subjects for granted and then to proceed with an analysis. If one is interested in understanding the world from the agent's point of view, for example, as composed of seemingly resistant social facts and already given problems, then it can plausibly be argued that one important component of analytic models and theories should be derived from, and to some extent be a copy of, the agent's common sense. However, if one is interested, as critical constructivists typically are, in going beyond the agent's point of view to examine those structures of meaning and social practices that are the conditions of possibility for the agent's self-understandings in the first place, then one needs to subject that common sense to critical scrutiny. This common sense is not truth; rather, it is what Gramsci called the "diffuse and unco-ordinated features of a generic mode of thought" (1971: 330 n) or what Hall has called the "categories of practical consciousness" (1986: 30). The process of denaturalizing is the result of this critical scrutiny. It seeks to defamiliarize—literally to make strange—commonsense understandings and so to make their constructedness apparent. Each of the analyses in this volume—whether implicitly or explicitly— engages in such a process of denaturalization. They denaturalize the putatively given agents, such as states and other communities; they denaturalize the relations among subjects; and they denaturalize as well the insecurities faced by those subjects as apparently objective threats.

That said, one might take issue with the claim that security studies is guilty of naturalizing the insecurity of organized political actors by noting that all analyses must take something for granted; everything cannot be problematized at the same time or no research can take place. We recognize that this is true. But the issue of naturalizing in security studies is not so much that researchers in the field typically make an *analytic* assumption that organized political actors and their insecurities can be treated as givens for the purpose of a particular analysis. Instead, it is that they make an *ontological* assumption of givenness. States and other political actors simply exist, it is assumed, as do their insecurities. The task, then, is to make them more secure. The problem for us, as for other critical scholars, is that this particular form of naturalization ends up expressing the point of view of the (insecure) political actor, generally the state. Making such an ontological assumption forces the analyst, willy-nilly, to define and investigate security and insecurity from the point of view of the (naturalized) state, with the consequences both that other sites of insecurity are ignored and that insecurities themselves are understood to be natural facts rather than mutable social constructions. It is hardly surprising, then, that most work in security studies adopts the standpoint of the state, takes state insecurities to be given rather than constructed, and neglects the investigation of other loci, or indeed victims, of insecurity.[18] To avoid this problem, the chapters in this volume all seek to denaturalize various generally taken-for-granted subjects—both states and communities of various kinds—and their understandings of insecurity.

Although it should already be obvious from the preceding discussion, it is perhaps worth emphasizing that an expressly *critical* social constructivism will, minimally, challenge some of the naturalized assumptions of the dominant representations of the world. A critical analysis does not, as does a "problem-solving theory," take the world as it finds it, "with the prevailing social and power relationships and the institutions into which they are organized, as the given framework for action," and so see as its general aim "to make those relationships and institutions work smoothly by dealing effectively with particular sources of trouble" (Cox, 1986: 208).[19] A critical theory, in contrast, "by disturbing comfortable understandings of the world and revealing their arbitrariness, can open up an awareness of new possibilities—of our ability to make the world anew" (Gusterson, 1993: 8). All of the essays in this book are not only attempts to contest or deconstruct privileged constructions of the world; they are also attempts to reimagine the world that are themselves partial and situated. As Donna Haraway has argued, all knowledge is situated knowledge and the "god trick of seeing everything from nowhere" (1988: 581) is an illicit move. This being so, it follows that we would be hypocritical to claim an Olympian objectivity for our own perspective that we seek to deny to others. At the same time, however, we also agree with Haraway that analyses that confess their own situated and partial nature are, paradoxically, more objective than those that, in claiming to be objective, deny it.

TWO MODELS OF INTERDISCIPLINARY ENGAGEMENT

At the outset of this project, some of us adopted—more or less unconsciously—a model of interdisciplinary engagement broadly similar to free-trade models in neoclassical economic theory. Within such a model, disciplinary communities, each endowed with potentially tradable factors (theories, concepts, methods, data, and the like) and exercising their legitimate sovereign ownership over those factors, enter into exchange with other similarly endowed communities. Engagement is modeled on the exchange typical of a capitalist market, often with little or no sensitivity to the complex contexts within which theories, concepts, and methods have been produced. Suitably enriched after exchanging goods and services, disciplines remain sovereign, discrete, and essentially the same as they were before.

Such a logic of engagement seemed well suited to our own cross-disciplinary effort. From within international relations, the logic of the "turn to anthropology" seemed straightforward: culture was becoming a topic of discussion; anthropology was the keeper of culture within the academy; therefore, international relations scholars should go and talk to anthropologists about culture. The positive response to the project from colleagues and funding agencies seemed to confirm the good sense of such reasoning. What was most likely to emerge from our project, then, was the reproduction of the existing division of labor within the academy. The anthropologists would tell international relations scholars about "culture," while the scholars of international relations would tell the anthropologists about the state, the international system, and "security" in particular. Indeed, at our first meeting, held at the University of Minnesota in the fall of 1994, many of our conversations took the form of consciously translating the commonsense argot of one field so as to make it intelligible to the other. Having enjoyed the gains from such interdisciplinary trade, we could look forward to returning to our respective communities, bringing back our profitable insights and added value from the "other side." The market logic behind such a model of interdisciplinarity was made explicit by invited commentators from the field of international relations who, treating anthropology as the project's cultural capital, persistently pressed the participants in this project to tell them what was the "value added" from engaging in exchange with anthropologists. This was necessary, they said, in order to assure "product differentiation" between our project (and this book in particular) and others engaged in the ongoing rethinking of security. As the project developed, however, we became suspicious of the logic that lies behind this model of interdisciplinary engagement. Bernard Cohn observes that we should be wary of purchasing used concepts from other disciplines: we do not know where they have been (in Dirks, 1996: 18). Not the least danger of such a logic is that it reinscribes and reinforces the authority of the established disciplines. Such a reinscription undercuts the emancipatory potential of a critical project committed to imagining the world in new ways.

It is a commonplace to observe that the modern state and the disciplines that speak for and to it "grew up together." Scholarly disciplines do not exist outside history or apart from relations of power but are indelibly marked by them. The production of knowledge is made possible not only by disciplinary codes of intelligibility but also by the institutional articulations between communities of understanding and wider patterns of social power. For instance, more than two decades ago Stanley Hoffmann observed that international relations was an expressly American social science (1977).[20] By detailing the close relationship between the state, the policy community, and the academic field, Hoffmann implicitly raised profound questions about how and why that field has taken a particular form, and about the likely consequences for the kinds of knowledge produced (see also Krippendorf, 1987). Similar articulations and their consequences are discernible in anthropology: John Borneman (1995) shows how American anthropology was shaped by the "rise to globalism" of the United States, traveling west and then abroad with the troops and reinforcing the conception of an American "self" that animated that project. In these and other ways, scholarly disciplines are marked by their relations with the state and other sources of social power, whether in terms of the categories they deploy, the definitions of problems or situations that they assume, or simply as they tailor their work in the pursuit of policy relevance and state and private funding. Economic models of cross-disciplinary exchange, we would argue, presuppose and reinscribe the conceptual categories and distinctions that constitute disciplines and that structure a common-sense world in which the state, the economy, society, and the international, for example, all refer to discrete entities that define disciplinary objects of knowledge. They thus reinscribe precisely those categories and distinctions that structure everyday life and through which the state is grounded in everyday technologies of power (see Litzinger, this volume), thereby hindering our ability to conceptualize and make the world anew.

Recognition of the ways in which disciplinary objects of knowledge have been shaped by broader relations of power brings into focus the politics inherent in concerns that cross-disciplinary exchange such as ours should take only appropriate forms, so as not to disrupt the intellectual coherence and "integrity" of the respective fields (Walt, 1991: 230 n. 44). For example, such concerns reinforce— whether consciously or unconsciously—a view of the proper role of security studies as speaking to and for the state, a role potentially undermined should the field itself be reconstituted in ways that do not readily correspond with state interests. From this point of view, anthropology becomes merely the owner of a method (ethnography) and data ("local knowledge") that can be purchased and thus appropriated for a substantially unaltered security studies. In turn, the claim of security studies to speak on and about insecurity, and to provide security-relevant knowledge to the state, is rendered more authoritative if bolstered with "cultural" inputs from the field of anthropology.

In contrast to this economic model of exchange, we prefer a model of interdisciplinarity as conversation, as dialogical, in which the disciplinary subject is at least potentially liable to be transformed through the encounter with the other.[21] Understood as conversation, interdisciplinary engagement entails a dialogical play between the taken-for-granted common sense of the two fields such that, insofar as we necessarily test our own prejudices against those of the other, we also risk undermining or transforming those prejudices. Implied here is not only a sense of interdisciplinarity as coming to know the other, but also a sense of coming better to understand ourselves. Thus, a conversational model has the more or less immediate implication that interdisciplinary engagement prompts a kind of reflexive reappraisal of the conditions of possibility of the conversation itself, among them our constitution as particular kinds of disciplinary subjects.

The implication of such a mode of engagement for theorizing insecurity—for both the subjects and the objects of knowledge—is straightforward. Such engagement draws attention to the peculiarity of the ways in which particular objects of knowledge have been defined. Put another way, it could be understood as foregrounding the "supplemental" relationship between, in our case, security and culture (cf. Dirks, 1996). Engagement across the disciplinary divide around the concept of culture (understood as a necessary addition to the conceptual arsenal of security studies, say) actually serves in this respect to highlight the inadequacy of the concept—security—to which culture is allegedly external. Adding culture, in other words, destabilizes the meaning of security insofar as it points to the inadequacy of the analytic distinctions that rendered the supplement a seemingly necessary addition in the first place. Modeled as conversation, cross-disciplinary engagement prompts a rethinking of the analytic distinctions the presupposed existence of which seemed to require that engagement: what is at stake is the construction of new objects of knowledge. The contrast with an economic model is direct: the latter in fact reinscribes those distinctions—thereby reinforcing disciplinary authority—and powerfully so.

For the subjects of knowledge—scholars of international relations and anthropologists, in the present case—the destabilization of our respective objects of knowledge implied by cross-disciplinary conversation is also potentially transformative. Our presumed relationship to a particular piece of reality—as owners and experts—is immediately put in question, and, by implication, so is our identity insofar as it depends on the stability of the object of knowledge itself. If "our" object of knowledge is in fact traversed through and through with the objects of knowledge of other fields, and this is a necessary feature of what "it" is, it follows more or less immediately that the retention of that "object" in anything like its original form— even after the appropriate refurbishing and redefinition—and our continuing authority with respect to "it" can only be a political choice, which will rely for its success on political/ideological labor. This is so not least because it will require the deployment of a set of claims regarding the continuing discreteness of the object, and the denial of its implication in and constitution by other objects. Of course, the state has a ready answer to the question of what is the appropriate object of analysis for security studies: the externally given insecurities of the state. Through its various instrumentalities of power, the state ceaselessly reiterates and seeks authoritatively to define the boundaries of the threatening and the dangerous. But the state is not the only site for the production of insecurity: others, too, seek to define it, both for themselves and for others. Confronting such claims in their multiplicity, we are driven to recognize our implication in the reproduction of particular worlds. Interdisciplinarity as conversation has direct antidisciplinary implications (cf. Mowitt, 1992). It is in this spirit that we present the following essays.

ORGANIZATION OF THE BOOK

All of the chapters in this volume emerge out of a set of shared analytic commitments. Within this collective and interdisciplinary framework, however, the authors have chosen to pursue what can be seen as two distinct approaches to our collective object of analysis: insecurity and its cultural production. Some, working in the spirit of George Marcus's injunction (see the Foreword) to seek an engagement with various disciplinary mainstreams and so to invite a response from them, are organized around events or puzzles—and thus around questions—that are standard in the field of security studies. This approach predominates in Weldes's analysis of the origins of the Cuban missile crisis and in Muppidi's explanation for the paradox of insecurity in Indo-U.S. relations. Others, in contrast, begin with the identity-securing practices of communities, seeking to follow these wherever they may lead, regardless of the distance this may take them from the questions and issues conventionally posed by students of international security. This latter approach is exemplified in Saco's investigation of efforts by the U.S. state to recolonize the Internet and in Litzinger's analysis of post-Mao efforts by the Chinese party-state to secure itself against its own population. Although these different strategies of engagement derive in part from the disciplinary backgrounds of the contributors, the chapters do not divide sharply along disciplinary lines. If they did, the dialogical model of cross-disciplinary work would have failed in this instance. More important, these different strategies reflect the diversity of possible questions and foci of analysis made possible by the analytic commitments of a critical social constructivism. Such commitments allow for the attempt to engage disciplinary mainstreams, on the one hand, and, on the other, for the creation of alternative spaces for analysis. Although each of the individual chapters leans toward one or the other of these two strategies for engaging with more conventional analyses of in/security, the volume as a whole follows both of these paths. It offers a sustained and critical argument that takes the traditional objects of analysis for students of international security—the state and its insecurities—and seeks to prompt a progressive rethinking of these objects by highlighting the cultural production of states, of other communities, and of their insecurities. The volume therefore both engages directly and critically with the assumptions of a state-centric security studies and creates a space for unconventional critical analyses by highlighting the centrality of processes of categorization and signification in discourses of insecurity.

The first three chapters in the book examine international crises, thus directly engaging a central topic in security studies. Jutta Weldes shows how the official U.S. state narrative of the Cuban missile crisis both constituted the events of October 1962 *as* a crisis and marginalized alternative understandings of these events, while simultaneously making possible the (re)enactment and (re)production of an always precarious U.S. state identity. Her chapter thus offers a critical analysis of an overtly state-centric narrative of identity and insecurity while demonstrating that the production of interstate crises is intimately bound up with narratives of state identity. But states are not the only producers of crises. Pamela Ballinger examines the production and deployment of historical narratives about the "Trieste crisis" by groups of Italian exiles who claim to have been "ethnically cleansed" from the former Yugoslav peninsula of Istria between 1943 and 1955. Such local histories challenge a variety of official, state-centric (e.g., Anglo-American, Italian, and Yugoslav) narratives. Ballinger illustrates the contested nature of such crisis narratives by investigating the "politics of memory" through which local and regional communities struggle to define their ethno-national identities, underwritten by always contested historical memories, and to privilege them as the historical truth. The question, and the consequences, of who narrates are also prominent in Jennifer Milliken's analysis of the reconstruction of "the West" as a collective interventionary subject in the case of the Korean War. Milliken shows how U.S. policymakers attempted to interpellate other states as followers in a U.S.-led international society of states. Focusing on how those representations were received, she shows that British policymakers were successfully hailed, thus enabling "Western" intervention in Korea. Not all such attempts at interpellation are successful, however. Part of what is at stake, as Milliken demonstrates in her comparison of the different forms of address deployed by U.S. state actors toward Britain and newly independent India, concerns the subjectivity, and the related status, accorded to states by the leaders of the international community.

The positioning of India by the United States raises the issue of international hierarchy in the production of insecurity and, in particular, of relations between "the West" and the rest. The next two chapters address this question. In his analysis of India's persistently insecure relationship with the United States, Himadeep Muppidi locates the structuring principle of India's "security imaginary" in the nationalist struggle with the British and shows how U.S. efforts to articulate the postcolonial Indian state in terms that aligned India with the United States in fact persistently and paradoxically violated the social practices that marked the boundaries of India's postcolonial identity. U.S. representations reproduced articulations of Indian identity as subordinate and colonial, thus producing insecurity in Indo-U.S. relations. Steve Niva offers a related analysis of the origins of regional discourses of insecurity in the Middle East. Niva shows that, contrary to Orientalist assumptions about the primordial nature of Arab and Islamic identities in the region, these identities and insecurities in fact emerged alongside and in tandem with processes of modern state formation and came to be understood in regional terms. These regional discourses of insecurity have informed both pan-Arabist and Islamic movements in the Middle East and have led to the construction of broader regional conceptions of security outside of the existing sovereignties of regional states. In both Muppidi's and Niva's analyses, what is at stake are competing representations of the international system, the place of particular postcolonial states and communities within it, and the relation between them and the West. A central theme of these analyses thus concerns the implications of colonialism and imperialism for the constitution of postcolonial identities, both of states and of the communities and societies with which they are entangled, and their profound legacies in contemporary international insecurities.

The production of insecurity, then, occurs at a variety of sites in world politics. Diverse communities—of states and of both local and regional subjects—reproduce or transform themselves in representations of their insecurities. In turn, they often produce insecurity for others as well. Michael Barnett's chapter vividly illustrates this point. Barnett explores the failure of the "international community," acting through the United Nations, to intervene in the face of genocide in Rwanda. He argues that the bureaucratizing of peacekeeping after the Cold War has ironically increased the potential for indifference in the face of evils such as genocide. Bureaucrats and officials alike justify their inaction through reference to the transcendental values represented by the United Nations as the expression of the possibility of international community. In seeking to secure the United Nations, they also produce insecurity for those—the people of Rwanda, in this case—whom they are ostensibly charged with protecting. Similar themes emerge in Joseph Masco's discussion of the implications of the reimagining of nuclear security concerns after the Cold War for the ethnic borderlands of the southwestern United States. He examines the "plutonium economy" associated with the nuclear weapons programs of the Cold War and traces out the complex network of relations it has spawned between the U.S. national state and the local and indigenous peoples of New Mexico. In analyzing the diverse ways in which the activities of the U.S. nuclear weapons complex are experienced by local communities, Masco questions the role of such weapons in the production of security and insecurity, and for whom, and forces us to rethink the relation between the U.S. state and its sovereign territory by demonstrating the contested and meaning-full nature of the various spaces over which the state seeks to exercise discursive authority.

The next three chapters also draw our attention to the ongoing imagining and reimagining of community identities and their insecurity problematics in relation to state power as the state endeavors to reimagine and redefine itself in the context of what is variously understood as late, hyper-, or postmodernity. Mark Laffey examines recent state efforts to rearticulate New Zealand as a multicultural place, the better to integrate the New Zealand space economy into the Asia-Pacific. Narratives of place and belonging constitutive of New Zealand as a white and European place generate modes of subjectivity and motivate practices that contradict the flexibility called for within the discourse of transnational liberalism. As the state and capital seek to redefine what it means to be New Zealand, there are produced new insecurities, for the state, for capital, and for other subjects, as this state project seeks to write over an already contested politics of culture. Diana Saco offers a related analysis of some of the ways in which the U.S. state and its insecurities are being reimagined in the new arena of cyberspace. Focusing on the debates over the Clipper chip, she highlights the multiple cultures of insecurity enabled by the technologies of the Internet, and demonstrates that both proponents and critics of this attempt by the state to regulate cyberspace construct their insecurities through a liberal discourse. That discourse, she argues, both places real limits on the ability of the liberal state to colonize cyberspace and foreshadows the likely future of that "anarchic" space. Finally, Ralph Litzinger examines some of the ways in which the post-Mao party-state in China is attempting to secure itself against both its own history and the Chinese people.

Litzinger focuses on the ethnic margins within China as a window onto ongoing struggles over how state and community security are to be defined and achieved as China is increasingly integrated into the world economy. Discourses of cultural recovery such as the return of Yao ritual practices, he argues, constitute a technology of rule through which ethnic minority cultures are being updated, transformed, and harnessed to the modernizing project of the Chinese state.

The volume concludes with two reflections on some of the practices and institutions through which scholarly communities—including our own—participate in the production of insecurity. Hugh Gusterson discusses some of the means through which American specialists in security studies, writing in the journal *International Security* in the late 1980s and early 1990s, constructed an influential discursive world "within which the indefinite continuation of the Cold War was plausibly presumed and what we would in retrospect narrate as signs of the impending end of the Cold War were rendered dubious or invisible." As such, the discourse of security studies, as exemplified in *International Security,* contributed to the production of the insecurities of the Cold War. Finally, John Mowitt locates this volume and efforts like it in relation to the contemporary politics of disciplinarity and interdisciplinarity within the North American academy. Drawing on the work of the late Michel Foucault, Mowitt sketches a geopolitical history of disciplines, in part by showing how insecurity and disciplinarity intertwine. In so doing, he not only raises questions about the politics of linking uncertainties over disciplinary objects of analysis with the "end of the Cold War," but also puts in doubt the claimed centrality of that end in provoking the insecurities of our time.

NOTES

Thanks to Itty Abraham, Pamela Ballinger, Michael Barnett, Lynn Eden, Akhil Gupta, David Holloway, Charles Lipson, Ralph Litzinger, Joseph Masco, Jennifer Milliken, Carolyn Nordstrom, Stephanie Platz, Thomas Risse, Diana Saco, Ivan Toft, and colleagues at Minnesota, Kent State, Stanford, and Chicago for comments on various versions of this chapter.

1. On culture as an object of analysis, see Lapid and Kratochwil (1996) and Katzenstein (1996). One of the ways in which culture has become an

object of analysis is by treating ethnicity as an increasingly important source of instability, conflict, and violence. Major funding agencies, such as the Social Science Research Council and the MacArthur Foundation, began targeting ethnicity as a security problem in the late 1980s (see Latham, 1995). The Council on Foreign Relations also established a committee/section on culture.

2. For analyses that demonstrate the implication of cultural processes in the Cold War, see, for example, Boyer (1985), Carmichael (1993), Carter (1988), Corber (1993), Lewontin et al. (1997), and May (1989). For cultural analyses of nuclear weapons, see Cohn (1987) and Gusterson (1996).

3. We recognize the contentious nature of claims about and periodizations of the end of the Cold War. For example, Agnew and Corbridge (1995) argue that the Cold War ended in 1980, whereas Cox (1996) argues that the Cold War has not ended.

4. As Alker and Biersteker observed in 1984, international relations is constituted as an interdiscipline, heavily rooted in political science but drawing extensively on models from neighboring fields such as sociology, economics, and history. One subfield of this interdiscipline is constituted by scholars and practitioners of international security. We use the phrase *security studies* to refer to that subfield. In much of the remainder of this Introduction, we focus attention on security studies, because cultural productions of insecurity are more central to its constitution as a subfield than they are to the constitution of other subfields of international relations, such as international political economy. But our primary objective is to foster theoretical conversation between sociocultural anthropology and international relations more broadly.

5. For other studies directed to rethinking security and insecurity, see Krause and Williams (1996, 1997); see also Lipschutz (1995) and Katzenstein (1996). On international relations and anthropology, see, for example, Eriksen and Neumann (1993); Boyarin (1994); and Shapiro and Alker (1996).

6. See Abu-Lughod (1991) for an argument, manifesting the increasing influence of Michel Foucault among anthropologists, that anthropologists should orient their analyses to "discourse" rather than "culture." See Yanagisako and Delaney (1995: 15–19) for a response that defends the analytical use of "culture" while, like Abu-Lughod, warning of the dangers of reifying it. Appadurai (1996: chapter 1) argues for a displacement from use of the noun form (culture) to the adjectival form (cultural) to reduce the tendency to reify.

7. With respect to social theory, there is often a greater degree of commonality between post-positivist scholars of international relations and those working in fields such as critical geopolitics (e.g., between Krishna,

1996, and Ó Tuathail, 1996), cultural studies (e.g., between Weldes, 1996, 1999, and Hall, 1988), and cultural anthropology (e.g., between Doty, 1996b, and Thomas, 1994, or Shapiro, 1994, 1997, and Appadurai, 1996) than with disciplinary peers employing natural science models and behavioralist assumptions.

8. This panel did, however, result in a special issue of *Human Peace,* edited by Robert Textor (1991).

9. See, however, Rubinstein and Foster (1988, 1989) and Turner and Pitt (1989). See Nader (1997) on the impact, largely unacknowledged in the field, of the Cold War on anthropology.

10. For an interesting argument that anthropology consists of core subfields (political anthropology, economic anthropology, psychological anthropology) that replicate the boundaries between neighboring social sciences while insisting on anthropology's authority over premodern instantiations of each discipline's subject matter, see Collier (1997).

11. The ways in which the ethnographic project of an earlier generation was deformed by colonialism has been brought into focus by a spate of writing on the subject. See Borneman (1995), Clifford (1988), Clifford and Marcus (1986), Foerstel and Gilliam (1992), Marcus and Fischer (1986), Rabinow (1977), and Wolf (1982).

12. For two edited volumes giving a sampling of this work, see Nordstrom and Martin (1992) and Nordstrom and Robben (1995). See also Borneman (1997).

13. On various approaches to the constitution of self and other in a wide variety of cultural processes, see, among others, Campbell (1992, 1994), Connolly (1991), Doty (1993), Drinnon (1990), Greenblatt (1991), Said (1978), Shapiro (1988), Spurr (1993), and Todorov (1982).

14. For a similar argument, one that draws explicitly on Connolly but limits its focus to the production of state identity, see Campbell (1992), especially chapter 1.

15. Relations of constitution differ from the conventional understanding of causal relations. The process of constitution is basically definitional: it explains how "a particular phenomenon is that phenomenon and not something else." It delineates the "possibility conditions for the existence of phenomena"; how, that is, within a discourse, some phenomena are possible such that they are defined in that discourse as those phenomena (Majeski and Sylvan, 1991: 8).

16. For a discussion of subject-positions, see Althusser (1971) or Davies and Harré (1990).

17. As Althusser (1971) has argued, ideas are in any case themselves material, if only because they have material effects.

18. Although he warns against too close a connection between security

studies and policy debates, Walt lauds this intimate connection of security studies to the state when he argues that "On the whole, security studies have profited from its [sic] connection to real-world issues; the main advances of the past four decades have emerged from attempts to solve important practical questions" (1991: 222).

19. Distinctions between problem-solving and critical theories, while not unproblematic, have a substantial history and are discussed by, among others, Fay (1975), Benton (1977), Bernstein (1978), and Cox (1986).

20. Such a claim is, of course, far less true today.

21. The following remarks have been prompted in part by reflection on Part III of Bernstein (1983), Dirks (1996), and Derrida (1974).

1

The Cultural Production of Crises: U.S. Identity and Missiles in Cuba

JUTTA WELDES

"On Tuesday morning, October 16, shortly after 9:00 o'clock, President Kennedy called and asked me to come to the White House. He said only that we were facing great trouble. Shortly afterward, in his office, he told me that a U-2 had just finished a photographic mission and that the Intelligence Community had become convinced that Russia was placing missiles and atomic weapons in Cuba" (R. F. Kennedy, 1971: 1). So began the "Cuban missile crisis."

The discovery of Soviet nuclear-capable missiles in Cuba was understood by U.S. state officials to signal the onset of a serious international crisis: the threat these missiles posed to U.S. security, and the concomitant existence of a crisis, were just plain obvious. Because of their offensive capabilities, the missiles were a grave "threat to peace" (J. F. Kennedy, in "October 27, 1962," 1987–88: 49) and their deployment was "intolerable and unacceptable" (Rusk, in "White House Tapes and Minutes," 1985: 172). As General Maxwell Taylor, Chairman of the Joint Chiefs of Staff during the crisis, has since explained, "there was no question about the problem. The President announced his objective within an hour of seeing the photographs of the missiles: it was to get the missiles out of Cuba" (in Blight and Welch, 1990: 77). And, according to Douglas Dillon, then-Secretary of the Treasury:

> While everyone at our first ExComm [Executive Committee of the
> National Security Council] meeting, specifically including the President, agreed that the emplacement of Soviet MRBMs and IRBMs in

Cuba was totally unacceptable and that they had to be gotten out one way or the other, I do not recall any specific discussion then or at later meetings of the ExComm as to just why they were unacceptable. *It just seemed obvious to all of us.* (In ibid., 49; emphasis added)

The essential character of the Cuban missile crisis *as* a crisis has been no more in doubt among (U.S.) scholars than among U.S. policymakers. The representation of the Soviet missile deployment and its immediate aftermath as a shocking foreign-policy crisis has been accepted and reproduced by most scholars, who have routinely taken U.S. decision makers' understandings of the events of October 1962 as the baseline from which to conduct their analyses (e.g., Abel, 1966; Allison, 1971). Although scholars have asked many questions about the events of October 1962, they have rarely asked whether or not these events actually had to be or should have been understood as a crisis. For example, Graham Allison's famous study of the missile crisis begins with four questions: (1) Why did the Soviet Union place strategic offensive missiles in Cuba? (2) Why did the United States respond with a naval quarantine of Soviet shipments to Cuba? (3) Why were the missiles withdrawn? and (4) What are the lessons of the missile crisis? (1971: 1–2). Rather than asking how these events came to be constituted as a "crisis," their status as a crisis requiring immediate action is assumed. Similarly, Ronald Pope argued in 1982 that the analysis of newly available Soviet materials could shed light on several important issues concerning the Cuban missile crisis, among them "why the missiles were sent to Cuba; what the significance of their deployment was; who, in the Soviet view, was responsible for the subsequent crisis; why the missiles were removed; who was responsible for ending the crisis; what the immediate results of the crisis were; and, finally, what lessons the Soviets seem to have drawn from this confrontation" (1982: 3). Again, the existence of a crisis, rather than being questioned or explained, is taken for granted from the outset.

But asking whether or not these events could have been understood otherwise than as a crisis is neither silly nor insignificant. After all, the Soviet Union lived with U.S. missiles in Turkey without insisting on a "Turkish missile crisis," so, crises are not inherent in the presence of enemy missiles, even nuclear ones, near one's borders. Furthermore, as demonstrated later in this chapter, alternative understandings of these events are not only plausible, but were available both to U.S. state officials and to subsequent commentators and analysts. That the Cuban missile crisis was a "crisis," then, is not in fact obvious; rather, the unquestioned status of these events as a crisis is a puzzle to be explained. In this chapter, I therefore ask: how did the events of October 1962 come to be understood as a crisis? In doing so, I hope to demonstrate that the Cuban missile crisis in particular, and crises more generally, are social, and specifically cultural, constructions.

The Cuban missile crisis is a useful exemplar because it has "assumed genuinely mythic significance" (Blight, Nye, and Welch, 1987: 170)—it has come to be treated, at least in the United States, as the paradigmatic Cold War crisis. It was "one of a few known nuclear crises in world history" (Thorson and Sylvan, 1982: 540) and one that exposed starkly the dangers of nuclear confrontation. During this "crisis," "the American people lived under the threat of disaster" (Divine, 1971: 3), as, of course, did many other people. Of equal importance is the canonical status achieved by the Cuban missile crisis as a masterpiece of "crisis management" (e.g., Richardson, 1988: 14). According to the orthodox U.S. narrative of these events, President Kennedy's "combination of toughness and restraint, of will, nerve and wisdom, so brilliantly controlled, so matchlessly calibrated . . . dazzled the world" (Schlesinger, 1965: 81).[1] Finally, in the fields of security and crisis studies, the Cuban missile crisis has received as much attention as any other crisis. In fact, it was this particular crisis that "spurred on" the development of the field of crisis studies in the 1960s and 1970s (Seeger, 1995: 17). Thus, if it can be shown that the Cuban missile crisis, this paragon of crises, was a cultural construction, then the case for the construction of all crises is rendered that much more plausible.

WHAT CRISIS?

Against the assumption that crises present themselves as objective facts, I argue that crises are social constructions that are forged by state officials in the course of producing and reproducing state identity. If crises are constructed in relation to particular state identities, events that are ostensibly the same will in fact be constituted as different crises, or not as a crisis at all, by and for states with different identities. The diverse ways in which the events of October 1962 were represented in the foreign-policy discourses of the United States, the Soviet Union, and Cuba offer a striking example.

For the United States, these events became known as the "Cuban missile crisis." The crisis was relatively short, spanning a mere thirteen days from October 16, when the presence of Soviet missiles in Cuba was confirmed and reported to the ExComm, to October 28, when the Soviets agreed to withdraw the missiles.[2] At issue in this crisis were Soviet missiles—it started with their discovery and ended with their withdrawal. The cause of the crisis was the Soviet missile deployment; responsibility for the crisis thus rested with the Soviet leadership. This missile deployment was a *crisis*, rather than, say, a mere nuisance, because the deployment of the missiles in Cuba by the Soviet other challenged the very identity of the United States, not only as the leader of the "free world" but also as the guarantor of freedom in the Western Hemisphere. At the same time, it provided an opportunity—realized through the successful U.S. quarantine— for the United States to reassert its leadership identity.

For the Soviets, in contrast, these events were the "Caribbean crisis" (e.g., Khrushchev, 1970; Gromyko, 1971). The situation was one of imminent U.S. aggression against Cuba. The time frame is much longer and includes not only the 1961 Bay of Pigs invasion but a prolonged history of U.S. aggression against Cuba. The issue was U.S. imperialism and the threat that it presented to socialism in general and to the socialist experiment in Cuba in particular. The cause of the crisis was, broadly, the threat of further U.S. aggression against Cuba and, more immediately, its unreasonable response to the defensive Soviet missile deployment. The identity for which these events were the "Caribbean crisis" is a subject—the Soviet Union— defined as the leader of the socialist bloc pledged to support socialist states and surrounded by a hostile other—the aggressive, nuclear-armed, global capitalist alliance led by the United States. The "crisis" for this subject, the urgent problem to be solved, was the threat to Soviet identity as the leader of the socialist world posed both by an imminent U.S. invasion of Cuba and the feared overthrow of Cuban socialism and by the U.S. insistence that the missiles be removed. This crisis also provided the Soviet Union with the opportunity—ostensibly realized in the U.S. pledge not to invade Cuba—to reaffirm its identity as the leader of the global socialist movement.

For the Cubans, what has come to be called the "October crisis" (e.g., Castro, 1992; Dorticós, 1962) is, yet again, substantially different. The situation was one in which the Cubans were attempting, with military assistance from the Soviet Union, to protect themselves against renewed aggression from their U.S. other. The time frame, unlike that of the "Caribbean crisis," is somewhat vaguely limited to October and November 1962 but, unlike the "Cuban missile crisis," it is understood to be embedded in the almost overwhelming insecurity brought on by relentless U.S. aggression (e.g., the Bay of Pigs invasion) and intervention (e.g., Operation Mongoose). The issue was fundamentally one of sovereignty: Cuba's right as an independent state to protect itself—its independence and its revolution—from imperialist aggression. The cause of the crisis was, again, the threat of renewed U.S. aggression and, more immediately, the act of war (i.e., the blockade) with which the United States responded to the Soviet missiles. The identity for which these events were a crisis was a small and vulnerable, yet sovereign, state attempting to protect and maintain its fledgling socialist revolution. The "crisis," the urgent problem to be solved, was the threat to this Cuban revolutionary identity posed by a hegemonic counterrevolutionary U.S. other poised, as the Cubans thought, for an imminent invasion and for the overthrow of the Cuban Revolution. Simultaneously, this crisis provided an opportunity—only partially realized in the U.S. no-invasion pledge— for Cuba to reassert its identity both as a sovereign state and as a successful socialist revolution.

As these contesting narratives indicate, the events of October 1962 have been constructed quite differently. The nature of this crisis, then, is not obvious. Although all three narratives represent these events as a crisis of some kind, albeit with notably different causes and issues at stake, it is worth pointing out that it was not inevitable—it was not given by any objective facts—that these events be read as a crisis. For example, had U.S. state officials represented the Soviet missile deployment as irrelevant to U.S. identity, the events of October 1962 would not have constituted a crisis for anyone. Such a representation is not unthinkable. Indeed, drawing on some of the arguments made by U.S. state officials, in particular those of then-Secretary of Defense Robert McNamara, one can quite easily generate a narrative in which these events were not a crisis at all (e.g., Weldes, 1996: 293–95).

On such a hypothetical account, the salient situation prior to

October 1962 was one in which the nuclear balance was strongly tipped in favor of the United States. Because the much-touted "missile gap" had been exposed as a fraud in February 1961, Soviet strategic pretensions had been deflated and its Cold War credibility undermined. The issue in October 1962 thus revolved around the nuclear strategic imbalance. Although Khrushchev deployed the missiles in Cuba in order to help the Soviet Union to "equalize what the West likes to call 'the balance of power'" (Khrushchev, 1970: 547), the United States nonetheless retained overwhelming strategic superiority. The Soviet deployment of missiles in Cuba, as McNamara more recently argued, simply "made no difference." As he explained,

> What difference would the extra 40 [Soviet missiles] have made to the overall balance? If my memory serves me correctly, we had some five thousand nuclear warheads as against their three hundred. Can anyone seriously tell me that their having 340 would have made any difference? The military balance wasn't changed. I didn't believe it then, and I don't believe it now. (In Blight and Welch, 1990: 23)

According to this representation, the Soviet missile deployment might have been understood as irrelevant to U.S. identity—whether as the leader of the Free World, as the leader of the Western hemisphere, or as the global nuclear superpower—and so need not have triggered any crisis at all. And if it had not been constructed as a crisis for the United States, then, of course, it would not have been a crisis for the Soviet Union or Cuba either. As these divergent narratives indicate, there are no objective crises out there waiting to be discovered or observed by state officials or analysts. Instead, events are differently constructed *as* crises, or not constructed as crises at all, in different cultural contexts and in relation to the discursively constituted identities of states.

THE PRODUCTION OF THE CUBAN MISSILE CRISIS

The Cuban missile crisis was produced in representations of the Soviet missile deployment in Cuba as a serious threat to, or the production of insecurity for, the deeply entrenched Cold War identity of the United States as the global leader in the battle with communism and as the regional leader of the Western Hemisphere. At the same time it provided the United States with the opportunity to reassert that identity, to attempt, yet again, to secure its always precarious self. At

the heart of the Cuban missile crisis, then, resides a culturally constituted subject—the United States—with a particular, discursively constituted identity.

A by now classic anecdote nicely illustrates the importance of the
identity of the United States to the production of the missile crisis.
During an ExComm debate over the advisability of launching an un-
announced air strike against the new-sprung missile bases in Cuba,
Robert Kennedy is reported to have written in a note: "I now know
how Tojo felt when he was planning Pearl Harbor" (in Schlesinger,
1965: 803). Later in the discussion, according to Schlesinger, Kennedy
insisted that

> he did not believe that, with all the memory of Pearl Harbor and all
> the responsibility we would have to bear in the world afterward, the
> President of the United States could possibly order such an operation.
> For 175 years *we had not been that kind of country.* Sunday-morning
> surprise blows on small nations were not in our tradition. Thousands
> of Cubans would be killed without warning, and hundreds of Rus-
> sians too. We were fighting for something more than survival, and a
> sneak attack would constitute a betrayal of our heritage and our
> ideals. (Ibid., 806–7; emphasis added)

The use of the Pearl Harbor analogy thus served to underscore for
U.S. decision makers what kind of subject the United States was
not—it was not a country whose traditions would countenance a
"sneak attack," at least not against a small country on a Sunday
morning. As a result, certain policy options were effectively foreclosed, at least in the short term, and the proposal to launch surprise
air strikes against Cuba was temporarily shelved. But the identity of
the United States, and specific arguments about what sort of subject
the United States was or was not, did not simply serve to score debating points among decision makers. Instead, U.S. state identity
was the linchpin around which the events of October 1962 were
constructed *as* a crisis. To demonstrate this, I highlight four central
and interconnected facets of the Cold War representation of "the
United States"—as global and hemispheric leader, as the bastion and
defender of freedom, as strong and resolute, and as credible—and
then show how the Soviet missile deployment was represented as an
acute and formidable threat—that is, as "a crisis"—in relation to
this discursively constituted identity.

U.S. COLD WAR IDENTITY

During the Cold War, "leadership" anchored the logic of an emphatically masculinist U.S. state identity. The United States was the "leader" of "the West" or the "free world" and the global champion of "freedom" and "democracy."[3] This leadership role was forcefully asserted in 1950 in NSC 68, a pivotal National Security Council policy planning document: "the absence of order among nations," its authors argued, "is becoming less and less tolerable" and "this fact imposes upon us [the United States], in our own interests, the responsibility of world leadership" (U.S. National Security Council, 1950: 390). Two assumptions were typically adduced to support the claim to U.S. leadership. First, it was treated as axiomatic that the United States won World War II and that this victory imposed on it the awesome responsibility of creating "half a world, the free half" in its own image (Acheson, 1969: "Apologia Pro Libre Hoc"). Already in 1945 President Truman had announced that "Whether we like it or not, we must all recognize that the victory which we have won has placed upon the American people the continued burden of responsibility for world leadership" (1945: 549). The successful outcome of World War II, that is, forced the United States, however reluctantly, to shoulder the burden of global leadership. After all, the United States was now "the only source of power capable of mobilizing successful opposition to the Communist goal of world conquest" (NSC 7) (U.S. National Security Council, 1948: 165).

Second, the United States was saddled with this "burden" as a result of its exceptional character. U.S. uniqueness resided in its "free society," which provided for the rest of the world an outstanding model of the way in which the "free way of life" and "free institutions"—in particular, representative or liberal democracy and a liberal market economy—could develop and flourish. As John F. Kennedy explained, "We [the United States] stand for freedom" (1961d: 396) because "our nation is on the side of man's desire to be free, and the desire of nations to be independent" (1961c: 369). This uniqueness, in turn, conferred upon the United States the "right to the moral leadership of the planet" (John F. Kennedy, quoted in Lundestad, 1989: 527). And the United States was not only the model but also the patron of freedom. Indeed, as the authors of NSC 68 argued, the United States had the obligation to "demonstrate power, confidence and a sense of moral and political direction" so that these same qualities could blossom elsewhere (U.S. National Security Council, 1950: 404).

Moreover, for the United States both to preserve its own unique freedoms and successfully to serve as a guide to others, it had to "foster a world environment in which the American system can survive and flourish" (ibid., 401). This need stemmed from the established Cold War axiom that freedom is indivisible: a threat to freedom anywhere is a threat to freedom everywhere. Truman, for example, justified U.S. participation in the Korean War on these grounds: "We cannot hope to maintain our own freedom," he argued, "if freedom elsewhere is wiped out" (1950: 610). In 1959, during the Berlin crisis, Eisenhower assured West Berliners that "We recognize that freedom is indivisible. Wherever in the world freedom is destroyed, by that much is every free nation hurt" (1959a: 30). As a result, as Kennedy asserted in 1961, "every time a country, regardless of how far away it may be from our own borders, every time that country passes behind the Iron Curtain, the security of the United States is thereby endangered" (1961b: 624). The indivisibility of freedom obligated the United States to "promote a world order" (George F. Kennan, in Gaddis, 1982: 27) in which freedom could prosper.

The indivisibility of freedom was particularly salient in the "Western Hemisphere" over which the United States, through the Monroe Doctrine and its successors and extensions, had established protective custody.[4] Although Khrushchev had announced in 1961 that the Monroe Doctrine was "dead" (Khrushchev, 1961: 6), the U.S. State Department made it clear at the time of the missile crisis that the principle embodied in the Monroe Doctrine "is just as valid in 1962 as it was in 1823, though the old imperialism of Western Europe has been replaced by the new and far more menacing political and ideological imperialism of international communism" (U.S. Department of State, Bureau of Public Affairs, 1962: 6). According to the Caracas Resolution of 1954, "The domination or control of the political institutions of any American state by the international communist movement extending to this hemisphere the political system of an extracontinental power would constitute a threat to the sovereignty and independence of the American states, endangering the peace of America" (in Atkins, 1989: 223). Kennedy drew on the logic of freedom's indivisibility in addressing the continued danger presented by the Castro regime in the aftermath of the Bay of Pigs disaster: "We intend to profit from this lesson," he argued, "We intend to intensify our efforts for a struggle in many ways more difficult than war. . . . I am determined upon our system's survival and success, regardless of the cost and regardless of the peril!" (1961a: 306). Communism in Cuba posed a threat to the "survival and success" of the U.S. system not, as Kennedy himself admitted, because "a nation of Cuba's size" was a direct threat to the United States, but because Cuba served as "a base for subverting the survival of other free nations throughout the hemisphere." As a result, Kennedy argued, "the real issue" in Cuba was "the survival of freedom in this hemisphere itself" (ibid., 305).

The pervasive rhetoric of "*burdens* of responsibility" implied that the obligations attendant upon U.S. leadership were at least in part an encumbrance. In fulfilling its leadership role, then, the United States was acting altruistically rather than strictly for its own gain. This altruism is captured in the notion of U.S. "commitments": commitments are pledges or promises that the United States is bound to honor, even though they may entail significant costs. The public-spiritedness of U.S. leadership implied by the term *commitments* was routinely opposed to the self-interested aggressiveness of the Soviets and of communists in general. In discussing the global struggle with "international Communism," for instance, Theodore Sorenson distinguished "U.S. commitment" from "Communist power involvement" in places such as the Congo, Laos, and South Vietnam (1965: 634).[5] Attributing "power involvements" to communists and "commitments" to the United States implied that "Communists" were engaged in aggression for the sake of private, self-interested gain (e.g., imperial expansion and ultimately world domination), whereas the United States was merely discharging, in other-regarding fashion, the responsibilities of a leader. The implication is clear: commitments made by leaders such as the United States are legitimate; the activities they warrant are worthy. The power involvements of communists, on the other hand, are illegitimate and their activities nefarious. The rhetoric of burdens of leadership, in part by differentiating the United States from the aggressive other it was charged with combating, thus constituted a U.S. identity that acts altruistically in the pursuit of admirable goals such as freedom and democracy.

A related contrast, between the "openness" of U.S. commitments and "the atmosphere of oriental secretiveness and conspiracy" (Kennan, 1946: 55) that marked Soviet aggression, helped to flesh out this U.S. identity. As Wymberley Coerr (then Deputy Assistant Secretary for Inter-American Affairs) asserted in 1961:

> Our objective toward the nations of Latin America is simple: We want the friendship of their governments and peoples. . . . We seek no satellites. We control no fifth columns or traitorous domestic parties with which to convert independent nations into satellites. We cherish the independence of the nations in this hemisphere as the key to their friendship for us, recognizing that it would suffer from undue exertions of our influence and that under Soviet domination it would die. (U.S. Department of State, 1961: 1)

On this account, the United States sought friendship and promoted independence while its Soviet adversary sought satellites, controlled fifth columns and traitorous domestic parties, and exercised domination. On the model of "Red Fascism" (Paterson, 1989), despotic "totalitarian" regimes were endowed with a penchant for secrecy and duplicity. "Our adversaries," Kennedy argued in 1961,

> use the *secrecy* of the *totalitarian* state and the discipline *to mask* the effective use of guerilla forces *secretly* undermining independent states, and *to hide* a wide international network of agents and activities which threaten the fabric of democratic government everywhere in the world. And their single-minded effort to destroy freedom is strengthened by the discipline, *the secrecy,* and the swiftness with which an efficient *despotism* can move. (1961c: 367; emphasis added)

The United States, in contrast, engaged in open rather than secret diplomacy, was forthright and trustworthy rather than treacherous, and used force only defensively, not for purposes of domination. As Adlai Stevenson explained in 1962, intermediate range ballistic missiles (IRBMs) had been placed by the United States onto the territory of various NATO members "without concealment or deceit, as a consequence of agreements freely negotiated and publicly declared" (1962: 729). Thus, U.S. missiles were deployed overseas "under open and announced agreements with sovereign states. They serve to strengthen the independence of those countries" (U.S. Department of State, Bureau of Public Affairs, 1962: 7).

Since creating a world, or at least half a world, in its own image demanded considerable effort, it is not surprising that this U.S.

identity narrative was preoccupied with the twin virtues of strength and will. Strength and will were essential in part because of the indivisibility of freedom. If an attack on freedom anywhere is an attack on freedom everywhere, then the United States, as the state bearing leadership responsibilities for promoting global freedom, required compelling strength as well as the courage to bring that strength to bear against aggressors. Strength and resolve were also necessitated by the specific character of the "totalitarian aggressor." The totalitarian penchant for "salami-slicing" tactics—for pursuing a series of "little encroachments not easily resisted . . . because one in itself seems trivial" (Bundy, 1988: 364)—and the related danger of "appeasement" required resolute displays of strength. Weakness would only invite further aggression. As Kennedy argued in 1961,

> The message of Cuba, of Laos, of the rising din of Communist voices in Asia and Latin America—these messages are all the same. The complacent, the self-indulgent, the soft societies are about to be swept away with the debris of history. Only the strong, only the industrious, only the determined, only the courageous, only the visionary who determine the real nature of our struggle can possibly survive. (1961a: 306)

U.S. identity, in short, was not only masculinist but aggressively macho. The fear of appearing weak—whether of arms or of will—loomed large because such a feminine characteristic would excite not the desired respect, but only contempt. "A weakling, particularly a rich and opulent weakling, seeking a peaceable solution to a difficulty, is likely to invite contempt," General Eisenhower explained in 1945, "but the same plea from the strong is listened to more respectfully" (1945: 109). U.S. identity was thus constructed not only in opposition to the external other of secretive and aggressive totalitarians but in opposition as well to an internal feminine other defined as weak, soft, complacent, and self-indulgent.

All three of these defining characteristics of the masculinized U.S. identity produced for the United States a pervasive and inescapable credibility problem. Claims to U.S. leadership, assertions to its guardianship of global freedom, and avowals of its strength and courage all involved a combination of promises and threats. To be of any use, these commitments had to be believed. But their very nature and extensiveness rendered suspect the claim that the United States could and would live up to them. Each of these aspects of the U.S. identity, then, simultaneously generated both a need for the United States to be credible and grave doubts about its credibility. As a result, the problem of credibility became central to U.S. identity.

The U.S. credibility problem was inextricably connected to the putative indivisibility of freedom. Because "a defeat of free institutions anywhere is a defeat everywhere" (U.S. National Security Council, 1950: 389), the free society so painstakingly nurtured by the United States both at home and abroad was always in danger. U.S. leadership thus demanded continual demonstration of its ability both to guide its allies and followers and to counter threats by actual and potential opponents; that is, the confidence of its allies (i.e., its leadership) and the reliability of its threats against its adversaries (i.e., its strength and will) had constantly to be (re)affirmed. This led the United States into ever-expanding commitments. As Gabriel Kolko has argued concerning the U.S. commitment to the Diem regime in South Vietnam: "the essentially open-ended undertakings inherent in this desire to sustain the confidence of its allies and the fear of its putative enemies had caused the United States to stake its role in the world on controlling events in relatively minor places" (1980: 293). But such expanded commitments created fresh areas in which U.S. credibility could be challenged.

The logic of credibility, of course, is ultimately self-defeating. For the United States to demonstrate its credibility as the "tough" leader in the fight for freedom, extensive commitments were required. But these commitments immediately became additional sources of insecurity because they became targets at which threats could be launched by an adversary, or even by an ally. A failure to respond to such threats then again challenged U.S. credibility. This Cold War narrative of U.S. identity thus embroiled the United States in a continuous and ultimately futile search for absolute credibility. Although all identities are, by definition, potentially unstable and insecure (as I argue later), the specific, discursively constituted Cold War identity of the United States was overtly and pervasively precarious. U.S. identity thus became a potent and persistent source and locus of crises that, while hazardous to U.S. identity, at the same time provided U.S. state officials with opportunities to reproduce that identity. The Cuban missile crisis is a good example.

U.S. IDENTITY AND MISSILES IN CUBA

The Soviet missile deployment in Cuba was constituted *as* a crisis, and that crisis rendered just plain obvious, in relation to this well-established masculinist U.S. identity. U.S. state officials staked U.S. identity on Cuba and in so doing created a locus of possible (one might even say probable) crisis. The representation of these events as a threat to U.S. identity both transformed the events themselves into a crisis and marginalized alternative narratives. U.S. identity thus enabled the production of the "Cuban missile crisis." Conversely, the cultural construction of the missile crisis enabled the (re)production of U.S. state identity; that is, constructing the Soviet missile deployment *as* a crisis offered U.S. state officials the opportunity to (re)assert the already precarious identity of the United States. At the same time, it enabled the (re)construction of a broader "we" around the identity of the U.S. state. The representational practices of the U.S. state surrounding the events of October 1962 thus had four significant consequences: they enabled the construction of a crisis; they marginalized other narratives; they made possible the reassertion of U.S. state identity; and they permitted the reproduction of a broader "we."

The Soviet installation of missiles in Cuba was constituted as a crisis by representing it as a serious threat to all four components of U.S. state identity. U.S. leadership, as well as the credibility of its claims to leadership, were at stake because the United States was pledged to promote freedom in and to prevent "Communist" incursions into the "Western hemisphere," to overturn or at least to contain the Castro revolution, and, more narrowly, to prevent the introduction of offensive Soviet weapons into Cuba (e.g., Kennedy, 1962a, 1962b). The basic elements of this crisis and its relationship to U.S. state identity are captured in Adlai Stevenson's depiction, in the UN on October 23, of the Soviet missile deployment: the "crucial fact" to be faced, he maintained, was that "Cuba has given the Soviet Union a bridgehead and staging area in this hemisphere, that it has invited an extra-continental, anti-democratic and expansionist power into the bosom of the American family, that it has made itself an accomplice in the Communist enterprise of world domination" (1962: 731). The threat to the United States posed by the Soviet missiles thus revolved around both global and hemispheric U.S. leadership. As Hans Morgenthau argued in November 1962, "the transformation of Cuba into a Soviet military base" was "detrimental to the political position of the United States in the Western Hemisphere in that it challenged American influence in an area which had traditionally been regarded as an American sphere of influence." As a result, he continued, "The Soviet presence in Cuba . . . affects the prestige of the United States as a great power" (1962: 9). Similarly, Zbigniew Brzezinski placed U.S. leadership and its credibility at the center of his depiction of the crisis: "the presence of Communism in Cuba," he asserted, "undermines the American claim that the Western Hemisphere is immune to Communist penetration and that the United States has the capacity to exclude Communism from this hemisphere. It thus forces the United States to back down from a traditionally proclaimed position and *imposes upon it a humiliation* which is bound to have international implications" (1962: 7; emphasis added). What was crucial to the United States during the missile crisis was living up to the masculinist identity constructed for it within the Cold War discourse of U.S. foreign policy: an identity built around leadership, freedom, strength and will, and credibility.

The missile deployment challenged U.S. leadership in that it was "aggressive intervention" into the Western Hemisphere (Rusk, 1962: 721); it was an "invasion of the hemisphere by a foreign power" (Douglas Dillon, in Abel, 1966: 117). This "provocation" and "attempted nuclear blackmail" (Sorenson, 1965: 700, 706), because it "was something that they [the Soviet Union] started in our own backyard" (Dillon, in Blight and Welch, 1990: 100), issued a direct challenge to U.S. leadership in the hemisphere that the United States was pledged, through the Monroe Doctrine and its successors, to defend. As a result, as Rusk argued in the ExComm on October 16, the United States had an "obligation to do what had to be done" ("White House Tapes and Minutes," 1985: 173).

The missiles posed a challenge to the U.S. status as freedom's defender as well. Because freedom is indivisible, a threat to freedom anywhere, even in a small island state such as Cuba, was a threat to freedom everywhere, including the entire Western Hemisphere and the United States itself. First of all, as Rusk explained to the OAS during the missile crisis, "this new Soviet intervention means a further tightening of the enslavement of the Cuban people by the Soviet power to which the Castro regime has surrendered the Cuban national heritage" (1962: 721). But more than Cuban freedom was at stake. This

"Soviet intervention" challenged freedom in the entire hemisphere because, as Stevenson argued in the UN, "an extra-continental, anti-democratic power" had, in the service of the "Communist enterprise of world domination," intruded into "the bosom of the American family" (1962: 731). "The most urgent problem confronting the hemisphere" in October 1962, Rusk explained to the OAS Council, was "the efforts of the Sino-Soviet bloc to convert the island of Cuba into an armed base for the Communist penetration of the Americas" (1962: 720).

The most overtly masculinist elements of U.S. identity—its strength and will—were under attack in the missile crisis as well. As Kennedy said at the ExComm meeting of October 16, allowing the Soviet missiles to remain in Cuba "makes them [the Cubans] look like they're coequal with us [the United States] and that—" "and that," Dillon concluded for him, "we're scared of the Cubans" ("White House Tapes and Minutes," 1985: 186). Such a perception would be intolerable, of course, because the maintenance of U.S. leadership required the maintenance of U.S. strength and the projection of U.S. resolve. The missile crisis thus "illuminates a feature of the American character that came to be considered a requisite personality trait of the cold war," namely, "toughness" (Nathan, 1975: 267). Of particular concern, then, was that Khrushchev had set a "trap" for the United States:

> The objective of the trap was both political and strategic. If the trap had been successful, our missile warning system would have been bypassed and the whole strategic balance overturned. But the President and his advisors put the main emphasis on the political objective. "If they'd got away with this one," says one member of ExComm, "we'd have been a paper tiger, a second-class power." (Alsop and Bartlett, 1962: 18)

The Soviet missile deployment, that is, raised questions about U.S. strength, its toughness and its will, and thus challenged the U.S. leadership identity by threatening to reduce the United States to, or to expose it as, a paper tiger.

As these examples already indicate, the credibility problem endemic to this masculinist Cold War U.S. identity was central to the construction of the Cuban missile crisis. In his speech to the American public on October 22, Kennedy explicitly pointed to the importance of U.S. credibility. The Soviet missile deployment "cannot be accepted by this country," he argued, because "the 1930s taught us a clear lesson: Aggressive conduct, if allowed to go unchecked and unchallenged, ultimately leads to war." As a result, the missiles could not be tolerated by the United States "if our courage and our commitments are ever to be trusted again by either friend or foe" (1962c: 5–6). Having said that the United States would not condone Soviet offensive missiles in Cuba (Kennedy, 1962a, 1962b), acquiescing in their deployment would have undercut U.S. credibility. This point was hammered home by Adlai Stevenson in the UN as well, in his insistence that

> If the United States and the other nations of the Western Hemisphere should accept this basic disturbance of the world's structure of power, we should invite a new surge of Communist aggression at every point along the frontier that divides the Communist world from the democratic world. If we do not stand firm here, our adversaries may think that we will stand firm nowhere—and we guarantee a heightening of the world civil war [i.e., the Cold War] to new levels of intensity and danger. (1962: 733)

This, in turn, would have threatened the identity of the United States *as* the legitimate leader of the free world. Had the United States allowed the missiles to remain in Cuba, the United States might have been perceived as a paper tiger, a second-class power, unable or unwilling to honor its promises or to make good on its threats.

The result was that the overarching U.S. interest in the missile crisis became precisely maintaining its credibility. Even a small slice off the salami required that the United States, bearing the burdens of leadership, enact its credibility. The pervasive problem of U.S. credibility central to the U.S. identity meant that the need to remove the missiles was obvious. The failure to do so would undermine the very identity of the United States *as* a leader, *as* the patron of freedom, and *as* the strongest and most resolute state in the free world. In other words, examining the discursively constituted U.S. state identity helps both to account for the way in which U.S. state officials constructed the Soviet missile deployment as the "Cuban missile crisis" and to explain why that U.S. construction seemed so obvious both to them and to subsequent commentators. It was this very identity that was at stake in the crisis and that helped to make the existence of a "crisis" self-evident to U.S. decision makers and U.S. observers alike.

This "crisis" was rendered self-evident as well by the success—that is, the persuasiveness—of this representation and its effective marginalization of alternative narratives. For example, the aggressive character of totalitarian states and of the "international Communist movement," and the contrasting obligation to defend freedom borne by the United States, marginalized any claims that the Soviet missile deployment was designed to defend Cuba against U.S. aggression. After all, aggressive totalitarian states do not defend the weak and small; rather, they dominate and enslave them. Conversely, the construction of the United States as the hemispheric and global leader with a moral obligation and formal commitments to defend freedom obscured what might otherwise have been considered U.S. intervention into the internal affairs of a sovereign Cuba. The U.S. response to the crisis it had defined—that is, the "quarantine" of Cuba, the demand that the missiles and other weapons be removed from Cuba, and its arrogation of the right to keep Cuba under surveillance—could have been understood, and was overtly represented in the story of the "October crisis," both as an act of war and as illegitimate intervention in internal Cuban affairs, as an attempt to dictate to Cuba its defense and alliance policies (e.g., "Text of U.N.-Cuban Notes," 1962; Castro, 1992). It could, quite simply, have been understood as U.S. aggression. This alternative understanding was ruled out by rendering commonsensible the claim that U.S. history, "unlike that of the Soviets since the end of World War II, demonstrates that we have no desire to dominate or conquer any other nation or impose our system upon its people" (Kennedy, 1962c: 5). Because of the construction of the United States as a "leader," this claim made sense, even in the face of the many overt military and covert U.S. interventions around the world between 1945 and 1962. U.S. "leadership" identity, devoted to the protection and promotion of "freedom," thus helped to transform blatant intervention into the internal affairs of a sovereign Cuba into, instead, an appropriate act of U.S. leadership "in freedom's cause." At the same time, it made common sense of the Cuban missile story by marginalizing the counterargument, offered in the stories of the Caribbean and October crises, that the Soviet weapons deployment was defensive, designed to deter renewed U.S. aggression against Cuba.

It also helped to render suspect any claim (as in the hypothetical strategic narrative offered earlier) that the weapons were irrelevant.

Because the Soviets had "power involvements" that were undertaken secretly and treacherously by a despotic totalitarian regime, the Soviet missiles were (necessarily) offensive and so by definition aggressive and illegitimate. In contrast, because the United States had "commitments" in which it engaged openly and without deceit, the extraterritorial missile deployments of the United States were (necessarily) defensive. U.S. missiles in Turkey, for instance, installed with the agreement of Turkey and NATO, were part of a U.S. "commitment" to defend its allies against communist, and specifically Soviet, aggression. As Kennedy reminded his audience on October 22, "our own [U.S.] strategic missiles have never been transferred to any other nation under a cloak of secrecy and deception" (1962c: 5). Their deployment was therefore legitimate and not offensive. Consequently, the U.S. missiles were not to be compared to the Soviet missiles in Cuba. The "symmetry" between the extraterritorial missile deployments of the United States and the USSR could thus be dismissed as "superficial" (Welch and Blight, 1987–88: 13) and any alternative narrative in which the Soviet missiles were irrelevant because of continued U.S. strategic superiority was successfully pushed beyond the "horizon of the taken-for-granted" (Hall, 1988: 44).

The particular way in which the narrative of the Cuban missile crisis was constructed around U.S. state identity, then, both rendered that crisis obvious and marginalized alternative understandings. In addition, this particular construction of the events of October 1962 enabled the reenactment of U.S. Cold War identity; that is, the Cuban missile crisis was not only enabled by a particular representation of the United States but simultaneously made it possible for that identity itself actively to be (re)produced. At the same time, this particular representation also contributed to the production of a larger "we" that, in its turn, legitimized the representation of these events as a crisis, reinforced the marginalization of alternative accounts, and normalized the reenacted U.S. identity.

Crucial to an understanding of the Cuban missile crisis, I want to suggest, is that it allowed U.S. state officials to reenact U.S. state identity, performatively reinscribing the four facets of that identity that had been challenged by the Soviet missile deployment. In creating an opportunity, and indeed the necessity, for U.S. action, the crisis allowed U.S. state officials to discharge U.S. leadership obligations, to defend freedom, to showcase its strength and resolve, and to demonstrate its credibility; that is, having defined a crisis into existence, responding to that crisis enabled the performative reproduction of U.S. identity.

For example, having defined the missile deployment as unacceptable, U.S. state officials decided, first, that a policy response was required. As Kennedy put it, "The latest Soviet threat must and will be met with determination. Any hostile move anywhere in the world against the safety and freedom of peoples to whom we are committed . . . will be met by whatever action is needed" (1962c: 10). They also decided that a "quarantine" would, at least in the short run, be an adequate response, and carried out that policy by deploying U.S. military might. The presence of a crisis, because it required that the United States make decisions and act, helped to reproduce the U.S. leadership identity. U.S. leadership, in other words, was reauthorized in its execution. Similarly, U.S. strength and will were enacted in its military deployments in the Caribbean in the form of the blockade, in its large-scale mobilization and redeployment of military resources within the United States, and, perhaps most important, in its ostensible willingness to "go to the brink" to get its way. The United States showed, in its response to the Soviet missile deployment, that it would actually use its military forces to defend the Western Hemisphere from the introduction of "offensive" Soviet weapons. In deploying its military forces and in acting out its resolve, in short, the United States performatively reproduced its own masculinist identity. As Abram Chayes (then legal adviser to the president) has explained, "The primary elements of the confrontation in the last weeks have been the ability and the will of the United States to deploy the necessary force in the area to establish and enforce the quarantine, and the mobilization of friends and allies—in the hemisphere, in Europe, and elsewhere in the world—in support of our action" (1962: 763). Perhaps most important, U.S. credibility was (temporarily) reasserted and validated by U.S. policy and actions. The United States showed, forcefully and concretely, that it would not allow the Soviet Union or "international Communism" to take a slice off the American salami. When it announced that offensive Soviet weapons would not be tolerated, it meant it; and it proved its credibility by forcing their removal. As Rusk allegedly said to McGeorge Bundy, the United States went "eyeball to eyeball" with the Soviet Union, which finally "blinked" (reported in Abel, 1966: 153). Nonetheless, the reproduction of U.S. identity in the Cuban missile crisis was not an unalloyed success because U.S. identity as the guarantor of freedom was only partially reproduced. By successfully forcing the removal of the Soviet missiles, the United States did demonstrate that its identity as global and hemispheric leader in the defense of freedom remained intact. But, because it had also been forced, if more or less secretly, to pledge not to invade Cuba, it did not fully reproduce its credibility as the guarantor of freedom.[6] In short, then, the U.S. triumph in resolving this crisis (created by U.S. state officials to begin with), reproduced, with significant although incomplete success, the four fundamental elements of Cold War U.S. state identity.

But it did more as well. Persistent invocations of U.S. state identity also created a broader "we" that, in turn, rendered this representation of "crisis" sensible and legitimate to most of the American public, reinforced the marginalization of alternative accounts of these events, and normalized the reenacted U.S. identity. Through processes of interpellation (Althusser, 1971; Weldes, 1996) or "implicit identification" (Burke, 1972: 28) of an audience with the U.S. identity, in other words, the Cold War U.S. foreign policy discourse produced a larger "we," an "imagined community" (Anderson, 1991) or, more generally, a "representation of belonging" (Tomlinson, 1991: 81). The production of crises, that is, is not solely about the production and reproduction of state identity; it is also about the construction of a broader identity—a "we"—that encompasses the state, its decision makers, and much of the public as well. In this "we," "the United States"—the anthropomorphized state subject of this discourse—became the identity of the individual speaker or hearer of statements made from within it. The typical response to such invitations was therefore one of recognition: "Yes, 'we' are like *this* (i.e., a tough leader, democratic, and in favor of freedom) and not like *that* (i.e., alien, despotic, and aggressive)." Once this identification had been produced, the description of the world provided, the logic of the arguments presented, and the warrants for action drawn from them all became quite persuasive. At the same time, alternative understandings were pushed beyond the boundaries of the intelligible. In conjunction with the characteristic representation of the Cuban missile crisis, then, the identity constructed for the United States and the interpellation of the audience into this subject-position helped to produce a persuasive logic that defined the Soviet missile deployment in Cuba as a "crisis"—as an obviously unacceptable situation that required a forceful U.S. policy response.

THE CULTURAL CONSTRUCTION OF CRISES

The literature in international relations and security studies has conventionally identified crises in one of two ways. Either state officials' representations of situations as crises are taken as the starting point of analysis, as is the case in much of the literature on the Cuban missile crisis, or crises are defined in terms of "objective behavioral data about conflictual interaction among states within an international system" (Brecher, Wilkenfeld, and Moser, 1988: 3). In either case, this literature has preoccupied itself almost exclusively with what Cox (1986) has called "problem-solving" rather than critical analysis of international crises.

In other words, this literature has tended to take the world as it finds it, "with the prevailing social and power relationships and the institutions into which they are organized, as the given framework for action," and so has pursued the objective of "mak[ing] those relationships and institutions work smoothly by dealing effectively with particular sources of trouble" (ibid., 208). This is clearly the case with security and crisis studies that focus on states' problems or insecurities as understood by state officials and attempt to solve those problems in ways that manage or minimize threats to state security. Walt thus argues for what he calls the "second norm" of security studies: "That even highly abstract lines of inquiry should be guided by the goal of solving real-world problems" (1991: 231). As a result of this problem-solving approach, exemplified in the literature on "crisis management," crisis studies crystallized around a specific and predictable set of questions. "The kind of knowledge that both policy makers and scholars might reasonably be expected to want about international crises," according to Hermann, includes answers to the following questions:

> When do crises lead to war or otherwise drastically alter the system in which they occur? As compared to non-crises do participants in a crisis behave more or less rationally—that is, behave so as to maximize their likelihood of obtaining desired goals? How can crises be averted? Can potential crises be detected in advance? Once a crisis occurs, how can it be managed? When can crises be used as opportunities to gain

political, military, or economic advantage? Under what conditions can a crisis be settled peacefully? When, and with what degree of certainty, is one crisis likely to manifest the same features as some previous one? Can the concept of crisis be usefully incorporated into theories accounting for a broad range of human behavior? (1972: 4)

All such questions are expressly oriented toward solving the problems of state officials. What such a problem-solving approach to crises fails to ask, and what, symptomatically, does not appear on Hermann's list, is how any particular situation comes to be understood as a "crisis" to begin with. It is to this lacuna that my argument is addressed.

Against the assumption that crises present themselves to observers as objective facts, I have suggested that crises are social constructions that are forged by state officials in the course of producing and reproducing state identity. Crises are social constructions in that they are fundamentally the outcome of particular social practices, including, centrally, practices of representation. This means that crises are cultural artifacts. The representations that constitute a crisis are produced in and through cultural processes and out of cultural resources—that is, in and through the "codes of intelligibility" (Hall, 1985: 105)—that both construct the reality we know and endow it with meaning. This constructive process is unavoidable for the simple reason (as was argued in the Introduction) that in order for the state to act, state officials must produce representations. These representations fix in place one particular set of features (out of the many that might be grasped hold of) that come to constitute "a situation" to which the state must then respond. State officials, in short, necessarily make decisions and act on the basis of culturally grounded representations and it is in these representations that crises are produced.[7] As Murray Edelman has argued, a crisis "is a creation of the language used to depict it"—it is "a political act, not a recognition of a fact or of a rare situation" (1988: 31).

The construction of crises, as I have tried to show, occurs in tandem with the construction and reconstruction of state identity. Crises are typically understood to issue from outside of the state and to disrupt its normal functioning. I have suggested instead that crises are internal to the functioning of states because they are inextricably intertwined with state identity in two complementary ways: first, state identity enables crises; second and conversely, crises enable state identity.

That state identity enables crises is the less problematic claim. After all, crises must be crises *for* some subject and, in the context of an international politics defined around states, that subject is typically, although not necessarily, the state.[8] The argument is quite straightforward. A crisis, in the most mundane sense of the term, can be understood as "an important situation" (Robinson, 1972: 20) and one characterized by a "critical or urgent problem" (Hermann, 1972: 4). But such a situation can only be recognized by asking: *For whom* is this situation a problem? *For whom* is this situation critical? *For whom* is this situation urgent? In the case of foreign-policy crises, the "whom" is generally a very particular subject—the anthropomorphized state subject produced in the foreign-policy discourses of institutional states (e.g., Campbell, 1992; Weldes, 1996). The "Cuban missile crisis," I have tried to show, was a crisis for the subject "the United States," while the "Caribbean crisis" was a crisis for the subject "the Soviet Union," and the "October crisis" was one for "Cuba." Defining a crisis thus depends on the discursively constituted identity of the state.

But crises also enable state identity. Crises are an important means, although certainly not the only one, for the production and reproduction of state identity. Paradoxically, although "crises" are, on the one hand, extraordinary events that threaten states and that state officials therefore want either to avoid altogether or to manage successfully, they are at the same time quite routine events that actually benefit states in two ways. First, they facilitate the internal consolidation of state power. As has been well established elsewhere, crises facilitate the building of state machineries (e.g., Barnett, 1992; Tilly, 1985), enhance the control exercised by a state over its population (e.g., Ayoob, 1983–84), and refine and elaborate the relations of power within the state itself (e.g., Bostdorff, 1994; Schlesinger, 1973). Second, and more central to the analysis I have presented here, crises allow for the (re)articulation of relations of identity/difference as a means of both constituting and securing state identity.[9]

This latter claim, of course, rests on a specific understanding of state identity. In particular, it rests on a conception of any identity, including the identity of the state, as always discursively produced in a relationship with difference. As William Connolly has argued, identity is always "established in relation to a series of differences that have become socially recognized. These differences are essential to its being. If they did not coexist as differences, it [identity] would not exist in its distinctness and solidity" (1991: 64). Identity and difference are mutually constitutive. Furthermore, as was discussed in the Introduction to this volume, securing an identity—fixing, or establishing the certainty of, its truth and goodness—is often accomplished by transforming mere difference "into otherness, into evil, or into one of its numerous surrogates" (ibid.). Difference, that is, might come to be defined, for instance, as evil (e.g., the Soviet Union and "Communism"), as debased or backward (e.g., the "Third World" or the "feminine"), or as mad (e.g., "rogue dictators")—in short, as other and dangerous. As a result, identity is always potentially insecure "not merely" because of "actions that the other might take to injure or defeat the true identity" but because of "the very visibility of its mode of being as other" (ibid., 66). Difference and otherness both constitute identity and threaten it. State identities, like all identities, are thus always potentially precarious: difference constitutes identity (e.g., they, the Soviet Union, are not like us, the United States); in order to secure that identity, difference is often transformed into otherness (they, the Soviet Union, are secretive, duplicitous, and aggressive); but this very otherness, in its otherness, can come to threaten identity (their aggressiveness and duplicity necessarily threaten our freedom). It is for this reason that I argue that crises and state identity are mutually constituting. Because state identity is always potentially precarious, it needs constantly to be stabilized or (re)produced. Crises present important opportunities for that reproduction.

CONCLUSION

As Benedict Anderson said of the French Revolution, its apparently self-evident "it-ness" was in fact the product of an extended process of social construction (1991: 80–81). The same is true of the Cuban missile crisis. According to McGeorge Bundy, what "made it so clear to Kennedy and to Congress in September and October [of 1962] that they should take a firm and flat stand against Soviet nuclear missiles in Cuba" was ultimately "*a visceral feeling* that it was intolerable for the United States to accept on nearby land of the Western

Hemisphere Soviet weapons that could wreak instant havoc on the American homeland." He has explained the self-evidently critical character of the Cuban missile crisis as the result of this *"strong national conviction"* (1988: 412, 413; emphasis added). What I have tried to demonstrate here is that this strong national conviction, this visceral feeling that the Soviet missiles in Cuba constituted a crisis for the United States, was a cultural construction. The events of October 1962 were not simply apprehended objectively by participants, by later analysts, or by other observers. Instead, the self-evident itness of this crisis was constructed, sometimes quite laboriously, out of the already existing elements of the discourse of Cold War U.S. foreign policy and in particular in relation to a discursively constituted and explicitly masculinist U.S. Cold War identity. And because this discourse was widely shared, the corresponding story of the Cuban missile crisis came as well to be accepted as the commonsense narrative of these events among a broader public, including many academic analysts. The constant, numbing repetition of the same stock phrases and descriptions—particularly the invocation of U.S. leadership, its freedom, its strength and will, its commitments, and its credibility—points to the tremendous ideological labor involved in eventually producing the thing that became known as the "Cuban missile crisis." This constant, numbing repetition constructed this crisis as a real object that could objectively be perceived as a self-evident threat to "the United States" and, in so doing, obscured the social conditions and processes of its own construction.

NOTES

1. The idea that the Cuban missile crisis was an outstanding example of crisis decision making and crisis management became virtual dogma in the study of crises (e.g., Sorensen, 1965; Abel, 1966; Allison, 1971: 39; R. F. Kennedy, 1971; and Janis, 1983). This positive evaluation of U.S. decision making resulted in large measure from "the apparently benign ending of the crisis" (Thorson and Sylvan, 1982: 540). If one questions either how benign that ending actually was, as do some revisionist historians (e.g., Nathan, 1975, 1992; Bernstein, 1979; Thompson, 1992), or the need for these events to have been understood as a crisis to begin with, as I do here, then the canonical status of this crisis as a precedent for dazzling decision making begins to be undermined. Other critiques of this ostensibly awesome display of

diplomacy can be found in Stone (1966), Steel (1969), Bernstein (1976, 1980), and Costigliola (1995).

2. This is the usual time span attributed to the missile crisis and its commonsense status has been reflected in and reproduced by the title of Robert F. Kennedy's *Thirteen Days* (1971).

3. The United States continues to be understood in this way, at least by Americans, but for reasons that, with the withering of the Cold War, are slowly being rearticulated (see Weldes and Saco, 1996).

4. The Monroe Doctrine, articulated in 1823, was extended in 1904 through the "Roosevelt Corollary" ("Monroe Doctrine Guards West," 1961: 3) and again extended, and made multilateral, in the Rio Pact (1947) and the Charter of Bogotá (1948), which created the Organization of American States (OAS).

5. This particular construction of identity and otherness was commonplace during the Cold War (see also U.S. National Security Council, 1950: 387).

6. The United States, however, "never issued any public or official statement of the commitment not to invade Cuba after the highly conditional statement by President Kennedy of November 20, 1962—the conditions of which (an international inspection in Cuba to verify the continuing absence of offensive arms) had not been met" (Garthoff, 1987: 94). Moreover, the no-invasion "understanding" reached between the United States and the Soviet Union during the missile crisis "was not really consummated until August of 1970, and not publicly confirmed until October of that year" (ibid., 97).

7. Crises between states are forged by officials of the state because these officials are both authorized and expected to determine if and when the state faces an emergency. But this does not mean either that official constructions always go unchallenged or that none save state officials can represent events as a crisis (as Pamela Ballinger's analysis in this volume of recent popular reimaginings of the "Trieste crisis" by various exile communities in Italy and the former Yugoslavia demonstrates). Because crises are political acts not facts, any particular crisis representation can be contested. In the case of the "Cuban missile crisis," the orthodox U.S. construction was immediately and forcefully disputed, although with little success in the United States, by the Soviet narrative of the "Caribbean crisis" and the Cuban narration of the "October crisis."

8. Sometimes the subject of a crisis is other than a state. For Robert McNamara, for instance, the missile crisis was less a crisis for the United States than for the Kennedy administration. As McNamara argued on October 16 in the ExComm, it was "a domestic, political problem" ("White House Tapes and Minutes," 1985: 192). At stake was the administration's

credibility with its domestic public in the face of its own repeated claims that it would not tolerate the stationing of Soviet offensive weapons in Cuba.

9. I am particularly grateful to Lisa Disch and Michael Shapiro for encouraging me to pursue this second aspect of the relationship between crisis and state identity.

The Politics of the Past:
Redefining Insecurity along the
"World's Most Open Border"

PAMELA BALLINGER

Tracking power requires a richer view of historical production than most theorists acknowledge. We cannot exclude in advance any of the actors who participate in the production of history or any of the sites where that production may occur. Next to professional historians we discover artisans of different kinds, unpaid or unrecognized field laborers who augment, deflect, or reorganize the work of the professionals as politicians, students, fiction writers, filmmakers, and participating members of the public. In so doing, we gain a more complex view of academic history itself, since we do not consider professional historians the sole participants in its production.
MICHEL-ROLPH TROUILLOT, SILENCING THE PAST

This chapter examines the production of historical knowledge for a canonical case in security studies, that of the post–World War II "Trieste crisis." In contrast to Weldes's discussion elsewhere in this volume of state-centric narratives about the Cuban missile crisis, I consider the Trieste episode from the angle of those historical "artisans of different kinds" whose interpretations were left out or silenced by such dominant constructions. Between 1945 and 1954, the Italo-Yugoslav territorial dispute known variously as the "Trieste crisis" or the "Trieste question" played out in British and American newspapers and strategy rooms as one battle in the broader, global struggle between communism and democracy, East and West. The dispute centered on long-standing territorial claims by both Italy and Yugoslavia to the region of Venezia Giulia (with Trieste as its capital); though Italy had acquired most of this area after World War I, the defeat of the Italian fascist regime, the establishment of a socialist state in Yugoslavia, and the Yugoslav military occupation of much of the territory reopened the question.

The conflict's dimensions expanded when the United States and Great Britain occupied Trieste at war's end in order to push back the Yugoslavs. Alfred Bowman, head of the Allied Military Government in Venezia Giulia from mid-1945 to mid-1947, claims that the Cold War began in northern Italy and that "its focal point . . . was the political and doctrinal confrontation at Trieste" (Bowman, 1982: 7). This confrontation set the stage for the (first) Trieste crisis, the Yugoslavs' withdrawal from the city and a provisional partition of the wider territory into Zone A (administered by the Anglo-Americans) and Zone B (run by the Yugoslav military). Zone B included the peninsula known as Istria (in Italian) or Istra (in Slovene and Croatian), a linguistically and ethnically mixed territory historically dominated by the Italian speakers concentrated in Istria's coastal cities and hilltop towns. Their fate tied to that of the "Trieste question," most of Zone B's Italians wished to remain part of the Italian state and feared the installation of a Yugoslav regime in Istria. Between 1943 and 1954, between 200,000 and 350,000 of these Italians left the peninsula in what became known as the Istrian *esodo* or exodus.

Although the term *exodus* suggests a unitary event (and, indeed, Istrian exiles have presented it as such) the departure of persons occurred for a variety of reasons (outright persecution by Titoists, fear, the Italian state's promise of a better life in Italy) and at different moments over a twelve-year period. The periodization of population movements from Istria mirrored shifts in the complex political wrangling over the broader territory. The first wave of people abandoned Istria in 1943, when the collapse of the Italian regime and army left vulnerable those individuals most compromised with the fascist state; a second wave followed at war's end, as the Yugoslavs used force and intimidation to install de facto control; and a significant number of Istrians legally "opted" for Italian citizenship as a result of the 1947 Italo-Yugoslav Peace Treaty, which awarded two-thirds of Istria to Yugoslavia (leaving in dispute the remaining territory). The question's final settlement in 1954 recognized the territory's partition (with

Trieste going to Italy and all of Istria to Yugoslavia) and prompted the last "Big Exodus" of those persons in Zone B who had held out hope of remaining in Italy. What the Great Powers understood as the Trieste question's resolution, then, Istrian Italians instead viewed as partition and population transfer.

After its formal resolution in 1954, the Trieste crisis was held up as a model case of conflict solving and border delineation (Sluga, 1994: 285). Although the negotiations were largely dictated by the Great Powers, who saw Italo-Yugoslav rapprochement as in their interest, the Trieste talks "are still studied by scholars of international relations as a classic triumph of the art of diplomatic negotiation" (Rabel, 1988: 159). A 1976 volume titled *Successful Negotiation: Trieste 1954*, for example, features diverse perspectives by participants to the talks, considered a successful model for dispute resolution. Similarly, a publication in the SAIS series uses the Trieste case as a teaching tool for students of international relations. The authors conclude that

> In the end, the Memorandum of Understanding produced by the secret Trieste negotiations of 1954 "settled" the Trieste impasse and has served as a binding agreement for more than 30 years. To be sure, the memorandum did leave open the possibility for future governments again to take up their territorial claims. But this has not occurred, and there is little on the political scene today—or anticipated—that suggests that this question will ever again arise to plague relations between Yugoslavia and Italy, as it did for so many years following World War II. (Unger and Segulja, 1990: 38)

Written in 1990 on the eve of the Yugoslav breakup that would resuscitate restitution demands made by those Italian "exiles" forced decades earlier to abandon their homeland as a result of the territorial dispute's "successful" conclusion, this assessment reflects the top-down, state-centric perspective common to traditional security analyses. Such a perspective does not take account of the continued resentments of those Italians whose exodus from the nearby Istrian peninsula played out within the jockeying of state and superpower interests discursively coded as the "Trieste crisis." Heeding the opening epigraph's admonition to "track power" by looking beyond the academic guild as the site for the production of both historical traces and silences, this chapter explores the ways in which the Istrian

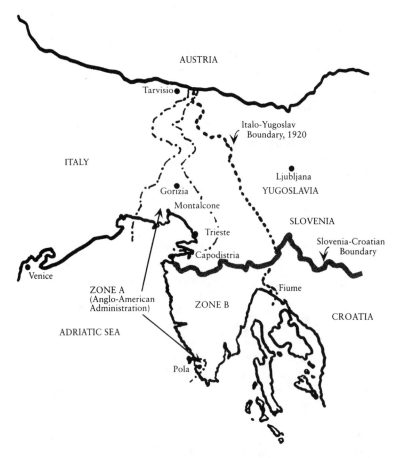

The division of Venezia Giulia, 1945.

esodo or exodus has been variously constructed and silenced as an event by different actors, including the Western Allies, the Italian and Yugoslav states, and Istrian exile groups.

The very notion of the Trieste crisis, within which this Istrian exodus unfolded, entailed the refraction of older narratives about competing Slavic and Italian nationalisms through the lens of an emergent Cold War discourse. The Cold War battle played out on the terrain of Trieste remained largely one of propaganda, with furious attempts by pro-Italian and pro-Yugoslav groups to address Allied opinion. In all their troublesome materiality, however, bodies (live and dead) became crucial to these propaganda efforts, which in turn resulted in all-too-real physical consequences for those Istrian populations who abandoned their homes. In this chapter's analysis of competing narrative constructions and their very real effects, then, I aim to address the hitherto largely "unresolved question . . . about who invests a form of discourse or of practical activity with authority" (Feierman, 1990: 3).

In answering this question, the chapter undertakes a "thick description" of the Istrian case, a story of ethnic and ideological conflict, Cold War partition, exile communities, and bitterly contested memories. This case has many obvious parallels to other divided territories and populations where the condition of displacement nurtures a nexus of deeply felt (and often explosive) claims about land, identity, and history; one need only look to Ireland, Palestine, Kashmir, or Bosnia-Herzegovina for other sites of contested partition and memory. Closer to home, the Cold War divisions separating Cuban exiles in Miami from their island homeland come to mind. Novelist Cristina García has written of Miami's "maddening" geographic proximity to Cuba and its almost unbridgeable distance: "Cuba is a peculiar exile, I think, an island-colony. We can reach it by a thirty-minute charter flight from Miami, yet never reach it at all" (1992: 219). Miami thus emerges, like Trieste, as "a place in which world politics and local power groups prey on people's most intimate desires and identities. . . . It is a city held in the clutches of international national security interest" (de los Angeles Torres, 1995: 39). Although the political environments of both Miami and Trieste have been largely shaped by the jockeying of international security, vocal exile communities in each city help sustain antagonisms by nurturing divisive histories that refuse to disappear. Typically overlooked by state-centric analyses, such groups may nonetheless revive issues—long presumed resolved or dead, as in the Trieste case—that complicate the international scene and confound confident predictions about conflict resolution.

In exploring such processes for the Trieste case, the chapter first locates my own project in a field of debate in Trieste about the recent past before turning to a critical reading of the state-centric narratives through which the Trieste crisis has been constructed as a diplomatic issue. I then consider efforts to reposition alternative histories of exodus in relation to those dominant narratives, pointing up the ways in which *esuli* or exiles morally authorize their claims to lost land and properties. These claims challenge the concurrent attempts, spearheaded by the small Italian minority that remains in Istria, to construct a transnational, regional entity in Istria. While the Istrian regionalists in Croatia also draw on the recent past in the fashioning of moral capital and in challenging Franjo Tudjman's centralizing regime, they possess yet another vision of Istria's historic identity and experience. By way of conclusion, I reflect on the Istrian case in order more generally to discuss the place of memory politics in the analysis of insecurity.

PRODUCING THE PAST IN TRIESTE

The history of World War II remains an intensely *public* topic of discussion in Trieste, a debate in which individuals feel authorized by their personal experiences to participate. Any given week in the city will undoubtedly feature several events that touch on the region's "traumatic" recent history. Conferences and talks given by scholars in Trieste are often met by impassioned personal testimonies and, at times, angry denunciations from audience members. Presentations I made in different forums in Trieste, for example, often prompted comments that began "With due respect to the *dottoressa americana,* who is too young to have lived through such events, I personally saw . . . ," after which would follow a long monologue about the individual's own experience.

Having come to Trieste to investigate the connections between historical memory and identity in the border region between Italy, Slovenia, and Croatia, I rapidly found myself drawn into charged debates over interpreting the events of the immediate postwar period. In conducting fieldwork between February 1995 and September 1996 in Trieste and Istria, I necessarily had to enter several different communities: those of the exiles, of the Italian minority in Istria, of the Slovene minority in Italy, and of academics in the regional circuit. As Barnett describes in this volume, participation within a community (in his case, the UN bureaucracy) inculcates a certain sense of identification that leads the ethnographer to fear that she is somehow betraying her informants. Most informants expressed their enormous satisfaction that at last their story would be known in the English-speaking world, for example, and each group assumed that I was simultaneously its advocate. I often felt conflicted, as if I was betraying one or the other group by consorting with the "enemy," although I exploited my position as neutral observer in order to explain away my potentially treacherous behavior.

Painfully aware of my precarious status as a young outsider, I also tried to listen respectfully to and note comments proffered by audience members at my lectures and other encounters in Trieste and Istria. At presentations I attended given by professional historians who were locally born, however, I often noted either a weary resignation to the audience's testimonies or the somewhat smug bemusement of an academic who "knew better." Triestine scholars who considered themselves serious historians often complained to me about living in a city where the past "refused to die" and thereby prevented the ostensibly dispassionate examination known as the "historian's craft."

Attending public events dedicated to Trieste's recent history, however, usefully revealed the active and lively contestation locally of broader narratives about the immediate postwar period. At the same time, locally dominant exile accounts themselves worked to efface other experiences and perspectives, such as that of the Slovene minority. In February 1995, for example, several hundred persons attended a public screening in Trieste of films only recently available from the Archives of the Republic of Slovenia, including footage shot by Yugoslav partisans in the course of their guerrilla war together with short pieces dating from the period of the Trieste crisis. Such clips showed manifestations of support for the Yugoslav "liberators" with enthusiastic demonstrators carrying signs, written in both Italian and Slovene, proclaiming "Long live Tito!" "Long live the Red Army!" "We are a part of Yugoslavia!" and so on. Most of these films dated from 1945–47, the period in which Winston Churchill imagined the Iron Curtain running from "Stettin in the Baltic to Trieste in the Adriatic" (in Rabel, 1988: 85).

The series of shorts concluded, however, with a breezy film from 1950 that presented a reconciliatory vision of life in the frontier zone. Set to the beat of jazzy xylophone music, the film featured both Trieste and Istrian Capodistria/Koper and showed the movement of peoples and goods between the two. The footage played up the similarity of life on both sides of the frontier and showed guards happily waving persons across the border. Such images anticipate the self-congratulatory propaganda about the "world's most open border," heard in the decades following the resolution of the border issue—at least to the satisfaction of the Great Powers—with the 1954 Memorandum of London.

Many members of the audience at the showing of the Slovene films on Trieste seemed particularly offended by this seemingly light film that concluded the presentation, its vision of coexistence along the border embodying the hypocrisy of both the Italian and the Yugoslav states after the formal resolution of the Trieste crisis. In the question-and-answer session following the cinematic program, several members of the audience asked on what basis the films were selected. One man complained that the films needed more contextualization, that in order to understand the postwar climate in the region one must first know the history of the "Forty Days" of Yugoslav "occupation" of Trieste (May–June 1945) and the events in the adjacent Istrian Peninsula.

These comments reflect a broader debate in Trieste as to whether the city experienced two "liberations"—one by Yugoslav partisans in the first days of May 1945, and another by Anglo-American troops the following month—or only one true liberation, that by the Western Allies. The organizers of an exhibition held in Trieste to mark the fiftieth anniversary of the war's conclusion, for example, found themselves confronted with this dilemma: given the highly divergent memories of the Yugoslav period in Trieste, how to represent this experience for a (fractured) general public? Within Trieste, for example, pro-Italians recall the brief period of Yugoslav occupation as the infamous "Forty Days," a time of summary arrests and executions with many Italians (as well as Slovenes) meeting their end in the karstic grottoes known as the *foibe*. In contrast, many members of the city's Slovene minority (as well as Italian communists) viewed the arrival of Tito's partisans as liberation from two decades of oppression at the hands of a fascist state bent on denationalizing Venezia Giulia's autochthonous Slavs. Given this complex situation in the immediate postwar period, any attempts to offer an exhibition for the general public in Trieste commemorating the city's "liberation"(s) prove fraught with tension. In the end, the organizers played down the role of the Slovene resistance, angering many members of the Slovene community and prompting intense discussions within the scientific committee that organized the exhibition. Nonetheless, this slighting of the Slovene contribution did not spare the organizers from charges of being philo-Slavic (given the mere mention of the Slovene contribution), reflecting the persistence and depth of anti-Slavic sentiment in Trieste.

As this example suggests, the Istrian case plays out on a field of politics in which various groups struggle to define their notions of identity, underwritten by historical memories, and to privilege them as the official historical truth. Having briefly sketched out the terrain in which historical debate takes place in contemporary Trieste and my own positioning in that landscape, I now turn to a detailed narrative analysis of the postwar Trieste crisis. First, I problematize the reading of events as a "crisis" focused on Trieste by examining the Cold War discourse through which the dispute was read. I also sketch out alternative nationalist readings in order to suggest the way in which older conceptual frameworks either articulated with or were effaced by these Cold War narratives of the "Trieste question." These narratives, in turn, underwent revision as a result of the Yugoslav–Soviet rift, a broad political shift that ultimately led the Anglo-Americans to push for the resolution of the territorial dispute. This change in Anglo-American views on Trieste—effectively rendering it a "non-crisis"—continues to anger the Istrian exiles, whose alternative accounts will then be explored in detail.

CONSTRUCTING AND CONTESTING THE "TRIESTE CRISIS"

Although the 1954 Memorandum of London ostensibly resolved the territorial dispute, in subsequent decades many Italian-speaking refugees from Istria scoffed at Italo-Yugoslav state propaganda celebrating "the world's most open border" and angrily denounced the sacrifice of their land and their culture in the name of Cold War security. Glenn Bowman (1995) has argued that in situations of war the refugee—symbol par excellence for the threat posed by the enemy to the national way of life—becomes central to the imagining of the national space. The Istrian exiles certainly occupied this symbolic slot for Italian nationalists during the immediate postwar territorial dispute. In a sense they became the professional victims described by Bowman and thus felt even more embittered when the nation had no further need of their symbolic capital and dropped their cause after 1954. Long after Trieste had been declared a "non-crisis" at the international level, then, some local actors nurtured the galvanizing spirit of combat, urgency, and profound insecurity that initially informed the postwar atmosphere in the city.

The following sections examine the standard constructions of security and insecurity against which *esuli* write their own personal and group histories of betrayal. Here I follow Trouillot's suggestion to examine processes of historical production at key moments by considering the making between 1945 and 1954 of sources, archives, and narratives about the "Trieste question." Particular attention will be given to the way that the situation of Italians in Istria either entered into or failed to figure in the story told by powerful actors, notably the Italian and Yugoslav states and the Western Allies, thereby offering one detailed case of the strategic silences engendered by traditional security readings.

PROBLEMATIZING THE "TRIESTE CRISIS"

The very labeling of events as the "Trieste crisis" or "Trieste question" shows how and where power enters immediately into the apprehension and construction of events at the war's close. Let us first problematize the "Trieste" aspect of the formulation. For many exiles, the more appropriate descriptive term would be the "question of Venezia Giulia" rather than one that privileges the fate of a city to the exclusion of its surrounding territory. Although one might argue for the "Trieste crisis" as convenient shorthand for the broader Julian question, the identification of the problem as centering on Trieste *does* matter. It not only reflects the Italian state's strategic emphasis (dating from before World War I) on the port of Trieste rather than on its hinterland, but more importantly signals the Anglo-American focus on the city as the "line in the sand" against the USSR and Yugoslavia.

The Anglo-American reaction to events in Trieste in 1945 rendered the situation an apparently unproblematic "crisis" (the second key term in our phrase), an evaluation that most exiles would not question or dispute. Yet, as Weldes demonstrates for Soviet missiles in Cuba, the naturalized appearance of crises works to efface the intense processes by which both security and danger, or insecurity, are continually (re)produced. It is not only the Great Power reading of the Trieste crisis that exiles find so questionable, but also the eventual Anglo-American definition of events as having been successfully resolved and thereby rendered a "noncrisis."

Events in Venezia Giulia first earned the designation "crisis" at the war's close when the Western Allies adopted an increasingly hardline stance toward the Yugoslav military. At the end of April 1945, the Yugoslavs were literally racing to "liberate" Trieste and Istria in advance of the Anglo-Americans, with the aim of installing administrative control there. The city of Trieste thus constituted an important border both physically and metaphorically, becoming an early and key point at which an emergent Cold War discourse began to be articulated. The (initial) Anglo-American interpretation of the Italo-Yugoslav border dispute as a thinly veiled act of communist expansionism prevailed over (even as it interpolated certain aspects of) competing interpretations emphasizing a complex history of nationalist contestation. Before expanding on the Cold War readings of events as a "crisis," I will consider the regionally specific interpretations put forward by supporters of both the Yugoslav and Italian positions. Doing so will elucidate the manner in which Cold War narratives at times incorporated and at other moments effaced elements of nationalist readings.

THE ITALO-YUGOSLAV DISPUTE: A CONFLICT OF NATIONALIST AMBITIONS?

One set of interrelated interpretations emphasized that Trieste and Istria had long been objects of Italian and Slavic irredentism. The 1915 Treaty of London, secretly concluded to ensure Italy's entrance into World War I on the Allied side, promised Italy Trieste, Istria, and Dalmatia. President Wilson's subsequent insistence that secret treaties not be honored opened up a phase of intensive propaganda and dispute between Italy and the nascent Kingdom of the South Slavs. With the Italian state's eventual "redemption" of Trieste and Istria and the installation of a fascist dictatorship after 1922, Slovenes and Croats living in these territories were subjected to an aggressive Italianization campaign. These policies only nurtured the hopes of many South Slavs that Istria and Trieste—now the object of Slavic irredentist passion—would ultimately be joined with the Yugoslav state, a goal to which Tito accorded much importance in his refashioning of the "second," socialist Yugoslavia. The arguments used after World War II to justify Yugoslav claims to the region were varied, ranging from ethnic composition and economics to the sacrifice made by South Slavs in the war. Pro-Italian tracts used and inverted the same principal arguments to refute Yugoslav assertions.

The quantity and presentation of pro-Yugoslav propaganda produced in English in the early period of the Trieste dispute suggest that the Yugoslavs outdid their Italian counterparts in pitching their appeal to an "Allied" audience. Anglo-American documents repeatedly refer to the "poor organization" initially demonstrated by pro-Italian proponents in their propaganda efforts. Many in the Allied camp appear to have remained unpersuaded by the more elaborate and abundant pro-Yugoslav propaganda produced in English, however, attributing this advantage to communist organization and careful, long-term preparation. An internal report titled *A Political History of Zone A of Venezia Giulia under Allied Military Government (12 June 1945 to 10 February 1947)* (Allied Military Government of Venezia Giulia, 1947), for example, describes the communists as using intimidation to create a false image of mass support. Furthermore, Italian violence is here posited as essentially reactive, merely responding to that initiated by Slav-communists. As these comments suggest, the Anglo-American interpretation of events in Trieste as following out of communist manipulation and aggression helped transform the inter-state dispute into a larger contest, the first "crisis" of what became known as the Cold War.

THROUGH A COLD WAR LENS: THE FIRST TRIESTE CRISIS

The initial Anglo-American reading of the Trieste question as a clash between communism and democracy recast a complex political and ethnonational conflict with deep historical roots. Intelligence officer Geoffrey Cox (1977) offers a Western account of the "race for Trieste" in May 1945 between Allied and Yugoslav forces, the scramble that set the stage for the (first) "Trieste crisis." For participant-observers such as Cox, the "Trieste crisis" consisted solely in this 1945 showdown between the Allies and the Yugoslavs for control of the city and regional administration. In Cox's estimation, the Yugoslav withdrawal from the city the following month and the establishment of Allied Military Government (AMG) in Venezia Giulia represented a Western triumph. He contends, "Trieste was the first major confrontation of the Cold War. . . . It was an exercise in what had not yet been termed brinkmanship" (ibid., 7). Cox further suggests that Trieste may have provided a reference point for Truman in the subsequent crises of the Berlin blockade and the Korean War (ibid., 8). Truman and Churchill, like Cox, constructed the crisis within the terms of an Anglo-American struggle against the "Moscow tentacle of which Tito is the crook" (Churchill, in ibid., 227). By reading the

Trieste crisis in Cold War terms, Cox and Allied leaders thus flattened out the social and political complexities of the situation in Trieste.

The historian Glenda Sluga has argued that many of the Anglo-Americans present in Trieste accepted long-standing Italian nationalist constructs—Latin versus Slav, civilized versus barbarian, West versus East—and grafted onto them the bipolar identifications characteristic of the Cold War. For the British-American representatives, "Slavs were a political communist threat from the East. The two connotations of the term overlapped politically and emotionally, enabling a rapport to be formed between the Allies and pro-Italian Triestines" (Sluga, 1994: 286). Cox's memoir illustrates this sense of Allied identification with the Italians. Contrasting friendly Italians with taciturn Yugoslav partisans, Cox and many others endorsed the pro-Italian thesis that the Slavs represented an unpopular occupying force imposed on the predominantly Italian Triestines (ibid., 287).

Sluga challenges many of the facile assumptions of such Western analyses of the situation with her attention to the ways in which the Allied administration, fitting the Trieste crisis into a Cold War mold, built on the understandings of pro-Italian groups in Trieste. Her analysis seems most appropriate, however, for the years 1945–48, prior to the Yugoslav–Soviet split. After 1949, U.S. attitudes and policies in Trieste altered significantly, provoking another "crisis" in 1953 when pro-Italian groups perceived the AMG to be hostile to the city's *italianità* or Italianness. The next section takes up the ways in which the political shifts of 1948 and 1949 led the Anglo-Americans to understand Yugoslavia in new terms and to redefine their role from one of protector (of democratic, Western Italians) to that of neutral mediator.

THE ANGLO-AMERICAN VOLTE-FACE AND THE "FINAL TRIESTE CRISIS"

Although some Anglo-Americans anguished over whether supporting *any* communists, even anti-Soviet communists, violated their basic principles, the Western powers soon decided to exploit the Soviet–Yugoslav breach and to embrace Yugoslavia's ambiguous position between East and West. In her study of Western Cold War perceptions of Yugoslavia, Beatrice Heuser (1989) argues that the years 1952–53—the period immediately preceding what became deemed the "final Trieste crisis"—represented the culmination of the West's opening toward Yugoslavia (and vice versa).

As a result of these broader shifts, in Zone A the Anglo-Americans increasingly adopted a more neutral position (Rabel, 1988: 131–36). This "betrayal" by their former defenders prompted various protests from pro-Italian groups, particularly those concerned with the fate of Italian populations in Istria. AMG suggestions for direct Italo-Yugoslav negotiations to resolve the impasse only deepened Italian nationalist anger (Novak, 1970: 358). In Trieste, nationalist protest against the AMG prompted a series of riots in 1952. These disturbances were harbingers of the violence that would erupt the following year.

Tired of a long and expensive military administration, the United States and Great Britain announced on October 8, 1953, that they would terminate the AMG and cede control of Zone A to the Italian state and Zone B to Yugoslavia. Both Yugoslav and Italian proponents responded angrily at the respective loss of half the desired territory. Tito rejected what he perceived as a humiliating and unilateral "fait accompli" (ibid., 431) while rumors of an irredentist coup d'état spread in Trieste. This atmosphere of panic and confused rumor set the stage for the riots of November 1953, sparked when Italian protesters provoked the fire of AMG police who entered a church where the demonstrators had sought refuge.

Italian nationalists interpreted these events as a spontaneous demonstration of patriotism by a long-suffering population. For proponents of *italianità*, events became violent as a result of the AMG's false portrayal of all Italian patriots as neofascists. A publication of the Committee for the Defense of the Italian Character of Trieste and Istria (1953) charges the AMG with brutal tactics and links the Trieste question directly with the fate of Italians in Zone B, sacrificed for the larger security interests of the Western powers. Written before the resolution of the Trieste situation, this document provides one example of the construction of an Italian discourse of betrayal at the time of the events. Yugoslav pronouncements from the period 1953–54 also express a sense of betrayal. Reading Italian policy toward Trieste in 1953 as a continuation of fascist imperialism, for example, Yugoslav leader Edvard Kardelj (1953) saw Western support of Italian aims as threatening to undo previous attempts at reconciliation with Yugoslavia.

Confronted by both pro-Italian and pro-Yugoslav discourses constructing them as betrayers, the Anglo-Americans renewed their efforts to extricate themselves from Trieste, serving as intermediaries in the negotiations that settled the territorial dispute. The 1954 Memorandum of London recognized the Italian acquisition of Zone A and the Yugoslav administration of Zone B, while assuring protection of the minorities in both territories. As noted earlier, the 1954 talks are still studied by scholars as a classic triumph of the art of diplomatic negotiation. Only in 1975, however, did the Italian and Yugoslav states succeed in finalizing these Great Power arrangements by means of the Treaty of Osimo.

PROTESTING THE RESOLUTION OF THE "TRIESTE CRISIS"

Not surprisingly, the Treaty of Osimo sparked an enormous popular protest that galvanized Trieste and temporarily re-created there the sense of urgency characteristic of the immediate postwar period. Out of a citywide petition drive denouncing Osimo was born the political party known as the Lista per Trieste, which has also worked to promote exile interests. My fieldwork period coincided with the twentieth anniversary of Osimo, an event that prompted a spate of newspaper articles and public meetings in Trieste (see *Il Piccolo,* November 10, 14, 1995). One program organized by an exile association took place on November 4, 1995, the traditional anniversary of Italy's victory in World War I or the "War of Redemption." The organizers chose this date, the "Festival of National Unity," in order to recall the infamous day in 1975 when national unity was shattered. Exile leader Denis Zigante commented that this meeting reflected the need to "always remember and denounce" Osimo, a treaty that legitimized the region's shameful partition.

Such meetings represent one aspect of the multilayered struggle to reject the official narratives of the "Trieste crisis"—and their very real consequences, that is, partition of Istria—that this chapter has outlined. I have focused on the perception and constitution of the crisis by the "Great Powers," both at the time and as a subsequent case for diplomatic histories and security studies. As should be clear from this discussion of the narrative constructions of the Trieste crisis, the problem of the exiles from Istria only entered consideration as a tangential concern, if a concern at all. This neglect continues to anger many exiles, who view themselves as victimized pawns in the struggle for Trieste.

Although for Italian national leaders Osimo merely ratified a

two-decades-long reality, then, for some exiles and Italian nationalists in Trieste the conflict was far from over. They refused to accept
the Great Powers' definition of Trieste as a "noncrisis" after 1954
(and, to some extent, after 1949). In the autumn of 1995, prompted
by the extensive commemoration of Osimo, prominent local historian Giampaolo Valdevit declared that "the Cold War never ended in
Trieste" (*Il Piccolo*, November 10, 1995). At the same time, as suggested by the location of Osimo in a narrative extending from the
"War of Redemption" to the contemporary Festival of Unity commemorating it, in Trieste a locally and highly specific Cold War narrative appears to link up temporally with those about World War I.
Perhaps, then, Valdevit would have been more accurate had he said
that "the irredentist struggle never ended in Trieste." I shall now
turn to continuities and discontinuities in both the production and
the reception of those contemporary exile narratives that draw on
earlier irredentist understandings.

RECONFIGURING THE EXODUS

Various publications repeatedly denounce the historical silencing of
the *esodo*, emphasizing that the exiles alone have preserved this story
in their collective memories. In reality, an extensive body of memori-
alistic and historical literature has been produced at the local level.
Outside of this regional circuit, however, the story of the exodus did
drop out of the national historical consciousness in both Italy and
Yugoslavia. Before turning to examine the content of exile narratives,
I will outline here the ways in which exiles have sought to bring their
history back into these national historiographies.

In Yugoslavia, the subject of the exodus—along with alternative
histories that depicted the glorious partisan war of liberation as a
bloody civil war—remained explicitly tabooed. For the small minority of Italians who did remain in Istria, the story proved fraught with
danger, as well as feelings of shame and resentment given that many
exiles accuse those who remained (the *rimasti*) of being communist
collaborators. Ironically, these same *rimasti* were sometimes labeled
"fascists" (or suspected of being so) in Yugoslavia. Croatian President Franjo Tudjman continues to deem members of the Italian
minority irredentists and fascists, a charge that angers many who
proudly remember the Istrian contribution to the antifascist struggle.
The historiographical debate about World War II (as either "antifascist

struggle" or interethnic conflict) that opened up in Yugoslavia with Tito's death has resonated in Istria, albeit in different ways than in Serbia and non-Istrian Croatia. Whereas in Croatia and Serbia revived histories about wartime atrocities proved useful for politicians wishing to incite nationalist violence, in Istria discussion of the "open wound" left by the exodus is posited as *strengthening* the peninsula's pluri-ethnic fabric.

In contrast to Tito's Yugoslavia, within Italy the facts of the matter were in no way unknown but found little reception outside of Trieste. Until the beginning of the 1990s, the story of the exodus proved not only an embarrassment to the national government and an obstacle to friendly relations along the "world's most open border," but also a painful reminder of the divisive civil war fought in northern Italy during the years 1943 and 1945. Within the antifascist tradition, the fact that socialist Yugoslavia had been abandoned by its Italian population needed to be explained away. The Italian Communist Party (PCI) did so by painting the *esuli* as fascists, rendering the *esuli* suspect in many eyes (Colummi et al., 1980: 265).

This wholesale depiction of all refugees from Istria as fascists merely reinforced the widespread exile conviction that "Italy lost the war but we paid [the price]." The *esodo* not only raised unsettling questions about a fascist regime within which most people proved complicit to varying degrees (DeGrazia, 1981; Passerini, 1979, 1987), however, but also about whether the Italian state instrumentalized *esuli* by urging them to leave Istria in order to evidence the "illegitimacy" of the Yugoslav regime there. With the demise of that Italian state—the Christian Democratic political machine that ruled Italy from 1945 until the electoral victory of Silvio Berlusconi in 1993— the *esuli* have at last found an audience for their politics of memory as they reposition their histories vis-a-vis larger historiographies.

The exile associations based in Trieste have been at the center of these efforts to make the Istrian experience more widely recognized. The three main organizations—the Unione degli Istriani, Comunità Istriane, and Associazione Nazionale Venezia Giulia Dalmati—have also been involved with the issue of restitution of lost properties. Although in the past some exiles received minimal compensation from Italy, many others never received any restitution. The exile associations thus demanded that Slovenia and Croatia compensate the exiles for their properties as a precondition of entrance into the European Union.

The aim in reviving these contentious property claims, which complicate interstate relations in an already destabilized area, lies in the desire for justice at three levels: financial, historical, and moral-spiritual. Although most *esuli* agree that the demand for lost properties proves significant in principle, little consensus exists over either what exactly that demand consists of or what the best means are for achieving it. Some exile figures even view this as a politics of illusion, opportunistically exploited by various politicians and ultimately dividing the exile community. Despite a considerable overlap in leaders and members, the associations have generally been seen as linked to particular political parties and positions. This fracturing of the associations along party lines has diminished the capacity of the exiles to speak with a unitary voice, revealing ongoing struggles to speak for the exiles. In spite of these divisions, however, the interpretation of the exodus as the "first ethnic cleansing" in Yugoslavia appears to unite many otherwise discordant positions, as the following section will explore.

NARRATIVES OF BETRAYAL

In repositioning their group history within broader historiographies, the exiles have labored to construct the story as an act of "ethnic cleansing." Narratives describe the exiles' betrayal at several levels: (1) betrayal by ungrateful Slavs who, having enjoyed the benefits of the Italian state from 1920 to 1945 (and Italo-Venetian culture for several centuries), treacherously turned on their Italian neighbors in ethnically cleansing Istria; (2) betrayal by those Italians in Istria who supported the communist revolution there and by members of the Italian Communist Party; (3) betrayal by the Great Powers, the Italian state, and/or specific Italian political leaders; and (4) betrayal by those Italians who met the Istrian refugees with hostility and suspicion. Given that ideological and ethnonational motivations for the exodus appear inextricably bound up with one another, this exile account of betrayal and ethnic cleavage struck me as too facile. In addition to Italians, for instance, Slovenes and Croats left postwar Istria in significant numbers. The presence of those Italians who chose to remain in Istria—together with a small number of committed Italian communists (estimated at between two thousand and three thousand)

POLITICS OF THE PAST · 81

who emigrated to Yugoslavia immediately after the war—further complicated a straightforward account of Italians driven out solely for being Italian.

Despite the existence of some exiles who recognize the complicated intersections of ideological and ethnonational claims in motivating the exodus, since Yugoslavia's breakup the exile associations and their leaders have had considerable success in Italy promoting a narrative of the exodus as a unitary event following out of a premeditated plan to Slavicize Istria. Such narratives may be likened to morality plays, as Malkki (1995) suggests for accounts told by Hutu refugees in Tanzania. In constructing the Istrian exodus as an act of ethnic cleansing and casting it in fundamentally *moral* terms, exile narratives in Trieste silence competing voices. Conflating Istrian Italian culture/history with all *Istrian* culture/history, these accounts posit the exiles as the only authentic Istrians.

Whether as oral testimony or written memoir, exile accounts tend to follow a general schema describing pre-exodus Istria, the exodus itself (the encounter between Italians and "barbarian" Slavs), the difficult conditions of the exiles' arrival and incorporation into Italian society, and/or the destruction of Istria's cultural integrity. These narratives feature the theme, common to literature on genocide (e.g., Patterson, 1992), of silence: the silence of the deserted cities and countryside of Istria; the silence of the nation and the world, which expressed no outrage at this event; the silence of the dead. This genocidal trope of silence literally silences the voices of those who lived alongside Istrian Italians for centuries and who now occupy the post-exodus "wasteland" described by the exiles.

Almost all *esuli* I interviewed pictured a largely idealized vision of pre-exodus life in Istria for the years before the war. Even when the life is presented as an economically difficult one, it is pervaded with a sense of collective solidarity and religiosity. One man, for example, lamented the contemporary loss of the values of family and faith and recalled the Istrian people as "economic and good," as religious people who placed the family first. Such halcyon descriptions of an ordered, harmonious world set the scene for recounting the dramatic rupture that will follow, an event usually presented as completely unforeseen by the trusting and unsuspecting Italians.

Central to many of these narratives about the exodus itself is the description of the partisans' methods in Istria, which now merely confirm more widely held stereotypes of Balkan fanaticism and butchery. The war in former Yugoslavia has lent strength to exile stories of barbaric Slavic nationalism, making them persuasive to a larger public. Almost every exile I have spoken with, for example, has told me that the Yugoslavs are now inflicting upon each other what they inflicted upon the Italians of Istria fifty years ago. Descriptions of "Balkan" methods inevitably focus on gruesome accounts of executions in the *foibe*, those pits into which partisans threw Italians; such stories parallel narratives about war atrocities (past and present) in former Yugoslavia.

An elderly couple from a small village in the interior returned again and again to this theme of the *foibe*, describing the Slavs as beasts who murdered innocent people in the most barbarous way possible. They claimed that this genocide followed from an age-old hatred and envy by the Slavs toward the Italians, who, thanks to their work ethic, lived better than the Slavs. The Slavs neither knew how nor wanted to work—they were dirty and stank—and thus seized the opportunity to expel the Italians and steal their homes and lands. Similarly, a man I interviewed, an unrepentant fascist from Pola who left Istria in 1943 to join Mussolini's forces at Salò, likened the People's Tribunals formed at the end of the war to enact summary justice to those of the mob during the French Revolution. Enumerating Yugoslav tactics, he concluded that these methods are identical with those currently employed in the genocidal civil war in Yugoslavia: "the disappearance of people . . . they came to a house and beat [people] in the night. They beat with kicks and rifles in order to intimidate the wife, who was crying . . . the children around the mother and only a summary interrogation. After, the *foibe*. This is the terror that was propagated in the land."

These descriptions combine with scenes of the actual moment of exodus. In some cases, individuals recount dramatic escapes at night on foot or in small fishing boats. In other instances, the act of leaving Istria is described as relatively calm, with families choosing to legally "opt" for Italian citizenship. Exile stories then discuss the exodus's aftermath, arrival and life in Italy. During the course of my fieldwork I heard again and again the refrain that exiles feel "strangers in their own home." Istrians feel strangers in a double sense: on return visits to their natal land, Istria, which they no longer recognize and in

Italy, paradoxically both their adoptive country and their "home" country (country of origin).

In assigning the blame for this malaise, exile accounts vary. Reflecting on his experience in the delegation to the 1947 Paris Peace Treaty Conference, prominent exile figure Gianni Giuricin told me that Alceste De Gaspari, head of the Italian delegation, had sold out the Istrians by nixing the proposal for a pleibiscite in Istria. Although Giuricin criticizes the Italian state for failing to defend the Istrians' interests during the negotiations and after the subsequent exodus, he also accuses the Italian communists of spitting (in some cases literally) on the newly arrived refugees. In his 1993 memoir, Giuricin relates the quintessential story of the *esuli*'s betrayal by communists in Italy. He describes an incident where a train transporting Istrian refugees, many of whom had just arrived by ship from Pola and who still wore the insignia of the Istrian resistance, passed through Bologna, a stronghold of the Italian Communist Party. The train workers in Bologna refused to allow the refugees to stop and enjoy the hot meal prepared for them by the Red Cross, vowing to strike and paralyze train service if, as Giuricin puts it, "the train of fascists remained stopped in the station" (Giuricin, 1993: 205).

This same story has been repeated to me on several other occasions by informants. One man narrated the story to illustrate that the exiles were treated little better than beasts. As an epilogue to the episode, he notes that "Then they put the people in old convents, in barracks." After suffering such abuse by Italian communists, many refugees also found themselves placed in miserable refugee camps. In Trieste, some even inhabited the former Nazi extermination camp, Risiera di San Sabba. Many of the life histories I collected during my fieldwork feature bitter recollections of life in these camps, yet another example for many exiles of their betrayal by the *patria*.

The bitter irony that the *esuli*, having fled intolerable conditions on the promise of aid in the Italian homeland, were herded together in former concentration camps and prisons still rankles in the hearts of many. Exiles also encountered hostility from those Italians who viewed them as taking away scarce food and jobs. In addition, some exiles felt that Triestines looked down on them as unsophisticated country cousins; one woman who lived in Trieste before emigrating with her family to the United States describes her embarrassment at being shabbily dressed and speaking dialect. Faced with this situation, many Italian Istrians—as well as Slovenes and Croats who had left Istria—chose to emigrate abroad. This is interpreted by some *esuli* (e.g., Giuricin, 1993) as another phase in the cultural genocide begun by the Tito regime and its allies in the Italian Communist Party and abetted by the Italian state.

While employing a contemporary language of genocide, many of these stories told today by exiles about their lost land echo pronouncements made by Italian nationalist parties at the time of the Trieste crisis. Although today produced and received in a changed political environment, exile narratives thus reveal remarkable continuity over time. This should warn against a narrowly "presentist" view that sees the past as largely produced in the contemporary moment (see Halbwachs, 1992; Hobsbawm and Ranger, 1983). Exiles today speak of ethnic cleansing, for example, where they once decried "denationalization." Made at the time of events after World War II, these denunciations of the denationalization and Slavicization of Istria in turn built on deeper irredentist discourses, forged in the struggle against the Hapsburg Empire, that reflect deep-seated fears of a "Slavic threat."

Not surprisingly, then, reconciliation with those Slavs and Italians who currently inhabit Istria does not rank high among the priorities of the exile associations. As the previous discussion of exile narratives evidences, the sense of horror remains vivid for those who lived through such experiences. With the tragic end of Yugoslavia, some exiles feel vindicated, as they were never taken in by the reconciliatory post-1954 rhetoric of the Yugoslav and Italian states. For many, though certainly not all, *esuli,* the Slavs have not changed and thus cannot be trusted, even when as in Istria they don the guise of European regionalists.

The main exile associations in Trieste have generally refused to collaborate with the Istrian regionalist movement, founded in Croatia in 1990 with the birth there of a pluriparty system. The exile organizations do, however, have some contacts with the associations of the Italian minority in Istria. Many exiles nonetheless continue to view these Italians in Istria with suspicion, claiming that they stayed out of opportunism or may not even be genuine Istrian Italians. Although exiles often have friends and relatives still living in Istria, they nonetheless view the *rimasti* in general as a dubious lot, yet another group that has betrayed them. Conversely, I have also heard many of the Italians who remained in Istria claim that those who left were victims of Italian state-sponsored propaganda. One woman from Rovigno who worked as a partisan during the war maintains that Italian nationalists instrumentalized the exiles. De Gaspari had lured them out of Istria, she said, with the promise that they would be able to return eventually. Several persons I spoke with lamented that if only the Italians had not abandoned Istria, there would have been no motive for the Slavs to move in and change Istria; this suggests that those who stayed similarly feel betrayed by those who left. This difficult relationship between those who left and those who stayed is reflected in the exiles' skepticism when confronted by supporters of the Istrian regionalist movement, both Italian and Croat.

ALTERNATIVE VISIONS OF IDENTITY AND HISTORY: ISTRIAN REGIONALISM

The collapse of the Yugoslav state has led the Italian minority to break the long silence in Slovenia and Croatia about the exodus. In contrast to the exiles' exclusive and nostalgic invocations of a lost *Italian* world, many Italians in Istria today link a reconfigured collective memory to a forward-looking regionalist project underwritten by the concept of a hybrid, Latin-Slav Istrian identity. The centralizing nationalism of Tudjman's Croatia and its insistence on Croatian "purity" has led many Italians to conclude that the only potential protection for minority rights resides in such a regionalist scheme. Tudjman's denunciation of dual citizenship for (some) members of the Italian minority in Istria as evidence of an Italian imperialistic project to reclaim Istria further impels the *rimasti* to distance themselves politically from the *esuli*'s contentious demands for restitution of their lost properties (even as the *rimasti* paradoxically hope for some general reconciliation). For these reasons, members of the Italian minority have assumed a prominent role in the Istrian Democratic Assembly (DDI), a regionalist movement that seeks cooperation between the Slovenian and Croatian territories of Istria.

Regionalists promote a vision of Istria as historically characterized by linguistic and cultural hybridity. Like the exiles in Trieste, proponents of regionalism view Istrians as the continual objects, rather than subjects, of history—a history viewed as a constant jockeying between great powers. DDI vice president and party intellectual Loredana

Bogliun Debeljuh describes Istria as an "area of ethnic fluidity and a place always at the geopolitical margins of States . . . an area considered a land of conquest" (Debeljuh, 1993: 21). The DDI's project consists in turning this ethnic fluidity and hybridity into a strength that will enable Istrians to take their future into their own hands, as well as to come to terms with their difficult recent past, in particular the violence of fascism and the exodus.

At the most immediate level, the movement seeks to provide an alternative to the exclusive nationalisms that destroyed the Yugoslav state and left the Istrian peninsula divided between Slovenia and Croatia. This situation has given rise to a number of tensions between the Slovene and Croatian states over once-shared infrastructure, fishing rights, and the protection of the Italian minority. By establishing a transnational, regional entity within the framework of the European Union, DDI proponents argue, such tensions can be overcome and more stable state relations established in the region. Invoking the language of new social movements, the DDI gives particular attention to the preservation of Istria's environmental and cultural patrimony.

DDI vice president Debeljuh stresses that an appreciation of Istria's cultural diversity must underwrite the political project of the DDI. This is necessary to heal what Luciano Delbianco, former president of the Istrian region, has called an "open wound in the collective memory." According to the DDI, the dual traumas of fascism and communism rent the fabric of coexistence in Istria. It is this tragic history that has convinced many DDI supporters that the only possible strategy for the future lies in ethnic cohabitation or *convivenza* and the celebration of tolerance and difference. According to Fulvio Tomizza, a well-known exile writer of self-described Slavic blood and Italian culture, an Istrian need not make an exclusive choice in declaring himself or herself Slovene, Italian, or Croatian. Rather, the only possibility exists in declaring oneself Istrian, a concept in some ways reminiscent of the failed Yugoslav identity.

Not surprisingly, this freedom of nonchoice remains under critical attack in Croatia. Such differences emerged at the First World Congress of Istrians held at Pola/Pula (Croatia) in April 1995. As one of the organizers and a DDI deputy to the Croatian Parliament explained there, "When we say we're Istrians, the state institutions say we can't be." In line with this state opposition to regionalism, Tudjman supporters reserved two hundred of the eight hundred places

at the congress and made a consistent effort to disrupt the proceedings. At the closing, these nationalists hoisted a Croatian flag and tried
to drown out the chant "Istra, Istra" with shouts for "Hrvatska,
Hrvatska" (Croatia, Croatia). The visibility of this internal Croatian
political debate at the congress confirmed the fears expressed by many
exiles that they had been largely ignored in the planning of the event,
which in their opinion had nothing to do with Italian–Croatian reconciliation but rather reflected Croatian domestic politics. Many
esuli stayed away and in the months preceding the conference had
sent letters of protest to the Triestine paper *Il Piccolo*.

   Given the prominent role played by the Italian minority in this regionalist movement, many exiles felt that the DDI Congress, like the
DDI more generally, represented an opportunistic strategy by the
rimasti and their Croatian allies to gain benefits and power. The fact
that as many as five thousand individuals have suddenly declared
themselves Italian since 1991 strikes the exiles as suspicious. As one
exile I interviewed put it, "Where did all these 'Italians' come from,
if all the towns [in Istria] were deserted after the war by the Italians?"
For this woman, Slavs now claim to be Italians in order to gain financial benefits from the Italian government. Another exile told me that
most so-called Italians today living in his native town of Capodistria
do not have genuine Capodistrian names. Given this, he concluded,
one cannot say that an autochthonous Italian community exists in
Istria. Such statements bring together the criteria of authenticity that
dominate many *esuli* accounts and that take a number of markers of
rootedness (names, genealogies, ancestors in cemeteries) as evidence
of the exiles' historical right to Istria. A host of secular and religious
practices reinforce these narrative strategies (see Ballinger, 1996;
Bogneri, 1993: 180). Such practices include the preservation of bits
of soil or stones from Istria, which at times are invoked in a kind of
literal "communion" with the lost homeland. The man from Pola
who fought at Salò described his brother's funeral; for the last rites,
he used a bit of soil from Pola bathed in Istrian seawater. Through
such rituals of exile (rooted in the traditions of Catholicism and Italian irredentism), some exiles have continued to nurture the bipolar
Latin-Slav/civilized-barbaric distinctions abandoned by the Yugoslav
and Italian states after 1948. In doing so, they forcefully reassert
their moral and legal right to their properties in Istria and contest the
vision of Istrian hybridity promoted by the DDI.

CONCLUSION: HISTORY, MEMORY, AND
THE INSTRUMENTALITIES OF POWER

Focusing on the kind of communities often overlooked by state-centric analyses, this chapter has employed an anthropological approach to reconsider a classic case study within the diplomatic history and security literatures. Viewing discourses of history and memory as social artifacts, my analysis has highlighted the power relations inherent in the production of particular histories of the Trieste crisis and in their reception at various levels. Within the local political field in Trieste, a powerful group history and identity has been articulated in the intersection of Great Power, national, and regional politics. *Esuli* claims to land and to their status as victims of ethnic cleansing rest on their construction and deployment of discourses about a historic Italian culture destroyed in Istria; such accounts compete with and necessarily seek to silence discordant conceptualizations, including those that view Istria as historically a multi-ethnic culture or alternatively as a Slavic land, as well as Great Power readings of the Trieste crisis as the first Cold War showdown.

In the Trieste case, then, discourses of group memory and history provide an entry point for reevaluating what various histories and security analyses necessarily silenced. Official neglect notwithstanding, the exiles' tenacity in nurturing their alternative histories and demands for justice reminds us that the victims of mass expulsions do not forget their homeland, even fifty years after the fact. Those memories, moreover, do not simply persist but are actively reproduced, contested, and politically deployed. These rather obvious points should not be neglected in addressing the massive refugee problem created by the Yugoslav wars of the 1990s and in working for retribution, resettlement, or repatriation for these refugees.

Sitting at the geographic and figurative borders of the broader contemporary crisis over the Yugoslav past, this case also underscores the general lack of serious consideration given to such "memory politics" within both the wider international relations field and the policy world. Security-focused analyses in particular have proved silent on the subject of memory politics (past and present) in the Balkans. Despite the outpouring of works in English on the current Yugoslav crises, for example, virtually none devotes attention to the ways in which memories of interethnic conflict and the challenging of state-sponsored narratives of the partisan war proved central to the ethnonational identifications that emerged in former Yugoslavia since the late 1980s.[1] As the ongoing contestation over the Istrian exodus makes clear, the centrality of "history" and "culture" to conceptualizations of identity proves crucial to understanding the production of insecurity for many of those, such as the *esuli,* whose voices have been drowned out by the official histories of the state.

Examining the Istrian case thus provides an interesting parallel to the way in which nationalist hatreds were created in post-Tito Yugoslavia through a reexamination of the past and in particular through questioning of the official narratives that depicted World War II as a war of partisan liberation rather than as a civil conflict. Many parallels exist between the exiles' litanies about the Yugoslav partisans' mass executions of Italians in the *foibe* and the "discoveries" in the 1980s of Serb-Croat massacre sites in Yugoslavia (see Denich, 1994; Hayden, 1994). In both cases, these collective graves have become sites for commemoration and have (re)produced a sense of ethnic difference and group victimhood. Not surprisingly, many of the same kinds of chauvinisms and hostilities heard in former Yugoslavia are also found within the exile community in Trieste, thereby putting into question those explanations attributing "primordial" ethnic hatreds to Balkan peoples.

Issues of memory and identity not only matter for security studies, then, but also force us to rethink power (its sites and operation) as we bring "culture" into such analyses. Understanding the politics of memory that has asserted itself so forcefully in many contemporary cases entails not merely adding in culture as another "variable" but taking seriously Trouillot's comment that "Power does not enter the story once and for all, but at different times and different angles" (1995: 28–29). As he puts it, "Power is constitutive of the story. Tracking power through various 'moments' simply helps emphasize the fundamentally processual character of historical production, to insist that what history is matters less than how history works" (ibid., 28).

Investigating the practices of power, particularly in the production of narratives of memory and identity, requires attention to both nonstate actors and specific state formations. The Istrian case, like the Yugoslav war, demonstrates the need to go beyond older views of identity formation as moving out from the center in order to account for a possibly more dynamic interplay between center and peripheries; the analysis here of the "Trieste crisis" has revealed the local appropriation (by elites and others) of discourses and practices, as well as ways in which locally generated practices may influence broader constructions. The limited success of the exile associations in promoting their political aims reminds us, admittedly, that the exiles continue to operate within a landscape of nation-states that, despite increasing trans-state flows of people and capital, still retain considerable power in delimiting the boundaries within which issues of identity may be negotiated.[2] Nevertheless, as sites of power become "unbundled" (Ruggie, 1993) and reconfigured in new ways within that landscape of states, nonstate actors such as the exiles have found a space for their demands in a variety of forums (including the UN and the European Court of Human Rights) not limited to those of the nation-state. In the analysis here of the constitution of those demands and their changing receptions, I have sought to "track power" and thereby chart one possible course for a reconceptualized security studies.

NOTES

This paper builds on fieldwork carried out in Istria and Trieste in the summers of 1992 and 1993 and for twenty months between 1995 and 1996. I am grateful to the following agencies for funding this project at various stages: Center for International Security and Cooperation at Stanford University, Council of European Studies, Department of Hispanic and Italian Studies at Johns Hopkins University, Fulbright, Institute for the Study of World Politics, Newcombe Foundation, NSF, SSRC-MacArthur, SSRC-Western Europe, and Wenner Gren. Thanks as well to the staffs at the Istituto Regionale per la Storia del Movimento di Liberazione nel Friuli Venezia Giulia, the Istituto Regionale per la Cultura Istriana, and the Centro di Ricerche Storiche di Rovigno. I am also indebted to the participants of the workshops held in Minnesota and Kent and in particular the editors for their reading of various drafts of this paper.

1. For two typical examples of such works, consult Gow (1992) and Crawford and Lipschutz (1994).

2. The resolution of the Italo-Slovene negotiations in 1996, with Italy voting in favor of Slovenia's entrance into the European Union (EU), illustrates this point. With the redefinition of Italian and U.S. state interests, efforts to link Slovenian membership in the EU with resolution of *esuli* claims for compensation were explicitly overruled by Italian state officials. This followed out of the electoral defeat of the exiles' political sponsors in the Berlusconi government by a center-left coalition in Italy in April 1995.

3

Intervention and Identity: Reconstructing the West in Korea

JENNIFER MILLIKEN

Contrary to how it is sometimes presented in security studies scholarship, the Cold War was not simply a conflict between the United States and the Soviet Union. It also included political-economic groupings of states, those of the "West" and the "East," and their battleground, variously represented as the "Free World" or the "Third World." These collective subjects were knit together through a web of political, economic, and cultural exchanges. They also came to life through military aid, the meshing of command and control systems, and the creation of security organizations such as NATO and the Warsaw Pact. And, in a less regular but nonetheless important fashion, the collectivities were constructed in interventions. Western states, predominantly but hardly exclusively the United States, intervened overtly with ground forces more than fifty times between 1945 and 1989.[1] Such interventions were occasions on which the intervenor(s) articulated and defined not just individual state interests but collective identity and collective threat.

This chapter examines cultural processes of collective identity formation as played out in Western intervention in the Korean War. Like so many subsequent conflicts, the Korean War was on the Free World periphery of the West. It was nonetheless a particularly significant moment in the broader process of (re)constituting the Western security collectivity. In Korean War diplomacy, state representatives had to declare the boundaries of justifiable international behavior, with whom they sided in international politics, and the price they were willing to pay for this stance. Declarations made about the Korean War also entailed other enrollments—bodies, machines and money, organizational structures, and historical memories rechanneled—that came to affect the daily practices of collective security for those states. Passage through Congress of the funding package for NSC 68, the planning document that served as the basis for the U.S. national security state, was justified in part by Soviet aggression in Korea. So too were agreements to station U.S. forces in Europe. On the other side of the Atlantic, the conflict was translated into a need for Britain to increase its defense spending (the Labour government's social policies being thereby waylaid), and for Europeans to permit German remilitarization.

Interventions are premised on insecurities. But what made these insecurities? And how did state collectivities figure in (or how were they made to figure in) this process in the Korean case? I will claim that state insecurities like those for the United States and its allies in Korea are not given but are (re)constructed through discourse, an ordering of terms, meanings, and practices that forms the background presuppositions and taken-for-granted understandings that enable people's actions and interpretations.[2] Discourses provide people with the capabilities to represent a situation to themselves and to others. Those capabilities give ways of naming and characterizing the subjects and objects of international relations, including states and collections of states such as the West (cf. Muppidi and Niva, this volume). They also provide ways of relating these subjects and objects, for example, in standardized narratives for how one state can threaten others through conquest, or how a community of states may collapse from internal divisions. My particular concern here is to elucidate how policymakers drew on and reconstructed security discourses so as to produce Korea as a site of collective insecurity for the West.

After briefly outlining concepts for my study, the argument unfolds in three parts. First, I seek to show how, for U.S. policymakers, intervention in Korea was made possible through "threats" to the collective identification of European and Asian states with Western-led international society and U.S. alliance leadership in that society. Using primary sources, my study examines the articulation of such "threats" in the first weeks of the conflict (June 25–July 21, 1950). Through primary and secondary sources, I also sketch the discursive emergence of collectives of the West and the Free World in the previous three decades of U.S. foreign policy.

Second, I examine how the United States' interventionary diplomacy "hailed" (attempted to interpellate) other states as followers of the U.S. interventionary lead. Here my study is based on meeting notes and diplomatic memoranda from the first month of the war. It draws out how U.S. diplomacy constructed differentiated categories of states as followers of U.S. leadership.

For Western states in particular, United States diplomacy opened up a subject-position of makers of collective unity secondary to the United States in the West and the Free World. In the third part of the chapter, I examine British reception of this subject-position, concentrating on British policy documents from the first month of the war. The conclusion is that Britain too intervened in Korea for the sake of collective identification, but this time predominantly for that of the United States with the West.

ON THE CONSTITUTION OF COLLECTIVITIES

Most of the security studies and international relations literature dealing with culture and discourse has been broadly poststructural in orientation. This literature also offers the richest set of concepts for understanding how political identity is constitutive of state insecurities. But work in this area has so far had little to say about collective insecurities among states; as in conventional (neorealist) security studies, this has been a secondary subject.

Consider, for example, the work of David Campbell. Campbell develops a theory of foreign policy as discursive practices that, rather than serving the interests of a predefined national community, constitute that community by drawing its borders conceptually and securing its identity as "a particular state with a definable character" (1993: 24). Central to these discursive practices are policymaking narratives entailing a sovereign, ethical "self" of the state and an anarchic "outside" to this state. In and through this narrative dichotomizing, threatening "others" that the state must combat and resist come to be identified. Such discursive construction of "danger" is legitimated through its being spoken and written by authorities (ibid., 7). The narratives make sense to policymakers and the public alike inasmuch as they draw on and reconstruct historical myths and tropes that are part of a state's culture. American Cold War discourse of the threatening Soviet "other," for example, acquired "epistemic realism" in part by drawing on the nineteenth-century myth of the frontier to reconstruct "us" as civilized and "them" as barbaric (ibid., 6; 1994: 159).

As this sketch suggests, Campbell's work remains focused on nation-state identity as a sovereign "self" defined against threats and dangers "out there." Such a focus is problematic for U.S. Cold War security policy (the main discourse of identity that Campbell studies), because it leaves aside issues of collective state identity and how insecurities are constituted for groups of states. During the Cold War, U.S. policymakers narratively opposed the United States to the Soviet Union, but interwoven with these oppositions were constructs of various collective subjects—for example, the Free World and the West—to which the United States belonged. Part of the United States' discourse of identity included relations of distinction between such collectivities and others "out there"—for example, the democratic, advanced, peaceful West versus the totalitarian, backward, aggressive Communist bloc. Also involved were relations of distinction within the collectivities: the United States as the leader of Western civilization and the Free World, and developing states as quasi children being brought up to become, in time, full members of the West (cf. Weldes, this volume). Such constructions would seem to invite a more nuanced reading than Campbell's field of anarchic, dangerous "others" residing "outside" the United States implies.

Besides the question of collectivities of states in U.S. security discourse, Campbell's work also bypasses questions of states' collective identity in a second way. This occurs when, at various junctures, Campbell presents U.S. discourse and its objects and relations as describing more generally a Western state discourse. For example, in analyzing the Persian Gulf War, Campbell writes: "that which distinguished the just and righteous American (or Western) 'self' from the evil and abominable Iraqi 'other' thus constituted the transgression of the territorial boundary as a crime and inscribed for the protagonists the ethical borders of their state identity" (1993: 26). But this asserts an equivalence between U.S. discourse and that of other Western states. Certainly the American discourse might be dominant, hegemonic, or otherwise representative of other Western states, but if this is in fact the case, the question remains: by what processes has a collective Western discourse been constructed and reconstructed?[3]

In this regard, Cynthia Weber's (1995) work offers a more promising line of investigation. Weber studies justifications given by diplomats for nineteenth-century European and twentieth-century American interventions to give an account of the shifting historical constitution of state sovereignty. In diplomatic justifications for interventions, she argues, state officials articulate "what it means to be a state at a particular place and time" (ibid., 1995: 29). However, Weber also points out that interventions "raise the question of the constitution of a community of states":

> In offering justifications [for intervention] . . . diplomats of intervening states simultaneously assume the existence of norms regulating state practices and an interpretive community that will judge intervention practices in accordance with those norms. But . . . it is international practice that constitutes the boundaries and capacities of . . . international interpretive communities. Rather than diplomats addressing their justifications for intervention to an already formed community, the form of a justification in effect participates in the constitution of . . . the interpretive community to which the state's justifications are directed. (Ibid., 5)

Weber here highlights how, in diplomatic exchanges, an act such as intervention is accounted for by intervening state diplomats with respect to the members of a particular international community, their legitimate modes of acting, and the dangers and threats they face. But the representations officials use are not neutral descriptions of fact: in naming and characterizing a state collectivity, diplomats of intervening states define it and its insecurities, possibly (Weber would say inevitably) altering how it can be understood and the activities that can be taken in its name.

In its focus on a diplomacy of intervention, Weber's project begins to locate the construction of collective state insecurity in an interesting way. Like Campbell, though, Weber remains indebted to the figure of the sovereign state and to theory that privileges it. This is made most clear in Weber's empirical studies, which focus almost entirely on speeches, memorandums, and diplomatic communications of an *intervening state*. Beyond the notion of "justification" (a rather broad label) there is little examination of this diplomacy as a set of activities undertaken by intervening state diplomats. Diplomacy is also communicative *interaction*, but the analysis only rarely extends to the response of officials of other states to the intervening state. Presumably the boundaries and capacities of an international community are constituted in this *reception* as much as in intervening state officials' representations.

As I use it, diplomatic reception is a process of communicative interaction in which policy elites seek to enroll others in intervention to give it political and material support. Such a focus seems to invite accounts of rational bargaining based on preformed state interests. My approach emphasizes instead the way that, in diplomatic representations, "subject-positions" are opened up into which other states are "hailed" (cf. Muppidi, this volume); that is, I treat diplomacy as a symbolic process, with modes of address about who "we" and "they" are, and especially, who "you" are, inscribed in what is said to other state representatives. Other states' responses depend on this address, its timing, its internal coherence, and whether and how it overlaps with those states' objects and narratives of discourse. Only if—as—the subject-positions of diplomacy are taken up as authoritative with respect to the social borders of and hierarchies within "us" will interventionary diplomacy succeed (Lincoln, 1989).

COMING TO LEAD INTERVENTION

If we read Korean War documents for traces of "community," one thing becomes clear: for U.S. policymakers, intervention in Korea was part of a project of securing collective identities of the West as a security "community" and the Free World as a Western-led alliance system (*Documents on British Policy Overseas* [hereafter, *DBPO*] 2/2: 268). Officials in the Truman administration moved to an intervention policy within several days of the June 25 outbreak of the conflict. This choice of action followed from a line of reasoning in which the North Korean invasion alienated Asian and Western states from the United States, and, more generally, from the Western alliance.

This reasoning actually began in policymakers' interpretation of Soviet responsibility for North Korean actions. U.S. officials had no proof of Soviet orders, of course, nor were Soviet forces involved. Rather, it was taken as self-evident that North Korea had no effective agency: it was a "puppet state" of the Soviet Union that was "completely under [the] Kremlin's control" (U.S. Department of State,

1976b: 149). The conflict was therefore a case of international "aggression" by the Soviet Union (ibid., 139).

This definition of (hidden but nonetheless clear) Soviet aggression excluded treating the conflict as Koreans fighting Koreans (i.e., civil war) and placed it instead in a context of state "imperialism." For U.S. policymakers at this time, the dominant interpretation of Soviet "imperialism" was global empire: the Soviet Union aimed to "to impose its absolute authority over the rest of the world" (Etzold and Gaddis, 1978: 348). A Soviet "move" in Korea might therefore have signified further military attacks on U.S. allies in Asia and Europe (ibid., 149). But such attacks were deemed "unlikely" by U.S. policymakers, because "Russia is not yet ready for war" (ibid., 157). Rather, the threat posed by the Soviet "move" lay in the damage it could do to allied confidence and solidarity.

One form of allied alienation followed from doubts about the United States' commitment to collective defense. On this reading, the North Korean attack was a "challenge" to U.S. "leadership . . . against Soviet Communist imperialism" (ibid., 150). If the United States did not "draw the line" in Korea to show its resolution, "a severe blow would be dealt US prestige throughout Asia" (ibid., 158, 150). States such as Japan would experience a strengthening of an existing "desire for neutrality" such that not even a commitment of "significant additional US military strength" would keep Japan allied (ibid., 151). In Europe, the core of U.S. alliances, "the capacity of a small Soviet satellite to engage in a military adventure challenging, as many Europeans will see it, the might and will of the US, can only lead to serious questioning of that might and will" (ibid., 154).

For U.S. policymakers, therefore, the stake in Korea was whether or not Asian and European states would identify with "us" and therefore be useful and reliable followers in alliances under U.S. leadership. But identification with "us" was also at stake in Korea in another way. Differentiating the Western side from the Soviet "camp" for U.S. policymakers was that the Western side alone stood for rule of law among nations (*DBPO* 2/2: 268). Western commitment to a legally and morally ordered international politics was embodied in the United Nations, an institution created by "Western Powers" to realize the hope of a "permanent and stable world society founded on mutual interests and aims of all nations" (George F. Kennan, in Jensen, 1993: 28). Soviet aggression in Korea was aggression against a state created through "US-led UN action" (U.S. Department of State, 1976b: 139). Therefore, the attack was also a "test" of the United Nations and the Western-led society it stood for (ibid., 201).

European states, though Western, could themselves be estranged by a "compromise with justice" in Korea (ibid., 394). But implicitly, the states and peoples that could be most affected were non-Western: "colonial areas and backward or dependent peoples" (as Kennan called them), looking toward "the peaceful and hopeful concept of international life" offered by the West (Kennan, in Jensen, 1993: 17). If the UN failed its test, these members of the Free World would lose their belief in a Western-led society. Conversely, if the UN were to mobilize, this clear demonstration of "moral position" and "moral principle" would deepen Free World confidence in the organization and its order (U.S. Department of State, 1976b: 394, 454).

It is worth noting how contestable many of the premises of this reasoning were. If the Soviets were puppetmasters, they might still not have been attempting a global symbolic challenge to "the strength and determination of the West," but a limited local power play (Truman, 1956: 339). Moreover, both North and South Koreans had sworn to reunify Korea, by force if necessary. North Korea might be acting independently, or semi-independently, in what "in its essence" was "in the nature of a civil war" (Norwegian UN Representative, in ibid., 145). Especially given the latter, the conflict might not have been a symbol of the United States' and the West's commitments—until U.S. policymakers and diplomats created that symbolism through taking the conflict to the UN Security Council on June 25, returning there for UN sanction on June 27, and otherwise calling forth a "test" in a flurry of cables and meetings.

But it was not just the definition of the conflict that was contestable: so was the West-East context assumed for the intervention. The United States had replaced Japanese imperial control of southern Korea with a U.S.-dominated client state and was helping European states retain their colonies in Asia. Simultaneous with intervention in Korea, the United States increased its assistance to France for its colonial war in Indochina and sent the Seventh Fleet to Formosa, an island that was by international treaty part of mainland China. Read in this context, the Korean intervention was not a matter of Western action against the Soviets to guard the sovereignty and independence of Asian states. Rather, as Egyptian diplomats put it, the intervention was a continuation of "Western imperialism" in Korea and the Asian region (ibid., 261).

U.S. policymakers were aware of such alternative accounts. Indeed, they strategized how to counter them, for example, planning "measures" to be taken in the UN to meet "propaganda" that "the conflict in Korea is a war where white men are shooting Asiatics" (ibid., 363). But such strategies were about getting others to see the "facts" as U.S. policymakers understood them. U.S. officials otherwise took for granted their definition of the context of the conflict, what it was, and what it meant. They did so, in no small measure, because of discursive ways they and others before them had developed for characterizing and narrating international events.

Let us start with international society as an entity naturally to be led by the Western powers. This hierarchy among "us" was by no means obviously justified on grounds of "right" conduct in world affairs. Western states such as Britain and France practiced war-making balance-of-power politics and imperial conquest and repression—as nineteenth-century U.S. politicians frequently pointed out. But already long before the Korean War, U.S. discourses had come to construct an identity for Western states as a grouping superior to, and necessarily the leaders of, non-Western states. In the early twentieth-century, it was widely accepted that civilizations progressed from savagery to barbarism to civilization.[4] For Americans, the civilizational progress of states such as Germany or Russia was less than Britain or the United States ("military despotism" being less advanced than "democracy"). But just as clearly, these were all members of "Western civilization," which, as a grouping, was far advanced over "savage" Africa and "barbarian" Asia (Theodore Roosevelt, in Ninkovich, 1994: 14, 8). The qualities securing Western "advancement" included, among others, the superior rationality of Westerners as compared to the "racial slowness, and the low average intelligence" of non-Western peoples (Herbert Hoover, in ibid., 90). Also featured was the ability of "a great civilizing power" to create the "law, order and righteousness" lacked by non-Western peoples and governments (Roosevelt, in ibid., 8).

From this discursive matrix it followed "naturally" that Western states should control other peoples and places, ensuring that "each part of the world should be prosperous and well-policed" (Roosevelt, in ibid.). As Doty remarks in her analysis of U.S. imperialism in the Philippines, this was to construct a "Western bond" establishing a "right of conquest" for Western states (Doty, 1996b: 34). By the end of World War II, the Western bond had been reconstructed—now Western control was to give way to the sovereignty and independence of non-Western states. But still, for U.S. officials and the informed public, "the self-determination of peoples" was to be an "eventual" development to "take place in an orderly manner" (U.S. Department of State, 1974, 109). During and after the transition, Western states were to give "guidance" to others in becoming a "free society" (U.S. Department of State, 1976b: 237).

Like the earlier right to rule, the new understanding was grounded discursively in a presupposition, made repeatedly in U.S. policy and congressional representations, of Western "reason" and "rationality" as "fundamentally" advanced over Asian or African "emotion" and "passion" (Doty, 1996b: 88–91). Relatedly, Western states were constructed as "democracies," politically liberal and moderate, and capable and experienced in peaceful international competition. Western states were thereby paradigms of governance, and thus natural guides, for immature non-Westerners just beginning "experiment[s] in free government" and still learning how to have "autonomous, democratic self-rule" (U.S. Department of State, 1976b: 237; U.S. Department of State, April 1945, in Leffler, 1992: 94).

One of the key ways the identity of a democratic West was naturalized was through juxtaposition with the Soviet Union as a "totalitarian dictatorship" (U.S. Department of State, April 1950, in Ninkovich, 1994: 149). This juxtaposition placed the Soviet Union in a category with Hitler's Germany as states that subordinated individuals to the state, removed civil liberties and free speech, and took over the private economy for militaristic purposes. The essential identity of Western states as democracies emerged in their opposition to characteristics of totalitarians (see Weldes, 1993: chapter 8). For example, for President Truman in 1947, the West was home to a "way of life . . . based on the will of the majority, and . . . distinguished by free institutions, representative government, free elections, [and] guarantees of individual liberty." "[T]otalitarian regimes," in contrast, were a "way of life . . . based upon the will of a minority forcibly imposed upon the majority." Totalitarians relied "upon terror and oppression, a controlled press and radio, fixed elections, and the suppression of personal freedoms" (Truman, in Spanier, 1973: 41).

The opposition between "we democracies" and "the totalitarians" was casually and regularly used by Americans well before 1945 (see Paterson, 1989). Extended into the Cold War, it not only made a paradigm of Western democracies as morally superior forms of government—the ideal type for a Free World—but also constructed Western conduct in international society as morally superior. Because of the "supposedly immutable characteristics of totalitarians," Americans expected that "Russia in the 1940s would behave as Germany had in the previous decade" (ibid., 5): "totalitarian Russia," like Nazi Germany, was a duplicitous and aggressive state, seeking to make other states into "satellites" and "puppet political machines" (U.S. Department of State, 1973: 741, 763; Kennan, Jensen, 1993: 32). The Western democracies, in contrast, were neither aggressive nor duplicitous. Rather, as demonstrated in their engagement in the United Nations, they were "by nature" peaceful, open, and willing and capable of acting "in the name of all and for the welfare of all" (*Congressional Register*, 1945, 90/8: A265).

The prior naturalization of Western democracies as exemplary members of international society enabled the Truman administration's Korean policy to assume that Western powers should lead "us," and that charges of Western imperialism were "deep-seated misunderstandings" of UN intervention (U.S. Department of State, 1976b: 383). Also enabled by the "essential" difference previously constructed between the West and the Soviet Union were the alleged "facts" of complete Soviet control of its North Korean "puppet" and Soviet imperialist objectives in Korea. But how was it possible that President Truman declared on June 26, 1950, that "he had done everything he could for five years to prevent this situation. Now . . . we must do what we can to meet it" (ibid., 183)? How, in other words, was a right and responsibility of U.S. *leadership* of the Free World made so commonsensical?

The United States had long been understood by Americans as "first" in Western civilization: "God's best representative of law and order and justice on earth," and a state leading "our sister civilization in Europe" in "every social and moral aspect" (Senator Spooner, 1899, in Doty, 1996b: 32; Herbert Hoover, 1922, in Ninkovich, 1994: 87). This notion of the United States as the exemplar of Western democracy helped after World War II to anchor U.S. leadership. So too did the repeated invocation of the United States as by far the most powerful and vital of the Western powers, with power so great it could hardly avoid worldwide responsibilities. U.S. alliance leadership of the West and the Free World, though, was perhaps most naturalized through two narratives of totalitarianism versus democracy: that of world empire and that of appeasement.

The world empire narrative extended World War II projections of Axis threats of "world domination" to the "fact" that the Soviet Union was undertaking a "program for world conquest" (Clark Clifford, 1950, in Ninkovich, 1994: 153).[5] If that program were to succeed, it would not mean, any more than during World War II, that the United States itself would be conquered. But, as in World War II, "the civilization in which the American way of life is rooted" would be destroyed, and with it the material and moral basis of a free and prosperous United States (Truman, 1947: 516). Here, for example, is President Truman using this account to argue in 1947 for the European Recovery Program:

> In the event of a totalitarian Europe . . . the change in the power relationships involved would force us to adopt drastic domestic measures and would inevitably require great and burdensome sacrifices on the part of our citizens. . . . The sacrifices would not be simply material. With a totalitarian Europe which would have no regard for individual freedom, our spiritual loss would be incalculable. (In Leffler, 1992: 191)

The survival of the United States as "itself"—liberal and free—was dependent on the survival of an "us" of the democratic West and, secondarily, the Western fringe. That linkage between collective identity, U.S. identity, and U.S. survival is missed by scholars claiming that its vastly superior power meant that the United States after World War II did not need its allies in order to survive against the Soviet Union (e.g., Waltz, 1979: 169–70; Snyder, 1990). Certainly the United States could have withstood Soviet attack, but it would have had to *surrender the American way of life* in the process. U.S. alliance leadership, however "entangling,' " was on this understanding vastly preferable to "a world condition" destructive of "the survival of our national values" (Dean Acheson, March 1950, in Ninkovich, 1994: 153).

If the world empire narrative helped make sensible "why" U.S. leadership, the appeasement narrative helped inscribe "how." This narrative was first used by World War II interventionists to argue that the United States must not repeat European democracies' error at Munich. After 1945, "Remember Munich!" became a slogan both for how the Soviet Union would behave (like Hitler) and for why the United States needed to oppose the Soviet Union (to avoid appeasement). In the face of any aggressive step, the United States must stand firm. Otherwise aggression would continue and its fruits would grow as frontline states, losing hope, would seek neutrality or join the Communist side. Eventually, the United States would find itself "standing alone" (U.S. Department of State, 1977a: 207). This was what "the tragic history of the 30's demonstrates," as Dean Acheson put it (U.S. Department of State, 1976b: 347). President Truman's evocation of this lesson was that "each time that the democracies failed to act they had encouraged the aggressor to keep going ahead" (Truman, 1956: 33).

The appeasement narrative turned negotiations with the Soviets into a potential "sellout." It also rewrote U.S. "isolationism" not as a morally superior policy but as a "compromise with evil" that could not be countenanced (Truman, 1945, in Paterson, 1989: 12–13). The United States would therefore have to be courageous and responsible, applying its power to prevent another Munich. To "stiffen morale" in European democracies, it should create a North Atlantic system of collective security (U.S. Department of State, 1974: 49). To prevent "Communist domination of the Eurasian land mass," the United States should increase its military capabilities and build up allied military forces (NSC 68) (U.S. Department of State, 1977a: 253). It should also be prepared to intervene globally, for "aggression anywhere—not only in the North Atlantic area, but anywhere—is a matter of the greatest concern to us" (Dean Rusk, 1949, in Ninkovich, 1994: 182).

As the references to allied morale and anti-Communist resistance suggest, the appeasement narrative did not just construct an identity of interventionary U.S. leadership; it also simultaneously constructed an account of, and identity for, U.S. allies. Whether democratic or otherwise, these allies could adopt a neutral stance or join the Soviet camp. Free World states and colonies in Asia were subject to political, religious, and ethnic strife, and might "embrace ideologies contrary to our own" (U.S. Department of State, 1969: 6). European democracies might be exemplary states, but they were weakened by war and facing "a loss of trust in the national State [and] a large Communist element" (*British Documents on the End of Empire* [hereafter, *BDEE*]: 376). In short, the United States' allies were morally and psychologically doubtful. U.S. policymakers therefore worried about whether a "neutrality complex" was developing in Europe or "a certain bandwagon psychology" growing in Asia (U.S. Department of State, 1976a: 21; U.S. Department of State, 1974: 40).

With the prior construction of U.S. allies as uncertain, potentially undependable followers, we arrive at how South Korea was to become a site of intervention. All U.S. officials agreed and announced that South Korea was a client state with little strategic value. But this was "the first overt act of aggression since the end of the war" (U.S. Department of State, 1976b: 347), and "all Europeans to say nothing of Asiatics are watching" whether the United States and the UN would intervene (ibid., 174). It followed that, as Dean Acheson put it in a June 26 meeting, "something" must be done (ibid., 180).

LEADING INTERVENTION

To answer the Soviet challenge in Korea, it was not enough for U.S. policymakers that the United States alone intervene. The test to UN collective security promises—and the charges of U.S. imperialism—required that the intervention be backed by UN decree and involve Western and Free World states. From its inception, part of U.S. intervention therefore included calling on other states to "at least" give "moral support to collective action against aggression in Asia" (ibid., 236).

In their interventionary diplomacy, U.S. diplomats nuanced and fine-tuned what they would say to other officials. But their approach was crafted largely within the same configuration of objects and relations as policy. In both policy debate and diplomatic discussion, the North Korean attack was Soviet aggression. And unless Soviet aggression was checked, as Nazi aggression had been during World War II, it would threaten all states. For example, in an initial report (June 27, 1950) to the North Atlantic ambassadors, George Kennan represented the issue in Korea as follows:

The United States Government did not attach overwhelming importance to [the] strategic position of Southern Korea. The symbolic significance of preservation of the Republic was however tremendous . . .
if Korea went, Formosa would be next on the list. The Philippines
were of course sensitive to anything that might happen in Formosa
and there was a chain of reactions which, if it revealed weakness in
the attitude of the Western Powers, would cause discouragement
which would most likely spread to Europe after doing its damage in
Japan. (*DBPO* 2/4: 5)

Note Kennan's reported reference to "the attitude of the Western
Powers." It implies a joint *Western* interest in and responsibility for
the fate of Asian (and European) states that others did not have. This
understanding of Western leadership of international society was
also extended from U.S. policy to diplomacy. U.S. diplomats assumed
that, as the most powerful and vital Western nation (and with higher
moral standing), the United States should lead any action taken in
Korea. Taking this leadership for granted, U.S. diplomacy effectively
opened up two different subject-positions for states as followers. The
first, exemplified by U.S. diplomacy toward India or Yugoslavia (i.e.,
Free World states), hailed states as members of the UN that should
support collective action for its precedent value, which might some-
day be important to their own security. The second, exemplified by
U.S. diplomacy toward the Western democratic powers, hailed states
not just as supporters of but as *makers*—under U.S. leadership, of
course—of collective action.[6]

This selective hailing of states can be traced in U.S. diplomatic
conduct, in what was said to and asked of other governments in
interventionary diplomacy, and in the agency to shape collective action granted to Western powers, but not other UN supporters. Differences in diplomatic conduct were exemplified by U.S. diplomacy
toward Britain and India. Both of these states were on the UN Security Council, Britain as a permanent member. Their positions toward
the intervention therefore had greater visibility than those of other
UN members, and because (unlike General Assembly members) they
would be voting on UN action, their votes (and explanations of
those votes) would a priori represent the "voice of the international
community." In the first few days of the conflict, as U.S. officials organized the passage of two Security Council resolutions, they worked

with British officials, providing them with drafts of the resolutions and key U.S. government statements, engaging in exploratory talks before Security Council meetings, and giving the British access to U.S. field reports (U.S. Department of State, 1976b: 187, 189, 214; *DBPO* 2/4: 4, 6, 7). Indian officials, in contrast, had either to approach U.S. officials themselves to *ask* for developments in U.S. plans and statements or to depend on British sources. This selective treatment implied that India was in a different, and secondary, category from Britain, something that Indian officials remarked upon at the time, observing that it had a "dampening effect on [the] spontaneity of [the] GOI desire [to] support [the] US in its undertaking" (U.S. Department of State, 1976b: 234).

In what was asked of other states, and in how their participation was represented, U.S. diplomacy also opened up two distinctive categories of followers. Immediately after the June 27 Security Council resolution calling for UN members to "furnish . . . assistance" to stop the North Korean advance, U.S. officials approached Britain, France, Canada, and other Western governments to request that they contribute military forces (ibid., 211). In this approach, military efforts in Asia were framed as a joint Western "burden," with Korea as a place where "we [the United States] naturally expected to bear the brunt of the burden in view of the position of our forces" (ibid., 214). Western forces were therefore not (at this point) for allying military strength. Rather, as in the initial U.S. approach to the British, these forces were represented as helping to produce community solidarity for intervention. British force contributions would create "the effect . . . of *us all acting together* and demonstrating *our* unity of view," making for greater Free World "solidarity" (*DBPO* 2/4: 10, my emphasis; 8). Moreover, inasmuch as their participation would "make out that the United States is only one of a band of brothers . . . under the banner of the United Nations," the British could also help secure American public support (ibid., 23).

Under the United States, but similar to it, "makers" had authority in and responsibility for international society. Also under the United States, but similar to it, the choice of action of U.S. "brothers" could solidify the global political borders between "us" and "them." Contrast this claim to shared identity with the subject-position of "supporter" opened up for Yugoslavia and India. U.S. policymakers asked Yugoslavia to "stand up and be counted definitely on [the] side of forces opposing aggression"—a dramatically labeled but limited action (U.S. Department of State, 1976b: 216). Yugoslavia's support was not represented as solidarity building; rather, it was linked to how Yugoslavia, as a small and vulnerable state, was likely to need similar protection against Soviet attack (ibid., 178). Similarly, India was asked by U.S. officials only for "moral support for collective action" (ibid., 236).[7] With a "position of leadership in Asia," India was constructed as a state with some regional authority and standing (ibid., 242). But, like Field Marshal Tito, Prime Minister Nehru was lectured by U.S. diplomats that Indian interests would not be served if the "principles of [the] UN" were made "meaningless so far as Asia is concerned" (ibid., 236).

Inherent in these representations were differences in the agency constructed for makers versus supporters, in their rights to speak to and take action on issues. One of the clearest illustrations of this selective granting concerns the Soviet Union. The Soviet Union might be the real aggressor in Korea, but its hand was not directly evident. Should it be named as the guilty party—with an implication that the "police" should "punish" the Soviets as well as North Korea? And if the Soviet Union was the real aggressor in Korea, negotiations with the Kremlin could settle the conflict. But should negotiations be attempted—or would any settlement be "appeasement"? On both sets of issues, U.S. officials gave only limited standing to other states. But, within these limits, standing to speak and act for the collective was granted to Western states in a way that was not given to other Free World followers.

The very fact of including Western states in U.S. drafting of resolutions and speeches granted them some agency to speak to how Soviet involvement would be represented by "us." Western states also took up this grant of agency, as illustrated in the handling of a draft of Truman's first main presidential speech, given on June 27, 1950. If the Soviet Union was to be publicly named as the guilty party, this speech would have been appropriately placed (the U.S. president) and timed (early in organization of intervention). The draft originally announced that the "attack makes amply clear [that] centrally directed Communist Imperialism . . . [is] seeking [to] conquer independent nations and [is] now resorting to armed aggression and war"—a fairly direct naming of the Soviet Union as, Hitler-like, making war in Asia (ibid., 187). British policymakers, however, cabled an objection that the naming risked throwing a "challenge which the Russians might feel bound to take up," perhaps leading to a world war. In a context in which the Russians had not committed to backing the North Koreans, it was wiser to give them "an opportunity of beating a retreat" (*DBPO* 2/4: 3). The British objection was accepted in this case, not always the response of U.S. officials (see, for example, U.S. arguments in December 1950 over naming Communist China as an aggressor in Korea). But the point remains that some agency to shape "our" public stance was granted in U.S. diplomatic conduct—and it was granted only to Western states.

U.S. policymakers were hardly supportive of negotiations with the Soviets. Nonetheless, the "maker" identity endowed Western states such as Britain with sufficient agency that they could not be actively discouraged from exploring negotiations and their attempts were treated as serious affairs. When the British reported a Soviet suggestion in early July 1950 for "specific proposals," U.S. officials gave their agreement for the British to continue (U.S. Department of State, 1976b: 316). Note how the following passage from the cable giving that agreement constructs (in the first lines) an "us" whose solidarity must be protected—but for whom the British are therefore also acting:

> Although it is impossible to be certain that this is not an attempt to confuse the issue and weaken our common resolve, we are inclined to regard this as serious approach designed to find [a] way to end [the] Korean affair without undue prestige loss to [the] USSR but presumably for [a] price as yet undisclosed. . . . We believe there would be [an] advantage in [the] Brit[ish] Amb[assador in] Moscow playing [the] matter out somewhat further . . . in order to get [a] clearer picture of what [the] Soviets have in mind. (Ibid., 327)

A sharp contrast can be drawn with the handling of Indian talks with the Soviets at about the same time. As a state hailed as a supporter, India was not endowed with agency to engage the Soviets in settling the Korean conflict. The efforts of Indian diplomats were therefore steadily discouraged by U.S. officials. Far from treating these efforts as a serious project, U.S. officials privately ridiculed Indian diplomacy in terms that constructed the Indians as irrational nuisances (cf. Muppidi, this volume). As newcomers to world society, Indian diplomats might speak in "good faith" and with "earnestness," but they also appeared "vague and starry-eyed, rather professorial in manner" (ibid., 342, 366, 379). Indian settlement efforts were "confused," much like the "confused state of mind of [the] formulators of GOI policies" (ibid., 371, 376). As for the terms of settlement the Indians proposed, Acheson commented that "I have never been able to escape wholly from a childhood illusion that, if the world is round, the Indians must be standing on their heads—or, perhaps, vice versa" (Acheson, 1969: 420).

Within the same configuration of objects and relations as policy, U.S. diplomacy selectively hailed states as followers of different sorts. But how did other states receive this address? In particular, how did other Western states take up, or fail to take up, the identity—as makers of collective action and yet as subjects under a morally and materially superior U.S. leadership—constructed for them in U.S. interventionary diplomacy? To shed light on this question, I turn to the grounds of British participation in the Korean intervention. How the British took up American diplomacy, and the discursive conditions of their reception, is certainly not exactly the same as French, or Canadian, or Dutch reception, but it is an important piece of the making of a collective Western identity in the Korean War intervention.

SHARING THE WESTERN BURDEN

Reception might at first glance appear to be all or nothing, with persons either taking up as authoritative truths others' representations and the identities these construct, or receiving these as failed truth claims misdescribing the social order. But, as Bruce Lincoln has demonstrated, between total uptake and total rejection lie modes of reception in which people contest features of their hailing, and take up variants of collective identity represented to them (Lincoln, 1989: 27–37). This situation of partial contestation and variant reconstruction describes British reception of U.S. interventionary diplomacy. British policymakers first contested U.S. representations of the implications of the intervention, and therefore the U.S. call for British combat forces. By late July 1950, they did commit those combat forces, but through taking up a variant of U.S. hailings of U.S. leadership and British followership.

In the dominant U.S. construction, intervention in Korea would prevent a loss of confidence in U.S. leadership and Western-led collective security. British policymakers partly received this representation as fact, but they also partly contested it. The starting point of the contestation was the possibility that the attack in Korea might mean "the beginning of a Nazi technique of isolating and defeating one state after another" (*DBPO* 2/4: 32). Further Soviet or satellite moves could therefore follow "at increased tempo regardless of Western interests and reactions" (ibid., 20).

Nazi-modeled Soviet takeovers existed as an object in U.S. discourse, of course; unlike U.S. officials, though, British policymakers made it prominent as a reading of what was perhaps *now* the Soviet design. And on this basis, U.S.-led intervention in Korea was potentially as much a problem as a solution. Within the first week of the war, it was clear that the United States was entering a "prolonged struggle in the Far East" (ibid., 38). Beyond further attacks in Asia, this "commitment of Western military reserves," as the British called U.S. military actions, might well "tempt the Soviet leaders to increase diversionary pressure on our weak spots in Europe and the Middle East" (ibid., 55).

If American intervention had its drawbacks, so too did British groundforce commitments. Such forces, as constructed in the U.S. hailing, might indeed anchor political support. But their assignment to Korea, as the British constructed it, could also be "an unwise dispersion of forces and of effort which may be urgently wanted . . . at some more vital spot" (in Kim, 1993: 156). The initial British response to the U.S. request for ground forces was therefore quite negative. In light of possible Asian Communist attacks, it would be "strategically unsound to divert to Korea" British troops in Hong Kong or Malaya (*DBPO* 2/4: 70). As for British forces stationed in the Middle East or Western Europe, their diversion would be a graver error. Europe was *the* key region in the fight against Communism, the Middle East a "land bridge" to European defense (ibid., 421). It "would be dangerous" to risk these "vital areas" for the Far East, a "secondary . . . front" (ibid., 37, 425, 424).

British officials, then, did not initially take up U.S. calls for combat forces, receiving them as doubtfully grounded in facts of the Korean situation. Yet, despite this initial reception, within several weeks Britain did commit troops to the conflict. The policy reversal surely owed something to Truman administration promises to increase U.S. military forces and to secure more military aid for Atlantic Pact

countries. But the decision was not taken because these promises relieved British military concerns, or provided a financial "carrot" sufficient to change British calculations of their interests.[8] Rather, the
decision emerged from how, out of discussions with the Americans,
the British took up and reconstructed identities of the United States
as leader and Britain as a follower.

The U.S. hailing emphasized the United States' strength, exemplary democracy, and greater courage and responsibility in learning
the "appeasement lesson." This exceptionalist identity was not quite
what the British took up as the U.S. leadership identity. Instead, they
represented the United States as a sometimes emotional and irrational state that was new to world leadership. U.S. policymakers
were "vacillating between being the saviours of the World . . . and
protesting at the lack of support they were receiving from other nations in their act" (ibid., 69). The flip-flop U.S. attitude with its mix
of "rational and irrational elements" arose from "this for them [the
United States] unparalleled undertaking to act as a policeman in the
world" (ibid., 78). Being new to the world order game, and so emotional, the United States was liable to turn against states such as
Britain judged not to be sufficiently supporting it (ibid.). And if that
was not bad enough, a loose U.S. cannon, no longer listening to its
allies, might well "precipitate a general war in the Far East and thus
a World War" (ibid., 48).

In contrast to the Great Power clumsiness of the United States,
the British construction of their identity was of an old, wise power
with experience in global policing by dint of "centuries of world
leadership" (U.S. Department of State, 1974: 1114). As such, Great
Britain made an ideal "partner" for the United States, "unequal no
doubt in power" but "equal in counsel" (*DBPO* 2/4: 77, 257). This
"partner" construction, less secondary in nature than the "maker"
understanding of the U.S. hailing, suffuses the British debate over
ground forces. Sir Oliver Franks, the British ambassador to the
United States, claimed that the United States reasoned in the same
terms: that the United States would "test the quality of the partnership by our attitude" to ground forces (ibid., 69). The identities were
also written into accounts of how Britain could, and as a partner
should, keep an overwrought United States from adopting unwise
and risky policies:

The American attitude is likely to be highly charged with emotion so long as they are suffering casualties and so long as they are being driven back. It may be that our only hope of acquiring a status . . . which they respect will be to provide some ground troops to fight alongside theirs. This is clearly a most unpalatable proposition . . . [but perhaps] our only way of influencing American policy in a vital matter. (Ibid., 48)

Finally, the identities were written into the troop decision itself. Prime Minister Clement Attlee ordered British military officials to accept sending combat forces. There were indeed military reasons against this commitment. But the troops were needed for "strong psychological reasons"—reasons stemming from U.S. psychology (Attlee in Kim, 1993: 166).

Full British enrollment in the Korean intervention emerged from British representations not of an exemplary U.S. leader, but of a rather less dependable "superchild" needing the steadying advice of a more mature partner. This quite different British reception might seem to suggest that the hailings of U.S. interventionary diplomacy were irrelevant to British policy, which was adopted outside of any U.S. diplomatic address. But this is not so. As a partial demonstration of why not, let us examine three points of overlap between the U.S. hailing and the British reception.

First, British policymakers accepted as authoritative that the conflict was a test of Western-led international society and of U.S. leadership. If the UN did not act, its failure would "discredit" the organization (*DBPO* 2/4: 56, 32), dealing a "shattering blow to Western prestige" (ibid., 18). Thus, British policymakers *themselves* recommended on June 30 that "the Americans should be encouraged . . . to use land forces if necessary" (ibid., 22) and they proposed that "the necessary action should be taken under the United Nations 'umbrella'" (ibid., 24). When the Security Council gave its mandate for intervention, British policymakers celebrated this as "the most impressive piece of international co-operation which the world has ever seen. The United Nations flag is in the ascendant—thank God for that" (ibid., 33).

Second, British policymakers accepted and used the representation of the conflict as unfurling in a context of West–East confrontation and Soviet aims of world empire. Indeed, British officials put perhaps even more emphasis than their U.S. counterparts on how the West was threatened by the Soviets. Further Communist attacks would be on "*our* weak spots" in the West and the Middle East, meaning Western weak spots (ibid., 53). Similarly, British force contributions had to be weighed in terms of the "burden" that the British were already bearing on behalf of a communal Western defense. Britain was "holding the ring for the Americans" in the Middle East, "as we have been doing in South-East Asia" (ibid., 41). So British counterinsurgency operations in the empire, or their military presence in Egypt and Iran, were actions taken for the Western collectivity!

Third, as the reference to "holding the ring for the Americans" implies, British reception of U.S. interventionary diplomacy might have questioned the United States' leadership qualities and its commitment to leading, but not that the United States *should* lead the West in leading world society. This standing was woven into British praise for U.S. intervention as a "courageous initiative" creating "the first significant demonstration of the principle of collective security against aggression" (ibid., 43, 28). It was also the implicit parameter of British identity constructs of the United States and Britain. In the British variant, Britain was to be more than a secondary "maker"; it was to be a key "counselor." But for both the British and the Americans, the United States was the leader of Western-led international society.

The British debate about ground forces is thus a contestation and a construction largely taking up the social borders and hierarchies of U.S. interventionary diplomacy. I cannot trace out in detail here how those borders and hierarchies had previously been naturalized in British discourse.[9] But it is worth noting that, like U.S. policymakers, British officials could act in these terms partly because of "essential" juxtapositions repeatedly invoked in British discourse from the mid-1940s on between "the upholders of true democracy" in the West and "dictatorship" in the East (*BDEE*: 329). In March 1946, the British ambassador to the Soviet Union, Frank Roberts, for example, already represented the Soviet Union as a continuation in the form of "Communist tyranny" of the "Tsarist system" of authoritarian rule (Roberts, in Jensen, 1993: 44). The "Western democratic world," in contrast, was organized on "liberal ideas, tolerance, and the concepts of right and justice" (ibid., 51). This identity of "Western democracies" meant in British, as in U.S., discourse that the West was a paradigm for non-Western states and peoples still "politically immature and not ripe for self-government" (British officials, in U.S. Department of State, 1973: 756). It also meant, identical with U.S. discourse, that their "sense of world community" made "Western democracies" rightful managers of world society (Roberts, in Jensen, 1993: 54).

The question of Korea began for the British in this context of the Western Powers' right and responsibility to contain "Soviet imperialism" in Asia. But whereas U.S. policymakers drew global connections for containment, British policymakers held to the priority of guarding "our Western civilization" (*BDEE*: 317). They did not want Western European defense jeopardized. They thought that the Korean intervention could expose Europe or its reaches to attack. But still more dangerous was a United States without "a brake" on "adventurous policies," or a Europe without "the closest association with the United States" (ibid., 347, 346). To ensure that the Americans did not "retire into an isolation dangerous . . . for themselves and for Europe," the British would have to share the Western burden in Korea (ibid., 343).

CONCLUSION

Western intervention in the Korean War was constructed out of interlocking insecurities about the West, its status vis-à-vis its Free World, and its hierarchy of governance. For the United States, Western and Free World states were fragile and uncertain allies, with tendencies to appease. This made U.S. leadership key to meeting aggression even in seemingly distant and unimportant places. For the British, the United States was an emotional and unstable leader, with tendencies toward isolationism and dangerous conflict escalations. To keep the United States in check, and to keep it constructively engaged with the Western project, the British supported the United States in its police action, even when this seemed somewhat unwise.

Looked at in this way, from the point of view of British and U.S. policymakers, "the West" appears, for its members, as an artificial and fragile construct. Yet, it also had a hardier discursive status in its naturalization in prior security discourses, their objects and narratives. Both the British and the Americans defined their West as democratic, in juxtaposition to the authoritarian-totalitarian Soviet Union. Both defined their West as the leader of international society and of non-Western states. Finally, both defined their West as led by the United States. These discursive objects and relations, and the social purpose they inscribed, were not examined or justified; they simply were facts about the international system and guides for acting in international affairs. Put another way, both leaders and followers were subject-positions within a broader discourse that constructed the international system as a Western-led society of states.

Almost fifty years after the Western intervention on the Korean peninsula, it is worth asking how much has changed. The end of the Cold War has meant the disappearance of the East. But has this made meaningless the West? Some, such as Owen Harries, the editor of *Foreign Affairs,* argue that without a "life-threatening, overtly hostile 'East,'" the West no longer exists as a "political and military entity" (Harries, 1993: 41). After all, the enemy that U.S. troops face in Korea is no longer an outpost of the Eastern bloc; North Korea is a "rogue state" in a post–Cold War world dominated by a single superpower. Of course, Harries is engaging in an ongoing politics of identity in the United States and Europe that is far from settled. Western intervention in Bosnia points toward the complex politics involved. Perhaps the West was unraveling with its "capitulation to Serbian aggression," squabbles over "leadership" between the United States and its European allies, and organizational deadlock between the UN and NATO. But Western policymakers actually did work out something of a shared position: that perhaps the West could only sit back and wait until the ethnic groups feel they have no more blood to give. On this basis, they worked together and separately to contain the conflict to the former Yugoslavia; and when the conflict would not go away, NATO was used to intervene—for the first time in its history. Versus a simple unraveling, this looks more like a partial redefinition of the Cold War Western security identity. As in Korea, collective identity continues to be (re)produced through the reworking of older discourses of the West.

It would be foolish to try to predict an outcome to this process. Just as Cold War configurations of the West were not predictable until they had been regularized in practices, the post–Cold War West will not be either. But any attempt to offer even a preliminary characterization of this process is also limited by a lack of scholarly understanding. The nearest antecedent is the transformation of the World War II alliance into the Cold War West. Standard realist arguments about the balancing versus bandwagoning behavior of post-1945 states skip over how this Cold War West was constituted. Indeed, insofar as they emphasize how the United States really did not need its allies to secure survival against the Soviet Union, they make a mystery of the alliance rather than explaining it. Arguments about emerging threat perceptions of the Soviet Union do better in engaging partly with the construction of "them," but leave largely unexamined the creation of "us."

More important, as I have argued here, is the recognition made possible by a critical constructivism that what is at stake—both in Korea and in Bosnia—are competing representations of the international system and the variable success of efforts to hail state subjects into the positions of leaders and led within a Western community of states. Such an argument runs sharply counter to realist accounts of cooperation between pregiven subjects both because it makes state identity the central factor in explaining how collective insecurities (and hence interventions) are made possible, and because, turning realism on its head, it implies that state identity is at least in part a function of the collectivity of the West rather than the other way around. Thus, for example, U.S. insecurity derives in part from the subject-position of leader within a Western collectivity. To the extent that leaders must by definition have followers or cease to be, U.S. identity as leader is dependent on successfully hailing other states into the position of followers; failure to do so thus produces insecurity. In other words, U.S. identity is a product of the culture of insecurity through which the West is constituted as a collective subject of world politics.

NOTES

1. From a personal survey, drawn from histories and political science lists.

2. For more on this conception of discourse, cf. Milliken and Sylvan (1996) and Alker and Sylvan (1986).

3. Other works on Western security discourse—for example, Klein (1994) and Dalby (1990)—also suffer from this limitation.

4. Space limitations prevent me from a thorough examination of such earlier discourse. Besides the works cited in the text, see Stephanson (1995), Gong (1984), and Hunt (1987).

5. For the transition from less menacing definitions of the Soviet Union

to the world empire definition, see Nathanson (1988) and Klein (1994). For why Cold War world empire projections were questionable, see Leffler (1992: 439–40, 511–17).

6. These distinctions were neither absolute nor free of contradictions. Within each, one can find a range of forms of address (e.g., among states hailed as supporters, "friends" such as Turkey as opposed to nonaligns or independents such as Egypt or Yugoslavia), and on occasion, a supporter state would be hailed partly as a maker. Yet, the fact that the distinctions were fuzzy did not make them any less real in organizing U.S. diplomacy for multilateralizing the intervention.

7. India partly set this limit by warning that it "had no armed forces, money or materiel to contribute" (U.S. Department of State, 1976b: 236). But in July the Indians did offer to send a military field ambulance unit, which the U.S. government waited some forty days to accept (Kim, 1993: 219). Compare the pressure being placed on Britain at exactly the same time for combat forces.

8. Any immediate buildup in U.S. forces would have to go to the difficult campaign shaping up in Korea. Financially, more U.S. aid still meant that Western Powers would have greatly to increase their defense expenditures, resulting in a "lower standard of living" and "larger dependence on US aid" (Attlee, in Kim, 1993: 165, 167).

9. Scholars such as Ryan (1982) and Taylor (1990) have argued that British policymakers were Cold Warriors before the Americans, actually guiding U.S. policymakers into breaking with the Soviet Union. Deighton (1993) locates this guidance specifically in British engineering of a "Bevin Plan" to force a division of Germany in contradiction to the 1945 Potsdam Agreement.

4

Postcoloniality and the Production of International Insecurity: The Persistent Puzzle of U.S.-Indian Relations

HIMADEEP MUPPIDI

On December 4, 1995, the Union Home Minister of India, S. B. Chavan, participating in a discussion on Jammu and Kashmir in the Indian Parliament, accused the United States of entertaining "evil designs" on that region. Arguing that the United States wished to acquire a "foothold" in Jammu and Kashmir, Chavan noted that recent history showed a pattern of U.S. "instigation" of trouble every time the situation in that state improved ("Govt. Considering Legal Option on Polls in Kashmir," 1995: 1; see also Narula, 1995). The United States rejected these remarks as "absolutely baseless," but they met with a different response domestically (Katyal, 1995: 1). Within the Indian Parliament, according to one report, while the Treasury benches were "stunned into silence" by the "bluntness" of these remarks, the Home Minister's statement was greeted with the "thumping of desks" and endorsed enthusiastically by the leader of the Opposition. The Home Minister was even complimented by one member of Parliament for expressing "the sentiments of 90 crore [900 million] Indians" ("Govt. Considering Legal Option on Polls in Kashmir," 1995: 1).

Such accusations and denials are not new in Indo-U.S. relations. Indeed, the history of India's relations with the United States exhibits a recurring puzzle: although India had cooperative and conflictual relations with both the superpowers, it was the United States that emerged as a chronic threat to Indian national security (Kreisberg, 1985; Kux, 1992; Brands, 1990). Given that there was no great difference in the number of times each superpower assisted India militarily and economically or worked against its interests, how is it that it was with only one of them that India had an insecure relationship? This chapter asserts that conventional security theories are ill equipped to address such questions (Muppidi, 1995). It offers an alternative answer based on an interpretive conceptualization of Indian security policy as shaped around a specific postcolonial security imaginary.

The chapter is organized as follows: I first briefly demonstrate that Indo-U.S. insecurity is a puzzling phenomenon routinely noted by scholars of South Asia and Indo-U.S. relations but inadequately addressed by security theories. Tracing this inadequacy to the neglect of meanings in conventional security theories, I offer a constructivist alternative. My constructivist explanation begins with a reconstruction of the self-understandings involved in India's relations with the United States and, for contrast, with the Soviet Union. I examine these self-understandings as they manifested themselves in two historical events—the state visits to India of Soviet Premier Nikolay A. Bulganin and Communist Party Secretary Nikita S. Khrushchev in 1955 and of U.S. President Dwight Eisenhower in 1959. In order to facilitate a systematic inquiry into the self-understandings of these three states, I employ the heuristic of a security imaginary. After elaborating the concept and the ways in which it opens up for analysis "the politics of meaning fixing" (Dirks, Eley, and Ortner, 1994: 32), I demonstrate some of the ways in which India's security imaginary is postcolonial. I then derive a more limited set of social practices that mark the boundaries of this imaginary. This enables me to analyze the politics of meaning fixing in India's interactions with the United States and the Soviet Union and to show that, in the Indo-U.S. case, there is a relative disjuncture between the U.S. and Indian security imaginaries that leads to the constant production of insecurity. Thus, the persistent insecurity in Indo-U.S. relations can be explained in terms of the distinctive ways in which the U.S. security imaginary interacted with the postcolonial security imaginary of India.

The metanarratives that structure many existing accounts of Indian foreign policy, like much else in international relations, are peculiarly

U.S.-centric ones. The material conditions of production and distribution of the following analysis also orient it toward a world that is primarily Western, if not more narrowly centered on the United States. Within the confines of such a discursive network, alternative social realities—particularly non-Western ones—do not exist, at least partly because there are few conceptual resources available with which to grasp them. My analysis is a conscious attempt to make conceptual and substantive space for such alternative, non-Western realities within the field of security studies.

THE PROBLEM

Indo-U.S. relations have been astonishingly insecure. Scholars have characterized the relationship between these two states as "troubled" (Dutt, 1984: 52), "estranged" (Kux, 1992: 447), "strained," "fragile," "discordant," "oscillating" (Limaye, 1993: 5, 9), "stressful" (Rose, 1990: 57), and characterized by "tension rather than cooperation" (Brands, 1990: ix). At the same time, Indian relations with the former Soviet Union were generally far more positive. Indian security discourse thus presented the Soviet Union and the United States in starkly contrasting terms. Within this discourse, the Soviet Union was produced fairly consistently as a friend while the United States was represented in a variety of positions ranging from an "unfriendly friend" (Kunhi Krishnan, 1974) to an arrogant and bullying hegemon (Thomas, 1993: 10; see also "Billy the Bully," 1996). These basic elements of Indian security discourse have been crudely but accurately captured by Kreisberg, who observed that "Indians have seen the Soviets as friends, the United States and China . . . as adversaries, and Japan, France and Britain . . . as trading partners" (1985: 880). Or, as a staff report for the Committee on Foreign Relations of the U.S. Senate put it, "Ironically, the world's largest democracy has much closer political and military ties with the world's most powerful totalitarian state than with the most powerful democracy" (U.S. Senate, Committee on Foreign Relations, 1984: 22).

A closer look at the history of India's relations with the superpowers intensifies the puzzle in yet another way. The initial conditions for the development of secure relations with India were far more favorable for the United States than for the Soviet Union. Both the United States and India shared features such as a history of anti-colonialism, a commitment to constitutional democracy, and a belief in economic growth based on private enterprise. India, because of its connections to Britain, was seen by the "West"—the United States and its allies—as a potentially important partner, and newly independent India received a much more favorable response from the United States than it did from the Soviet Union. The Soviets denounced Gandhi's and Nehru's roles in the anticolonial struggle, did not recognize Indian independence as genuine, condemned nonalignment, and gave clandestine encouragement and support to the Indian communists who were being suppressed by the new state (Gupta, 1988; Kapur, 1972; U.S. Department of State, 1975). The Indian state also inherited from the British an institutional legacy that regarded Russia as the traditional threat to the South Asian region. Notwithstanding such unfavorable initial conditions, the Indo-U.S. rather than the Indo-Soviet relationship came to be characterized by insecurity. Although Indo-U.S. relations have not led to war—unlike those between India and Pakistan, for example—they were marked by the production of the United States as a consistent threat to Indian security. The United States entered into Indian security considerations as a state that sought to exploit or balkanize India and that was interested in undermining Indian stability in various ways, not least by encouraging centrifugal forces. When Indian politicians talked about the "foreign hand" (Thornton, 1988: 78) behind Indian domestic troubles, they were typically alluding to the United States, not the Soviet Union, Pakistan, or China. What explains the production of such paradoxical effects of security and insecurity?

Such insecurity is all the more puzzling if a common misconception about superpower "alliances" in South Asia is dispelled. Analyses of Cold War alliances have routinely assumed that Pakistan and India were aligned with the United States and the Soviet Union, respectively. Based on this, it could be argued that it was the U.S. military support for Pakistan, given Pakistan's disputes with India, that produced insecurity in Indo-U.S. relations. Such an interpretation, however, overgeneralizes from the pattern of alignments visible during the 1971 Indo-Pak war. A closer look at superpower involvement in South Asia reveals a more complex pattern of support to India and Pakistan (Appadorai and Rajan, 1985; Mansingh, 1984). The United States was swift in rushing to India's defense in its 1962 border war with China and the Soviets supported India in its 1971 war against Pakistan. The United States wavered in its support of India in disputes with Pakistan, but so did the Soviet Union. Both the United States and the Soviet Union stayed neutral in the 1947 and 1965 Indo-Pak wars. Both the United States and the Soviet Union furnished India with large amounts of economic assistance and arms transfers. Correspondingly, although sensitive to Indian concerns about arms transfers to Pakistan, both also refused to let India veto such moves. Both the superpowers were united in pushing for India to sign the nuclear nonproliferation treaty and not very receptive to India's efforts at demilitarizing the Indian Ocean. Both courted China at different times and unhesitatingly extended the Cold War into the South Asian region when they thought it necessary (Thakur and Thayer, 1992; Kux, 1992). Thus, notwithstanding conventional perceptions of Pakistan and India as U.S. and Soviet "allies," respectively, it would be wrong to argue that the United States was, on the whole, more supportive of Pakistan than of India. Moreover, "Indo-U.S. acrimony was noticeable even before the communist triumph in China; while the Soviet Union was still hostile to India and before the U.S. started giving military aid to Pakistan" (Singh, 1993: 231). This means, among other things, that explanations of Indo-U.S. insecurity based on discrete causes—such as U.S. military support to Pakistan and Soviet support to India—are theoretically inadequate because Indo-U.S. insecurity preceded such factors. It is difficult, then, on both substantive and theoretical grounds, to locate the causes of Indo-U.S. insecurity primarily in U.S. military support for Pakistan.

Existing security theories fail either adequately to conceptualize or to offer satisfactory explanations for such insecurity. These theories fail to take seriously the self-understandings of the actors involved and are therefore limited in their ability to explain the chronic insecurity to which specialized scholars of Indo-U.S. relations so routinely point.[1] My alternative explanation of Indo-U.S. insecurity is premised on a self-consciously interpretive reconceptualization of Indian security understandings. In what follows, I utilize the heuristic of a "security imaginary" to capture the self-understandings framing the Indo-U.S. encounter and then show how this notion helps us to understand the causes of Indo-U.S. insecurity.

SECURITY IMAGINARIES

The concept of a security imaginary refers here to a field of meanings and social power.[2] Operating as a field of meanings, the security imaginary provides an organized set of interpretations for making sense of a complex international system. Operating as a field of social power, the security imaginary works to produce social relations of power through the production of distinctive social identities. Both operations are moments of the same process: the security imaginary is thus constitutive of a field of interpretations and a field of social relations simultaneously.

The meaning of "security" is deliberately left open within this theoretical framework so that the term is available for different conceptualizations, including both state-centric and non-state-centric ones. The "imaginary," within this conception, refers to the structuring principle underlying a set of meanings and social relations and constituting them into an organized set of understandings and social identities that are productive of worlds. The imaginary in this sense is a social signification

> which is neither 'real' in the sense of being available to perception and empirical scrutiny nor 'rational' in the sense of being deducible via the rules of thought of a culture . . . the imaginary is *prior* to the real and the rational: it is the product of an act of cultural creation which is fundamental to any subsequent system of cultural representation. (Tomlinson, 1991: 156–57; emphasis in the original)

So defined, the imaginary is the key to understanding the distinctive representations of "reality," "rationality," and "security" that are operative within the security imaginary.

One of the primary ways in which the security imaginary operates is through its capacity to organize meanings in distinctive ways. Such an organization of meanings is also productive of specific social identities and, derivatively, of interests. The security imaginary has a mutually constitutive relationship with the social identities and the related practices that it produces. This means that while certain social identities and practices are only possible and only make sense within the security imaginary, the security imaginary itself is reproduced through the continued performance of those practices. The social identities that are produced and reproduced by the security imaginary cannot be specified a priori but can be established through a reconstruction of the sets of meanings operating within it. The discursive boundaries of the security imaginary are reached when particular representations of the world seem "unintelligible," "irrational," "meaningless," or "ungraspable" in and through the symbolic resources offered by the security imaginary. Moreover, the security imaginary is not a static field but a dynamic one and hence is in need of constant reproduction.[3]

How is that reproduction carried out? Two processes for the organization of meanings and power—articulation and interpellation—are of particular relevance here (e.g., Althusser, 1971; Laclau, 1977; Hall, 1985, 1988; Weldes, 1993, 1996). Articulation can be understood, at a minimum, as the establishment of certain compelling links between different elements of meaning. This process makes sense on the assumption that there is no intrinsically necessary connection between different elements of meaning and that the arrangement between such elements is conventional (or "arbitrary") but not logically given. For example, there is no logical or necessary connection between the term *Hindu* and the term *Indian*. The term *Indian* is capable of being linked or articulated to a variety of subject-positions such as *Muslim, Christian, Tamil, Jew,* and so on. All of these subjectivities could be socially produced in a nonconflictual relationship with *Indian*. It is also possible, however, to articulate these sets of meanings in an antagonistic manner such that, conventionally, *Indian* appears to connote a necessary relationship with *Hindu* and excludes alternative linkages with *Muslim, Christian,* or *Chinese,* for example. Both operations are political operations in that they have to be socially produced and reproduced and such productions involve political struggles over which combinations are legitimate and which are not. One way of ensuring such legitimacy is by producing some of these links consistently as the "unproblematic," "conventional," and "natural realities" for specific groups of people; that is, for such terms to be accepted by large numbers of people, what is required is political work that fixes some of these meanings in specific ways in the public or, in the case of state actors, the official mind.

Neither officials nor publics, however, are dupes waiting to be articulated one way or another. As amateur social theorists, they are all the time appropriating and reorganizing sets of available meanings to render meaningful their own lived reality and to function effectively within it. Hence, it cannot be taken for granted that because specific articulations are proposed they are also received unquestioningly by an audience. The concept of interpellation refers to the ways in which people, when "hailed" by discourses, "recognize" themselves in that hailing (Althusser, 1971: 174). Interpellation is a useful window onto the question of how compelling or convincing particular articulatory chains are to people. Do they recognize or see themselves in these hailings? Articulation and interpellation are thus two different moments in the political production of reality. Both moments participate in the "politics of meaning fixing."

THE INDIAN SECURITY IMAGINARY

The Indian security imaginary was a product of the nationalist struggle against the British.[4] Although the security imaginary made possible different understandings of "India," the specific version that was socially empowered and institutionalized in 1947 was the Nehruvian vision of India. Central to this security imaginary was the strong assumption of the Indian state as a "great" power (Nehru, 1961: 12). This claim to greatness was based less on material power capabilities than on a "civilizational identity" (Krishna, 1984: 270), "civilizational subjecthood" (Banerjee, 1994: 5), and "destiny" (Nehru, 1961: 18). As Nehru declared: "Destiny has cast a certain role on this country. . . . and so far as we represent this great country . . . we also have to act as men and women of destiny . . . never forgetting the great responsibility that freedom, that this great destiny of our country, has cast upon us" (ibid., 20). There was thus a strong sense that this newly won "freedom" and "great destiny" brought with it a certain "inevitable" responsibility that would lead India "to play an important role in world affairs" (ibid., 18). Playing such an important role in world affairs meant viewing problems from the "long perspective of destiny and of the world and of Asia" and "standing up for certain ideals in regard to the oppressed nations," without becoming a "camp follower" of any great power (ibid., 32). Could a materially weak country hope to stand up to the military might of the great powers? Nehru argued that while such a confrontation could be injurious to India, it would be far more destructive for it to submit without fighting for its ideals. Moreover, there was the recent past to draw on during which the Indian national movement had opposed "one of the greatest of world powers" (ibid., 32) and succeeded. It was on this basis that Nehru articulated the possibility of an active role for the Indian state in support of "certain ideals" without turning into a dependent "camp follower" of one great power or the other. What, then, were the social practices that the Indian state understood as appropriate expressions of its independence?

During the period of the Cold War, Indian "independence" manifested itself initially as a self-conscious intervention in, and a refusal to accept as legitimate, the attempts of the United States and the Soviet Union to define the nature of international reality for all other states. As Nehru observed: "It is said there are only two ways of action in the world today, and that one must take this way or that. I repudiate that attitude of mind. If we accept that there are only two ways, then we certainly have to join the Cold War—and if not an actual military bloc, at least a mental military bloc" (ibid., 80). The desire to avoid both an "actual" and a "mental military bloc" and to chart an independent course in the international system gave birth to the policy of nonalignment.

Nonalignment, as an alternative definition of international reality, specified a different set of appropriate modes of being and social practices in the international system to those offered by the superpowers. It became important, from within this interpretation, to resist any understanding of nonalignment as primarily a policy of "neutrality" in superpower conflicts (Appadorai, 1982: 5). The conflation of nonalignment with neutrality was resisted because it implicitly produced other states as "observers," "onlookers," and thus as "passive" objects on the international stage. Reducing nonalignment to a policy of neutrality in superpower conflicts therefore reinforced the positions of the superpowers as the primary actors on the international stage—as the shapers of history—and others as the objects of this history (Nehru, 1961: 79).

In contrast to the dominant U.S. production of Asia and Africa as the objects of history, the Indian state's identity was constituted through an imaginary that posited that Asia and India had arrived as historical actors and that it was time that "the West" accommodated this reality. "After long years of alien domination, colonialism and suppression, the countries of Asia and Africa want to think and act for themselves. They have rejected the idea of being told what to do and what not to do" (ibid., 84). Although the relative imbalance in military power was acknowledged, it was also partially delegitimized by the argument that there was no reason why "the possession of great armed might or great financial power should necessarily lead to right decisions or a right mental outlook" (ibid., 80). Furthermore, nonalignment was consciously distanced from efforts to depict it as a way of creating a "third bloc" (ibid., 11) because that move itself was seen as reproducing the discourse of the Cold War (ibid., 80).

In the case of India, then, nonalignment was not just a specific foreign-policy practice that asserted an active Indian presence in the international system but an alternative discursive construction of the international system itself—one that refused to be limited by the categories, definitions, and constructions of the dominant Western powers, and in particular the United States. Similarly, Indian non-alignment saw itself as inadequately captured by terms such as *realism* and *idealism* (ibid., 51). Collapsing the distinctions, Nehru argued that idealism was nothing but "the realism of tomorrow" and that the "practical person" who failed to look beyond the short term was "tumbling" constantly (ibid.). Rejecting such simple binary oppositions, nonalignment was articulated as both, and more. It understood itself to be a utopian vision expressive of the newly decolonized states and also as a realistic pursuit of national interests (ibid., 34). It refused to define itself as either against the United States or against the Soviet Union but saw itself as for and against both. While thinking in terms of national interest, it refused to see a focus on national interest as necessitating a conflict with others or as being in conflict with long-term world peace (ibid., 28).

The Indian security imaginary thus generated an alternative definition of appropriate relations in the international system and also an alternative practical agenda for international society. Within this imaginary, it was not the Cold War or European power struggles that emerged as the dominant and legitimate reality for states but anticolonialism, antiracialism, and the rapid economic betterment of "vast peoples" (ibid., 40–41). Security was seen as an effect of the pursuit of such an alternative vision. "Security can be obtained in many ways. The normal idea is that security is protected by armies. That is only partly true; it is equally true that security is protected by policies. A deliberate policy of friendship with other countries goes farther in gaining security than almost anything else" (ibid., 79).

This imaginary reproduced the dominance of the Indian state through a variety of different social relations—domestic and international, political, economic, and cultural. Two effects are of particular relevance to this project. The security imaginary worked domestically to construct the moment of national unity, of "Indianness":

By projecting India onto the world stage as an independent, free-wheeling entity pursuing its own national interests, Nehru held up before Punjabis and Bengalis and Tamils a mirror image of themselves as Indians. He believed that it would signify a fundamental lack of confidence for India to yield the stage deferentially to the super-powers. . . . Should India ever lose its sense of a great national destiny, Nehru reflected, it could all too easily succumb once again to divisive centrifugal stresses. (Selig Harrison, in Mansingh, 1984: x)

Internationally, the imaginary served to produce the moment of Afro-Asian unity. It did this by articulating its alternative definition of world politics as that of a hitherto dominated but now resurrected Afro-Asia emerging in a new relationship with the West. The dominant self–other relations involved were those of the diverse communities within India united in acting as "India" on the international stage, and of an ex-colonial India/Afro-Asia asserting itself against the colonizing West (cf. Niva, this volume).

POSTCOLONIALITY AS THE ORGANIZING PRINCIPLE
OF THE INDIAN SECURITY IMAGINARY

What were the boundaries of the Indian security imaginary? What were the outside limits of a security imaginary organized on the principle of the Indian state's "independence" on the international stage and expressed in the practices of nonalignment? What practices did the imaginary identify as negating the meanings and social relations it produced?

As noted earlier, the drive to be independent in international affairs was an important constitutive principle within the Indian security imaginary. Negatively, this expressed itself as a stubborn refusal to be "dictated to" (Nehru, 1961: 270–71). Articulating what he saw as the "new spirit" in Asia that no longer made it "passive" or "submissive," Nehru declared, "If there is anything that Asia wants to tell the world, it is that there is going to be no dictation in the future" (ibid.). Insistent though it was, this drive toward independence was not blind to the potentially detrimental consequences it could generate for India. It acknowledged, for instance, that India's independent practices in international affairs might not go down well with others, that they might either be misunderstood because of a lack of "imagination" or be seen as a "nuisance" (ibid., 46–47), and thus provoke the anger of some of the Great Powers whose response might be to withhold help to force a change in policy (ibid., 63). The appropriate response in all these cases, however, was to be persistence in the pursuit of an independent policy.

Within the Indian security imaginary, "independence" was linked to a set of practices concerning India's relations with other states. Although India was always willing to cooperate, cooperation had to emerge out of a genuine friendship and respect for India's independence, and could not be imposed or forced on the Indian state in any way (ibid., 11–12). Nehru was emphatic that India could only be influenced through "friendship and co-operation and goodwill" and that "any attempt at imposition" or the "slightest trace of patronage" would be "resented" (ibid., 9). Arguing that this did not mean a "dissociation" from other countries but "cooperation" as a "free nation," Nehru noted that "real co-operation would only come between us and . . . other nations when we know that we are free to co-operate and are not imposed upon and forced to co-operate. As long as there is the slightest trace of compulsion, there can be no co-operation" (ibid., 11–12). The limits to such cooperation were set by the willingness of others—especially the dominant Western powers—to recognize the Indian state as an "equal" (ibid., 270–71) and to respect its right to an "independent" (ibid., 11–12), possibly different, judgment on issues of international importance.

These markers of the limits of the security imaginary—the refusal to tolerate certain practices—are indicative of the structuring principle of the Indian security imaginary. It is instructive to invoke here Nehru's articulation of some of the core elements of the field of meanings organized by that principle: "We are not copies of Europeans or Americans or Russians. We are Asians and Africans. It would not be creditable for our dignity and new freedom if we were camp-followers of America or Russia or any other country of Europe" (ibid., 271–72). Nehru's strong assertion of the difference between Asians, Africans, and (by implication) Indians on the one hand, and Europeans, Americans, and Russians on the other, makes one wonder why anyone would have thought that Asians, Africans, or Indians were "copies" in the first place. Was it not obvious—given the different racial, ethnic, sociocultural, and political boundaries that each inhabited—that Asians and Africans were different? What factors threatened to erase these differences so that their reassertion became important? In other words, what were the historical conditions under which the assertion of this difference became meaningful?

In brief, it was the social relations and identities generated by the nationalist struggle against colonialism that continued to be salient.[5] For postcolonial identities such as that of India, the colonizer was the constitutive Other.[6] The Indian state was one of the actors produced through this struggle: it was in the successful practice of "securing" the Indian people against the colonizer that the Indian state first emerged and was legitimized. Its dominant identity and legitimacy were thus reproducible through and dependent on a demonstration of its ability to keep at bay the "threats" posed to the people by the colonizer. On such an understanding, although the achievement of independence pushed the colonizer from within India, the social practices and relations associated with colonialism—domination, subjection to the dictates of powerful others, inequality, racial discrimination, passivity, lack of freedom, economic exploitation, and the like—remained in the international system and needed to be resisted. Thus, it was India's postcolonial identity that was being expressed in the assertion of independence on the international stage. Resistance to colonial domination in the international system was less a matter of achieving specific interests than a new mode of being, a new way of life or social relationship that was sought by newly independent states such as India. The assertion of difference evident in Nehru's articulation of India and its place in the world can thus be read as an expression of the dominant social relationship—in this case a postcolonial one—productive of the Indian state.[7]

A reconstruction of the self-understandings associated with Indian nationalism thus suggests postcoloniality as the structuring principle of the Indian security imaginary. In other words, if the security imaginary is a field of meanings and social power, the dominant meanings and social relationships it produced were postcolonial ones. If postcolonial meanings, identities, and practices were productive of the Indian state, how did they relate to those generated by other security imaginaries?

EVENTS AND SECURITY IMAGINARIES

Why Analyze Events?

I investigate the interaction among security imaginaries as they came together in historical events such as the visits of heads of state for two reasons. First, faced with a mutually constitutive relationship between structures and agents—that is, between the security imaginary

and the practices that it produced—the "event" offers an appropriate analytic tool for cutting into the "manifold and endless" structuring of social reality. As Abrams explains:

> Structuring, the reciprocal flow of action and structure, is manifold
> and endless. To understand it we must somehow break into it, some-
> how construct moments or episodes within it which our analytical
> resources can manage. The event is such a construct—and it is an es-
> sentially apt construct because it preserves just that balance of agency
> and social order which so many of the constructs of history and soci-
> ology [and, one might add, following Wendt (1987), international re-
> lations] upset. (1982: 192)

A focus on events makes it possible for me to get away from a mode
of analysis that either brackets agential practices and focuses solely
on the powers of the security imaginary or, alternatively, brackets the
security imaginary and focuses on the innovative practices of the
agent.

Second, visits of heads of state are conscious attempts to forge
better understandings between states. This means that state officials
attempt, deliberately and consciously, to produce a shared reality between the two states: about each other, their respective policies,
strategic issues, and the international system that both states inhabit
(cf. Milliken, this volume). Such attempts are reflected, among other
things, in the various speeches made by the dignitaries, in the public
statements that are issued in visiting different parts of the country,
and in the joint communiqué that is released at the end of the visit.
All these are rich expressions of the attempt to produce a shared
reality between the two states and thus can be read as the outcomes
of the interaction of different security imaginaries.

If articulation and interpellation are two moments in the production of social reality, historical visits can be read in terms of the effectiveness of these moments in the production of a shared reality. As a
first step in the analysis of such a "politics of meaning fixing," I examine in some detail the articulatory processes apparent in two historical events in India's interactions with the superpowers—the visits
to India of Soviet Premier Nikolay A. Bulganin and Communist
Party Secretary Nikita S. Khrushchev in 1955 and of U.S. President
Dwight Eisenhower in 1959.

Why these visits? The 1950s represented a formative decade in

India's relations with the superpowers. Not only did a variety of significant foreign-policy events occur, but the specific relations between all the major players in the region—the United States, Pakistan, China, India, and the USSR—were in a state of flux. This fluidity allows me to focus better on the articulatory practices that were first deployed in the 1950s but acquired the status of common sense in later periods. These events are also useful cases because they were commonly read as historically significant (Gopal, 1984; Kux, 1992). Both visits were seen by scholars and the states themselves as highly "successful" (see U.S. Department of State, 1987: 301; "Triumph in Asia," 1959: 1E). Both represented critical efforts on the part of the United States and the Soviet Union to woo India.[8] Within the United States, there was a distinct awareness that Eisenhower's visit to India was meant to counteract the success of the earlier Soviet visit (see Baker, 1959: 16). These two visits thus provide rich concretizations of the interactions among the different imaginaries.

I also take the "success" of the visit as a sign of the availability of space for the workings of a politics of meaning fixing. Such space facilitates the analysis of a politics of meaning fixing when it had a good chance of working rather than when its operation was already limited by other factors. Although the three imaginaries interacted at a number of levels during these events, my analytic focus is confined to the public discourse—specifically the public addresses delivered by these state representatives during their visits to India. Within these addresses, I limit myself to exploring the distinctive ways in which each of the superpowers engaged in a process of articulation. I ask: How did each superpower represent itself and India? Which meanings and relations did it present as shared and which as different?

READING THE POLITICS OF MEANING FIXING

The Soviet and U.S. articulations mobilized fairly similar elements of meaning in seeking to "hail" the Indian state. Both condemned colonialism, racial inequality, and political domination. Both touched on India's contributions to world peace. Both talked about their commitment to global disarmament and the defensive nature of their own armament. Both highlighted their own role in advancing the economic welfare of newly independent countries such as India. Both articulations thus might seem to operate well within the common sense of the Indian security imaginary and, at least superficially, not to have violated its boundaries. Analyzed in these terms, there was little to differentiate the Soviet articulation of India from the U.S. one.

The Soviet and U.S. articulations nonetheless differed dramatically with respect to the ways in which these meanings were organized. This is most readily apparent with respect to the identity of the India "hailed" by the superpowers. Eisenhower, for example, observed in his speech to the Indian Parliament:

> All humanity is in debt to this land, but we Americans have with you a special community of interest.
>
> You and we from our first days have sought by a national policy the expansion of democracy. You and we, peopled by many strains and races, speaking many tongues, worshipping in many ways, have each achieved national strength out of diversity.
>
> You and we never boast that ours is the only way. . . . We both seek the improvement and betterment of all our citizens by assuring that the state will serve, not master its own people or any other people. Above all our basic goals are the same. (Eisenhower, 1959b: 15)

The U.S. articulation sought to fix meaning in terms of a "special community of interest" located in the shared features of democracy and diversity. Implicitly, the absent Other constitutive of such a shared identity was the undemocratic state, which did not respect "diversity," saw its way as "the only way," and sought not to "serve" but to "master" its own and other people. The United States and India could not, on this articulatory logic, share the same goals as this absent (Soviet) Other. The U.S. organization of meanings thus sought to constitute the United States and India as a community of shared identity and interests, in part by excluding an Other that did not share these characteristics.

Compare the U.S. articulation of India with the Soviet articulation:

> The friendship between our peoples has its origins in the distant past. Almost five centuries ago, even before the first European ships had reached the coasts of your country, the first Russian explorer Afanasy Nikitin visited India and wrote a book outstanding for its time about the wondrous country in which he lived for several years and which he ardently loved. This was the first "discovery of India" by the Russians. . . .
>
> The relations and mutual understanding between our peoples became even stronger after the victory of the great October socialist revolution in Russia. The principles of equal rights and self-determination

for peoples, which were proclaimed by our revolution, met with wide response in other countries, including India, which was then in colonial dependence.

Soviet people in turn sympathize from the bottom of their hearts with the unselfish and courageous struggle which your people waged against colonial oppression, for the restoration of your motherland's independence. (Bulganin, 1956b: 3)

In contrast to that of the United States, the Soviet articulatory process based itself not on a commitment to socialist democracy or diversity but on a shared anticolonial identity. Afanasy Nikitin's scholarly "discovery" of India was contrasted to the commercial and colonizing discovery by Europe. The self–other constructions operative in this case were those of nonexploitative Russians in a shared "community of interest" with newly independent Indians against the colonizing Europeans. For this articulatory process, then, it was the struggle against colonialism that signified the moment of identity between India and the Soviet Union.

It is important to note here that the production of articulations is not necessarily a question of "truthfulness." This is partially shown by the manner in which both U.S. and Soviet articulations sought to erase and rewrite history in their organization of meanings. The Soviet articulation, for example, invoked Gandhi's critical role in the nationalist struggle, declaring that "the ideas and the guidance of that outstanding leader of the Indian national movement, Mahatma Gandhi, were of great significance in this struggle" (ibid.). This was an explicit attempt to rewrite an earlier Soviet understanding of Gandhi as a "reactionary utopian" ("Gandhi as a 'Reactionary Utopian,'" 1949).

The U.S. articulation had a different problem to negotiate. It had to operate within an Indian security imaginary that located Eisenhower's "three evils" (political subjection, racial inequality, and economic misery) as originating in the domination of the colonizing West over the colonized East (1959b: 15; Gopal, 1984; Appadorai and Rajan, 1985). The U.S. articulatory process sought to displace such a linkage by asserting that the United States had been committed to defeating these evils from its "founding" (Eisenhower, 1959b: 15) and that it was still fighting them relentlessly. In other words, within the logic sutured by the articulatory process, the United States could not reasonably be seen as the source of these evils because it had been actively engaged in fighting them since its founding (ibid.).

A broader reading of the two visits thus offers the following contrast between the U.S. and Soviet articulations of India. As noted, the U.S. articulatory process posited a shared democratic identity between India and the United States, and implicitly constituted a Soviet Other that was not democratic and hence not a variety of other things democratic nations such as India and the United States were. It recognized an important Indian concern in combating the "three evils," displaced any U.S. responsibility for their perpetuation, linked the notion of these three evils to other evils—such as the violation of the "rule of law" (ibid.)—and by doing that presented the United States as a defender of important democratic principles in the international system. It acknowledged the important contribution of India in combating the three evils but linked the better achievement of these common goals to the successful realization of the broader Cold War project of the United States in the international system. Thus, the shared democratic identity of the United States and India and the understandings derived from that identity were privileged at first, and did a lot of work in making the overall discourse appear reasonable, rational, and persuasive. But the U.S. articulation also sought to engage the Indian security imaginary in ways that would affirm the Cold War meanings of the U.S. security imaginary.

Like the U.S. articulatory processes, the Soviet articulation also sought to engage the Indian security imaginary in ways that would affirm the Cold War meanings of the Soviet security imaginary. But, in contrast to the U.S. imaginary, the Soviet articulatory process organized these around the anticolonial meanings within the Indian imaginary. It regretted the continuing failure of the European powers to awaken to the new Asian era with its growing intolerance of colonialism (Bulganin, 1956b: 5). It asserted that colonialism had many forms; one of these was the dependence of a country's economic development on foreign capital and foreign industry. On this logic, independence from colonialism was "real" only when the national economy was freed from such dependence (Khrushchev, 1956f: 6). It then claimed that colonialism, in its different forms, presented a threat to all independence-loving, anticolonial forces. To the extent that this included newly independent India and the vigorously anticolonial Soviet Union, both needed to come together to resist oppression. Like the U.S. articulatory process, the Soviet articulation also sought to write its Cold War meanings over the Indian imaginary, though it focused on the anticolonial meanings within it.

One significant feature of the Soviet articulation, however, was the attentive demarcation of and respect for the differences between India and the Soviet Union. This came through in many ways. It was apparent in Khrushchev's careful disagreement with Nehru when the latter declared that both India and the Soviet Union were following socialist paths of development (Khrushchev, 1956b: 4). It was evident in the constant assertion that, although the Soviet Union was willing to help, it would do so only if India explicitly wanted its help. Unlike Western nations—the implicit Other being invoked here—the Soviets presented themselves as having no intention of forcing their aid, capital, and technology on, or taking advantage of the industrial weakness of, newly independent countries such as India (Khrushchev, 1956f: 7). There was thus a strong recognition of difference, but this recognition was also used to strengthen shared identity by stressing the bonds of commonality and mutual interest in other, ostensibly more central, goals. The articulatory logic was in each case premised on a successful suturing of a shared identity within the discursive terrain of the Indian security imaginary. Thus, within the U.S. discourse, the shared identity of "democracy" furnished the rationale for respecting the "rule of law" in the international system, for avoiding the imposition of one's own way on others, for seeing the state as a "servant" rather than a "master" of its citizens, and for creating the correct international conditions for the achievement of freedom, human dignity, and economic development. An interlocutor skeptical of the shared social relationship of democracy was unlikely to move very far on this chain of significations. A similar case could be made for an anchoring in anticolonialism that was necessary to make the Soviet chain of significations socially meaningful.[9] The U.S. organization of meanings generated an articulatory process that sought out the democratic self-understanding of the Indian state to establish a relationship of identity. The Soviet articulatory process, on the other hand, sought to establish a relationship of identity through the postcolonial self-understanding of the Indian state. This difference, I will argue, is critical to understanding the different degree to which the two articulations compelled recognition in their "hailings" of the Indian state.

Before I do that, however, I need to locate my reading of these two events within the broader security imaginaries of the United States and the Soviet Union. The specific mechanisms of articulation that I illustrated in the case of the U.S. and Soviet imaginaries were from the better moments in the history of U.S. and Soviet state interactions with India. Although this makes them relatively limited in terms of their generalizability, it also provides a marker for judging the articulatory logics in cases where there was more than enough scope for a successful politics of meaning fixing. In order to facilitate generalization, however, I will situate the articulatory processes apparent in these better moments in relation to some general propositions about the U.S. and Soviet security imaginaries as they sought to come to terms with postcolonial India.

THE U.S. AND SOVIET SECURITY IMAGINARIES COMPARED

Three features of the broader U.S. and Soviet security imaginaries are of particular relevance to my argument. First, both the Soviet and the U.S. imaginaries initially denied the reality of Indian independence. The U.S. imaginary denied this reality by seeing independent India as akin to British India and therefore as a continuing part of the Western Free World and hence a natural ally against the Soviets (U.S. Department of State, 1972a; U.S. Department of State, 1975). When Indian practices did not fit this conceptualization, deviations from this vision were laid at the door of the Indian state's lack of realism about the international system, its "anti-Westernism" (U.S. Department of State, 1977b: 1672), its failure to be either "balanced" or "objective" (ibid., 1676), its unwillingness to recognize threats to its own security, Nehru's "negativism" and "passivism," which were rooted in "Hindu emotion and philosophy" (ibid., 1691), India's "emotional barriers" arising out of wrongly associating the United States with "European colonialism" and "color discrimination" (U.S. Department of State, 1983: 1090), Nehru's "innate feelings of personal superiority and proud and obstinate character" (ibid., 1100), and so on. The organizing sign of such efforts was captured nicely in a study prepared by the U.S. embassy in India when it pointed out that "India is Asian and Indians, no matter how westernized, are Asians and often unpredictable to Westerners" (U.S. Department of State, 1987: 397).

It was understandings such as these that structured the measures taken to combat the "error of India's foreign policy of neutralism" (U.S. Department of State, 1977b: 2173). Negatively, the U.S. imaginary empowered a whole series of educative measures (U.S. Department of State, 1983: 1092, 1139) to get India to see the "fallacious basis" (U.S. Department of State, 1977b: 1678) of its reasoning. India was, in a variety of ways, to be helped in achieving greater "stability" through association with the "older," "more mature," and "more stable" powers (U.S. Department of State, 1983: 398). Positively, the imaginary sought to construct India as a democratic alternative to communist China that should be encouraged in its efforts to develop economically.

The Soviet imaginary also initially denied the reality of Indian independence. It expressed this understanding through practices that differentiated between the Indian state and the Indian masses and saw the former as having betrayed the national liberation struggle and the Indian people. Gandhi and Nehru were denounced in no uncertain terms and Indian "independence" was understood to be the collusive outcome of a deal between the Indian bourgeoisie and Anglo-American imperialists. India's nonalignment was then read as a covert way of siding with the British and the Americans. Soviet support to the Indian communists—as the real representatives of the Indian people—seemed therefore to be an appropriate way of relating to the real India (Kapur, 1972; Remnek, 1975; Gupta, 1988).

Second, although it was possible within the limits of the U.S. and Soviet imaginaries to express different, even contradictory, understandings of India, nevertheless some understandings dominated over others. Within the Soviet imaginary, contestations between different understandings of India were typified by the disputes over the true processes under way in the international system and, relatedly, over the reality of Indian independence. Soviet scholars such as Eugene Varga, F. I. Mikhalevsky, and E. M. Zhakov ("The Economists' Debate on Their Shortcomings and Tasks," 1949) argued about whether India had achieved genuine independence from the domination of colonial Britain or whether the Indian state continued to be a colony of Britain even after its formal independence. Such contestations over what India really was affected Soviet assessments of India's ability and willingness to exploit differences between the United States and Britain to its own benefit. These debates were extremely significant in shaping Soviet policies toward India (Remnek, 1975: 101–26).

Contestations over what India really was were also common within the U.S. administration. Representative of prominent alternative understandings were people such as Chester Bowles and John Galbraith who argued for making anticolonialism a major plank of relations with India (U.S. Department of State, 1983: 1652; Schaffer, 1993; McMahon, 1994). Debates over alternative understandings of India were resolved not by policymakers progressively approximating the reality of India but by the overall logics of meaning and power within each security imaginary. Thus, Bowles's support for anticolonialism was not read as a sign of his greater understanding of a different reality—that of postcolonial India—but as an indication of his inability to grasp the "overall reality" of U.S. security policy. This was not an experience peculiar to Bowles. Galbraith, under a Kennedy administration much more favorably inclined toward India, ran into the same problem on Goa (U.S. Department of State, 908–13). The critical point is that outcomes of policy debates were inextricably also contestations of social power within the broader security imaginary.

It is beyond the purview of this chapter to examine how particular understandings of India maintained their dominance within the Soviet and U.S. discourses or why they changed—from their initial denial of Indian independence—more easily in the former than in the latter. The broader point I want to foreground here is that although there were alternative, often contradictory, understandings within each discourse, their presence did not automatically translate into social practices appropriate to the reproduction of India's postcolonial identity. Between the different understandings and the actual practices there often fell the shadow of power working to legitimize some and disempower other understandings and practices.[10]

These were the two common features shared by the U.S. and Soviet security imaginaries as they interacted with India. However, from the perspective of articulatory processes, there was a third feature: one wherein the U.S. security imaginary's articulation of India also exhibited a critical contrast with the Soviet one. The appeal to a shared democratic identity, as described earlier, marked a significantly better moment of the U.S. imaginary insofar as it was meant to articulate India in a way that enabled Indians to "recognize" themselves. Other moments, however, were marked by articulatory processes that unhesitatingly violated the most negative markers of the postcolonial security imaginary.

By far the best illustration of such an articulation was the "short-tether" (Kux, 1992: 247) policy of the Johnson administration. In 1966, facing severe drought conditions and an acute shortage of food from domestic production, the Indian government approached the United States for surplus stocks of wheat to stave off famine. President Lyndon Johnson personally coordinated the authorization and release of every shipload of grain that left U.S. shores in order to force a change in Indian domestic and foreign policy. As Mansingh notes:

> Releases of U.S. commitments to the World Bank earmarked for India, as well as each foodgrain shipment, now required the President's personal authorisation. Authorisation was frequently delayed until the last possible moment, keeping everyone concerned in agonised suspense, and necessitating frequent calls by Ambassador B. K. Nehru on the Secretary of State. Johnson decided to substitute one-fourth of the wheat shipments with sorghum and milo, used as feed for the animals in the U.S. and produced in surplus by Texas. His decision was made regardless of how problematic this was for shippers and unloaders, how distasteful for the human palate, how insulting in its connotations, or how embarrassing for the U.S. envoy Bowles to explain. . . . Throughout the fiscal year 1966–67, the President maintained this kind of pressure on India despite criticism from within his administration. (1984: 111)

During such moments, the U.S. articulatory process unproblematically took on all the signs associated with the colonizer in the postcolonial Indian security imaginary. India was dictated to, pressure was applied, the United States refused to recognize the right of the Indian state to disagree or to have an independent judgment on domestic or international issues, aid was tied to immediate concessions, and so on. Chester Bowles's observations on Johnson's "short-tether" policy are revealing in this context: "LBJ's performance remains beyond comprehension or belief. . . . It is a cruel performance. The Indians must conform; they must be made to fawn; their pride must be cracked. . . . It is in this way that distrust and hatred are born among people who want to be our friends" (in Schaffer, 1993: 282).

The U.S. security imaginary's articulatory processes toward India thus ranged from an appeal to its democratic identity to an unequivocal "hailing" of India as a colonized subject. Conspicuous by its absence, however, was any articulatory process that sought to fix anticolonialism as the moment of identity. What the U.S. security imaginary could have done but never did—even in its "best" moments—was to privilege the postcolonial self as the moment of identity between the two states. This was definitely not because anticolonialism was somehow not recognized or acknowledged as an important aspect of the Indian state. As innumerable memorandums, telegrams, discussions, and position papers indicate, there was a definite awareness of the strong role that anticolonialism played in shaping the Indian government's actions. What was missing was any sustained attempt to produce an articulatory chain of significations based on that anticolonial moment.

Paradoxically, it was the Soviet imaginary that persistently privileged the anticolonial moment as the moment of Indo-Soviet identity. The practices empowered by the Soviet imaginary also steered clear of colonial markers that articulated India in the position of the colonized. Symbolic of such practices was the willingness of the Soviet Union to let the Indian delegation draft the joint communiqué that was issued after Nehru's visit to the Soviet Union in 1955 (Menon, 1963: 118–19). This strategy of allowing the Indians to author or coauthor the joint relationship could be seen as an organizing sign of the Indo-Soviet interstate relationship. Strong support for nonalignment, for Indian initiatives on a variety of anticolonial issues, and the overall Soviet aid, trade, and military agreements with India were all in keeping with this focus on joint authorship of the relations between the two (Allison, 1988).

THE PRODUCTION OF INSECURITY

What, then, is the explanation for the differential generation of insecurity in these cases? How do we understand the movement from different articulatory processes to the generation of security or insecurity? One way is to see interstate interaction between India, the United States, and the Soviet Union as the coming together of different security imaginaries. If security imaginaries are distinctive fields of meanings and powers, then the analyst can examine whether interactions between these imaginaries are reproducing a relay of

POSTCOLONIALITY AND THE PRODUCTION OF INSECURITY · 143

meanings, identities, and power, where a relay is an effective transformation of articulatory processes into interpellative ones.[11] A relay
thus results in the production of an intersubjective social reality.

From this perspective, U.S. articulatory processes were singularly
ineffective in transforming themselves into interpellations within
the Indian security imaginary. U.S. articulatory processes sought to
fix meaning at the level of a shared democratic identity or at the
level of the colonizer–colonized relationship. Although the democratic identity was not central to the identities generated by the
postcolonial security imaginary, the colonizer–colonized relationship directly contravened the postcoloniality of the Indian security
imaginary and was destructive of the meanings and social relations
that the Indian security imaginary sought to reproduce. Given this
disjuncture between the imaginaries, the Indian state either did not
recognize itself well in the ways in which it was addressed by the
U.S. security imaginary or saw a representation of itself that
negated its dominant self-understandings.

This meant that every coming together of the two imaginaries
was marked by failed attempts to generate a set of mutually shared
social meanings and relations. Such a disjuncture of imaginaries generated insecurity by producing every interaction as an uncertain
event whose social reproduction—in terms of shared social meanings
and relations—could not be taken for granted. In other words, each
interaction was a potential "crisis" (see Weldes, this volume, on the
cultural production of "crises" in interstate relations).

Such "crises" continue to affect Indo-U.S. relations. They range
from issues with apparently trivial signification—the failure of the
Clinton administration to appoint an ambassador to India during
much of 1992–93, a leaked Pentagon draft suggesting the curbing of
Indian "hegemony" in South Asia (Kux, 1992: xvii), a modification
by the U.S. State Department in its ritual reiteration of U.S. neutrality
over Kashmir ("U.S. Questions Kashmir Accession," 1993: 23554–5;
"Protests Greet Raphael," 1994: 23903), the simultaneous arrival in
New Delhi of the Iranian president and the U.S. secretary of the treasury, to the embarrassment of the latter (Naqvi, 1995: 1; see also
Malhotra, 1995)—to those with ostensibly greater substance, such
as disputes over nuclear proliferation, intellectual property rights,
trade barriers, a ban on the sale of high-technology items to India,
and human rights. My point is not that some of these issues are

intrinsically more important than others but that all of them end up as diplomatic "crises" in the Indo-U.S. encounter because each of these events is implicitly an occasion for the affirmation and reiteration of a postcolonial identity that is not in fact relayed in the coming together of the two security imaginaries.

The Soviet state, on the other hand, obtained a secure relationship with India because of the way in which the Soviet security imaginary articulated India as a postcolonial state. For the Indian state, the Soviet offer of joint authorship reproduced and validated its postcolonial identity in ways that no amounts of economic aid or military weapons alone could have done. This definitely should not be taken to mean that the Indo-Soviet interstate relationship was a benevolent interaction free of struggles over meanings, interests, or power. On the contrary, it was precisely the "co-authorship" of the overall set of understandings productive of the Indo-Soviet relationship that enabled struggles over specific disputes to take place without disrupting the relationship between the two or generating distrust. Thus, even in cases where Indian and Soviet interests differed, the effect on security was not significant.[12]

Indo-U.S. insecurity has its effects in the domestic arena also. The postcolonial Indian security imaginary functions, in domestic debates, to disempower meanings that closely overlap with those of the U.S. state. Those who argue, for example, for renouncing the nuclear option, for signing the Comprehensive Test Ban Treaty, for supporting the monitoring of human rights violations, or for opening the domestic economy to external competition (see Gupta, 1994; "BJP Is Opposed to Ties with US," 1995; "The Foreign Devil," 1995; Narula, 1995; Cooper, 1996)—positions that overlap in important respects with those of the United States—have overtly to distance themselves from the U.S. position to be taken seriously. Their arguments are tougher to make and their political credibility more easily delegitimized within the Indian security imaginary.

Such a disempowerment is not easily mapped onto conventional ideological positions of left or right or onto specific political parties. The postcolonial security imaginary produces Indo-U.S. insecurity with a certain blindness to party affiliations. Notwithstanding the past dominance of the Congress Party at the level of the central government, Indian foreign policy has enjoyed a fair degree of consensus across political parties. That consensus continues to shape Indian foreign policy in the present. The coming to power of the United

Front government in 1996 did not change the situation to any significant extent. On being asked about India's relations with the United
States and the latter's application of pressure on various issues, the
then minister for external affairs (and later prime minister), I. K.
Gujral, observed:

> We are not egoists but we have our self-pride as a nation. So there-
> fore those who care for being our friends must respect our dignity. It
> is for them [the United States] to decide on what issues to "press."
> The only thing I can say is that we have two legs and we will stand
> firmly on them. We will not make friends with anybody on our
> knees. (In Chengappa, 1996: 39)

"Self-pride," "friendship," "dignity"—strains of a postcolonial song
that has been performed many a time, by many a minister since Indian independence. One could say that all of these ministers were, in
a variety of ways, reproducing a postcolonial India. Or, one could
say, more correctly, that it was the Indian security imaginary that
was composing them, performing them, playing their refusals, again
and again, to Uncle Sam, and through such refusals re-creating a
postcolonial India. One could be certain about one thing, however.
This did not sound like the beginnings of a beautiful friendship.

NOTES

This chapter has benefited from the criticisms of Anjuman Ali, Sanjoy
Banerjee, Tarak Barkawi, Shampa Biswas, David Blaney, Chris Chekuri,
Evelyn Davidheiser, Lisa Disch, Lynn Eden, Naeem Inayatullah, Prabhakara
Jha, Frank Klink, Jeff Legro, George Marcus, Ido Oren, Richard Price,
Vakulabharanam Rajagopal, Rajesh Rajagopalan, Velcheru Narayana Rao,
Diana Richards, Michael Shapiro, Asha Varadarajan, Alex Wendt, the con-
tributors to this volume, and members of the South Asia Contact Group of
the School of International Studies, Jawaharlal Nehru University. Thank you
for forcing me to think through this argument more carefully.

1. See Muppidi (1995) on the limitations of rationalist theories in explaining insecurity in the Third World.

2. I have adapted this conception of the "imaginary" from the work of
Cornelius Castoriadis (1987); see also Tomlinson (1991) and Kaviraj (1992).

3. Thus, the heuristic of a security imaginary is meant to facilitate analysis by conceptually freezing a set of social relations, identities, and boundaries that are always in process, not fixed, and variously contested.

4. On Indian nationalism, see Chandra (1993), Chatterjee (1986, 1993), Chatterjee and Pandey (1992), and Kaviraj (1992). I have limited my discussion here to the conception of nationalism that was empowered in the juridical relationships that came into existence in 1947. I have relied, in mapping this nationalism, on the published texts of Nehru's speeches and writings. This is because Nehru not only had a long and influential stint as prime minister of independent India, but also was a prolific writer and prime articulator of the vision behind Indian foreign policy. He was, as Sankaran Krishna (1994: 193) so aptly notes, "the lyrical bard of Indian nationalism." That Nehru's composition was not an idiosyncratic one is evident in the overall consensus that shaped Indian foreign policy for many years. Nehru's writings, however, represent only one entry point into a reconstruction of the Indian security imaginary. This reconstruction, in principle, should be compatible with others based on sources such as biographies of other political leaders, memoirs of state officials, or readings of popular culture.

5. A complete answer to the questions just posed requires a thorough explication of the politics of post-coloniality, of the historical attempt of colonialism to subjugate the otherness it encountered in its colonizing mission and to produce subjects who were, in Thomas Macaulay's terms, "Indian in blood and colour, but English in taste, in opinions, in morals, and in intellect" (1995: 430). But see Laffey and Muppidi (1993).

6. On postcoloniality see, for example, Alavi (1972), Krishna (1993, 1994), Nandy (1983), and Prakash (1992b).

7. One could argue that the Indian state was only one of the products of this security imaginary. Other actors (e.g., the diasporic Indian community) can also be seen as partially constituted by this security imaginary.

8. See Khrushchev (1956a–f) and Bulganin (1956a–b); see also "The Heart of India" (1959) and Kux (1992: 139–79) on Eisenhower's trip as a "public relations triumph."

9. To reinforce this point, I would ask readers to imagine how compelling would be an articulation that fixed meanings in terms of a shared imperial past between India, the United States, and Britain—as subjects of the crown—and sought to promote an anti-Soviet alliance based on that loyalty.

10. What is opened up for investigation, then, is not the question of how some specific administration could work to improve its "India policy" but a more structurationist focus on the overall workings of the security imaginary that consistently empowers particular articulations and practices and disempowers others.

11. I am grateful to Lisa Disch and Michael Shapiro for suggesting the notion of a "relay" between security imaginaries.

12. For example, although the Soviet selling of arms to Pakistan in the late 1960s became a cause for concern in India, it did not generate the sort of insecurity that U.S. arms sales to Pakistan traditionally did.

5

Contested Sovereignties and Postcolonial Insecurities in the Middle East

STEVE NIVA

The Iraqi invasion of Kuwait in August 1990 once again raised divisive questions about the very sovereignty of states in the Middle East established by the colonial powers after World War I. That many Arab leaders sided against Iraq masked the deep divisions across the region provoked by the crisis. Before the end of the Gulf War in 1991, massive public demonstrations in support of Iraq and in opposition to the military buildup of the U.S.-led coalition had taken place in almost every country in the region (Karmi, 1991; Seddon, 1991). This opposition emphasized the common interests and bonds of solidarity between Arabs and, more broadly, between Muslims against Western intervention (Piscatori, 1991).

The Iraqi invasion of Kuwait and its claim to have liberated its "eighteenth province," however, were initially greeted with little regional support and even provoked demonstrations by many across the region, who were quite familiar with Saddam Hussein's brutal rule and ruthless opportunism. Yet, there was a dramatic shift in popular attitudes once the United States began its historically unprecedented military buildup in Saudi Arabia and quelled diplomatic prospects for an "Arab solution" to the conflict (Niva, 1991). A growing perception of the threat posed by the largely Western-orchestrated and overwhelmingly U.S. interventionary force, its presence near Islam's most sacred cities, and the prospects of a permanent Western military presence in the region took precedence over initial concerns

147

about the threat posed by Iraqi aggression (Esposito, 1991: 259–67). As an observer of Arab popular opinion at the time put it:

> If Saddam Hussein was not considered a big liar in the eyes of his masses . . . it was not because he enjoyed any credibility but was, first, due to the total lack of credibility of the U.S. and its allies. The fear of U.S. hegemony was and still is the main concern, particularly after the disintegration of the Eastern bloc which, as many people rightly or wrongly think, had created a monopolar world system controlled by the U.S. (Abd al-Jabbar, 1991: 215)

These concerns about the threat posed by Western intervention became discursively linked to appeals for broader regional unity and solidarity among Arabs and, in some cases, among Muslims. The significance of territorial boundaries between regional peoples gave way to an imaginary geopolitical boundary based on a different conception of "us" and "them." Sovereignty was no longer simply equated with defending and preserving "lines in the sand." The defense of Kuwaiti sovereignty against Iraq was seen as equivalent or even secondary to the defense of the independence and agency of the Arab or Muslim world against external Western intervention and its international domination. Many opposed to the U.S.-led coalition rallied not to Saddam Hussein and his violation of Kuwaiti sovereignty but to the confrontation between the West and the Arab/Muslim world. An Islamist activist from the Arab world who had been highly critical of Saddam Hussein in the past confessed to siding with Iraq because "U.S. intervention has forced many Arabs to choose sides between foreign intervention/presence and Arab independence and solidarity" (Esposito, 1991: 263).

The ensuing destruction of Iraq by the U.S.-led coalition did not lead to the mass uprising of Arab and Muslim peoples that some observers had predicted. Nevertheless, the broader Gulf crisis and war highlighted an important and often overlooked dimension of what could be termed, following Barry Buzan, the Middle Eastern "security complex" (1991: 190).[1] Since the establishment of territorial states in the region, the boundaries of the community to be secured from a dangerous outside have often not been coextensive with nor coincidental to the political fields constituted by the territorial boundaries of modern Middle Eastern states. Despite an intense preoccupation on the part of most Middle Eastern states with "national security," there has also existed a powerful discourse of regional insecurity about the threat to the region posed by the West and Western powers. This discourse of regional insecurity has been central to recurring calls for regional solidarity over and above the claims of any single state to sovereignty and security. It has been most powerfully expressed, albeit with different emphases, by pan-Arab nationalist movements associated with Egypt's Gamal Abdel Nasser in the 1950s and by regional Islamist movements that have gained prominence in the past few decades.

Security analysts and scholars who study the region have had a difficult time addressing, let alone explaining, such enduring regional expressions of insecurity about the threat posed to the region by the West, which go far beyond a simple concern with direct military intervention to issues of economic, cultural, and political security. This is particularly the case for conventional realist security studies, which theoretically equates "security" with the defense of the sovereign state from external military threats and claims that "security" is reducible to an objective set of threats (Walt, 1987).[2] For example, Stephen Walt's impressive realist-inspired account of security dynamics in the Middle East often notes the linkage between widespread regional aspirations for Arab unity and anticolonial insecurities and yet he still theoretically reduces regional security dynamics to a list of "objective" external threats confronted by given state actors.

A more promising approach to understanding regional insecurities has been adopted by security analysts who draw on security literature on Third World states to argue that Middle Eastern regional insecurities and aspirations for unity are related to the fact that regional state formation and development is "lacking" or "incomplete" in comparison with modern European states (Korany, Noble, and Brynen, 1993).[3] Following Jackson's (1990) argument that Third World states are "quasi states" that lack "empirical sovereignty," this work argues that the sociological condition of state "weakness" in the Middle East explains the existence of contending "state" and "communal" notions of security that are based on enduring "precolonial" affinities and identities. Thus, the Middle Eastern security environment has been riven by a persistent conflict over whether security should be understood in terms of sovereign states or on the basis of "precolonial" collectivities, whether the "Arab Nation" or some other—usually Islamic—form.[4] Ayoob contends that "Arab states are less sovereign, even in a theoretical sense, than other members of the system of states. Such a diminution of sovereignty, even in the abstract, opens the way for more intervention and intramural conflicts within the Arab world, thus detracting from the 'national' security of individual Arab states" (1993: 49).

This explanation of regional notions of insecurity that transcend the individual sovereignties of regional states is problematic, however, for a number of reasons. The most glaring problem is that the sociological notion of "state weakness" in comparison to European states depends on a Eurocentric teleology built into most "Third World" histories, which turn on "references to 'absences' or 'failures' of a history to keep an appointment with its destiny" (Chakrabarty, 1992: 5). Framing political dynamics in non-Western contexts in comparison to models and trajectories of European state formation overlooks the transformative regional encounter with Western colonialism and the continuing dominance of European powers within the state system. Recent scholarship in postcolonial studies emphasizes that we should not focus on the "failures" to replicate the Western experience but turn our attention to the aftereffects of the unequal encounter with Western colonialism, which Prakash describes as "the violent institution of a set of racial, political, epistemic, and economic systems" (1992a: 177).[5] Talal Asad points to the necessity of recognizing the "radically new form and terrain of conflict inaugurated by it—new political languages, new powers, new social groups, new desires and fears, new subjectivities" (1991: 322–23).

The failure of recent security literature on Third World states to consider the aftereffects of the colonial encounter leads it to substitute an investigation of the broader regional insecurities that have animated regional political life since that encounter with a static and ahistorical distinction between "state" and supposedly "precolonial" affinities and identities. The Orientalist assumption of an unchanging "precolonial" cultural essence leaves one unable to register how novel *postcolonial* articulations of Arab identity and Islamic tradition have arisen *alongside* modern state formation and have informed both statist and oppositional interpretations of sovereignty, legitimacy, and security (al-Azmeh, 1995; Hovsepian, 1995; Abu-Rabi, 1996).[6]

Further, it leaves one unable to recognize how such postcolonial regional discourses of insecurity since the colonial encounter have been preoccupied with both the problems of "weakness" and the perceived dangers posed by the Western-dominated cultural, economic, and political structures of the existing international system. Rather than assume a sociological condition of state "weakness," other scholars have noted that Third World states and peoples have been constituted as "weak" and less than sovereign members of the international society because of their positioning within the hierarchical structures and exclusionary discourses that characterize the *postcolonial* international system (Blaney, 1992).[7] Siba Grovogui traces how, from the mid-sixteenth century, the relationship between European powers and non-European peoples was constructed on the twin principles of either denying or suppressing the claims to sovereignty of the latter (Grovogui, 1996). Different forms of imperial authority and colonial rule were enabled and justified by a powerful "colonial discourse" that constructed non-Europeans as languishing in a primitive developmental stage long surpassed by Europeans and lacking the attributes of "civilization" that would enable full participation in the international system (Gong, 1984; Spurr, 1993).

What may be unique about the Middle Eastern regional security environment, therefore, is not the existence of contending "state" and "precolonial" notions of identity and security so much as the struggles between existing regimes and opposition movements over contending interpretations of sovereignty and security in the postcolonial international system. Opposition movements in the region frequently contend that the present global order subordinates the rights of the colonized and postcolonial states to the requirements of the self-defined national interests and security concerns of the West. For them, decolonization and sovereign recognition have not completely transformed the institutional contexts of Western hegemony in the global international order and the marginalization of the formerly colonized peoples within it. This cultural understanding of regional weakness and victimization, rather than a sociological condition of "weakness," has led these movements to emphasize the necessity both of regional unity and of affirming an "authentic" cultural heritage in order to claim the right to sovereign independence. These opposition movements should be understood as postcolonial "counterstate" movements precisely because they have not opposed existing states on the basis of "precolonial" affinities as much as they have challenged the sovereignty of existing states on the basis that they are not *truly* sovereign, decolonized, and independent of the West.[8]

Drawing on a constructivist approach to the production of insecurity, this chapter will trace the origins of regional postcolonial discourses of insecurity to several foundational moments in the colonial encounter between the region and the West. It will outline how different constructions of the dangers posed by the West came to be understood in regional terms and led to contending views about how best to confront this threat. It will then explore how these discourses of insecurity have informed oppositional pan-Arabist and Islamist movements in the Middle East. It will examine the ways in which their different interpretations of the threat of the West to the region and conceptions of effective sovereignty in the international system have led these movements to construct broader regional conceptions of security outside of the existing territorial boundaries of regional states.

As David Campbell has argued, the construction of a threat entails the differentiation of a community from a threatening "other," thereby producing a boundary between the community inside and the threat outside (Campbell, 1992). The production of this boundary, however, is neither static nor fixed and can be constituted in a variety of ways that privilege certain conceptions of a community over others. The constructivist approach to security enables one to investigate how the boundaries of community to be secured from a dangerous "other" have often been neither coextensive with nor coincidental to the political fields constituted by the territorial boundaries of the Middle Eastern states, without relying on essentialist notions of "precolonial" identities and community. That security dynamics have never simply been confined to rigid interstate dynamics and state security elites has been exceedingly difficult to address because "conventional analyses of security are incapable of discussing security without taking the state for granted. . . . it often seems to be forgotten that the contemporary state system is a modern invention" (Dalby, 1992: 106). Because security studies has paid little attention to the emergence of the modern state system through Western imperialism and colonialism, "other forms of either historically existing social responses to threat or possible nonstate forms of security provision are excluded" in these analyses (ibid.).

REGIONAL INSECURITIES AND THE COLONIAL
ENCOUNTER IN THE MIDDLE EAST

Postcolonial discourses of regional insecurity in the Middle East have their origins in the new social and cultural terrain created by the regional encounter with the colonial West, long before the creation of Arab territorial states after World War I. The incorporation of the region into the Western state system and capitalist world system was mediated by the complex network of social relations, cultural traditions, and political structures that had been given political form through the Ottoman Empire that emerged in the fifteenth century (Islamoglu-Inan, 1987). Since the sixteenth century, significant commercial, military, and cultural interactions between the Ottomans and Europeans profoundly shaped both regions.

But a series of devastating military defeats and the growing involvement of European diplomats and commercial agents within the Ottoman Empire in the late eighteenth century generated a growing insecurity about the very existence of the empire. This insecurity was heightened by Napoleon's invasion of Egypt and the direct arrival of European forces into the Ottoman hinterland in 1798 (Hourani, 1983: 34–66). The French invasion inaugurated a new chapter of European expansion into the region as well as dramatic internal transformations in the form of the *Tanzimat* reforms, which initiated the adoption of modern European legal codes, private property, and the harmonization of its social practices with those of European states (Owen, 1981). These reforms dissolved the empire's distinctive intermediary institutions—abolishing notions of *dhimma* (non-Muslim subjects) and of Muslim extraterritoriality in the empire—and set the empire on a new "modern" basis in which adherents of all religions would be equal and patriotic members of the political community. This grand policy of cultural homogenization constituted new forms of subjectivity based on more bounded notions of identity and community (Anderson, 1991: 6; Mitchell, 1991a).

Ottoman–European interactions during this century were governed by what European diplomats called the "Eastern Question," in which competing European powers struggled among themselves to determine the eventual fate of the Ottoman empire (Anderson, 1966). England's policy of preventing the unilateral dismemberment of the empire by any single European power did not prevent European

powers from carving out spheres of influence and occupying Ottoman provinces. European powers were united by a colonialist discourse that constituted their identities as "civilized" and "advanced"
and those of regional peoples as "backwards" and "uncivilized"
(Gong, 1984: 106–19; Grovogui, 1996). The empire was assumed to
be unqualified for sovereign recognition; it was required to justify its
authority in terms of cultural standards defined by European states.
This new regime enabled the European powers to institutionalize unequal treaty arrangements, assert extraterritoriality, impose capitulations, and acquire outright jurisdiction in the name of civilizational
superiority (Gong, 1984). The Capitulations system, which granted
rights of extraterritorial legal jurisdiction to Europeans operating in
the Ottoman Empire, was a particularly important symbol of Ottoman inferiority because it gradually signified the inability of the Ottomans to uphold "civilized" standards and laws and prevented the
Ottomans from regulating European activities.

The threat of external dangers was amplified by an increasing
doubt in the universal claims of the empire and in the cultural resources necessary to confront the new dangers (Hourani, 1983: 104).
Perennial questions of communal order, moral dangers, and legitimate authority were shaped by the new conditions and modalities of
communal order and identity. Typical of the questions being asked
were: What was the secret of Western superiority? Why were we defeated? How was it possible to establish new and authentic foundations of community in order to restore the unity necessary to confront the West? It is precisely these questions, which are at the heart
of a distinctive regional discourse of insecurity in relation to Western
power and influence, that continue to inform contemporary regional
political discourses and practices.

Differences among regional elites over the nature and severity of
the threat of Western colonialism and how it should be confronted
emerged at this time. Many elites and members of the Ottoman intelligentsia contended that the dangers of the West could be met by
grafting its cultural and social achievements on to a reformed Ottoman and Islamic framework of political and moral authority. These
Westernizing elites became the most socially empowered class determining the course of developments within the empire (Cleveland,
1994: 78). For example, the Egyptian dignitary Rafi' al-Tahtawi
called for social transformations and the development of a national

culture along the lines of European civilization. For Tahtawi, as Sharabi points out, "Europe appeared as less of a threat than a promise" (1970: 27).

For others, the threat of the West was interpreted in a more sinister way. This interpretation emerged around 1870 when the West started to make deep inroads into the Ottoman Empire and European imperial penetration of the Islamic world extended from Morocco to Indonesia. By 1880, the Palmerstonian doctrine of preserving formal Ottoman integrity was replaced with the view that the Ottoman Empire was doomed to disintegrate. These inroads generated a widespread reaction led by both religious conservatives and secular-minded intellectuals against those "Westernizing" Ottoman reformers who were held responsible for the growing dismemberment of the empire and for making it subservient to the West.

For the influential Jamal al-Din al-Afghani and his religiously inclined followers, nothing was more important than confronting the Western threat and fundamentally transforming the existing social and moral order (Esposito, 1991: 46–52; Hourani, 1983: 103–29). The inner weakness of the Muslim community enabled the external political and cultural advancement of European imperialism. These "Islamic modernists," or the Salafiyya movement, as they became known, called for a revitalization of the classical Islamic heritage of the ancestors (salaf). This current was co-opted by Sultan Abdulhamid II, who was convinced that European powers were ready to partition the empire and believed that the emerging European norm of ethnic-linguistic identity would make disintegration of the Ottoman state inevitable (Karpat, 1996: 26–35). Because of this construction of the Western threat, the Sultan revived the idea of an Islamic umma under the rule of a single caliph who would adopt the role as protector of Muslims throughout the world.

A different understanding of the threat of the West became associated with a coalition of bureaucrats and intelligentsia known as the "Young Ottomans" (Mardin, 1962). After the European advances of the 1880s, this current took a more virulent form as the Young Turk movement, which accepted as a truism that England and France were determined to occupy the Middle East. But rather than challenge the political values of the West, they sought acceptance as equals with Europeans. They denounced the pan-Islamist policy of Abdulhamid and constructed a doctrine of antireligious secularism

156 · STEVE NIVA

and a "Turkish" ethnic-linguistic national identity as the basis of the empire. They demanded that it be treated equally as a European power and sought an end to the odious Capitulations and other "unequal" treaties. For Feroz Ahmed, nothing describes the ambitions of the Young Turks better than their claim to be the "Japan of the Near East" (Ahmed, 1984: 12). Japan had become an iconic example to many non-Europeans of a polity that was able dramatically to "civilize" its institutions without losing its cultural distinctiveness and had obtained near-complete sovereign recognition from the European powers without colonial occupation.

What is significant about these regional discourses of insecurity is that we find the first expressions of what could be considered the modern "problematic" of insecurity in which the construction of community is linked to the problem of defining a boundary between community inside and a threatening "other" on the outside (Campbell, 1992: 41–59). To a great extent, it was European imperialism, conquest, and social engineering that had engendered a strong sense of shared historical experience and unity among regional peoples, and that had compelled many to abandon "precolonial" affiliations in order to construct a new basis on which to confront the European powers.

REGIONAL INSECURITIES AND THE MANDATE SYSTEM

The second formative moment in the emergence of regional discourses of insecurity followed the partition of the Ottoman Empire after the Ottomans sided with the Germans in World War I. This development brought to an end the European "Eastern Question" and, more broadly, the formal existence of the Ottoman framework that had governed regional political life for five hundred years. Regional discourses of insecurity were reconstituted in response to three dramatic developments. The first was the establishment of the Mandate system of territorial states in the former eastern Arab *wilayets* (provinces) of the now defunct empire according to the boundaries drawn up in the secret 1916 Sykes-Picot agreement in which France controlled Syria and Lebanon and Britain controlled Iraq, Jordan, and Palestine (Fromkin, 1989). The second development was formal dismemberment of the Ottoman Empire in the Treaty of Lausanne in 1923 and the abrogation by the Turkish nationalist Mustafa Kemal Atatürk of the sultanate in 1922 and the Islamic caliphate in 1924.

The third development was England's Balfour Declaration of 1917, which promised predominantly European Zionists a Jewish "national home" in Palestine.

Contrary to the assumptions of conventional security studies, the arrival of the modern state system did not create an entirely new ordering of identity and difference and insecurities tied exclusively to the problems of territorial states. Fears of the threat posed to the region by Western colonialism and aspirations for unity and cultural renewal survived World War I and were even intensified because of the greater presence and visibility of the West. The central issue of regional political life remained the desire to end European colonial rule and to achieve self-determination and sovereign independence. World War I had intensified nationalist discourses and empowered the drive to eliminate racial discrimination and national oppression in the international system. The League of Nations' promise of eventual autonomy and even statehood to the populations of mandated territories provided the vocabulary and principles from which Arab intellectuals and activists could draw in their attempt to combat colonial rule. The resolution of the General Syrian Congress in 1920 stated that the "Arab nation" had taken part in the war on the basis of

> President Wilson's open declaration of the noble principles calling for the freedom and the independence of peoples, large and small, on a footing of equal rights, the ending of the policy of conquest and colonization, the abolition of secret treaties which are prejudicial to the rights of nations, and the granting of the right of self-determination to the liberated peoples. (Khalil, 1962: 5)

Aspirations for self-determination were now constructed around a new geography of self and other in which Arabic-speaking people increasingly began to think of themselves as a distinctive "Arab" people with corresponding rights to sovereign statehood (Khalidi et al., 1991). But once again there existed different interpretations both of the nature of the threat posed to the region by Western colonialism and of the boundaries of community from which to claim sovereign independence from the West.

The dominant interpretation of Arab independence and nationalism was embodied in broadly the same class of notables and elites who had been locally dominant under the Ottomans (Khouri, 1991). This highly Westernized group had a narrow view of the problem of the West. To be independent and sovereign, in the language of the time, was to have internal autonomy and be a member of the League of Nations. But it did not exclude (in fact it almost implied) a permanent relationship with the former occupying power: the maintenance of military bases and economic and cultural links, the subordination of policy in major matters of foreign relations (Hourani, 1983: 345). Arab nationalism was understood more in terms of a cultural orientation than as an ideology with political consequences. As Khalidi has pointed out, "contrary to the mistaken impression held by many, it is not the case that Arab Nationalism was or is necessarily synonymous with pan-Arabism, that is, with the idea that all Arabs should live in a single great Arab nation-state" (1991: 1365). During this period, this general platform for Arab unity was largely in the hands of the dynastic ambitions of the pro-British Hashemite rulers of Iraq and Transjordan who sought geographically specific forms of "Fertile Crescent" unity or "Greater Syrian unity," respectively, both of which excluded Egypt and the Arabian peninsula from their schemes (Porath, 1986: 4–22). These views eventually led, with British blessing, to the establishment, by the representatives of Egypt, Syria, Jordan, Iraq, Lebanon, Saudi Arabia, and Yemen, of the Arab League of States in 1945 based on the principle of respect for the sovereignty of its member states. The primary security concern of these states was understood in terms of limited self-determination, aligned with Britain, prevention of mass-based anticolonial movements, and the preservation of elite rule in politics and economics.

This position was opposed by largely oppositional figures and movements who believed that these elites had not recognized the Western intention to perpetuate colonial domination by other means (Hourani, 1983: 341–73). These groups held up the secret Mandate division of the region, Britain's Balfour Declaration of support for a Jewish homeland in Palestine, and the strict limitations on regional independence as examples both of Western hostility toward the Arabs and of Arab weakness (Dawn, 1988). For Arabs to become *truly* independent and sovereign, they had to resist the West's political, economic, and cultural imperialism and its attempt to divide regional peoples. This more radical set of beliefs was first announced in the Arab National Covenant formulated at the Arab National Congress meeting in Jerusalem in 1931, which was based on three principles:

1. The Arab countries constitute an indivisible unit; the Arab nation does not acquiesce in any sense to the fragmentation which it has been undergoing.
2. The efforts of all the Arab countries shall be directed towards one objective, namely their complete independence and unity, and the combating of every idea which aims at restricting Arab efforts to local and provincial policies.
3. As imperialism, in all its forms and types, is diametrically opposed to the dignity and great objective of the Arab nation, the Arab nation will reject it and resist it with all its might. (Khalil, 1962: 8)

Moreover the conflict with colonialism came to be conceived in a way that sharpened the notion of an irreconcilable cultural contradiction between the East and the West. They rejected the narrow territorial nationalism that had not liberated them from colonial rule, in favor of broader suprastate unities from which to confront colonialism (Gershoni and Jankowski, 1995: 215).

This oppositional discourse of regional unity found its most severe expression in the rise of more explicitly pan-Arab nationalist and Islamic groups and movements in Egypt and the Arab East such as the Ba'ath Party and the Ikhwan al-Muslimin (Muslim Brotherhood). Despite similarities, each had a different view of the specific danger posed by the West.

Radical pan-Arab nationalists sought to sever more completely the region's ties with the West. The Ba'ath Party, founded in Damascus in the 1940s under the slogan "one Arab nation with an eternal mission," played an important role in spreading the pan-Arab nationalist idea in Lebanon, Jordan, and Iraq, as well as in Syria (Devlin, 1991). This Arab nationalist view stressed the natural unity of the Arab peoples and the severity of the threat posed by Western colonialism to Arab society and culture (Dawn, 1988). Its leading ideologue, Michel Aflaq, condemned the West for fragmenting the Arab world and for culturally corrupting it by "Europeanizing" Islam (Donohue and Esposito, 1982: 107–12). In a somewhat mystical register, the Ba'ath claimed that what was needed was a double transformation: first of the intellect and soul and then of the political and social systems. This new form of Arab nationalism was not hostile toward Islam, but it was seen less as a divinely inspired faith than as an integral element of the Arab heritage. Influenced by the rise of socialist and communist movements in the region, the Ba'ath Party

gradually placed a greater emphasis on the need for social revolution, including programs for the redistribution of wealth, national
ownership of public resources, and limitation of private ownership
of land (Devlin, 1991: 1398–99).

The belief that the West was the central military and cultural
threat to the welfare of Islam and Muslims was given political expression by a number of Islamic groups and movements that developed extensive networks of activists across the region, notably the
Ikhwan al-Muslimin founded by Hassan al-Banna in 1928. One of
the central aims of the Ikhwan was to revive the Islamic caliphate in
order to counter the divisions among Arabs and Muslims that made
them vulnerable to colonial aggression (Abdelnasser, 1994: 34–36).
The greatest danger was cultural Westernization through the introduction of European laws and educational systems that were believed to be designed to guarantee the West's permanent domination
of Muslim countries and peoples (Donohue and Esposito, 1982:
78–83). As Ikhwan founder Hassan al-Banna argued, "[t]his drastic,
well-organized campaign had a tremendous success, since it was rendered most attractive to the mind, and would continue to exert a
strong intellectual influence over a long period of time. For this reason, it was more dangerous than the political and military campaigns
so far" (in Abu-Rabi, 1996: 81).

The Mandate period witnessed the crystallization of contending
discourses of insecurity among Arab peoples. Despite the growing
differences between Arab nationalist and Islamist movements over
the nature of the Western threat, neither believed that the struggle
against Western colonialism could be limited to simply obtaining the
sovereign recognition of separate regional states from the West.

PAN-ARABIST DISCOURSES OF INSECURITY

The termination of the colonial mandates following World War II
sharpened the debate over the actual terms of independence and sovereignty of regional states because European powers still controlled
the foreign and domestic policies of most Arab states. The establishment of the state of Israel in 1948 and the belief that the Arabs had
"lost" Palestine heightened concerns about regional weakness and
disunity. The "loss" of Palestine instigated a far-reaching debate
about the reasons for Arab failure. It was seen as a reminder that,
whatever had been Arab glories and achievements in past, the Arab

world was now in decline and at the mercy of others in its own region.

The widespread belief that the Arab states and elites had failed to defend their fellow Arabs in Palestine largely because they were too closely identified with the Western powers led to a series of coups and challenges to the veteran state elites (Seale, 1986). The spread of pan-Arabist discourses of insecurity was strengthened by Nasser's rise to power in Egypt after 1952. Nasser adopted a view of regional insecurity that came to coincide with the discourses of insecurity that informed the many pan-Arabist groups and activists who were challenging regional elites and Western colonial rule. As Nasser claimed at the peak of pan-Arab nationalism in the region in 1958:

> The forces of imperialism have spared no effort in their active attempts to alienate the heart of the Arabs and to divide them artificially into countries, states, clans and parties, and to sow the seed of discord and hatred among them. These forces have likewise sought to destroy Arab nationalism at the very heart of the Arab Nation, in Palestine, and to establish Zionist nationalism in its place. (In Abdel-Malek, 1968: 258)

How Nasser gradually came to adopt this position is instructive. Initially, the most pressing concern for Nasser was the continued presence of foreign troops in the region, including the British in Iraq, in Jordan, and especially along the Suez Canal in Egypt. He "regarded the perpetuation of Britain's and France's privileged position in the Suez canal as incompatible with the kind of sovereignty that they would claim for themselves and, in principle, all states" (Piscatori, 1990: 134). But it was the pressure put on Nasser to join a U.S.-orchestrated "Middle East Defense Organization" linked to NATO that eventually led him to adopt a more expansive security agenda (Gerges, 1994: 21–40). The Western powers made Egyptian requests for arms and loans for economic development projects conditional on joining such a collective security pact, which led Nasser to consider such conditions a threat to Egyptian political and economic security and sovereignty.

Nasser's own views were profoundly influenced by his involvement with the nonaligned movement of Third World states that sought to remove themselves from the status of objects of the Cold War rivalry between East and West (Abdel-Malek, 1968: 222–29; cf.

Muppidi, this volume). This movement claimed that Third World states had been denied "equal sovereignty" with other members in the international system, which was understood as the right and capacity of all states to pursue their independent state missions in the world (Bull, 1984: 220). The primary threats to the achievement of equal sovereignty lay in external pressures to enter into Cold War security alliances, in "neocolonial" privileges still maintained in many Third World states, and in the broader hierarchies of wealth and power that characterized the international system. Nasser claimed that "our participation in any pact would destroy our sovereignty, would make us followers in regard to our foreign policy and would completely destroy Arab nationalism" (Khalil, 1962: 281). With their sovereignty compromised, it was necessary to forge international alliances with like-minded Third World states in order to enhance and protect their sovereignty (Gupta, 1992).

Nasser adopted this concern for equal sovereignty and nonalignment but redefined it in the terms of pan-Arab nationalism. Nasser drew on the emerging discourses of Arab nationalism but, unlike the Ba'ath Party's concern for cultural renewal, his primary concern was the struggle for equality in the international system and the fight against political and economic neocolonialism. Nasser's confrontation with the Muslim Brotherhood in Egypt in 1954 and his opposition to the pro-Western path chosen by overtly Islamic countries such as Saudi Arabia, led him to adopt a more clearly nationalist-secularist attitude in his version of Arab unity (Gerges, 1994: 39–40).

This discourse of regional Arab insecurity informed Nasser's forthright opposition to the Western-inspired regional security scheme known as the Baghdad Pact, founded upon a Turkish-Iraqi-Pakistani military alliance in 1955 under British sponsorship with indirect U.S. participation (Seale, 1986). Nasser made the refusal to join the Western-sponsored pact a central marker of the boundary between legitimate Arab nationalists and illegitimate collaborators with imperialism: "any Arab state which thinks of acceding to the Turco-Pakistani Pact would not only forsake the Arab League but would also bind itself with Anglo-American imperialism" (in Meyer, 1980: 91). To the pro-Western Arab states, the paramount security concern was the threat of Communism and internal social revolution. They believed that it was natural for them to side with the West in order to defend themselves from that threat (Gerges, 1994: 26). For the pan-Arabists, external security alliances of any kind were considered a threat to regional independence and sovereignty based on a broader Arab solidarity. Such a stance toward the meaning of sovereignty exasperated and confounded U.S. policymakers, such as Secretary of State Allen Dulles, who stated his concern:

> Now the thing we are up against is a rather extreme view which the Arab countries in general, and Egypt in particular take on this thing which they call nationalization and "sovereignty." Nasser can hardly speak more than a couple of sentences but what he has to bring in "sovereignty"—"sovereignty"—they apparently conceive it as being the right to prove that you can step on other people's toes with impunity. But we all know, who have some maturity in these matters, that sovereignty—its best expression involves the harmonization of policies, coordinating them and working for the common good. But countries that have newly won their wings of independence incline toward taking initially an extreme view. They are hypersensitive about this thing. (March 24, 1957; in Meyer, 1980: 29)

The struggle between these contending visions of sovereignty and regional security was heightened following the 1956 Suez crisis in which Nasser, after Britain and the United States refused to fund the Aswan High Dam, defied the West and nationalized the Suez Canal. Nasser claimed to be asserting the right of economic sovereignty and laying the economic foundations for Arab unity. Despite being rescued from sure military defeat by the United States and USSR following the invasion of Egypt by Israel, France, and Britain, Nasser's prestige and popularity intensified in the region. The crisis provoked massive demonstrations in support of Arab unity and forced the pro-Western regimes onto the defensive (Gerges, 1994: 64). Many of the pro-Western regimes, such as Iraq, Jordan, and Saudi Arabia, were compelled to distance themselves from the 1957 U.S. announcement of the Eisenhower Doctrine, which pledged to defend the region against the threat of Communist subversion (ibid., 80–81).

One of the most startling examples of the relationship between pan-Arabist discourses of insecurity and individual state sovereignties was the Egyptian and Syrian merger in 1958, which created the United Arab Republic. Nasser had initially opposed such a complete merger, preferring a more limited form of Arab solidarity on the grounds that the time was not right to collapse the existing regional states into larger units (Seale, 1986: 325). But Western opposition to pan-Arabist aspirations and fears of Western intervention in Syria heightened insecurities such that comprehensive Arab unity was seen as a necessary response. Nasser clearly articulated the linkage between Arab unity and security:

> By Arab nationalism we mean that we should be independent and that independence is born of our conscience. We should no longer be in servitude to any other country or to imperialism, any more than we should be a part of any sphere of influence. That is what Arab nationalism is: Arab nationalism is union, unity, solidarity, which should be erected on the rights, the interests of the Arabs and not on those of imperialism or spheres of influence. . . . That is why, from the very first day of this Revolution, we were led to declare that *Arab nationalism constituted the only possible security for an Arab country.* We said that the defense of the Arab nationalism should arise out of its own inner being and not from pacts dominated by the Great Powers. (In Abdel-Malek, 1968: 258–59; emphasis added)

The United Arab Republic collapsed in 1961, because of the belief by many Syrians that it had become an instrument of Nasserist hegemony. Although this development was a blow to Nasser's vision of Arab unity, it did not significantly alter the contending discourses of regional insecurity that divided the region in the following decade. By the end of the 1960s, however, Nasser became a victim of the very pan-Arabist discourse of insecurity that he had labored to produce. In the pan-Arabist view, Israel was not seen, as in the West, as a tiny nation struggling for its existence, but rather as an international colossus serving as the vanguard of Western imperialism in the region (Peretz, 1966). Therefore, when Israeli attempts to divert water from the Jordan River led Syria to call for a united Arab front against Israel, Nasser was compelled to conclude a comprehensive defense agreement that committed Egypt to Syria's defense in case of an Israeli attack (Piscatori, 1990: 139–40). Nasser was thrust into an alliance with the new Ba'ath leadership in Syria, which was bent on restoring the Arab nationalist revolution across the Middle East. When Nasser finally took confrontational steps toward Israel by calling for the removal of UN forces from the Sinai Peninsula in May 1967, the Israeli military struck in lightning fashion, taking the Golan Heights, the West Bank, the Gaza Strip, and the entire Sinai Peninsula in six days.

ISLAMIST DISCOURSES OF INSECURITY

Since the 1967 war, the region has witnessed the emergence of a new oppositional discourse of insecurity that has challenged the sovereign claims of many states and regimes. A central reason for this development lay in the complete and decisive Arab defeat at the hands of Israel, which shattered confidence in Arab nationalism and confirmed for many the belief that the West was innately hostile to Arab interests (Haddad, 1980). Despite the end of the Mandates and national independence, the Arab world remained at the mercy of external powers, symbolized by Israeli military domination within the region. Moreover, European colonialism had been replaced by the United States' extensive regional military presence, its multinational corporations, and its unquestioned support for Israel.

The defeat of 1967 was seen not simply as a military defeat but as a moral judgment on the leaders and political projects who were responsible for it (Esposito, 1991: 154–55). Was the speed and ease of Arab defeat not a sign that there was a deeper problem, that something was corrupt about their societies and even their moral systems? Many began to turn away from Arab nationalism and toward the heritage of Islam (Donohue, 1983). This emphasis on Islam manifested itself across the Middle East in a growing split between regimes and their opposition, a split based in part on different interpretations of the nature of the threats that confronted the region.

For states and elites, the ascendance of Saudi oil wealth provided vigorous Islamic direction to the Arab world. King Faisal set in motion diplomatic conferences, funded academic programs and activities throughout the region promoting an Islamic alternative to the radical pan-Arab nationalism that had always threatened Saudi claims to sovereignty. A series of unparalleled developments during the 1970s was widely interpreted as signifying a change in Muslim fortunes. The most important was the Arab–Israeli war of 1973, led by Egypt and Syria, which became known as the Ramadan War after the sacred month of fasting during which it occurred. The surprising initial success of the Egyptian and Syrian forces was seen as a reversal of the Arab defeat of 1967 and widely interpreted as an "Islamic victory" (Esposito, 1991: 155). Its code name was "Badr," the first major victory for Islam led by the Prophet himself. The Arab oil embargo demonstrated Arab/Muslim economic power and instilled a new sense of regional strength. Even regimes based on more secular ruling ideologies, such as those in Syria, Iraq, and Algeria, began adopting Islamic symbols and certain elements of the *shari'a* (Islamic law) as the basis of legislation and law.

The initial emphasis on a return to Islam was directed primarily by regional state elites and, more importantly, by those states closely allied to and heavily dependent on the United States, such as Saudi Arabia and Anwar Sadat's Egypt. These states downplayed the confrontation with the West, focused on narrow issues of social and cultural authenticity, and sought to diffuse more radical attempts to ground Islamic revivalism in a confrontation with the West (Roy, 1994: 107–31). In contrast, the widespread popular disaffection with the West and criticism of its double standards in its dealing with Israel and the Arabs began to take a more central role in the discourses of oppositional Islamist movements that began to emerge in nearly every Arab state (Haddad, 1996: 424–26). Where regional elites saw growing regional strength, these movements saw increasing weakness and dependence on the West.

The stunning success of the 1979 Islamic revolution in Iran emboldened many Islamist activists in the region and fortified their belief that steadfast commitment to the cause of Islam could topple a regime armed and supported by Israel and the United States. For example, in Saudi Arabia, Islamic insurgents took over the main mosque in Mecca in 1979; in Iraq, underground Islamic groups challenged the Ba'athist government; in Egypt, Islamist activists confronted Anwar Sadat's regime, which launched a massive roundup of its Islamic political opponents in 1981, which eventually led to his assassination; and in Syria, a 1982 armed Islamist uprising in the city of Hama was brutally suppressed.

What was new about this oppositional Islamic activism was neither the call for an Islamic revival in order to confront the threat of the West nor the criticism of the corruption of existing Muslim elites. What was new about this Islamic activism was both its desire for a more severe break with the West and its unwillingness to compromise with existing states and regimes. The beliefs of these new radical groups had crystallized in the 1960s, especially among circles of Muslim Brothers imprisoned under Nasser. The main articulator of this new radical outlook was Sayyid Qutb, who had been jailed and executed by Nasser (Abu-Rabi, 1996; Choueiri, 1994). Qutb had argued that the postcolonial nation-state and nationalist movements did not stem the tide of Western domination and cultural hegemony. By contrast, Qutb argued that the governments and societies of the contemporary Muslim world had slipped back into *Jahiliyya* (a period of religious unbelief). Qutb argued:

> We are also surrounded by *jahiliyah* today, which is of the same nature as it was during the first period of Islam, perhaps a little deeper. Our whole environment, people's beliefs and ideas, habits and art, rules and laws—is *jahiliyah*, even to the extent that what we consider to be Islamic culture, Islamic sources, Islamic philosophy and Islamic thought, are also constructs of *jahiliyah*. (In Abu-Rabi, 1996: 180)

It was incumbent on Muslims, therefore, to restore the central role of Islam, particularly the *shari'a*, in society and to establish *hakmiyat allah* (sovereignty of God) on earth in order to reestablish a moral link between government and society (Choueiri, 1994: 123–24).

This radical perspective has led to a polarization within the regional Islamic movement as Qutb's followers moved increasingly into opposition movements across the Arab world, and others even withdrew from *Jahiliyya* society and formed more militant groups. Some of the latter groups prepared for martyrdom and military opposition, resulting in the assassination of Anwar Sadat in 1981 and the disastrous attempt by the Muslim Brothers in Syria to overthrow the regime of Hafiz al-Asad in 1982. By contrast, the mainstream of the Islamic movement, consisting of the Muslim Brotherhood within and outside Egypt and a great many sheikhs and Muslim activists, has avoided the risks of imposing Islamization by force and seeks to build a vibrant and unified Islamic society from the bottom up through gradual social reform and political pressure (Dekmejian, 1995: 213–20).

Despite significant differences among regional Islamist groups and activists, there has emerged a remarkably similar discourse of insecurity centered on the need to establish an authentic cultural basis from which to assert the sovereignty of Arab states and to achieve true decolonization (Abdelnasser, 1994; Abu-Rabi, 1996). This discourse differs from that of the pan-Arabists because it defines true sovereignty in terms of a radical alterity or alienation in relation to European international society rather than in terms of equality within the existing international system.[9] While pan-Arabists largely located threats to the region in the practices of external actors and their control of local collaborators, Islamists have focused on the way in which external threats have been internalized in the very practices of Middle Eastern states. The primary threat for many Islamic activists is the capitulation of regional leaders and societies to cultural Westernization. The primary goal of Western colonialism has always been the weakening of Islamic doctrine and, ultimately, of Muslims themselves in order to perpetuate Muslim subordination. As a result, a major premise of contemporary Islamism is that Islam cannot be practiced except in the context of an Islamic political system. This assumption has led Islamist activists to seek to establish Islamic states—based on a comprehensive system of Islamic law, government, education, and ethics—across the region.

For more radical currents of Islamic activism, for whom the threat of the West is understood in terms of a cultural invasion and for whom the existing states and regimes have sunk into a state of *Jahiliyya,* there has been a renewed call for unity through the revival of the Islamic *umma* (Abdelnasser, 1994: 96–116). The defeat of 1967 was a defeat of Arab nationalism and of the logic of the nation-state that had claimed the monopoly of legitimacy in Arab countries. In contrast to Hasan al-Banna's call in the 1930s for respecting Arab nationalism as a step toward Muslim unity, the call for Islamic unity is now often based on the demand for eradicating the narrow-minded nationalism or ethnic patriotism that divides Muslims (ibid., 99). Although many believe that Arab nationalism remains a step toward Islamic unity that should be accommodated, for others it has become outmoded and should be superseded.

In these Islamist discourses of insecurity, Israel is still seen as an extension of Western imperialism in the region. The dramatic victory of Israel in 1967 and the capture of the holy city of Jerusalem was interpreted by many Islamists as part of a broader Western plan to frustrate Muslim aspirations. Israel, supported by the United States, was seen as committed to keeping Muslims in a subservient state. The Lebanese Islamist leader Muhammad Husayn Fadlallah claims that Israel and the question of Palestine are central to contemporary Islamism:

> To my mind the question of Palestine, as a result of its unique nature, position, allusions and the political impact it has had on the Muslim

world, summarizes in a nutshell the movement of Islamic history in this age. In its genesis, the Palestine question represents the conflict between Islam and British colonialism, that was intersected by a conflict between Islam and the Zionist movement. The Palestine question has led to a general conflict between Islam and the West. (In Abu-Rabi, 1996: 240)

Muslim fears were magnified both by Israeli policies in the 1970s, which called for the "Judaization" of Jerusalem and the remainder of historic Palestine, and by the coming to power in 1977 of the Likud Party, which referred to the occupied Palestinian territories by the biblical names of Judea and Samaria (Haddad, 1992: 268). The 1982 Israeli invasion of Lebanon, and its relentless bombardment of "Muslim" West Beirut, among other things, enhanced the perception that only Islamic unity of some kind could empower people to liberate Palestine and confront the broader "Crusader-Zionist" efforts to destroy Islam (ibid., 270). But the problem of Palestine is also seen in terms of Muslims being recognized as having full rights and equal status in determining their own future, a belief that cuts across the spectrum of Islamist opinion.

The present Islamic revival and its discourses of insecurity cannot be reduced to the misleading label "fundamentalism," which implies a literalist and conservative attitude to the Scriptures that is not found in contemporary Islamic revivalism (Utvik, 1995: 30–31). Nor can it be reduced to a homogeneous, antimodernist, and irrationally anti-Western movement (Lewis, 1990). Like other religious traditions, Islam is composed of many heterogeneous elements and disagreements. Yet, what is arguably the most important feature of contemporary Islamism has been its call for cultural decolonization and independence from the West (Abu-Rabi, 1996). At its broadest, the Islamist movement is an effort to reconnect with an indigenous system of references in order to change the rules of political discourse by compelling political debate to adopt a language in which references are taken from the moral traditions of Islam. As two astute commentators argue:

The ideological and symbolic terrain now provides the framework for seeking a balance of power after decolonization. . . . One cannot express the rejection of the West, using its language and its terminology. How better to mark the distance, how better to satisfy the demand for an identity, than to employ a language that is different from its own, along with a system of codes and symbols that seem foreign to it? (Burgat and Dowell, 1993: 64)

What most observers have been unable to recognize is that, in Bobby Sayyid's formulation, this project amounts to a "continuation and radicalization of the process of decolonization," a decolonization whose scope lies far beyond that of Arab nationalist programs articulated immediately following colonialism, and whose terms of enunciation may have no "precedent in modern political discourses" (Sayyid, 1994: 281).

CONCLUSION

The regional responses to the Iraqi invasion of Kuwait and the Gulf War with which this chapter began can be traced to contending interpretations of security and sovereignty resulting from the region's colonial encounter with the West, which profoundly shaped the nature of communal identities and orientations to danger. Since that time, the region has witnessed a linkage between a pervasive discourse of insecurity about Western power in the international system and recurrent calls for regional unity and solidarity at the expense of individual sovereign states. This linkage was clearly articulated during the Gulf War. Such a linkage cannot be understood in terms of an enduring "clash of civilizations" (Huntington, 1993) or an endemic anti-Western "Muslim rage" (Lewis, 1990). Nor can the regional discourses of insecurity about the West be reduced to a sociological condition of "weakness" and an ahistorical clash between "state" and precolonial "communal" notions of security.

Politics in the Middle East, as elsewhere, is an effect of global power relations and struggles in the region are located within the broader discursive economy through which global power and authority are exercised. The frequent disregard for the security and sovereignty of existing regional states by regional actors is a product of the widespread regional belief that sovereignty and self-determination cannot be obtained with the existing Western-dominated regional and global order. This challenge has led many Western policymakers to consider such movements as pan-Arab nationalism and contemporary Islamism to be major threats to the international system. If the specter of Islamic "fundamentalism" replaces communism as the principal perceived threat to Western civilization and norms, as seems to be the case, then it is incumbent on scholars and citizens to examine not only the insecurities and aspirations that drive such movements but also the historical processes that constructed the cultural opposition between "our" supposed civilization and international norms and "their" imagined backwardness and fanaticism.

NOTES

1. This chapter will focus primarily on the discourses of insecurity that have characterized those states of the modern Middle East created out of the remains of the Ottoman Empire whose dominant linguistic and cultural identity has been constituted as Arab.

2. It should be noted that Walt, working within the positivist research tradition, uses the case of the Middle East in order to test his amended formulation of the standard realist theoretical approach to state action and "security dilemmas" best represented by Kenneth Waltz (1979) and Robert Jervis (1978).

3. For work on security in the Third World, see Ayoob (1995), Buzan (1991), and Job (1992).

4. For example, the Korany volume argues that the lack of congruence between cultural communities and territorial borders "goes deeper than problems of border demarcation and is related to the imposition of an (alien) state structure on a (forged) nation. The result is the impression of a state at war with its own society . . . and also that society at war with itself" (Korany et al., 1993: 12).

5. This chapter seeks to further an engagement between the study of international politics and security and the growing interdisciplinary field of postcolonial studies (Darby and Paolini, 1994; Walker, 1984; see also Muppidi, this volume). Some important statements of the general concerns of postcolonial theory and criticism include Breckenridge and van der Veer (1993), Prakash (1995), and Moore-Gilbert (1997).

6. The tendency to ascribe political dynamics in the Middle East to inherent and unchanging essences peculiar to the region is symptomatic of a longstanding tradition of thought and analysis that Edward Said (1979) has tellingly critiqued as the discourse of Orientalism.

7. My use of the term *postcolonial* in this context should not be understood as a monolithic or temporal category that overlooks the multiplicity of contexts that may be termed postcolonial and the continuities with "colonialism" that are often referred to as "neocolonialism." See the important

critical commentaries on the term *postcolonial* by McClintock (1992) and Shohat (1992), as well as Stuart Hall's review of this debate (1996).

8. This conception of "counterstate" movements has been shaped by Richard Ashley's discussion of what he called "transversal struggles," which are "conflicts that traverse all political boundaries because they are conflicts over the interpretation of the sovereign man in whose terms states, domestic societies, and their political boundaries shall be defined" (Ashley, 1989: 270). These struggles are not simply interstate conflicts or domestic conflicts but rather trans-state conflicts because they are conducted by both state and nonstate actors across existing political boundaries.

9. This formulation draws on the arguments of Blaney (1992: 220) about pan-Africanist movements.

6

Peacekeeping, Indifference, and Genocide in Rwanda

MICHAEL N. BARNETT

I was on the Delta Shuttle from New York to Washington on April 6, 1994, when I first learned, by way of the *New York Times,* that the plane carrying President Juvenal Habyarimana of Rwanda mysteriously crashed as it approached the Kigali airport. My first response was to study the face of the dead president; after closely covering his comings and goings for the past several months, it struck me as odd that the first time I would see his face was in a newspaper article announcing his death. Then I felt frustration bordering on exasperation. As a political officer at the U.S. Mission to the United Nations who was assigned to cover Rwanda, I had spent the last part of March consumed by the negotiations on the mandate extension of the United Nations Operation in Rwanda (UNAMIR). Peacekeeping operations are given six-month operating periods. Toward the end of the term, the Secretariat writes a report with observations on and recommendations for the operation, and the Security Council then debates the conditions for extending the mandate, and whether to continue it at all.

Although many of the debates have a scripted quality that foreordains renewal, this instance was uncharacteristically lengthy and contentious. UNAMIR was charged with overseeing the implementation of the Arusha Accords, the blueprint to end the civil war between the Tutsi-backed Rwandan Patriotic Forces (RPF) and the Hutu-dominated Rwandan government and to install a new, more representative, government. For some months the Rwandan government had been dragging its heels and failing to produce the transitional government, leaving many on the Security Council increasingly irritated. The U.S. position was that the Rwandan government should be notified that unless it quickly established the transitional government, the UN operation would be closed. How strong these signals should be, and how serious should be the threat to close the operation, was a principal point of contention during these negotiations over the mandate's extension. The Security Council approved an extension just as the mandate expired in early April, the United States was satisfied that its concerns were communicated to the Rwandan government (which happened to be a member of the Security Council), and I was relieved finally to have Rwanda off my desk and now to be able to turn my attention to other matters. The president's death changed all that, for bad and for good. Exhausted from the hectic pace, I would now not have my long-awaited break. Still, Rwanda rarely commanded front-page news as it was now doing, and I could look forward to a thankful departure from the daily monotonous routine.

As it so happens, I was going to Washington to meet the various people in the State Department from whom I received my instructions on Rwanda and other peacekeeping operations. Beginning in January 1994, I was assigned primary responsibility for the peacekeeping operations in Rwanda, Burundi, and Mozambique, and became the backup officer for the rest of sub-Saharan Africa. Such responsibilities entailed a never-ending stream of phone calls to various parts of the State Department that had some input into these operations. Before the death of Habyarimana, the agenda for my trip to Washington was to make the rounds, meet my bureaucratic counterparts, and discuss the various operations. Now I was anxious to hear about what was happening in Kigali.

I was greeted by my contact person from the Bureau of International Organization, who had little news but was eager to bring me upstairs to the recently established Situation Room. The "Sit Room"—assembled at the outset of any crisis as a nerve center for receiving and coordinating information—had three banks of phones, roughly twenty people milling in and out, and a makeshift map of Rwanda on the wall, the only marker of why we were all there. As we entered the room, my contact person gathered everyone's attention to relay news of the current situation on the ground in Kigali, which was rather little and highly speculative. She then asked each of us to introduce ourselves. When my turn came I was given a special introduction by my contact: I was the person at the U.S. Mission to the United Nations who followed Rwanda. The subtext was that I was a Rwanda expert. My credentials established, those nearest to me immediately asked me to provide some basic background on the country, as well as the military positions and strengths of the government; the RPF and the UN forces; their anticipated moves; and what the Security Council was likely to do. To my amazement, I handled these and other questions with a degree of assuredness and authority expected of someone of my position. I then called my contacts at the UN Department of Peacekeeping Operations (DPKO), who gave me a more alarming and complete picture of developments on the ground. I relayed the information to those around me, solidifying my credentials as an expert on Rwanda.

That I might be presented as a Rwanda expert still strikes me as rather incongruous. After all, I teach international politics at the University of Wisconsin, feel most comfortable in the world of theory rather than in the world of facts, and any claim to regional expertise is limited to the Middle East. That I became an expert on Rwanda is a testimony to the Council of Foreign Relations, which offers a unique fellowship program that places academics somewhere in the government ostensibly to carry out a research project, but in fact to become part of the policy-making process. I served at the U.S. Mission to the United Nations from August 1993 to August 1994, and held the title of Adviser for Peacekeeping Operations (at least so my business cards announced) at the suggestion of my immediate superior. More accurately, I was a political officer (sometimes referred to as an "action officer"). My responsibilities included reading cable traffic on my issue, writing talking points for the ambassadors, hosting various Washington officials when they visited the United Nations, covering my issue in the Security Council and writing cables on its proceedings, receiving instructions from Washington and transmitting them to the UN, and generally acting as a conduit between Washington and the UN. Sometimes I would be asked to work on more "policy-oriented" issues such as peacekeeping reform and Security Council expansion, but by and large most of the action revolved around, well, "action."

On my arrival, I was assigned to help cover Somalia, but by December the issues that I was following had all but disappeared because of the anticipated American withdrawal. So I was assigned to other parts of Africa. When Rwanda became part of my "account," my knowledge of it did not extend much beyond my ability to identify it on a map or that it was the country that had the gorillas, and my first association of Mozambique was the song of same title by Bob Dylan. My lack of knowledge seemed to trouble only myself; my superiors were, perhaps, reassured by the experience I had already gained covering Somalia and the fact that they would closely supervise my activities, and they knew better than I that in-depth knowledge of the country was not necessary to carry out my daily activities. I was a seasoned veteran of Rwanda for nearly four months when President Habyarimana of Rwanda was killed and hell erupted.

BECOMING A BUREAUCRAT

That I might be plausibly presented as a Rwanda expert can only be understood in the context of the foreign-policy bureaucracy. The foreign-policy bureaucracy, like all bureaucracies, organizes and privileges knowledge in particular ways, and in this context the knowledge that matters most was not the particulars about Rwanda but rather about the policy-making process in the U.S. government and the UN. Specifically, my standing as an expert depended on the following factors: As political officer I was, by definition, an expert. No one ever asked me for my credentials, and it would not have mattered; because Rwanda was my account, I was a Rwanda expert. It hardly mattered that when Rwanda became part of my account I knew little of its political, economic, and social structures. Although I soon learned the basic parameters of the country and the conflict, my day was consumed with back-to-back "fires" that precluded the luxury of "getting smart" on the subject. The other political officer at the U.S. Mission who covered Africa could claim greater expertise by virtue of the fact that she had been covering the topic in recent years, not from any formal training or visits. Expert status, in short, had little to do with real knowledge and much to do with my bureaucratic position. My status as an expert also derived from my possession of the "facts" of the bureaucracy: who handled what issues, who had access to key decision makers, who my counterparts were in other missions to the United Nations and other departments in Washington, what had transpired in the Security Council, and what the precise language of past mandates was. Knowledge of some of these facts and having the Rwanda account went some distance in defining me as an expert.

More fundamentally, my expertise derived from my knowledge of the culture of the foreign-policy bureaucracy, that is, its discourse and rules for appropriate language selection, the symbols that are connected to that language, and the norms of interaction, in both practices and language choice, that mark insiders from outsiders. This knowledge of the culture enabled me to understand what knowledge was relevant; the symbols that were emotionally charged; the subtext to conversations; what was said and what was not said; how to formulate questions, responses, and talking points; how information was framed and arguments were constructed; and generally how to use language that was consistent with the understandings and discourses of my superiors and my colleagues. Whether I was accepted and effective, my very status and credentials in the eyes of my colleagues were dependent on acting in a manner that was consistent with that culture.

My awareness of and becoming comfortable with this culture was a slow and often awkward process. When I first arrived at the U.S. Mission I knew little of the language and understood few of the symbols. My colleagues could speak full sentences in acronyms that I had never heard of, slang that referred to events and processes that I had no knowledge of, and easily transformed nouns such as *démarche* into verbs. Unable to speak the language or understand the subtext to conversations left me feeling generally alienated and confused. Events and symbols that would make my colleagues take notice would have little effect on me; other incidents and symbols that would cause me to panic would leave my colleagues paralyzed with boredom. My general bewilderment frequently led my colleagues to make somewhat playful but also derogatory references to my "academic" status. I had left the ivory tower for the real world, they told me. Although I never conceded that their world was the "real" one, there was no arguing that this was a world that had its own internal logic, symbols, and language, and I was truly an outsider. Still, within several months I became comfortable with the cultural terrain.

A good illustration of this was my experience learning to write reporting cables, accounts of events, meetings, and developments that might be relevant to U.S. policy or someone, somewhere, in the foreign-policy bureaucracy. A good cable has various characteristics, and at first my cables had few of them. Initially my cables were "academic," reminiscent of my notes from graduate seminars: exhaustive, analytic, dense, aspiring to reach some mythical Archimedean point that incorporated the complexities of the issue, the details of the meetings, and the views of all those in attendance. Yet, this attention to detail and assumption that cables were to report the "facts" completely overlooked the basic point that cables are political documents; and, as political documents, cables are expected to articulate a narrative that weaves together various worldviews, perspectives, and interests that derive from personal, bureaucratic, and U.S.-centered positions.

My task as a political officer was to report on events in which my superiors were directly involved or interested, or for which they had bureaucratic responsibility. Simply put, I had to "clear" these cables by the same individuals on whom I was reporting or who had a direct interest in the issue. Not surprisingly, they were concerned at least as much with making sure that they were presented favorably and protected from bureaucratic rivals as with "getting the story right." A good cable, I learned, is not only clear and succinct; it also offers an account of an event that is consistent with the interests, both personal and bureaucratic, of one's superiors. For instance, my cables had to portray the U.S. representatives as sharp, alert, and probing. Their gaffes, no matter how consequential, nearly always went unreported, and the sequence of events could be rearranged if it improved their presentation. An important goal of any cable, in short, is to present a narrative that protects and promotes one's superiors.

Yet, cables also were to reflect the bureaucratic interests and the worldview of the U.S. Mission to the United Nations in general and the Political Section in particular. Those in Washington believed that we in New York had "gone native," that is, that we were reflexively pro-UN and peacekeeping, had little sensitivity to how U.S. policy toward the UN was to reflect the interests of the United States and not the UN, and were naive about U.S. domestic and Washington politics. We in New York believed that those in Washington had little understanding of either the "politics of the UN" or how resolutions were crafted and drafted, and saw our job as having to explain to Washington how the UN and the Security Council worked and how our proposed policies were, in fact, consistent with the United States' interests. In this way, our understanding of U.S. interests was shaded by our bureaucratic position. Over time, I learned a conception of the U.S. national interest that supported the UN and peacekeeping.

An effective cable is one that is likely to be read, and a cable will only be read if it organizes knowledge and uses language in much the same way as the potential reader does. Slowly I developed the capacity to present information so that it paralleled how other bureaucrats understood and organized the world; to couch and frame my issue in ways that made sense to those on the distribution list; and to organize the narrative in order to promote the issues that I was covering and the interests that I was protecting. I became more skilled at cable writing as I more fully understood and felt comfortable with the culture.

Slowly I acquired more than the skills of a political officer—I developed the mentality and mind-set. Not only had I entered the bureaucratic world, but the bureaucratic world had entered me. My long days of intense interaction with my colleagues were slowly transforming how I understood, identified, and presented myself. Whereas once I had adopted certain practices and discourses because of their instrumentality and strategic value, now I did so because they felt consistent with who I was and how I understood myself. At various instances when I comfortably embraced the language and the practices of a political officer, my colleagues would comment on my "socialization" with chuckles and tongue-in-cheek congratulations. If once I thought of "me" and "them," I now began thinking in terms of "us." Although my identity as an academic and a visitor never disappeared for either my colleagues or myself, my presentation and practices were less strategic and mimetic and more authentic.

My new identity was tied to a particular set of interests. Whereas once I was bewildered by my colleagues' logic as they defended or promoted a particular policy, I soon became sympathetic to and supported their positions. More dramatically, if once I judged, promoted, and criticized policies depending on how they related to my "academic" preferences, I had "swallowed a dose of reality" and was now situating policies according to whether they were good or bad for the interests and reputations of, first, the United States, and, second, the UN. I more fully identified with my role as a representative of the United States to the United Nations, and I slowly identified with, developed a greater loyalty to, and took my identity from these organizations. I began to defend the policies of the United States and the potential of the UN not because to do otherwise might cause my colleagues to sanction me, but rather because I came to identify with these organizations and to see the world as those around me saw it. I was now a Rwanda expert.

RWANDA

The twenty-four hours after the death of President Habyarimana on April 6 produced the feared bloodshed. With only 2,500 lightly armed peacekeepers scattered throughout Rwanda, UNAMIR was unprepared to confront the wave of terror unleashed by Hutu extremists against Tutsis and Hutu moderates. UN troops were instantly confronted by two increasingly untenable tasks: protecting the lives of civilians and defending themselves. The tension between these two goals became immediately apparent when ten Belgian peacekeepers were brutally murdered protecting moderate Hutu politicians during the first days of the violence; the remaining Belgian troops were widely believed to be marked for assassination. If the non-Belgian peacekeepers were not at immediate risk from Hutu forces, they were running dangerously low on fuel, water, and food; moreover, resupplying or rescuing them was becoming increasingly questionable as the airport became a major battleground, raising the real possibility that any approaching aircraft might suffer the same fate as Habyarimana's. To make matters worse, the RPF was now assembling and preparing to march on Kigali. Therefore, the meager and badly supplied UN forces were confronted by two wars: the Rwandan government's terror campaign against its "enemies" and the brewing civil war between the RPF and the government.

Back in New York, the Security Council had to decide quickly what would be the future of UNAMIR and the UN's response to the growing violence. The Security Council was in almost constant session, meeting sometimes twice daily and long into the night. As I watched and participated in the debate over the Security Council's response during this critical period, I (and others around me) came to believe that the only responsible decision was to reduce UNAMIR's presence and mandate. Three factors, in my view, were most important for driving this decision. First, the Secretariat (namely, Secretary-General Boutros Boutros-Ghali's office and DPKO) gave an impression of distance and aloofness from the emerging tragedy, which only reinforced the disinclination among many member states in the Security Council to propose a greater role for UNAMIR.[1] DPKO exhibited a "business-as-usual" approach; few whom I encountered displayed much urgency. Boutros-Ghali also emanated indecision to the point of complacency. He happened to be in Europe in early April, and decided to keep to his schedule rather than returning to New York. This decision, in my view, reflected a disturbingly distant stance from the unfolding tragedy and demonstrated a troubling abdication of responsibility and leadership. Other stories concerning his demeanor were even more disturbing.

The most consequential expression of this distance was the failure by the Secretariat to offer any options to the Security Council regarding the future of UNAMIR. The Secretariat, through its recommendations and reports, shapes the Security Council's deliberations and potentially its decision. The Secretariat's agenda-setting influence was potentially enhanced in this instance because few if any member states had independent sources of information and therefore relied heavily on the Secretariat for intelligence on the conditions on the ground and for recommendations regarding UNAMIR's future. Yet, the Secretariat's reports were evasive and noncommittal, insistent that it was unable to present options at that time. My overall impression, shared by others on the Security Council, was that the Secretariat was "not up to the task" of crisis management, either being overwhelmed to the point of paralysis or insensitive to the dead peacekeepers and the escalating violence. At this moment, I became convinced that the Secretariat should not be given the responsibility of commanding troops in dangerous situations and that UNAMIR's size and responsibility needed to be reduced.

A second reason for the decision to reduce UNAMIR's role was that no country was willing to contribute its troops for an expanded operation or mandate. Although there was a brief discussion concerning the possibility of UNAMIR intervening to halt the escalating bloodshed and to protect the civilian populations, I was (and still am) unaware of a single member state that offered its troops for such an operation. Consequently, those on the Security Council, largely the nonpermanent members, who were arguing for intervention had little ammunition: the Secretariat, which would be responsible for carrying out the mandate, was silent, and silence was widely interpreted as disapproval; and no troop contributors were volunteering for an expanded force. Indeed, soon after the death of its soldiers,

Belgium, which represented the backbone of UNAMIR, announced its immediate withdrawal, and no state offered replacements.

Third, with UNAMIR's mandate to oversee the Arusha Accords effectively over, with no country willing to send its troops into an increasingly chaotic environment, and with access to the airport increasingly precarious, the Security Council had to protect its peacekeepers and the UN's reputation. This was a line most forcefully argued, in particular, by the United States; it and others consistently argued that the Security Council had a duty and obligation to protect the lives of the peacekeepers and that the failure to do so would result in a more difficult time obtaining troops for future operations, and, perhaps, a further decline in the UN's reputation. Although the Security Council was divided over the extent and timing of the drawdown, after much debate there was a general recognition that peacekeepers, unprotected and exposed, could do little good and much harm to themselves and the UN's reputation and future. I fully shared and supported this decision. On April 21, the Security Council decided to withdraw the bulk of UNAMIR and to leave in place a skeletal force to assist the ultimately unsuccessful attempt by UN Force Commander General Roméo Dallaire to fashion a cease-fire agreement between the RPF and the government.

No sooner had the Security Council voted to reduce UNAMIR's presence than it and Boutros-Ghali revisited whether and how the UN might respond to confront the increasingly evident genocide. Now recovered from his bout of indecisiveness, Boutros-Ghali began to take a visible lead, using his bully pulpit to formulate options and to urge the Security Council and the member states to respond vigorously to the continuing massacres. The Security Council, highly embarrassed that its only answer to the bloodshed was a reduction of UNAMIR, began to debate the possibility of an intervention force. But there were no volunteers for such a force. It seemed that the daily reports of carnage and brutality only contributed to the belief that it was highly improbable that a modest-sized outside force could halt the terror, and no member state was enthusiastic about sending its troops into such chaos.

When the Secretariat finally unveiled its long-awaited plan in late April, it was greeted with considerable enthusiasm by the Security Council, though more because it created an image of a UN that was poised for action than because the plan was likely to contribute to ending the genocide. Simply put, this proposal was merely symbolic and highly impractical: it proposed to dispatch five thousand troops to Kigali, acknowledged that the forces might not be located for months (if ever), and confessed that it had no real idea what they would do once they arrived. Still, the Security Council embraced this unworkable scheme not because it would rescue the Rwandans but because it would rescue the Security Council from any further embarrassment associated with its inactions. The United States rightly criticized the plan as little more than smoke and demanded that the Secretariat and others on the Security Council design a realistic proposal rather than constructing a Potemkin village. The United States, in response, circulated its own suggestions for protecting and providing relief to the growing number of refugees. Because the United States objected to this initial proposal, it was widely portrayed in the media as representing the sole obstacle to military intervention by the UN. But the U.S. position, in my view, only blocked the adoption of a proposal that was designed to save face for the Security Council and diverted energy away from recommendations that might actually help those on the ground.

No international action would be taken until late June when a UN-authorized French operation went to southern Rwanda to protect the refugees. The Security Council was unenthusiastic about France's proposed intervention. France had long-standing military and political ties to the very Hutu military that was now accused of genocide, and the Security Council feared that France would use the pretext of a humanitarian intervention to intervene on behalf of the Hutu military. But because there were no other viable options, the Security Council set aside these concerns and reluctantly approved the French operation. Soon thereafter, the United States and other states contributed humanitarian assistance (though outside the UN umbrella) to try and alleviate the suffering of an estimated 2 million refugees. UNAMIR returned to Kigali in greater numbers that fall, long after the RPF had captured the country and between five hundred thousand and eight hundred thousand people had perished in the genocide and one-quarter of the country's population had become homeless.

I left the U.S. Mission in June 1994 and returned to academic life.

As I began to write on peacekeeping and its future, I highlighted the policy implications of Rwanda and other peacekeeping operations. Most of the lessons derived from the need to protect the UN's resources and to better define the limit and scope of future UN operations in order to salvage the UN's reputation and to ensure the continuation of the member states' support. Although troubled by the Security Council's failure to take even the most minimal steps to alleviate the suffering in Rwanda, I justified the lack of action based on the assumption that anything short of a massive and dramatic intervention would not have stopped the genocide, the knowledge that no states were offering troops for such a campaign, and the belief that another "loss" after Somalia would jeopardize the UN's future. Such horrors existed and would continue to exist, I told myself and others, and the UN could not be expected to intervene wherever danger and bloodshed occurred. In short, I developed both an articulate understanding of the politics and pragmatics of peacekeeping and an ability to reflect and represent my understanding of the interests of the future of the UN and the basis of U.S. support for peacekeeping operations.

In April 1995, I was watching a television special commemorating the first anniversary of the genocide of Rwanda. The narrator emphatically contrasted the genocide and the refugee crisis with the minimal efforts of the international community. My first response was my standard line: there had been no effective basis for UN intervention, and the Security Council had a responsibility not only to Rwanda but also to the UN and its peacekeepers. Upon further reflection, however, I began to question why I, along with so many others in the Security Council and the Secretariat, had quickly concluded that the needs of the organization overrode those of the targets of genocide. Why was there little evidence, for instance, that the Secretariat or any state vigorously petitioned the Security Council to assemble an intervention force? Why were most apparently more exercised by the need to restrain the UN from any further involvement than they were by the need to dispatch assistance? Raising such questions led me to pose the reason for inaction in a more brutal manner: the UN had more to lose by taking action and being associated with another failure than it did by not taking action and allowing the genocide in Rwanda. The moral equation was: genocide was acceptable if the alternative was to harm the future of the UN.

THE BUREAUCRATIZATION OF INDIFFERENCE

I am increasingly drawn to the conclusion that the bureaucratization of peacekeeping contributed to this indifference to the suffering of the very people peacekeeping is mandated to assist. As I, for one, more closely identified with the United States and the United Nations, I found it easier to remain indifferent to the occasional evil in deference to their interests. There is, in my experience, an intimate connection between the discourse of acting in the best interests of the United Nations and the international community, the bureaucratization of peacekeeping, and production of indifference.[2]

The traditional view offered by international relations scholars is that states pursue their "security interests," and thus no matter how grieved member states were by the genocide in Rwanda, they were unwilling to commit money and manpower to any operation because it remained outside their "interests." This is part of the answer. But it does not adequately capture the dynamics of the Security Council's debate over Rwanda, nor explain why the Security Council agonized over its decision, nor why I and others were adamant that the UN's reputation was part of the moral calculus. What is missing from the traditional approach is an understanding of how the decision not to halt the genocide came to be understood and defined as ethical and moral.

Michael Herzfeld's *The Social Production of Indifference: Exploring the Symbolic Roots of Western Bureaucracy* offers a conceptual apparatus that I find useful for thinking about these issues, as it asks: "how and why can political entities that celebrate the rights of individuals and small groups so often seem cruelly selective in applying those rights?" How can bureaucrats justify their acts that violate the values of the community and their own indifference to members of the community? I can only simplify his argument here, highlighting those claims that inform my discussion of the relationship between peacekeeping and indifference.

Bureaucracies are not only instruments of domination, they also are symbolic markers of boundaries between "peoples" and are expressive of the societies that produced them. These boundaries and markers exhibit criteria that define who is a member of the community, enabling bureaucrats to determine who will receive their attention and who will not. "Compactly expressed . . . indifference is a rejection of those who are different" (Herzfeld, 1993: 33). The most intuitive marker, of course, is citizenship, and it is expected that bureaucrats will attend to citizens and be indifferent to noncitizens. Bureaucrats, as members of the nation-state, use "national" identity to determine who will receive their attention and who will not.

Yet, bureaucrats also are known to disregard many citizens of the state, the very individuals that they supposedly represent, and to selectively apply rights and dispense preferential treatment to members of the community. There are several reasons why. One is that the politically and economically powerful are frequently favored, and so too are those who possess the defining qualities and characteristics of the community, including race, religion, and gender. Another reason for this selective attention is that bureaucrats identify not only with their fellow citizens but also with their bureaucracy, thus exhibiting a loyalty not only to the community but also to the organization. A final reason for bureaucratic indifference is that bureaucrats also will pursue their personal agenda. There are many sources of indifference.

How is it that society and even bureaucrats themselves cope with and explain their indifference? To address this issue, Herzfeld deploys the concept of secular theodicy, building on Max Weber's concept of religious theodicy (ibid., 5–7). Briefly, Weber was interested in how religious systems account, in Herzfeld's words, for the "persistence of evil in a divinely ordered world" (ibid., 5). Weber (1962: 138–39) observed that the "legitimation of every distinctively ethical prophecy has always required the notion of a god characterized by attributes that set him sublimely above the world." The more a religion holds to a conception of a transcendental deity, however, the greater is the problem of how to reconcile the "problem of the extraordinary power of such a god . . . with the imperfection of the world that he has created and rules over." Different religions have offered different responses that allow them to maintain their belief in transcendental principles, notwithstanding the existence of evil. Such responses constitute theodicy, as Herzfeld uses the term.

Herzfeld transports the concept of theodicy from the religious to the secular domain of "Western" nation-states, suggesting that these states exhibit a secular transcendentalism bound up with the nation, claiming that members' sins cannot undermine their shared ideals; that individuals who are part of the nation-state must also cope with and explain away evils and disappointments committed by the bureaucracy that is situated in a democratic context that potentially calls into question those transcendental values; that societies and bureaucrats explain the presence of evil—and even justify their own indifference—with reference to abstract moral principles that derive primarily from the nation and secondarily from democracy; and, therefore, that indifference is tolerated by societies and bureaucrats because of the continuous belief in the transcendental purpose of the nation-state and the retreat to secular theodicy.

Most important for my purposes here is that bureaucrats, who routinely express indifference and author laws that seem far from the values that define the community, justify their behavior with references to the sanctity of the transcendental. Such references can be strategic or genuine; in either case, such discourse allows them to live with themselves. To be a servant of the state that espouses transcendental values while following bureaucratic rules means that disappointments are delivered on a daily basis and the occasional sin is excused, ignored, or justified with reference to abstract moral principles. Such indifference is a testimony to the dominance of the needs of the organization over those of the individual, a testimony to the primacy of the universal over the particular. In general, the notion that actions occur with reference to and are embedded within a community context allows bureaucrats and other members of society to accept disappointments, if not evil.

Important differences exist between national and international bureaucracies, such as the UN, but the comparison between national bureaucracies and the UN is apt for three reasons. First, both the national and the international community are invested with transcendental principles by their members; where Herzfeld looks to the nation-state, I look to the international community. Indeed, UN officials, according to David Rieff (1996: 20), often talk about the UN as if it were a church, suggesting that they are guardians of a religion whose tenets are transcendental. Second, the UN is founded on the "principle of identity" and the existence of a "community, whose members' individual sins cannot undermine the ultimate perfection of the ideal that they all share" (Herzfeld, 1993: 10). The UN symbolically defines who is and who is not part of the "international community," selectively applies the rights of the community among its members, and produces difference and indifference by differentiating members of the community from nonmembers. Third, UN officials and member states identify with and protect the UN's interests and reputation, strategically and sincerely evoke the discourse of the transcendental while ignoring the plights of the individual, and express their own brand of indifference and secular theodicy. These three points provide the points of departure for revisiting the Security Council's debates on Rwanda.

A complex and contested feature of the UN is its constituency and the articulated and working definition of the community: does the UN represent individuals or states? The United Nations maintains that it represents the peoples of the world, and claims that there exist a set of moral principles that are transcendental, existing across time and space, and state sovereignty can do little to abrogate or silence such principles. Yet, the UN Charter also observes that a guiding principle of international society is state sovereignty and the principle of noninterference. The United Nations is an intergovernmental organization, its membership is limited to states, only states are part of the General Assembly and the Security Council, and states alone determine its policies. Throughout its history, the UN has generally promoted and honored the principle of sovereignty, which meant that any tension over the UN's constituency—that is, who composes the community—is most often resolved in favor of states and against individuals and peoples. Because throughout the Cold War the UN favored states over peoples and individuals, the focus was on the security of states.

The end of the Cold War raised the UN's visibility in global affairs, led to a debate over the definition of security, and triggered a reconsideration of the definition of the international community. During the Cold War, the UN expressed a statist definition of security that focused almost exclusively on interstate conflict. The end of the Cold War, however, unleashed a spiraling number of proposals and statements that called for shifting the definition of security away from states and toward individuals and peoples. Those in and around the UN increasingly voiced the concept of "human security" in various guises, suggesting that what matters is the security of individuals and not states, that states can be a source of insecurity and not a unit of protection, and that domestic rather than interstate conflict is a greater threat to individuals' security in today's world. Boutros-Ghali, for instance, would frequently stress the "human" foundations of security, arguing that the UN must be as concerned with the security of individuals as it is with the security of states.

Tied to these questions of "whose security" was a reconsideration of the working definition of the international community, which resuscitated the tension between the community as defined by sovereign states and the community as defined by peoples and individuals. During the Cold War that tension was resolved in favor of sovereign states. But beginning in the mid-1980s and accelerating after the end of the Cold War in the face of the new security challenges, the working definition of international community was expanded to more fully include individuals and identity-based groups residing within the state. There was, if you will, a shift of representation as various statements from the Secretariat and the Security Council offered that the UN was to protect not only the community of states but also individuals and peoples.

Peacekeeping operations reflect the UN's growing prominence in global affairs, the reconsideration of the definition of security, and the debate over the UN's constituency and working definition of the international community. To begin, the UN's post–Cold War popularity translated into an explosion of peacekeeping operations. There were eleven operations between 1956 and 1988, and no new operation was authorized between 1978 and 1988. Between 1988 and 1995, however, the Security Council authorized twenty-four new operations. The UN was anxious to prove its promise, and the Great Powers, who now discovered the UN to be a useful place to dump intractable conflicts, encouraged that sentiment.

Perhaps more impressive than the growing numbers were the ambitious tasks assigned to these "second-generation" peacekeeping operations that reflected a changing definition of security. Prior to 1988, peacekeeping concerned interpositioning lightly armed UN troops between two states that had agreed to a cease-fire. After 1988, peacekeepers were now being deployed to confront humanitarian disasters and to facilitate domestic conflict resolution and the post-conflict process of nation building; soon the UN was running elections, creating new police forces, repatriating refugees, and overseeing the demobilization of armies and the reintegration of deeply divided societies. Many UN officials with whom I spoke recalled a sense of excitement and exhilaration during these first post–Cold War days; not only were they unshackled from the Cold War but their activism was directed at helping people rather than states. "There are greater rewards," recalled one official, "from helping the victims of political turmoil than from helping its instigators." The UN, as exhibited through its peacekeeping operations, was shifting away from state security and toward "comprehensive" and "human" security.

As the UN became increasingly concerned with human security, however, it continued to operate in state-centric terms: human security most often meant "saving failed states." To save a failed state, in turn, meant creating a democracy. For many member states and UN officials, "democratic" states became the type most worthy of emulation and were accorded legitimacy and prestige. Democracy was equated with being "civilized" and was said to be a foundation of "peace and security." That "democratic states don't go to war with one another" became a cliché for many member states and UN officials, and Boutros-Ghali himself stated that democratic states are more legitimate than others and were less likely to have domestic conflicts or become embroiled in regional wars (1995). It should come as no surprise, then, that UN officials were busily forwarding numerous proposals that concerned how the UN might help expand the number of democracies. In sum, being a "democracy" came to define full membership in "the elect" of the UN's "international community."

Most of the post–Cold War peacekeeping operations have been a direct extension of the view that domestic stability in general and democracy in particular are related to international order and define membership in the international community. Indeed, as the UN looked to end an operation, it used the symbol of a "free and fair" election. Few genuinely believed that one election at the end of a peacekeeping operation was enough to institutionalize democratic practices, but the ritual of the election symbolized how peacekeeping operations were to help rehabilitate fallen members of the community.

This highly ambitious and increasingly crowded security agenda overwhelmed a bureaucratically and organizationally underequipped UN. Such developments led to a series of reforms that were designed to rationalize and expand peacekeeping activities, an absolutely essential undertaking if an antiquated and inefficient organization was to meet the challenges of the day and to carry out its mandated responsibilities. One by-product of this bureaucratization process, however, was to encourage individuals and states to develop a vested interest in peacekeeping and the UN. Some benefited materially from their involvement in UN operations, and, therefore, championed their continuation. Others argued that peacekeeping was an important instrument for interstate and intrastate conflict resolution. Still others, however, came to identify with the idea of the United Nations, its symbol as transcending power politics. The common denominator of all three, however, was an identification with the UN, its interests, and its future.

An additional feature of the bureaucratization of peacekeeping was a greater consideration and elaboration of the conditions when an operation was likely to be successful, and, relatedly, should be approved. Whereas in the early 1990s it seemed that no operation was too small, large, or complex to deserve the UN's attention, by the fall of 1993 many state and UN officials grumbled that such automatic authorizations were leaving the UN stretched thin and increasingly ineffective; it was time, they said, to exhibit greater self-restraint. The sobriety was driven in part by the "failures" of Somalia and Bosnia, and the Security Council now began to incorporate a more restrictive set of criteria to inform its decision to approve or extend a peacekeeping operation (United Nations Security Council, 1994b). With bureaucratization came rationalization.

These criteria, however, contributed to the production of indifference. The bureaucratization of peacekeeping, in terms of both its means and the conditions for its deployment, was generally couched in terms of the organization's needs. The future of peacekeeping, according to many, depended on the Security Council's elaborating a tighter set of conditions for considering the authorization or extension of an operation. The absence of criteria had led the UN into a series of high-profile disasters, and there was considerable fear that any more UN "failures" would spell the end of the UN. Accordingly, these criteria took into account not only the conditions under which peacekeeping was effective but also the desire to keep the UN from being saddled with operations that had little chance of success. The desire by UN officials and member states to pick winners and to avoid losers meant that the UN was as interested in human security as it was its own. "Select wisely," became the adage, "because the next selection may be your last."

The concern for the UN's reputation and interests affected the operations that were selected. The Security Council now frowned on peacekeeping for humanitarian intervention or during moments of domestic turmoil. Illustrative was the Security Council's decision not to intervene in Burundi in October 1993, when nearly one hundred thousand died. Living in the immediate shadows of Somalia, many members of the Security Council argued against intervention on the grounds that there was "no peace to keep" and the need for the UN to avoid obvious quagmires. Many UN officials and delegates breathed a sigh of relief when the Security Council opted to abstain from the conflict, whispering that the UN had to conserve its energies for "winners." The desire not to intervene in Burundi exemplified the shifting sentiment at the UN concerning the feasibility and desirability of humanitarian intervention. Those who opposed such interventions contended that crises are a by-product of wars, wars are defined by instability, and a modicum of stability is a precondition for effective peacekeeping. The UN could only be effective when there was a "peace to keep."

Moreover, whereas once the Security Council and the Secretariat routinely noted that they had a responsibility to help those who could not help themselves, now they were suggesting that they could only help those who were willing to help themselves. The language that began to creep into nearly all Security Council statements as a consequence of Somalia was that an operation was justified only so long as the parties to the conflict demonstrated a resolve to work toward political progress; the Security Council, for instance, emphasized how "the people of Somalia bear the ultimate responsibility for achieving national reconciliation and for rebuilding their country" (United Nations Security Council, 1994a). Such statements are highly defensible. The UN, stretched thin and facing a nearly inexhaustible number of potential crises, must decide who deserves its attention, and one reasonable criteria is the active support of those whom it is helping. Yet, the shift in language represented a search not only for accuracy but also for political expediency, a desire to defend the UN from its critics who claimed that it had failed. Whereas once the UN and member states recognized that "the people" were the victims of violence and needed protection, these same officials were now, for all intents and purposes, using the failure of the "people to take control of their lives" as a justification for inaction. Who were "the people" of Bosnia? of Somalia? of Rwanda? By and large, "the people" no longer meant the victims of violence but those who controlled the means of violence. The UN was stepping away from its initial post–Cold War concern for human security and retreating to the traditional tenets of peacekeeping that stressed the need for stability as a precondition of deployment and the focus on state security. This shift, according to many, was defensible on the grounds that the UN could only help those who were willing to help themselves, and absolutely necessary to protect the UN's reputation and future.

The siren of secular theodicy was detectable in these developments. Many at the UN appealed to the interests of the UN, represented as a symbol of both the international community and universal human rights, to reconcile the uncomfortable tension between the transcendental and their reluctance to act. Although the UN was still committed to the same transcendental values, they argued, the conditions under which it would henceforth become involved in attempting to secure and promote those values had been justifiably tightened. The secular and politically expedient decisions that were being offered in place of actions were clothed in universalism and the need to protect the international community's defining organization. The occasional evil could be tolerated so long as it did not damage the greater collective good. These developments and this discourse imprinted the Security Council's debate over its response to the violence in Rwanda in April 1994.

A RETURN TO RWANDA

Member states could not simply and silently watch the unfolding genocide from the sanctuary of the Security Council. Rather, as "agents" of the "international community" they had to negotiate the fluid and contested relationship between their respective "national interests" and the "international community." States serve on the Security Council and thus represent state interests. Delegates are, after all, citizens of their states, representatives of their national capitals from whom they receive their instructions. What matters to these states are national interests. Yet what are these "national interests," and are they inconsistent with the concerns of the international community? I noted earlier that, from my bureaucratic position, I learned an interpretation of the U.S. national interest that supported a more prominent role for the UN and involvement in activities that were

not directly connected to traditional understandings or core definitions of national security. Although there were numerous occasions
when events that exercised the Secretariat remained outside my conception of what should animate and involve the United States, over
time my understanding of U.S. interests, the means and ends of U.S.
foreign policy, became more fully connected to the UN and its operations. "Working" these UN issues had shaped my definition of U.S.
interests, and my learning a definition of U.S. interests had shaped
my support for the UN.

My experiences and observations thus suggest that those who serve
on the Security Council view themselves not simply as handmaidens
of states but also as representatives of the international community.
What is the "international community" and what are its interests?
Earlier, I argued that there has been a continuous, though varying
degree of, tension between the notion of the international community
as composed of sovereign states and the international community as
composed of peoples and individuals. One of my observations of the
workings of the Security Council was that although its members pursue their state (or "national") interests, there also is a strong hint of
cosmopolitanism in their language and movements. For instance, the
Security Council's documents refer to itself as a representative of the
international community. Although it is easy to dismiss such language as diplomatic blather, states take seriously such blather and
shifted their policies accordingly. The Security Council was not alone
in presenting itself as the representative of the international community and responsible for protecting its interests; other actors—
notably the media, private human rights groups, and other states
who were not on the Security Council—also identified the Security
Council in this manner. During the debate over Rwanda, those in the
chamber referred to themselves as the "international community,"
and when the meeting adjourned, the president of the Security Council greeted a media who wanted to know if the "international community" had formulated a policy.

In general, the existence of the UN and the participation by member states in the Security Council remind member states that they
should avoid stark self-interested strategies and pursue more enlightened policies that reflect a sense of cosmopolitanism. Interstate cooperation at the UN, therefore, was not merely a technical feat but
is also, as Émile Durkheim might suggest, a connection to a moral

order (Zabusky, 1995: 23, 113). Through their discourse and practices, member states were not only overcoming problems associated with interdependent choice, but also attempting to connect themselves and their activities to a set of transcendental values.

Throughout the Security Council debates there was a negotiation between, first, state interests and the obligations to the international community, and, second, the competing demands on the Security Council that derived from its responsibilities to the UN and the Rwandans. Although pained by the unfolding bloodshed, member states did not view their interests as suitably engaged to justify the involvement of their own troops for a risky intervention. Because this was an intrastate rather than an interstate conflict, whether this crisis constituted a "threat to international peace and security" was also an uncertain and contested point. Still, no state represented its unwillingness to get involved as a matter of strategic calculations; rather, member states couched their reluctance in terms of the needs of the UN.

The United States, for instance, argued that the Security Council's overriding responsibility was to its peacekeepers, and if there were more fatalities the consequences would be more criticism of, and a dimmer future for, the UN. To further support its case for withdrawal, the United States employed the previously mentioned criteria for whether the Security Council should approve or extend an operation. Consequently, the United States was able to argue persuasively that by the Security Council's own criteria, which were intended to rationalize and formalize its debates and decisions, UNAMIR had no business being in Rwanda. UNAMIR's immediate withdrawal was in the best interests of the UN.

The Clinton administration's stance was also designed to protect itself and the UN from a hostile Congress. During the debate over the mandate extension in late March, the United States advocated reducing UNAMIR in order to send a strong signal both to the Rwandan government to establish the transitional government, and to Congress, which had declared open season on the UN, that the administration could be tough on peacekeeping operations. Such displays of "toughness," suggested one administration official at the time, would benefit the UN because the administration would better shield it from further congressional attacks. "Tough love," he offered.

Two points bear emphasizing. First, to make the case for intervention required connecting such action to interests. Yet, the language of interests is largely the language of states, and state interests were hardly engaged by the unfolding tragedy in Rwanda. Indeed, member states and members of the U.S. Mission framed any prospective intervention in the language of obligation. I, for one, viewed the violence as lamentable but could not make the necessary strategic link to justify the deployment of U.S. troops. Simply put, Rwanda activated the language of obligation rather than interests, but to expect and justify the involvement and possible sacrifice of one's troops generally demands a connection to the language of state interests rather than of international obligations. In such a situation, state interests will nearly always trump transnational obligations. Second, those member states who opposed intervention for self-interested reasons were reluctant publicly to display such calculations; much more morally palatable and defensible was the argument that the Security Council had an obligation and interest to protect its peacekeepers, and, relatedly, the future of the UN. Indifference was presentable through the appeal to the transcendental.

Some nonpermanent members of the Security Council, however, demanded robust action to protect civilians, couching their arguments in terms of the "international community" to refer to a moral order that transcended state boundaries. At the time, however, I feared that such language was designed to lure the United States into doing the work of and for the "international community." Over the course of the year, I became increasingly frustrated by the fact that when a humanitarian nightmare unfolded somewhere in the world, the world looked to the UN, and then the UN looked to the United States. Accordingly, I was suspicious that when other states evoked the "international community," they were, in fact, pointing to the United States. New Zealand and Czechoslovakia, which I often referred to as the "conscience of the Council" in both derision and admiration, supported robust action by the UN and were critical of those members who resisted the intervention temptation. While they were arguing for action, however, they were not volunteering their own troops and were only subtly insinuating that the United States should go first. As some of us at the U.S. Mission would joke about other proposed and existing UN operations, the international community seemed willing to fight down to the last American. The rhetoric of the international community, then, became something to fear and reinforced my defense of U.S. national interests. In general, member states used the language of the international community and the defense of the UN to hide their own unwillingness to get involved and sometimes to implicate others.

Where was the Secretariat during these discussions? Earlier, I noted that its comments were limited to sketchy and noncommittal appraisals, failing to offer any concrete recommendations and thus forfeiting its agenda-setting powers. At the time, I attributed its lack of direction to "not being up to the task" of crisis management. Yet, a highly authoritative and exhaustive report on Rwanda suggests not amateur but rather instrumental and strategic behavior (Steering Committee of the Joint Evaluation of Emergency Assistance to Rwanda, 1996). During these first, highly critical, days, the Secretariat was receiving concrete recommendations from its Force Commander General Roméo Dallaire, who was cautiously optimistic that a limited military intervention could halt the bloodshed. The Secretariat, however, did not communicate UNAMIR's recommendations to the Security Council. I can only speculate as to why the Secretariat failed to do so, but one very real possibility is that it feared becoming embroiled in a conflict that spelled failure. Although the motives are unknown, the consequences of the Secretariat's noncommittal stance are more certain: its failure to offer any recommendations or hint that an intervention had any chance of success played directly into the hands of those in the Security Council who demanded UNAMIR's immediate withdrawal. Member states were not the only ones who could hide their personal agenda.

Members of the Security Council were trying to negotiate not only between state interests and the international community, but also between their responsibility to the Rwandans and to the UN. This tension, which was a central and underlying feature of the debate, slowly gravitated toward the view that, however tragic for the Rwandans, the only responsible and feasible option was to withdraw UNAMIR. To place peacekeepers in harm's way would not only betray a singular responsibility of the Security Council but potentially lead to a further deterioration in the UN's stature. In the shadow of Somalia and in the midst of the drama of Bosnia, there was little doubt that a failure in Rwanda would translate into greater trouble for the UN. The Security Council's reluctance to act, in this view, was morally defensible because it protected the international community's organization.

The language of "international community" now was as likely to be evoked to urge restraint as it was for action. This possibility became painfully apparent as the Security Council became increasingly aware that what was transpiring in Rwanda was not "massacre" but rather "genocide." At first, the Security Council was reluctant to utter the word *genocide*. Its very mention had the raw, discursive capacity to demand action; its mere rhetorical presence might be enough to shame and embarrass the Security Council into doing what it resisted. Accordingly, there appeared to be a tacit understanding to avoid such inflammatory language. As the days passed, however, occasionally a member state would implore action because of genocide, but soon thereafter the discussion slowly descended on the recognition that little could be done, that the Security Council had to protect the UN's interests, and that under no uncertain terms should a member of the Security Council use such explosive—that is, irresponsible—language outside the room. What was once a demand for action in the name of the international community because of genocide soon became inaction in the same name.

After lengthy deliberations, the Security Council voted on April 21 to reduce UNAMIR's presence and mandate. For those who opposed this decision but failed to offer troops to back their diplomatic pleas, this was the best that could be gotten. And those who insisted on reducing UNAMIR were reluctant to demand a complete withdrawal for fear of portraying themselves and the Security Council as morally bankrupt. By maintaining a token presence, the UN was able to symbolize its continued concern and, perhaps, help effect a cease-fire.

Under the watchful eyes of the Security Council, five hundred thousand to eight hundred thousand Rwandans fell victim to genocide. No one can be certain that a modest intervention at the outset of the crisis might have halted this tragedy; the record is that the Security Council did little until it was too late and safe. And the stark truth is that although some states called for intervention, few if any volunteered their own services. In this regard, the UN's indifference reflects the indifference of the member states; nothing more, nothing less. Yet, the bureaucratization of peacekeeping imprinted the Security Council's debates and contributed to the production of indifference. The Security Council saw itself as a representative of the international community. One of the dilemmas it faced was choosing between its charge in Rwanda and its protection of the peacekeepers. Any more peacekeeping fatalities, I and many others argued, would undoubtedly mean more criticism and fewer resources for the UN. This was the moral equation and the justification for inaction. Such inaction was made palatable and morally defensible, invested with ethical distinction, as it was given support by appeals to the transcendental value of preserving the international community's central organization. Officials in and out of the UN were able to explain the evils of Rwanda and their own indifference by pointing to the secular religion of the international community and its cathedral, the UN.

CONCLUSION

As I continue to think about peacekeeping and the lessons of Rwanda, I do so differently than when I completed my tenure at the U.S. Mission. To be sure, many of my initial "policy-relevant" recommendations still inform my views of peacekeeping, its functions, and its future; learning has taken place concerning what states are willing to support and when peacekeeping is likely to be effective, and the pragmatics of peacekeeping are understandably part of any decision regarding its possible employment. Yet, part of making peacekeeping, according to the slogan of the Clinton administration, "effective when selected" required giving the UN the means and resources to do the job. Professionalizing peacekeeping was absolutely necessary if peacekeeping was to have a future. But this bureaucratization entailed that individuals come to have a stake in and identify with the bureaucracy, begin to evaluate strategies and actions according to the needs of the bureaucracy, and, accordingly, begin to frame discussions and justify policies in a different manner. I became part of this bureaucratization process; I, too, altered how I judged and evaluated UN peacekeeping. Sometimes this meant that I had a heightened awareness of the complexities of the issues involved and the stakes of the game. Yet, at other times, this involved a shift in what I thought was desirable and valuable; I became as interested in protecting bureaucratic and organizational interests as I was in employing the UN to help those it was supposed to serve. The UN might be above power politics, but it is not above politics.

Nor is the UN immune to a culture of insecurity. The UN's formal intervention in Rwanda came in fall 1993, and as a third-party force its mission was to contribute to the production of security in Rwanda by overseeing its political and social reconstitution. But the UN became as interested in its own security as it was of those whom it was mandated to assist. Because the UN's reputation and future viability were dependent on whether the operation was deemed a success or a failure, those in and around the UN came to define Rwanda as a potential threat to the organization. Accordingly, the Security Council and the Secretariat attempted to disentangle the UN's fate from Rwanda's by distancing it from the bloody happenings through the moral discourse of the international community and the need to preserve the integrity of the UN. If once member states used the discourse of the "international community" to justify intervention in Rwanda's political affairs, they now used the same discourse to justify distance and indifference.

This rendition of the politics of international organizations is somewhat more complicated, therefore, than that offered by many political scientists who don liberal lenses as they gaze on the construction and hypothesized function of international institutions. Specifically, self-proclaimed neoliberal institutionalists are interested in identifying the conditions under which states will construct international institutions and abide by international agreements because of the presupposition that such developments enable states to eschew short-term gains for the greater benefits associated with long-term cooperation. International institutions, in this view, are critical to sustained cooperation (Keohane and Martin, 1995). This leads to an implicit tendency to see the mere creation of international organizations as cause for celebration. Yet, why make this assumption? Why the automatic applause? Not only will states construct institutions for purposes other than the attempt to maximize their material interests, but the very creation of these international institutions can become a site for new political identities and definitions of interests that can be inconsistent with their original intent.

Are we, then, to imagine that all international bureaucracies will exhibit indifference? I have no desire to essentialize bureaucracies or to suggest a global "banality of evil," but I do want to call attention to this underappreciated feature of international organizations. Although Herzfeld limits his discussion to "Western" bureaucracies and is reserved about whether his discussion travels to non-Occidental or international contexts, there is scattered but highly compelling evidence that his analysis and the story of Rwanda are not an isolated phenomenon. Stacia Zabusky's (1995) *Launching Europe* demonstrates how Herzfeld's analysis can survive the journey; Liisa Malkki's (1996) recent reflections on the United Nations High Commission for Refugees (UNHCR) in Central Africa offers similarly disturbing observations about the relationship between international organizations and the individuals in whose names they act; and evidence from Bosnia, eloquently argued in David Rieff's *Slaughterhouse* (1995), also suggests a relationship between the bureaucratization of peacekeeping, the concern for the organization's interests, and the production of indifference. In general, an intriguing, though equally disturbing, implication is that the dynamics and developments that Herzfeld locates among Western states are an increasingly globalized phenomenon. On the intellectual agenda of an era defined by globalization-cum-bureaucratization should be a more nuanced understanding of the consequences of global bureaucratization.

But the UN is more than a site of indifference, a place where state inaction and organizational interests come to have an ethical content and moral luster. The Security Council and the United Nations also are sites of a struggle over individuation and connection, a place where member states define themselves and their interests through their engagement and confrontation with a set of transcendental values. In this regard, the UN offers a sanctuary for individuals to contemplate a moral order that transcends their local confines, a place where member states mimic, learn, and express a set of transcendental values that are above, beyond, and before the sovereign state. It is this UN, as the international community's secular cathedral, that allows many, including myself, to maintain a belief in the transcendental, even in the face of the occasional evil that exposes the sins of the members.

NOTES

This chapter is a shortened and slightly revised article that previously appeared in *Cultural Anthropology* 12(4): 551–78. I benefited from the reactions and observations of many colleagues in diverse fields, and to them I owe a collective thanks. I want to thank James Fernandez, Marty Finnemore, Michael Herzfeld, Diana Saco, Victoria Shampaine, three anonymous referees at *Cultural Anthropology*, and the editors of this volume. I owe a particular debt to Dan Segal. Finally, this article could not have been written without the support of the U.S. Mission to the United Nations, the Council on Foreign Relations, and the MacArthur Foundation's International Peace and Security Fellowship. The views expressed are entirely my own.

1. Because the UN is an international organization that also is representative of states, it can be understood as both the sum of its parts and as an independent actor. I will refer to the Security Council, the fifteen member states who are designated to preside over matters of international peace and security, when discussing the UN as a representative of its member states. I refer to the Secretariat when considering the UN as an independent actor, and refer most frequently to the office of the secretary-general and DPKO.

2. I want to add two critical caveats. First, I am representing my personal reflections after a period of distance and attempting, as best as possible, to represent and interpret the events unfolding around me; I have no doubt that others would tell a different tale. Relatedly, I observed these events from the U.S. Mission to the United Nations, and I expect that people in Rwanda, the UN, or other delegations would offer a different view. Second, I have tremendous respect for the integrity and values of many of those with whom I worked; these were highly dedicated individuals who worked long hours and labored under difficult conditions. I have no doubt that they would object to my characterization of their supposed indifference.

7

States of Insecurity:
Plutonium and Post–Cold War Anxiety
in New Mexico, 1992–96

JOSEPH MASCO

Although it is a historic arena of anthropological inquiry, New Mexico is not often thought of as an important site in which to study global (in)security, or, for that matter, to assess the local costs and consequences of the Cold War. Within security studies, after all, the continental United States has traditionally been imagined to be the one stable entity in an anarchy-filled world, the one territorial space that can remain untheorized in the face of a volatile and dangerous international order (see Campbell, 1992). The end of the Cold War has made this conceptual lacuna visible, however, just as the dissolution of the Soviet Union has powerfully demonstrated the fragility of even "superpowered" nation-states. With this in mind, it is important to examine how the end of the Cold War has affected visions of "security" in the West, and within the United States in particular; for the 1990s revealed that the global, dual-structured, oppositional nation building of the Cold War did not transmute insurgent regional identifications or ethnonationalist desires as perhaps once thought.[1] Local ethnic and regional identities were not necessarily unified or superseded by Soviet—or, as I would like to argue here, U.S.—Cold War policies but were complexly and asymmetrically harnessed to them (see Litzinger, this volume). The end of the Cold War, then, not only has necessitated a radical rethinking of the terms of scholarly

204 · JOSEPH MASCO

inquiry into the nature of global order, but also has left a complicated political and cultural legacy as communities express identities,
ambitions, and fears once rendered invisible or subsumed under the
Cold War dialectics of the nuclear age.

The end of the Cold War is of particular importance in New Mexico, as it was there that the first atomic bomb, as well as the majority
of nuclear weapons in the U.S. stockpile, were designed. In significant ways, New Mexico's nuclear weapons laboratories might even
be said to have coauthored the Cold War with their scientific counterparts in the Soviet Union. Consequently, this essay investigates
how reorganizations in global political and economic structures at
the end of the Cold War are influencing regional articulations of self
and nation in New Mexico, America's own ethnic borderlands. It
does so by examining how the activities of the U.S. nuclear weapons
complex are experienced by communities in New Mexico, by examining how, in fact, diverse racial, (ethno)national, and political groups
that usually fall under the rubric "U.S. citizens" define and experience "U.S. national security" at home. Thus, this essay explores the
social imaginaries where concepts of "national security" meet practices of "national sacrifice," where the interests of the sole remaining
global superpower collide with those of marginalized indigenous nations, and where U.S. national identity is complexly negotiated and
challenged in the everyday life practices of local citizenry. By looking
at how neighboring communities alternately experience the "national security" offered by the U.S. nuclear complex in New Mexico,
this essay reveals that the nuclear standoff of the Cold War precluded attention to another set of (inter)national relations internal to
the United States; it also shows how the end of the Cold War has
made visible new spectrums of insecurity that both exceed, and are
produced by, U.S. national security policy in the Southwest.

The essay develops in three parts: first, I (re)introduce New Mexico as a subaltern *international* space, whose populations were complexly harnessed to a Cold War nation-building enterprise through
the U.S. nuclear weapons complex; second, I examine how the quintessential commodity of the Cold War—plutonium—continues to
generate widespread insecurity in New Mexico; and, in a concluding
section, I draw on the New Mexico context to explore the value of
expanding, and significantly decentering, concepts of "security" in
the post–Cold War era.

RETHINKING (INTER)NATIONAL RELATIONS IN THE U.S. SOUTHWEST

To investigate "national security" in New Mexico requires engaging the complex histories and competing national identities that inform everyday life in the U.S. Southwest, which is among the most politically contested regions in North America. Consider for a moment the diverse claims now made in New Mexico on historical presence, territorial identity, and legal status. The U.S. Southwest is a geographic area first inhabited by the scores of Native American nations that have maintained a territorial sovereignty there "from time immemorial."[2] The Southwest, it should be remembered, was an (ethno)national borderlands long before the arrival of Europeans, and from an indigenous perspective alone remains a remarkably complex cultural region. Today, seven indigenous languages are spoken by twenty-two tribes in New Mexico. And in just the one hundred-mile stretch of the Rio Grande River roughly bounded by Los Alamos National Laboratory (Los Alamos, New Mexico) to the north and Sandia National Laboratory (Albuquerque, New Mexico) to the south, sixteen pueblos maintain territorial sovereignties manifested in their own tribal governments, police forces, courts, and legal codes.

This indigenous reality is complicated by the fact that when the U.S. Declaration of Independence was signed in 1776, much of the Southwest (and notably what is today New Mexico) had already been an established part of the Spanish Empire for nearly two hundred years. After the war of independence with Spain in 1821, the Southwest became the northern half of the United States of Mexico, before falling twenty-seven years later to the United States of America in the Mexican-American War. With the Treaty of Guadalupe Hidalgo in 1848, the United States gained more than a million square miles, nearly doubling its total territory and thereby securing its control of North America (see del Castillo, 1990; Meinig, 1993). Most important for local communities, the U.S. Southwest was taken in a war of conquest with Mexico, providing ethnic groups in New Mexico, both indigenous and European, with a visceral experience, and an ongoing negotiation, of U.S. colonization. Today, the extensive land grants given by the Spanish and Mexican governments to their citizens, which were reaffirmed by the U.S. government in the Treaty of Guadalupe Hidalgo, remain in legal dispute in the area and are a perennial source of regional tension.[3] For much of the

Nuevomexicano (or Spanish-speaking) population, New Mexico is alternately a Hispano homeland, a unique enclave of Spanish cultural identity, or "Aztlán," the sacred homeland of the Aztec empire, and thus the geographic center of an indigenous Chicano nation.[4] A consistent theme within both contemporary Native American and Nuevomexicano experience is, therefore, the battle to overcome the historical amnesia in American political life and to communicate the continuing social impacts of being forcibly incorporated into the United States.[5]

Remarkably, the same area of the north-central Rio Grande Valley that has been the epicenter of cultural resistance movements in New Mexico from the Pueblo Revolt of 1680 through the Hispano land-grant battles of the 1890s and the Chicano activism of the 1960s, has also been subject to U.S. government appropriations of land under "national security" guidelines since the atomic bomb project came to Los Alamos in 1943 (Rothman, 1992). Today, New Mexico, like much of the Southwest, remains a U.S. military colony: it is the center of the U.S. nuclear weapons complex, where the first atomic bomb was developed and tested, home to two of the three U.S. nuclear weapons laboratories (Los Alamos and Sandia), the only permanent repository for U.S. military nuclear waste (the Waste Isolation Pilot Plant), the largest above-ground missile-testing range in the United States (the White Sands Missile Range), and other military installations.[6] In the post–Cold War period, New Mexico's military role has only expanded in importance, with increasing evidence that the twenty-first-century U.S. nuclear weapons complex might be consolidated along the Rio Grande (U.S. Department of Energy, Secretary of Energy Advisory Board Task Force, 1995).

Each of these "national imaginings"—Native American, Nuevomexicano, and U.S. military-industrial—evokes a different sense of territorial identity as well as a different approach to "national security" (Anderson, 1991; cf. Ballinger, this volume). I want to argue here that traditional approaches to U.S. national security policy quickly become problematic if one acknowledges the complicated, power-laden, and historically suppressed international politics that surround national security institutions in the U.S. Southwest. A close analysis of how "security" issues are elaborated in contested regional spaces such as New Mexico, in fact, demonstrates that the universalistic approaches to "sovereignty," "security," and "citizenship" that have typified Cold War security studies render invisible the political tensions and human experiences that structure everyday life in much of the world. For example, what conceptual space is there in Cold War security studies or international relations theory for the national security of a "domestic, dependent nation" (the official legal definition of Native American territories in the United States)? The ambiguous international legal standing of nations that are "domestic" and/or "dependent" has enabled ongoing violence throughout the Americas toward indigenous populations, yet these kinds of conflicts have rarely entered into the formal debates about foreign policy, international relations, or national security. Similarly, how should we now talk about the "security" of the traditional Spanish-speaking populations in New Mexico, who have periodically taken to armed protest against the U.S. government to assert their ownership of land and to affirm cultural rights validated by the Treaty of Guadalupe Hidalgo (e.g., see Gardner, 1970; Rosenbaum, 1981; Pulido, 1996)? It is within this ambiguous legal and national context that the U.S. nuclear weapons complex operates in New Mexico, folding the logics of "U.S. national security" back on themselves and requiring a more expansive conceptual approach to the production of (in)security. Today, in fact, New Mexico might best be approached as a *multinational,* multicultural state, an arena of proliferating and contradictory visions of national identity, where the U.S. government is merely the most dominant legal entity.

But how should we approach a territorial space this complex, where the Cold War rhetorics of "communist containment" become eerily resonant with the reservation system in the United States, or where Nuevomexicano residents will sometimes self-identify more with downtrodden Palestinians than with other "U.S. citizens," or where living next to a nuclear facility may present more immediate threats to personal health and safety than the thermonuclear arsenals of countries overseas? In this essay, my approach has been to "decenter" security studies, to explore how neighboring communities alternatively experience danger and risk, and to investigate how they express that danger in relation to one another. More specifically, my method has been to look at how local populations mobilize strategically to forward ethnonational identifications and/or U.S. citizenship in their engagements with federal authorities and with each other, and to search out those areas where contesting "national imaginaries" collide (see Anderson, 1991). This essay stands, then, as a kind of case study, an example of how, by looking at the engagement of cross-cultural/international logics in their local complexity, one can see arenas of insecurity once rendered invisible, or as emerging out of the Cold War. By recognizing indigenous sovereignty rights, investigating subaltern legal formations, and placing cultural logics in a comparative perspective, we can not only discover how these diverse national-cultural imaginings in New Mexico are mutually dependent and interconnected, but also realize how people occupying the same territorial space can nevertheless live in radically different worlds. To make this case, I follow the path of plutonium as it circulates between communities in northern New Mexico, for to do so allows us to locate viscerally and to identify precisely the complex articulations of security and insecurity that now structure everyday life in the U.S. Southwest.

THE PLUTONIUM ECONOMY:
INSECURITIES IN POST–COLD WAR NEW MEXICO

Plutonium is not an arbitrary choice for an analysis of (in)security; it is a material that has been crucial to definitions of U.S. national security since World War II and has been equally instrumental in defining areas of "national sacrifice" within nuclear states (see Kuletz, 1998). In fact, one might argue that the unique capabilities of plutonium enabled the Cold War to take the shape that it did (see Rhodes, 1986, 1995). Plutonium remains instrumental in structuring global relations of power in the post–Cold War era, and will be an ever-increasing presence in New Mexico as the U.S. nuclear complex slowly collapses back to its point of origin and the decades of Cold War nuclear research exact their environmental toll. In fact, by tracing how plutonium, as a material commodity, moves in and out of different "commodity phases" and national "regimes of value" in the Rio Grande Valley, one can identify how competing "national insecurities" are articulated there and begin to appreciate how the legacies of the Cold War will continue to generate insecurity for generations to come (Appadurai, 1986a; see also Beck, 1992).

Consider the social contradictions plutonium evokes: First, plutonium is a material that rarely, if ever, has existed in nature, yet because of its quarter-million-year life span and the effects of atmospheric nuclear testing, it is now, for all practical purposes, a permanent aspect of the global ecosystem. Second, as one of the world's deadlier poisons, it is a material whose military production (from uranium mining to weapon testing to nuclear waste storage) has inevitably produced ecological devastation, but it has, nonetheless, been the basis for definitions of "national security" since 1945.[7] Put differently, in the name of protecting territorial borders from attack, nuclear powers have practiced an internal cannibalism in the form of multiplying "national sacrifice zones"—areas that are too contaminated for human habitation. Indeed, nuclear states have pursued the "security" offered by plutonium production to the point of bankruptcy, mutual annihilation, and at an unforeseeable cost to future generations.[8] This complex articulation of national identity through plutonium has also always hidden a colonial dynamic, for lost in the polarizing logics of the Cold War were the most direct victims of nuclear proliferation, the indigenous nations around the globe who have predominantly borne the physical consequences of radioactive material production, weapons testing, and waste storage in their communities.[9]

This reality was implicitly acknowledged in New Mexico in 1992. As officials at Los Alamos National Laboratory (LANL) watched with some incredulity as the Soviet Union fell apart, they turned their attention toward the nations within. After a half century of silence and in the context of growing public concerns about local cancer rates and environmental damage, LANL set up formal government to government relations with four neighboring Pueblo nations who by default have been intricately involved in the plutonium economy right from the very beginning of the nuclear age. The Pueblos of San Ildefonso, Santa Clara, Jemez, and Cochiti (who have lived with the sound of explosions echoing off canyon walls and wondered about the toxicity of the clouds that drift over their territories from Los Alamos since 1943) achieved a new, post–Cold War, legal recognition of their sovereign status solely by virtue of their forced entry into the plutonium economy. This was not simply an altruistic move by LANL, however, as new environmental laws suddenly put these Pueblo nations in the legal position to set environmental standards for the air, water, and land they share with the laboratory. Although this is an ongoing process, the United States' premier nuclear weapons facility is now responsible to the environmental regulations of four sovereign Pueblo nations. This has contributed to an entirely new political dynamic in New Mexico, one providing new legal power to some indigenous communities, while energizing others, particularly Nuevomexicano and antinuclear groups, to mobilize in an unprecedented manner formally to engage the national security mission of Los Alamos National Laboratory.

MILITARY-INDUSTRIAL INSECURITIES: LOS ALAMOS NATIONAL LABORATORY

The plutonium economy in northern New Mexico begins, of course, with the U.S. nuclear weapons complex and specifically at LANL, an institution with a complicated administrative structure. LANL is owned by the Department of Energy in Washington, D.C., but is managed by the University of California from Oakland; it is funded by Congress, yet it has written its own mission statement since the end of World War II. With its regulatory structures on both coasts, LANL has, until very recently, enjoyed a remarkable autonomy in New Mexico. Perched at 7,200 feet on the Pajarito Plateau above the Rio Grande Valley, LANL's central mission has been to pursue scientific answers to U.S. national security questions. The unique explosive capabilities of plutonium have been the laboratory's raison d'être. National security at Los Alamos has meant primarily deterring the Soviet nuclear threat through new and improved nuclear weapons. Thus, national security at LANL has traditionally been something that began first overseas; by the 1980s, for example, a Soviet thermonuclear missile could reach the United States with less than ten minutes' warning. Consequently, Los Alamos scientists developed a uniquely global plutonium-mediated vision: national security issues were everywhere, but the ones of most concern were outside the U.S. territorial borders and far away from New Mexico, requiring a global surveillance system and a militarizing of earth, sea, and sky.

The traditional mission of the laboratory, however, dissolved alongside the Soviet Union. Like any culture that has experienced the loss of a cosmology, elder nuclear bomb designers in the 1990s were worried about how to preserve their cultural knowledge in the face of a rapidly changing world. Some at the laboratory began to describe designing nuclear weapons as a "folk art." Unable to perform underground nuclear tests since 1991, and with a significant weapons dismantlement project under way around the country, weaponeers began archiving their nuclear weapons "folk" knowledge while pursuing a new set of high-tech facilities that would allow them to continue work on nuclear weapons without ever actually exploding one. Increasingly, nuclear weapon scientists will be working in the virtual worlds of computer simulation and not in the hard world of physical experimentation, an important cultural shift that many see as an end to the nuclear weapons complex of the twentieth century and the beginning of the twenty-first (cf. Saco, this volume). Simultaneously, the U.S. nuclear weapons complex is slowly collapsing back into New Mexico, with LANL increasingly positioned to become the United States' centralized design and production facility. In the U.S. nuclear stockpile of the mid-1990s, five of the seven nuclear weapon systems were LANL designs and the laboratory had begun, for the first time since the late 1940s, to produce the plutonium "pits" that are the core components in nuclear weapons. By 1995, national security in Los Alamos was defined less through actual deterrence—who exactly was there to deter?—and more through maintaining the ability to resume nuclear weapons production should a new Cold War arise. LANL's official post–Cold War mission was redefined to "Reduce the Global Nuclear Danger" (Los Alamos National Laboratory, 1995), an expansive mission that recentered the institution on nuclear weapons and materials on a global scale, even though no new weapons are officially being designed, and money for cleanup of Cold War military production sites in the United States has been repeatedly cut back.

This new mission, however, has still not provided the laboratory with a clear-cut task or identity. Weapons scientists say privately that "reducing the global nuclear danger" could mean anything and therefore is an inadequate mission statement, except for those few working directly on the nonproliferation of nuclear materials and technologies (see U.S. General Accounting Office, 1995). They yearn for a giant organizing structure, a scientific project on the scale of the Manhattan Project, the Strategic Defense Initiative (SDI), or the technical and strategic targeting problems of the Cold War. These projects presented real technological challenges and required unprecedented financial backing. The Brookings Institute, for example, has estimated the total Cold War costs of the U.S. nuclear weapons arsenal (including development, delivery systems, and cleanup) at more than $4 trillion—roughly the total U.S. national debt in 1995 (S. Schwartz, 1995). Security expenditures on this scale were a reaction to the perception of a massive exterior threat to the nation. What could fill this void in the post–Cold War era? In the immediate scramble to justify the laboratory's continued presence, the Soviet nuclear threat was soon replaced in Los Alamos by talk of giant killer space asteroids that might need to be pulverized with thermonuclear weapons to protect the Earth from the kind of catastrophe that ended the dinosaur age. This was, however, merely a transitional effort in oppositional mission building, for the Persian Gulf War soon provided a more terrestrial threat, that of the now ubiquitous "rogue" or "terrorist" state. This conceptual innovation has proven to be a remarkably successful tactic, effectively institutionalizing Cold War–level military expenditures in the United States (Klare, 1995).

One nuclear weapons scientist described the post–Cold War challenges to the laboratory to me in this way:

> The problem is we've overdesigned our weapons for safety reasons. It's part of the craziness surrounding nuclear weapons and there is a lot of that. For example, we were ordered to take beryllium out of nuclear weapons because it's a poison. Now think about it, you're worried about the health effects of a bomb that's in the megaton range! Today you could shoot a bullet through a weapon, light it on fire, drop it out of a plane, and it still won't go off or release its nuclear components. We developed a form of high explosive that will just barely go off as well. We also worried about how to prevent a weapon falling into the wrong hands—so we designed elaborate security systems and codes on each device that prevent that. Today these weapons will just barely detonate they're so complicated. Since the end of the Cold War we have had what you call a paradigm shift. We used to think that all the weapons being designed were as complicated as ours—so you would want to track specific nuclear materials associated with those designs. Now we realize that if you aren't concerned about the safety of your troops or about containing nuclear fallout, and if you just want one bomb, you can do it very quickly. Now some of us have been thinking about how someone might use fertilizer to set off an atomic yield. We've seen what could be done with that in Oklahoma City. We now realize that it's much easier to build a single bomb than we ever thought before. So the question we are asking about proliferation today is: Do you monitor materials or people? I say people because there is too much nuclear material floating around out there to ever effectively monitor it. You've got to track the people with the know-how.

Thus, Los Alamos, a technoscientific community that prides itself on having saved the "Free World" from both fascism and communism, and believes it prevented a third world war by implementing a global targeting system for mutually assured destruction, has been reduced, of late, to trying to figure out just who might have the technical knowledge to set off an atomic bomb with fertilizer. This is a far cry from the heady days of the Strategic Defense Initiative in the 1980s when, quite literally, weapon designers were working on a geoplanetary scale (see Gusterson, 1996; Broad, 1992; Rosenthal, 1990).

Although the laboratory has developed skills suited to global nuclear threats—those presented by governments with huge military capabilities, or needed to track the spread of nuclear materials and weapons components—it has stumbled in dealing with the concerns of local populations in New Mexico, for local populations do not fit any of the categories developed during the Cold War for international relations. Local populations include indigenous nations that have no standing army, fewer than a thousand citizens, whose political leadership changes every year, and that have a sudden ability directly to influence research activities at the laboratory. Similarly, the laboratory has struggled to negotiate the activities of local nongovernmental organizations that are part of a global antinuclear and peace movement, and are thus not only unwilling to accept LANL's vision of "security" at face value, but also quite interested in focusing international attention and applying legal pressure on LANL activities. Thus, whereas laboratory officials justify the institution's purpose to Congress by talking about intercontinental threats, this kind of "national security" discourse does not necessarily elicit the support of local communities, who, in some cases, are either diametrically opposed to the laboratory's interests and/or find themselves to be only marginal U.S. citizens.

INDIGENOUS INSECURITIES:
THE NATIONS OF SAN ILDEFONSO AND POJOAQUE

A thousand feet below Los Alamos at San Ildefonso Pueblo, national security is a much more immediate business than on "the hill," and of foremost concern is protection against the social and environmental impacts of Los Alamos National Laboratory.[10] Government officials at San Ildefonso Pueblo self-identify as the only Native American nation whose recognized territory borders directly on a Department of

214 · JOSEPH MASCO

Energy site. The Pueblo also has had an aboriginal land claim standing in the courts since 1967 for return of the entire Pajarito Plateau, which Los Alamos has occupied since 1943. For San Ildefonso, national security is a brutally local affair: in addition to the perceived health effects of living next to a nuclear facility and recovering the land lost to the Manhattan Project in 1943, national security for the pueblo involves protecting the local ecosystem as well as the thousands of archaeological and religious sites on the plateau from ongoing laboratory activities. It means engaging the present with a long-term view of the future. Having already outlived the Spanish and Mexican territorial governments, Pueblo leaders assume that their nation will also outlive the United States, and today must wonder about the environmental damage they will inherit when the laboratory closes down. In the future, the most serious environmental impacts may derive from the nuclear waste dump that the laboratory has installed on a plateau directly above the Pueblo. The accumulation of radioactive waste buried in shafts and pits at what is known as "Area G" has made it a "national sacrifice zone": an important unresolved question, however, is, for whose nation? San Ildefonso's forced entry into the plutonium economy now presents a "national security" problem of indefinite longevity for the pueblo. Pueblo leaders are responding to these millennial problems by working to train a new generation of Pueblo youth as environmental scientists. The future of the pueblo will increasingly involve monitoring LANL activities and mobilizing environmental laws to protect the physical, spiritual, and financial security of the tribe from the local effects of U.S. national security policy.

The unique legal status of Pueblo Nations in North America infuses such negotiations with a complicated international context. Pueblo communities were incorporated into the United States in the Treaty of Guadalupe Hidalgo in 1848. Unlike many indigenous nations, they did not enter into individual treaties with the U.S. government but were incorporated as "Mexican citizens." Their aboriginal status, however, was debated for the next sixty years during which many Pueblo communities lost much of their land base before the U.S. government took up formal trust responsibility in 1913 (Simmons, 1979: 213–15; Ortiz, 1980). Although the Treaty of Guadalupe Hidalgo theoretically made all citizens of Mexico in the ceded territories U.S. citizens in 1848, and the U.S. Congress theoretically granted all Native Americans full citizenship in 1924, Pueblo members did not actually achieve the right to vote in either state or federal elections until 1948 (Sando, 1992: 102). Moreover, Native American nations in the United States are legally designated as "domestic, dependent nations," an ambiguous status that allows state and federal bureaucracies to redefine indigenous sovereignty rights on an issue-by-issue basis (see Cohen, 1941). This relegates Native American communities to the paradoxical position of being, as John Borneman (1995) has insightfully pointed out, entities that are "simultaneously domestic and foreign" to the United States. Today, Pueblo members maintain a dual citizenship with the United States and their respective pueblos.

It is important to acknowledge that the people who arguably paid the most immediate price for the Manhattan Project in the 1940s did not at the time even have the right to vote in New Mexican or federal elections.[11] Many of the shrines and pilgrimage sites that Pueblo members identify as having been spiritually important "since time immemorial" were destroyed by laboratory installations, roads, weapons tests, and the town of Los Alamos.[12] Moreover, revelations about LANL's environmental impacts and the amount of nuclear materials on the highways have alerted Pueblo leaders to the frightening fact that one nuclear accident on the highways crossing Pueblo land could potentially destroy their entire nation. I asked one Pueblo member about the environmental justice implications of nuclear weapons work at LANL:

> What your people have done here is more than racism or environmental racism. It's genocide against my people. It's part of the system of apartheid in America. South Africa is not the only place with apartheid, you know. It's part of a system where Europeans came to this area and because we didn't have a written system, a written title, took the land and placed us on reservations. Little areas of land that restrict our movement and culture. I thought in the 1940s we were fighting against Nazi experiments on humans and the creation of a Nazi "superman." That's why we helped the government at Los Alamos. But now with all the revelations about human experimentation here, the U.S. government was doing the same things. There's no difference.

The reference to human experimentation is a pointed one. Many in northern New Mexico fear that the laboratory has poisoned the land

and the people. This concern is exacerbated by the fact that current epidemiological models are unable to evaluate statistically the cancer rates in the small-scale communities of northern New Mexico, leaving such fears on an ambiguous scientific terrain. LANL's techno-scientific approach also falters when confronted with Pueblo cultural and religious concerns. In response to Pueblo demands to protect the undisturbed religious sites on the forty-three square miles of what is now laboratory territory, LANL officials offered to map these sites and design future construction projects around them. However, the strict prohibitions within Pueblo societies about speaking to the non-initiated about religious matters—a tactic developed to fight the missionary zeal of seventeenth-century Spanish officials and reinforced by the aggressive ethnographic collecting of early twentieth-century anthropologists—makes such an approach impossible. Thus, Pueblo negotiations with LANL and Department of Energy officials have historically faltered over two very crucial national security issues: the health and religious rights of Pueblo nations. In the end, Pueblo governments who believe their health, territorial borders, and spiritual security have been compromised by U.S. national security work at Los Alamos must face the reality of fighting an institution with a $1 billion annual budget (which is vital to the national security of the world's sole remaining superpower) and of doing so in U.S. courts.[13]

If we follow the plutonium economy one community further to the east in the New Mexico landscape, to Pojoaque Pueblo, which lies immediately adjacent to San Ildefonso and fifteen miles north of Santa Fe, we find a very different articulation of a plutonium-mediated national security. Pojoaque is a pueblo with a difficult history. It has, as its governor says, "died twice" because of epidemics in the eighteenth and nineteenth centuries, and was only reconstituted in the 1930s. Pojoaque entered the plutonium economy in 1994 with a public announcement that it was going to pursue nuclear waste storage as a form of economic development. By 1995, Pojoaque had taken only the first steps in this process, a series of conceptual studies, but its national security strategy shows how mediated by nuclear issues indigenous politics in New Mexico has become. In the late 1980s, the Department of Energy began a process of soliciting all indigenous nations about nuclear waste storage projects on tribal lands (Hanson, 1997; Stoffle and Evans, 1988). This was, and is, an explicit attempt to break the gridlock around nuclear waste caused by middle-American fear of living near nuclear materials. For many tribes, new recognition as a "sovereign nation" is quickly followed by invitations from federal bureaucracies and corporations for lucrative nuclear waste storage projects. By 1995, the initial outlines of a transnational Native American nuclear waste storage economy were beginning to take shape in New Mexico: the Mescalaro Apache began building a short-term nuclear waste storage facility in southern New Mexico and signed agreements with an association of northern Canadian Cree nations for permanent storage of U.S. nuclear waste. The North American Free Trade Agreement (NAFTA) explicitly marked radioactive waste as a nontariff item, paving the way for this kind of transnational indigenous nuclear waste infrastructure (see Hanson, 1994, 1997).

Pojoaque's nuclear waste storage project was, however, also a political tactic designed to underscore what was at stake for the pueblo in debates over casino gaming. National security for the few hundred people that make up Pojoaque Pueblo today means economic independence. The government at Pojoaque Pueblo has been among the most vocal supporters of Indian gaming in New Mexico, and today the pueblo has one of the most successful casinos in the state. Its "City of Gold" casino plays off the ancient myth of the seven golden cities of Cibola that energized the Spanish conquest of the Southwest, and today it extracts money, with almost surgical irony, from the mostly Spanish-speaking counties of northern New Mexico. In 1995, the legality of Pueblo gaming operations in U.S. courts remained in doubt, even though compacts had been signed by the governor of New Mexico and approved by the U.S. secretary of the interior. The consequences of these negotiations could not be more serious; as there are few industries more profitable than casino gaming or nuclear waste, quite literally, millions, and possibly billions, are at stake in these decisions. It is hardly surprising, then, that in response to a steady stream of new legal roadblocks on gaming from state and federal officials, a coalition of nine Pueblo nations in the mid-1990s repeatedly threatened to shut down the highways in northern New Mexico (all of which cross Pueblo lands) if the gaming compacts were not honored.[14]

In their public announcement, Pojoaque representatives specifically stated that they were interested in storing plutonium from dismantled U.S. nuclear weapons, precisely the weapons that were designed a few miles up the road at LANL. The plutonium economy has come back to Los Alamos and the role of nuclear materials in defining national security. Pojoaque's leadership played off of fears of nuclear waste in Santa Fe to press claims about tribal gaming. Pojoaque Pueblo's tactical consideration of placing a nuclear waste site on tribal lands, however, not only is an example of the high-stakes international politics that have taken place around nuclear materials in New Mexico since 1943, but also suggests a strategy that privileges an economic-based national security over all other concerns. Thus, as the national security of San Ildefonso is compromised by the environmental and social costs of the laboratory's nuclear waste dump, neighboring Pojoaque, a community that has already "died twice" in its history, can still forward nuclear waste storage as the ultimate means of achieving its own national security. Pojoaque's strategy is, however, a direct consequence of the interior colonial dynamic between Native American communities and the United States. Thus, although no indigenous nation currently produces nuclear waste, all are potential candidates for the disposal of the nuclear materials produced by the U.S. nuclear complex.[15]

POSTCOLONIAL INSECURITIES: NUEVOMEXICANOS AND THE TRI-ETHNIC TRAP

If we follow our plutonium economy ten miles north from Pojoaque along Highway 68 to the town of Española, a different, but equally charged, set of security issues is evoked. Española is a majority Spanish-speaking community. Many Española residents are direct descendants of the first Spanish settlers in the region in 1598, and can self-identify as "twentieth-generation New Mexicans." LANL is the area's largest single employer, accounting for roughly half of the jobs in greater Rio Arriba County. Before Los Alamos was built in the 1940s, most Nuevomexicano families in the area lived on small-scale farms and spoke primarily Spanish (Weigle, 1975; Forrest, 1989). Many had to work as migrant laborers all across the Southwest to support their families. Currently, there are three generations of men and women from the tiny villages of northern New Mexico who have worked almost exclusively at the laboratory. Traditionally they have been the security guards, laborers, and support staff. Although more Nuevomexicanos are working in technical fields at the laboratory, in the early 1990s very few had careers as scientists or project managers. Thus, an extreme cultural and economic, as well as geographic, divide separates Los Alamos from "the valley." According to the U.S. Census, Los Alamos County is 94 percent white, with the highest number of Ph.D.s per capita in the nation. Rio Arriba County is 75 percent "Hispanic" (although few in New Mexico recognize this term), with only 10 percent of the population having completed college degrees. The average income in Los Alamos is three times that of Rio Arriba County. Unemployment is 2 percent on "the hill," but more than 27 percent in "the valley." In other words, for most people in Rio Arriba County who desire a middle-class lifestyle, Los Alamos National Laboratory is the only game in town.

One Hispano, who recently retired from a thirty-five-year career as a construction foreman at LANL, put it this way, jabbing his finger into my chest for emphasis:

> I'll tell you what to write in your book—you write that the lab saved everybody in this valley! Without Los Alamos, all these little Spanish villages wouldn't exist. Everybody tries to work at the lab—because its good, steady work. Before the lab, all the men in the valley had to go all over the country trying to find work—they would see their families only once or twice a year. With the lab, we have good jobs that allow us to stay with our families. People drive from all over New Mexico to work at the lab—from Albuquerque, from Tierra Amarilla—because it's such good work. People from the valley built Los Alamos and there are always big construction projects there, there's always work.

This narrative of an endless economic security broke down in 1995, however, as the laboratory (for the first time ever) laid off more than a thousand people, predominantly Nuevomexicanos from the valley, and forecast more post–Cold War layoffs to come. Within this political context, Nuevomexicanos began expressing long-standing concerns that LANL holds northern New Mexico hostage economically, that it is more responsible to officials in Washington, D.C., than to local communities. Employees began to talk openly about racism at the laboratory, about a "glass ceiling" in promotions, and about how Nuevomexicanos do most of the dangerous and dirty work. Outside the laboratory, residents of the valley discussed the long-term effects on Nuevomexicano culture of having to speak English at the laboratory, and, as always, note when LANL employees began pronouncing their Spanish surnames with an English accent. Without the security of employment provided by an endlessly expanding national laboratory, the public sphere surrounding LANL in northern New Mexico in the mid-1990s was being radicalized and racialized, with an increasingly public portrayal of LANL as a colonial institution. The laboratory's layoffs in the fall of 1995, for example, were immediately interpreted by some in Española and neighboring communities as a federal declaration of war on northern New Mexico.

It is important to understand the historical context of such a conclusion. From the Nuevomexicano point of view, the 1848 Treaty of Guadalupe Hidalgo has never been honored by the United States (Chavez, 1984; Acuna, 1988). Explicit provisions in that treaty for the protection of the culture and land of Mexican citizens incorporated into the United States were negotiated and then stricken by Congress at the last moment. The Mexican government demanded, and received, further assurances that its citizens' land rights would be protected in the United States (del Castillo, 1990). The land grants that were the basis for both Spanish and Mexican social and economic organizations were, however, quickly broken apart by U.S. territorial judges, who affirmed legal ownership of small plots of land to individuals, but not the large collective landholdings that had traditionally been used for cattle grazing and that were the basis for communal life. Only a fraction of Nuevomexicano land claims were upheld by the U.S. courts in the late nineteenth century, and many were stolen outright by a corrupt legal system. Literally millions of acres changed hands, leaving almost every Nuevomexicano family in northern New Mexico with a story about how the U.S. government or someone manipulating the U.S. legal system took part of their land and impoverished their communities (see Briggs and Van Ness, 1987; Ebright, 1994). Consequently, much of the U.S. national forest land in New Mexico remains hotly contested to this day and is a perennial source of regional tension. In a discussion about California's recently passed Proposition 187, which denied public services (including hospitals and schools) to undocumented Mexican immigrants in California, one Hispano activist summed it up with a casual shrug: "The United States and Mexico never signed the same treaty in 1848—they are still at war."

For many Nuevomexicanos, and those who do not work at the laboratory in particular, there is bitter irony in the fact that New

Mexico is now the center of the U.S. nuclear weapons complex. Indeed, the U.S. government saturates everyday life in northern New Mexico, monitoring land and water use through the U.S. Forest Service and the State Engineers Office, housing and welfare through Housing and Urban Development (HUD) and other agencies, and regulating employment through Los Alamos National Laboratory. Thus, although the U.S. nuclear weapons complex provides an important job base in New Mexico, (the third poorest state in the United States), federal and state officials nonetheless practice a historical amnesia about treaty obligations and the long-standing land claims of Nuevomexicano residents. As one Chicano land-grant activist put it:

> The real problem is dealing with white politicians, most of whom came to New Mexico very recently. You go to a public hearing and talk about land grants and the Treaty of Guadalupe Hidalgo and they look at you like you're from another planet—they don't know what you are talking about. They treat you like you just got off the boat from Juárez and they want to see your green card. We've been here for hundreds of years. The real immigrants are all those people from New York, Boston, and California that come to live here and know nothing about us.

This political dynamic is what anthropologist John Bodine has called a "tri-ethnic trap" (1968), a situation in which the legal and cultural position of Nuevomexicanos is doubly marginalized by white structures of power and by the cultural status of Native Americans as the "first Americans." Thus, although Pueblos as sovereign governments have gained a new post–Cold War legal discourse with the laboratory, equally impacted Nuevomexicano communities have gained no such legal voice. In this context, Nuevomexicano concerns about the economic and environmental impacts of the laboratory can be dismissed, as they were by the LANL leadership following the 1995 layoffs, as an expression of a "welfare state mentality" and not of legitimate political concern (*Santa Fe New Mexican*, September 12, 1995). Nuevomexicano participation in the plutonium economy is therefore double-edged: it has allowed many access to a middle-class life, but it has also meant participating in an ongoing consolidation of northern New Mexico to Anglo-American and U.S. governmental interests. It is with new post–Cold War anxiety, then, that many

Nuevomexicanos continue to look to LANL as the future of northern New Mexico. Others, however, underscore their resistance by referring to the laboratory and town site simply as "Los Alamos, D.C.," acknowledging that, more than five decades into the Manhattan Project, Los Alamos remains, in their eyes, more properly a suburb of Washington, D.C., than a legitimate part of New Mexico (Romero, 1995).

NONGOVERNMENTAL INSECURITIES: ANTINUCLEAR ORGANIZATIONS AND THE NEW TRANSNATIONAL IMAGINARY

Our exploration of the plutonium economy concludes in Santa Fe, which is twenty miles equidistant from Española and Los Alamos and is home to several antinuclear nongovernmental organizations (NGOs), which have been instrumental in organizing community debates about the laboratory in the post–Cold War era. The membership of these NGOs, notably the Los Alamos Study Group and Concerned Citizens for Nuclear Safety, is mostly Anglo, first-generation New Mexican, and self-identifies as citizens of the United States. These antinuclear NGOs have become extremely adept at utilizing environmental laws to gain a voice in nuclear weapons policy at LANL. In 1995, for example, they halted construction of the Duel Axis Radiographic Hydrodynamic Test Facility (DARHT), which the Department of Energy has identified as *the* premier post–Cold War facility for ensuring the safety and reliability of the U.S. nuclear weapons stockpile (U.S. Department of Energy, 1995b). They did so by forcing LANL, through U.S. courts, to do an environmental impact study of DARHT and to justify publicly the need for the project. In the 1990s, these NGOs have provided the first consistent, technically and legally informed, public critique of U.S. nuclear weapons work at LANL. They have also sought to provide technical information about the laboratory and its environmental impacts to a fragile coalition of diverse Pueblo, Nuevomexicano, and Anglo interests.

For many in these organizations, the real achievement of the Manhattan Project was not the atomic bomb but the institutionalization of a system of government secrecy, and with it the curtailing of democratic process when it comes to U.S. national security policy. They view their work as combating the secrecy and public manipulation of an insurgent military-industrial complex and, more specifically, as exposing the environmental, social, and global security impacts of nuclear weapons work at LANL. As one Anglo peace activist put it: "Everything having to do with nuclear weapons is born secret in the United States—and the division between what is secret and what is not secret is also secret." Thus, for antinuclear activists, U.S. citizens are eliminated from the decision-making process because federal authorities can argue that, by definition, citizens never have the information necessary to make informed statements about U.S. national security policy.[16] Consequently, antinuclear NGOs in Santa Fe initiated a new project in 1995, that of lobbying the World Court to outlaw nuclear weapons globally.[17] By appealing directly to a global legal body, NGOs not only call into question the legality of U.S. national security policy in New Mexico, but also dramatically demonstrate that the federal government does not represent their national security interests. This act not only underscores a profound distrust of the United States when it comes to nuclear weapons policy, but also exemplifies how the local is now intersecting with the global, how individuals are beginning to imagine their community as part of a post–nation-state world order. Through such actions, NGOs publicly challenge and reject the state's right to define authoritatively the meaning of "security" and "danger" for their communities.

For members of these groups who fear environmental contamination from the laboratory and/or identify nuclear weapons of any kind as the greatest threat to their personal security, the U.S. government remains the most immediate danger in the region. For many, LANL is both the symbol for, and the realization of, a society in love with violence. As another Anglo Santa Fe peace activist put it, the central question is:

> How are we going to put an end to this monstrous development of weapons? How are we going to put an end to an institution which so far has existed, as far as I can see, primarily as an institution developing means of threat, an institution which works to instill fear in people, an institution basically which has devoted itself for over fifty years now to violence? We're all very aware of the violence that we have around us. What is it like for young people to grow up in this city and to look out and see those lights every night and know what's going on up there, that [LANL] is an institution devoted to violence . . . that Los Alamos is a place of death?

Antinuclear NGOs critique LANL, therefore, on moral and ethical as well as environmental grounds. They point out that the majority of the nuclear weapons in the current U.S. stockpile were designed *after* the United States signed the Nuclear Nonproliferation Treaty in 1968, in which government leaders promised to "achieve at the earliest possible date the cessation of the nuclear arms race and to undertake effective measures in the direction of nuclear disarmament" (*Treaty on the Non-Proliferation of Nuclear Weapons, 1968*: 1). In the mid-1990s, even as a comprehensive test ban was being negotiated by the Clinton administration, activists feared that the arms race was simply going into a new phase, emphasizing the design and testing of nuclear weapons in virtual reality. This is a major structural change in the nuclear complex, one that will generate few environmental impacts, thus eliminating one of the primary legal tools that NGOs have for influencing U.S. nuclear weapons policy. These are not unfounded concerns, for U.S. weapons laboratories will receive more than $40 billion in new facilities for their "science based stockpile stewardship programs" from 1996 to 2006 (Zerriffi and Makhijani, 1996). The DOE has proclaimed these facilities necessary to ensure the "safety and reliability" of nuclear weapons in a world without underground nuclear testing, but these programs will also provide a "state-of-the-art" complex (with the world's fastest computers, as well as numerous new aboveground testing facilities) equally capable of designing new nuclear weapons as testing old ones (see Zerriffi and Makhijani, 1996; Gusterson, 1995). Thus, the post–Cold War period has produced unexpected, and new, forms of insecurity for local antinuclear NGOs as the United States has ignored the opportunities for large-scale disarmament, renewed its commitment to a plutonium-mediated national security, and begun retooling for a new generation of nuclear weapons work.

CONCLUSION: DOING ANTHROPOLOGY IN AN INSECURE STATE

I have tried to demonstrate in this essay that "national security" in New Mexico is not simply a question of how to defend the territorial borders of the United States; it evokes the contradictory and competing worldviews currently attached to military-industrial, aboriginal, postcolonial, and antinuclear subject-positions in North America. Moreover, each of these ideological positions involves a specific constellation of racial, ethnic, national, and territorial identities, while maintaining distinct internal politics as well. Communities in New Mexico are mobilizing historical identities, and pursuing new forms of subaltern nation building, by challenging U.S. national security policy in international forums, in U.S. courts, and in the everyday context of living next to a major nuclear facility. What does this political fragmentation surrounding the plutonium economy in New Mexico tell us about the new global context or insecurities in the post–Cold War era?

The end of the Cold War inaugurated a reorganization of global political and economic structures, generating new internal and external pressures for some regional populations. New Mexico, for example, is now part of a transnational economic arena in which the sovereignty of Native American nations has become an attractive means through which corporations can manipulate legal restrictions on dangerous substances such as nuclear waste. Current DOE regulations for burying nuclear waste, for example, require that permanent storage facilities have a ten-thousand-year operative plan, an unprecedented legal requirement that is still just a momentary blip in the social life of plutonium. Here, the dilemma of the "national sacrifice zone" is finally revealed: that of designating which nations—past, present, and future—must bear the costs of the Cold War nuclear economy. I have argued here that the Cold War reliance on a plutonium-mediated national security has already surpassed the ability of the United States to control its mutating effects, unleashing materials and social logics that will be generating diverse insecurities for generations to come. Concurrently, the post–Cold War effort in Congress to do away with unifying national programs and policies in favor of individual state programs—what might be called a national *unbuilding* project—promises to put poor states, such as New Mexico, which rely on federal dollars for basic services, at ever-greater risk. This dynamic is exacerbated by the marginalizing of local ethnic groups in New Mexico, many of which were instrumental in fighting the Cold War and which are now being targeted by corporate and U.S. national interests. U.S. national security policy has, therefore, produced a wide range of effects in the Southwest over the last half century, leaving many in the post–Cold War era to search out their own forms of security.

To understand these realities, we might consider the advantages of a "decentered" approach to the production of (in)security. *Decentered* means moving beyond the nation-state to nation-state dynamic that has in different ways dominated both security studies and anthropology, to pursue projects that investigate multiple subject-positions and that explore how specific experiences of place are constructed in the tension between the global and the local. As I have tried to demonstrate in this essay, approaching the production of insecurity with universalistic definitions of sovereignty, security, or citizenship means erasing the cultural and political complexity of many geographic spaces in the world, such as northern New Mexico, and rendering invisible areas of ongoing, and potential, conflict. This has been amply demonstrated in the immediate post–Cold War period. Only a few years ago, for example, it was still possible to describe the former Yugoslavia as an example of a working multiethnic, pluralistic society. And who could have predicted that the most significant struggle in recent North American history would erupt among indigenous communities in Chiapas over the terms of the 1994 North American Free Trade Agreement? In both of these situations, the relationship of memory to land, race, and ethnicity has combined with historical shifts in geopolitical relations to produce regional volatilities that challenge Cold War assumptions about the foundational bases of security and even national stability.

To understand cross-cultural anxiety and (inter)national conflict in the post–Cold War era, we need to move beyond a model of security studies based primarily on alignments of weapons and armies to include investigations of how people experience insecurity across a broader sphere of relationships, from those of economic exploitation, to environmental degradation, to racial conflict and geopolitical marginalization. This poses several distinct disciplinary challenges. For anthropology it means moving beyond the implicit Cold War emphasis on using one's home nation-state as the ultimate point of reference for identifying difference. As John Borneman has pointed out (1995), anthropology has always been involved in a subtle form of foreign policy, in that, by exploring the boundaries of "otherness," anthropologists have also been implicitly reenforcing national borders. This is most clearly evidenced in the traditional requirement for entry into the field of anthropology as a profession: the completion of an ethnographic project that takes place *outside* the territorial borders of one's own nation-state. From this perspective, anthropology has been involved, however obliquely, in a particular state and nation-building project right from the very beginning. Consequently, it may well be that in the future we will look back on the anthropology of the Cold War as a distinctive global project (see Nader, 1997). Recent interest in examining global processes from an ethnographic point of view has produced a number of innovative efforts to expand the possibilities for ethnographic research (e.g., see Appadurai, 1991; Friedman, 1994; Marcus, 1995a). Because the Cold War provided much of the energy and funding for the development of area studies programs, however, the challenge that remains is to articulate a compelling new understanding of the value of cross-cultural research, one that is not tied to the kind of state and nation-building projects that characterized the Cold War, but one that also does not abandon programs that are, in fact, producing both cross-cultural and international understanding.[18]

Decentering security studies is a more profound challenge, given that it is largely a creation of the Cold War, and because of the close interactions that many security scholars maintain with government policymakers. As this essay purports to be a case study, we might locate one conceptual blind spot in Cold War security studies by reviewing institutional responses to the "national security" debates in New Mexico. With few exceptions, security studies agencies in the mid-1990s found the security issues raised in this essay to be simply unrecognizable.[19] Two issues seem to inform readings that positioned the regional debates about Los Alamos outside the purview of security studies: (1) the ambiguous legal standing of indigenous nations within international relations theory, and (2) the absence of an area studies category devoted to investigating security issues *internal* to the United States. These conversations at times provoked curious results. For example, I was informed by one security studies agency that if I could demonstrate that the political context around Los Alamos had international implications—something that might affect arms-control agreements, for instance—then this project might be considered a contribution to security studies. Then, while readily acknowledging the territorial sovereignty of Pueblo nations in New Mexico, and thus seemingly an international context, that agency concluded that because the Pueblos were unlikely to "break away" from the United States, the regional context surrounding LANL lacked the criteria to be relevant to security studies. A paradoxical vision of sovereignty was revealed in these exchanges, one defined by an ability to threaten the United States within this paradigm. Because Pueblo nations do not have standing armies, and cannot militarily challenge the United States, there are no legitimate security concerns in the region. Consequently, indigenous nations can only enter the world of security studies by taking military action, and even then they can enter it only as a threat to U.S. national security, not as national entities with security concerns unique and valid unto themselves. The broader security implications of building (and, after the Cold War, potentially consolidating) the U.S. nuclear weapons complex in an area of New Mexico that is territorially contested (with sixteen indigenous nations and numerous land-grant controversies), racially and ethnically unique (a majority Nuevomexicano and Native American region), and poor (one in three people around Los Alamos live below the poverty line) were rendered invisible, in this case, by devotion to a specific Cold War–era internationalism.

A vigorous interdisciplinary debate is now taking place over the conceptual and institutional outlines of a post–Cold War global studies. Undoubtedly, the twenty-first century will witness new parameters both for what counts as security as well as for the more ominous issue of whose insecurity it is important to understand. One test of the institutional ability to disengage from Cold War structures, I suggest, is whether North America, and the United States in particular, is included within a revised security studies topography. Certainly, the kinds of issues being debated in New Mexico—which involve state and quasi-state entities, asymmetrical legal structures, territorial memory, alternative definitions of citizenship, and fundamental questions of environmental justice—argue for a move away from a strict focus on state-to-state interactions to enable investigations into how people actually experience insecurity in everyday life. Given the embedded cultural and institutional legacies of the Cold War, however, it may well be that in order to study insecurity at the dawn of the twenty-first century, we may have to embrace it as well.

NOTES

Earlier versions of this essay were presented at the 1995 Annual Meeting of the American Anthropological Association on a panel organized by Adriana Petryna and Mariana Ferreira, and to the Peace Studies Program at Cornell University. I am very grateful for the commentary and discussion received in each of these forums. I would also like to thank Michael Meeker, John Borneman, and Stefan Senders for valued support and criticism. Shawn Smith has been a generous reader and critic of this work.

1. For an analysis of the dual-structured, oppositional nation building in the Cold War Berlins, see Borneman (1992).

2. "From time immemorial" is a legal phrase used in land- and water-rights cases in the United States to designate that Native American claims are prior to any other (see Cohen, 1941).

3. On the history of conflict surrounding Spanish and Mexican land grants in New Mexico, see Briggs and Van Ness (1987); Ebright (1994); Rosenbaum (1981); Gardner (1970); Nostrand (1992); Ortiz (1980); and Pulido (1996).

4. On the concept of New Mexico as a Hispano homeland, see Nostrand (1992). On "Aztlán" see Anaya and Lomeli (1989); Barrera (1988); and Chavez (1984). This split within the Spanish-speaking community in New Mexico over whether to forward Spanish or Native American ancestry in terms of contemporary identity politics is demonstrated in the conflict over naming in northern New Mexico. In the Spanish-speaking villages of northern New Mexico residents are likely to refer to each other as "Mexicano/a," but probably use "Hispano/a," or "Chicano/a" when speaking in English or to outsiders. "Chicano/a" is more commonly used by Spanish speakers in the larger urban areas, but current usage varies considerably and is politicized. In this essay I use the collective term *Nuevomexicano* to refer to all Spanish-speaking people in northern New Mexico; and I use *Hispano* or *Chicano* only when people self-identified to me that way in conversation.

5. For example, see Ortiz (1980); Jaimes (1992); Churchill (1993); Acuna (1988); Chavez (1984); and Pulido (1996). For detailed studies of the relationship of U.S. nation building to race and territory in the ninteenth and early twentieth centuries, see Drinnon (1990) and Horsman (1981).

6. In fact, the state of New Mexico is eclipsed only by Maryland and Virginia in per capita federal dollars. In 1995, this included $2.7 billion from the Department of Energy (DOE) and more than $650 million from the Deparment of Defense (DOD) (see the *Santa Fe New Mexican*, June 18, 1996). Overall, one out of every four workers in New Mexico is employed by the federal government (*Albuquerque Journal*, July 1, 1992), and the DOE is directly responsible for 13 percent of the total economy of the state (see Lansford et al., 1995).

7. I am speaking here specifically about plutonium-239, which was developed for use in nuclear weapons. See International Physicians for the Prevention of Nuclear War and the Institute for Energy and Environmental Research

(IPPNW and IEER) (1992) on the physics and health risks of plutonium, and IPPNW and IEER (1991) on the cumulative health and environmental effects of nuclear weapons tests.

8. The DOE has estimated that it will cost $230 billion over the next seventy-five years to clean up those nuclear production sites that can be cleaned up and simply to stabilize the most serious sites, which remain beyond our capabilities to remediate (see U.S. Department of Energy, 1995b, 1995c).

9. During the Cold War, all nuclear weapons tests by the acknowledged nuclear powers (the United States, Britain, France, China, and the former Soviet Union) took place on contested indigenous lands (see Nietschman and Le Bon, 1987; also Hanson, 1997; LaDuke and Churchill, 1985; and Kuletz, 1998).

10. The Pueblo nations surrounding Los Alamos explicitly articulate their security concerns within a discourse of territorial sovereignty. The difficulty many U.S. officials and security scholars have in accepting this discourse as presented, or in translating the ambiguities around Native American sovereignty into a more familiar discourse of national security, is precisely one of the problems facing indigenous communities in New Mexico, and throughout the Americas.

11. I do not mean to suggest that having the vote would have influenced the Manhattan Project in any way, as it was a top-secret project on which even Vice President Harry Truman was not briefed until after he had been sworn in as president (Rhodes, 1986: 617). I am simply pointing out the legal disparities at work in New Mexico that were instrumental in the development of Los Alamos.

12. On the importance of shrines and pilgrimage sites in Tewa cosmology, see Ortiz (1969).

13. Pueblo governments do have the option of trying to mobilize international opinion and law on their behalf, as several tribes in the Southwest have, in fact, attempted to do. However, there are inherent difficulties in finding international allies that are willing to challenge the United States over internal nuclear weapons policy. Because the United States can evoke the "supreme national interest" clause in any international treaty or agreement to protect the nuclear weapons complex from suit, local Pueblo nations face an uphill battle simply locating an international forum willing to consider their case.

14. Pojoaque Pueblo did, in fact, shut down U.S. highway 84/285, just north of Santa Fe, on March 21, 1996, to protest the lack of progress on gaming issues in the state.

15. See Randy Hanson's pathbreaking analysis of the economics and geopolitical forces behind the Mescalaro Apache's decision to initiate a nu-

clear waste storage project (1994, 1997). On nuclear politics and environmental justice, see Kuletz (1998); LaDuke and Churchill (1985); Eichstaedt (1994); Grinde and Johansen (1995); Stoffle and Evans (1988). On concepts of environmental justice, see Bryant (1995); Bullard (1993); and Pulido (1996).

16. For example, the DARHT lawsuit was ultimately settled in favor of the DOE/LANL only after the DOE provided a classified supplement to the federal judge adjudicating the case. NGOs argued that they should be able to find a representative with a security clearance to review the classified documentation in order to mount an adequate rebuttal, but they were denied that option. Ultimately, NGOs in Santa Fe succeeded in delaying the DARHT project for sixteen months, and put LANL on notice for the first time that the public could significantly influence nuclear weapons projects at the laboratory.

17. In 1996, the World Court in the Hague did rule that using nuclear weapons in a first-strike capacity was against international law; however, judges left room in their decision for a "defensive" use of nuclear weapons.

18. My intent here is only to point out the structural role that the Cold War played in shaping the development of area studies; it is not to make any claim on what individual scholars did within those area studies categories (see Rafael, 1994; Lewontin et al., 1997).

19. The notable exception was the MacArthur Foundation, which supported the conversation leading to this collection of essays.

8

Adding an Asian Strand: Neoliberalism and the Politics of Culture in New Zealand, 1984–97

MARK LAFFEY

Since 1984, successive New Zealand governments have aggressively pursued neoliberal policy reform.[1] In a remarkably short time, they have achieved a degree of social, political, and economic transformation far beyond that of the Reagan and Thatcher regimes more commonly associated with such policies (Kelsey, 1995). International institutions such as the International Monetary Fund (IMF) and the Organization for Economic Cooperation and Development (OECD) as well as international media such as the *Economist* and the *Wall Street Journal* celebrate New Zealand's neoliberal reforms as an international success story and an example for the rest of the world (for a summary, see ibid., 5–8).

The celebration of structural adjustment policy in New Zealand is but one element in the emergent discourse of world politics that Agnew and Corbridge (1995) term transnational liberalism or, as it is more popularly and less precisely dubbed, "globalization" (e.g., Mittelman, 1996). Despite the oft-repeated claim that "globalization" has rendered the nation-state defunct or at best powerless in the face of hypermobile capital, it is more correct to see states as "agencies of the globalizing trend" (Cox, 1996: 155). Contrary to the "millennial dreams" of capitalist postmodernity (Smith, 1997), capital is still both grounded in and dependent on the state even as

233

the state is busy reshaping relations between the territory over which it holds sway and the world economy. Whether through the enforcement of property laws and policing, the maintenance of the "order" necessary to doing business, or more generally the production of the conditions under which accumulation takes place, state power is "an essential prop to the political management of global accumulation" (Drainville, 1995: 69).

Among the conditions of capital accumulation in which the state plays a key role are processes of subject formation. In this chapter, I argue that the discourse of transnational liberalism prompts a heightened interest on the part of at least some states in reasserting the national identity of their citizens, albeit an identity reworked in ways that render it compatible with the requirements of flexible accumulation as these are shaped by particularities of site and situation.[2] A significant feature of the emergent regime of flexible accumulation brought into being by policies of structural adjustment, then, is the production of new social subjects—"flexible" subjects, as it were—through state efforts to renarrate the nation (Smith, 1997: 81–84). Reflecting the fact that it is often through the language of culture and "culturalisms" that identity politics is mobilized at the level of the nation-state (Appadurai, 1996: 15), the reworking of national identity associated with transnational liberalism is effected through a new and overt politics of "culture." I elaborate this argument through an analysis of the politics of "culture" in contemporary New Zealand.

Pred and Watts argue that "how things develop depends in part on *where* they develop, on what has been historically sedimented there, on the social and spatial structures that are already in place" (1992: 11). In New Zealand, discourses of global competitiveness and flexibility confront subjects already spoken for by public narratives of national identity structured around conceptions of place and belonging—New Zealand as white and European—that, through the practices they motivate, are in certain respects inconsistent with the new regime of accumulation. In the face of the rise in the 1980s of a "dynamic" East Asia within the world economy—often articulated as part of the "Asia-Pacific" (Cumings, 1992a; Dirlik, 1992)—and growing relations between New Zealand and states in that region, such narratives, as I will show, generate orientations to the world inconsistent with neoliberal narratives of flexibility and the pursuit of markets solely on the basis of comparative advantage.

Rendered insecure by the requirements of flexible accumulation, the state and corporate capital responded by setting out to reimagine New Zealand as a multicultural part of the "Asia-Pacific" rather than as (an admittedly distant) part of Europe.[3] Such a reimagining aims in part to facilitate the integration of New Zealand into the "Asia-Pacific" by convincing potential investors and immigrants that it is not a racist place. But the rewriting of New Zealand identity is only partly directed to an offshore audience. At least as important from the point of view of the state and capital is the production of new social subjects in New Zealand appropriate to the needs of flexible accumulation in the South Pacific. It is for this reason that, in reaction to the difficulties white and European narratives of place and belonging generate for the neoliberal state, the extended state and capital have, in part through the Asia 2000 Foundation, sought explicitly to renarrate New Zealand as multicultural and part of Asia, and thereby to produce new subjects who will look to and actively engage with East Asia.

This new politics of "culture" is not peculiar to New Zealand. As I will show, the discourse of "globalization"—of flexibility and competitiveness in the context of a reconfigured world economy—prompts similar efforts to rearticulate the nation in other places. Shaped by local circumstance and the specific histories of particular places, transnational liberalism effects and is effected through a new politics of "culture." In this chapter, I examine New Zealand state efforts to renarrate the nation as both an exemplary instance of, and as a window onto, the politics of "culture" in the context of transnational liberalism.

The argument unfolds in two steps: first, I sketch the new international imaginary of competitiveness and flexible accumulation and show how it produces insecurities for the state and capital in general and in New Zealand in particular; and second, I trace the effects of this imaginary in the contemporary politics of culture in New Zealand. Specifically, I examine recently enacted neoliberal immigration policies and the associated contests over national identity, outline some of the institutional means through which new narratives of self and other are being produced, and discuss efforts to rewrite New Zealand's history. In the conclusion, I draw out the implications of my argument for thinking through the politics of culture in the context of "globalization."

TRANSNATIONAL LIBERALISM AND THE PRODUCTION OF GEOECONOMIC INSECURITIES

Despite newfound or rediscovered concerns about rogue states, horizontal nuclear proliferation, and ethnonationalism, according to many Western intellectuals of statecraft, the central drama of world politics after the Cold War is geoeconomic rather than geopolitical in character. Economic competition between liberal capitalist states is the new ground on which hopes and fears, opportunities and threats are being constructed. This particular reworking of the Western international imagination is in turn one more expression of the ongoing expansion and restructuring of what is now claimed to be a transnational or global capitalism (e.g., Dirlik, 1994; cf. Smith, 1997). Of course, none of this means that more traditional geopolitical concerns about alliance formation, the strategic environment or the size of one another's arsenals have been forgotten by state managers and their research and planning departments. Narratives of competitiveness and flexibility presuppose rather than challenge the continuing centrality of U.S. military power to world order (e.g., Cumings, 1992b). But discourses of the post–Cold War world by and large foreground the geoeconomic rather than the geopolitical as they imagine into existence a brave new world of transnational liberalism. If the key concept of the Cold War was national security, it is competitiveness that now comes more often to the lips of governments and policy analysts the world over.

Transnational liberalism brings with it a set of claims about how competitiveness is to be achieved that, taken together, constitute a developmental model (Lipietz, 1992). An exemplar of this model, at least according to authorities such as the World Bank and the IMF, is New Zealand. Prior to the election in 1984 of a Labour government that embarked on an ambitious and rapid program of neoliberal reform, New Zealand was regularly described as one of the most heavily regulated economies in the world. A decade and a half later, New Zealand rated high on indexes of international competitiveness. According to the Swiss-based World Economic Forum, for example, in 1995 New Zealand ranked eighth in the world in competitiveness; by 1996, it was third, behind only Singapore and Hong Kong (but cf.

"World Competitiveness On-Line," 1997). Despite what was, by most indicators, only weak economic performance and a simultaneous assault on the standard of living and the security of many of its citizens (Kelsey, 1995), the "New Zealand model" rapidly became a benchmark in international policy circles for the privatization of public assets, the reform of state structures, and the deregulation of labor markets, among other things. Although by 1998 it had dropped to thirteenth in the global competitiveness ratings, New Zealand was briefly the very model of a flexible and competitive place.

Regimes of accumulation are always embedded in specific material spaces, defined by particular logics of identity and difference through which they are constituted and positioned in larger sets of relations and processes. Those logics of identity and difference emerge to a significant degree out of histories of nation-state formation: for instance, projects of state formation have typically been carried out in part through the imagining of "communities of shared blood and heritage as well as language," of shared histories and spaces, in which "the ethnic identity of the dominant group is privileged as the core of the imagined community" (Alonso, 1994: 390–91). For most of its history, New Zealand has been narrated and constituted by the dominant settler or Pakeha[4] community as a white, European, and specifically British place (cf. Larner and Spoonley, 1995; True, 1996). A Japanese scholar who in 1995 spent six months in New Zealand observed that "Asians have traditionally perceived this country as 'a bit of Britain in the Southern Hemisphere,' and they have done so with justifiable reasons. In the eyes of the Asian people, New Zealand is still an enclave of Europe in the deep South Pacific" (Kamiya, 1995: 3). This identity was secured and reproduced through policy—"Our immigration is based firmly on the principle that we are and intend to remain a country of European development" (Department of External Affairs, 1953; cited in Brawley, 1993: 36)—and reinforced by New Zealand's positioning within Imperial, British, and Commonwealth circuits of industrial, financial, and cultural capital and both British- and U.S.-centered networks of geopolitical relations. White and European narratives of place and belonging were also rendered plausible partly through the progressive dispossession of Māori land by the state and, until recently, their ongoing cultural, political, economic, and social marginalization (e.g., Walker, 1990). Not surprisingly, everyday experience served to confirm the truthfulness of narratives of British, European, and white belonging (A. Bell, 1996; C. Bell, 1996). These narratives and the practices through which they were reproduced served to naturalize and embed in place a British settler capitalism in the Antipodes (e.g., Berg and Kearns, 1996).

Bundled together under the label of "nationalism," "national identity," or simply "culture," narratives of place and belonging are both materialized through practices of regulation in the apparatuses of the state—immigration policy, for example—and also serve as the systems of meaning through which New Zealanders and other subjects (to the extent that they recognize themselves in such narratives) represent the world to themselves and to each other. Systems of representation—"concepts, ideas, terminology, categories, perhaps also images and symbols" (Hall, 1986: 39)—such as those reproduced in narratives of belonging and place enable us to know the world and to function in it; they locate us in relation to specific social processes and prescribe social identities for us. Such narratives "make a material difference, since how we act in certain situations depends on what our definitions of the situation are" (ibid.). Complexly entwined with class and other dimensions of difference, conceptions of place and belonging expressed in narratives of national identity animate and motivate practices such as news coverage and language training, as well as reactions to foreign investment and immigration, all of which have become topics of public discussion and concern for the New Zealand state and other actors in the context of the rise of East Asia. Decisions about which parts of the world are important and which are not, which items to include in the evening television news, what subjects to study in school, where investment opportunities are to be found, and so forth, all derive in part from narratives of place and belonging that position us in relation to ongoing social processes and relations, at home and overseas. In these and other ways, narratives of place and belonging, and the logics of identity and difference through which they operate, have consequences for the kinds of practices we engage in and for how we are oriented to the world.

Within the discourse of flexible accumulation, articulations of "culture" and the narratives of place and belonging through which they are fleshed out become both a strategic resource for the state and a potential threat to it. Transitions from one regime of accumulation to another must negotiate those regulatory practices and sedimented

narratives through which capitalist social relations have been embedded in particular social formations (e.g., Rupert, 1997). Narratives of place and belonging structured by historical processes of
nation-state formation can motivate practices that render the neoliberal state insecure. The effective pursuit of foreign markets may be
hindered by narratives that inform practices that do not readily enable successful competition: the overproduction in New Zealand of
French-speaking high-school students, for example. Such narratives,
however, can also be rearticulated in ways more compatible with
state projects. Thus, we see efforts to redefine the nation—the "ideological alibi of the territorial state" (Appadurai, 1993: 412)—to rework the logic of identity and difference through which it has been
constituted in order to produce subjects more compatible with the
state's accumulation function (Offe, 1984). These strategies are designed to enable the state to continue to bind subjects—sometimes
over great distances—to attract both their skills and their investment, and so to secure their active engagement in and support for
state projects of capitalist modernity (Ong, 1997).

The significance of the practices motivated by existing narratives
of place and belonging for the neoliberal state is readily apparent in
relation to the contemporary rise of East Asia as a center of capitalist
accumulation and the growth of relations between New Zealand and
states in the region. Like New Zealand, the "miracle economies" of
the "Asia-Pacific" are also often constructed as exemplary and, at
least prior to 1997, as *the* new locus of capitalist accumulation in the
world economy (Cumings, 1992a; Palat, 1996b). For New Zealand,
flexible accumulation requires, among other things, social subjects
who in pursuit of comparative advantage will look to and actively
engage with "Asia." By 1996, more than 40 percent of New Zealand
exports were going to Asian countries—an increase of 62 percent
since 1990—as compared with only 13 percent in 1971. Seven of
New Zealand's top ten markets were in East Asia (Japan, South
Korea, Hong Kong, Taiwan, China, Malaysia, and Indonesia) and
the rate of growth in exports to these markets had been considerable: exports to South Korea, Taiwan, Hong Kong, and Malaysia
grew 492.6, 278.5, 250, and 206.4 percent, respectively, between
December 1985 and December 1995. Tourism—New Zealand's
largest foreign-exchange earner since 1988—from the region had
also grown; by 1996, more than 30 percent of tourists came from

Asian countries (Gibson, 1996; Export Institute of New Zealand, 1996; D. McKinnon, 1996b).

Despite this rapid increase in relations, however, state actors and others have repeatedly expressed anxiety about the continuing lack of popular interest in the region and a persistent cultural orientation toward Europe and Britain (e.g., Kamiya, 1995). For example, in March 1995, Deputy Prime Minister Don McKinnon complained that, despite growing trade relations with "the Asian region" and its importance to New Zealand's future prosperity, there were no New Zealand news correspondents in Asia ("McKinnon Blasts NZ Press," 1995). In response, the New Zealand Press Association's chief executive, Paul Cavanagh, former editor of the *Wellington Evening Post,* cited the high cost of stationing a journalist in Asia—always assuming it was possible both to identify just where "it" was and thus where best to locate him or her. He also noted that "In terms of a newspaper, the readers come first. . . . Newspaper surveys show that Asia does not figure high on their list. They are not signaling they are frantic for Asian news" ("Asian News Gathering," 1995: 5). In a similar vein, Dr. John McKinnon, of the Geography Department at Victoria University, reported that

> Initially my students can really only talk about Asia as an under-developed part of the world that needs New Zealand help. It's depressing. They have an image of Asian cultures as being quaint and ethnic. But that's not the reality. There's no sense of the terrific wealth and sophistication in Asian countries. On their mental map, New Zealand is somewhere in the middle of the Atlantic. There's an unwillingness to admit to the actual world that's sitting on their doorstep. (In "Asian Studies Workshop," 1994)

Narratives of place and belonging that prompt New Zealanders to situate themselves "somewhere in the middle of the Atlantic" and to identify Europe and North America as the sources of important international news—to cite only two examples—run counter to the perceived requirements of flexible accumulation in the South Pacific, thereby rendering both capital and the neoliberal state insecure.

By the 1990s, New Zealand's identity as white and European had become a matter of considerable concern to state actors and business leaders as they attempted to reposition themselves in relation to the "dynamic" space-economies of the "Asia-Pacific." That identity is seen as a hindrance to the active engagement of New Zealanders with Asia, and a barrier to the attraction of Asian investment and the integration of the New Zealand space-economy into the region. Faced with the threat apparently posed by white and European narratives of belonging and the practices they inform for the future of trade, investment, and tourism from East Asia, and more generally for the production of the flexible subjects required by post-Fordist regimes of accumulation, both the extended state and local capital have begun to engage in a set of strategies designed explicitly to rewrite narratives of New Zealand's white identity and to transform the practices through which they have been reproduced. They have set out to reimagine New Zealand. Perhaps the most striking, and egregious, example occurred in 1993 when then-Prime Minister Jim Bolger introduced himself to a Tokyo audience as an Asian leader, causing an instant uproar at home—and doubtless some bemusement among his listeners. The Leader of the Opposition, Helen Clark, retorted: "clearly he is not an Asian leader . . . to say that New Zealand is an Asian nation 'is hyperbole and a very generous interpretation of what constitutes Asia'" (1995: 3, quoting Stephen Hoadley). If not plausibly "Asian"—Bolger and other cheerleaders for regional integration have since taken to saying explicitly that New Zealand is *not* Asian—the state is nevertheless determined at the very least to "add an Asian strand" (Bolger, 1994: 20) to New Zealand identity, so as more readily to locate itself within the "Asia-Pacific."

It is in this context that state actors, business leaders, and representatives of the culture industries have begun to renarrate New Zealand as a multicultural rather than a monocultural (i.e., white and British) or bicultural (i.e., Pakeha and Māori) place, and to 'educate' the New Zealand public anew about the realities of New Zealand's site and situation. As Bolger put it: "New Zealand was never a European country situated in the South Pacific though many thought of us like that. We always had a bicultural dimension and now that in turn has developed into a truly multicultural community" (ibid., 23). The necessity of this reimagining is linked explicitly to the claim that "The countries to our north in the Asian region had become the engines of world growth" and to the preservation of "what had been achieved through the difficult years of restructuring" (McKinnon, in "Launching of Asia 2000," 1994: 2). It is for these reasons that New Zealanders "urgently needed to be aware of what was happening in Asia and to acquire the skills and knowledge to deal more comfortably and effectively with Asian nations" (ibid., 3). Failure to do so risks turning New Zealand into an "isolated backwater in the South Pacific" (Bolger, in ibid., 2). In place of an ethnic nationalism, New Zealanders are now enjoined to embrace some form of civic nationalism (e.g., Yeatman, 1994; M. McKinnon, 1996: 9) as they belatedly discover that they have in fact been multi-cultural all along: "The most remarkable thing about the evolution of New Zealand's national identity is not that we have come to real-ize that it has an Asian dimension, but rather that we have post-poned that realization for so long" (Bolger, 1992: 23).

Efforts by the New Zealand state to redefine New Zealand iden-tity in the context of a putatively global capitalism and a new geo-economic imaginary, and its focus on a politics of "culture" as a means for doing so, are neither isolated nor unusual. Related efforts to bind populations to state projects of capitalist modernity are being pursued elsewhere. Many of these other projects are also articulated through a set of claims about "culture." In Canada, for example, the Multiculturalism Act of 1988 explicitly links multiculturalism with identity, nationhood, and progress. Prime Minister Brian Mulroney made the connection to competitiveness clear: "In a competitive world, we all know that technology, productivity, quality, marketing and price determine export success. But our multicultural identity gives us an edge in selling to that world" (Mulroney, in Mitchell, 1996: 239). Similar articulations have been made in recent Aus-tralian policy. For instance, Prime Minister Paul Keating linked a vi-sion of Australia as a multicultural republic to a "neoliberal agenda of an open, competitive economy integrated into the new global in-dustrial and communications world" (Frankel, 1997: 25). In East Asia, concerns about the potential fragmentation of the nation in the face of "globalization," for example, or the existence of large dias-poric populations, have led to what Spivak (1987: 205) terms "strategic essentialisms"—contingent articulations of identity that purport to refer unproblematically to the real nature of their ostensi-ble referents—on the part of the state as East Asian capitalism is ar-ticulated through narratives of Confucian, Chinese, or Asian culture (Ong and Nonini, 1997; Huat, 1996). Euro-American imaginings of the Asia-Pacific that privilege culture as the marker of difference have been picked up and reproduced by those whom they allegedly are about, often in self-Orientalizing ways (Dirlik, 1992; 1997): diasporic Chinese entrepreneurs narrate their success in terms of an essentialized and ahistorical Confucianism suspiciously similar to the moral virtues espoused by Horatio Alger (Ong, 1997). "Globalization," understood as the internationalization of capitalist social relations of production and the generation of a new global division of labor, thus both prompts and is made possible through a new politics of "culture."

THE POLITICS OF CULTURE IN AN EXEMPLARY PLACE

In the transition from Fordism to flexible accumulation, the role of the New Zealand state in "the production of cultural difference within a structured system of global political economy" and the attendant redefinition of the "territory–identity relation" comes more clearly into view (Pred and Watts, 1992: 12). Efforts to rework what it means to be New Zealand occur at a number of sites and take a variety of forms. Two of the most conspicuous are the ongoing revision of immigration policy and the state's "Asia 2000" initiative, which has set out explicitly to renarrate New Zealand's histories.

Neoliberal Immigration Policy and the Logic of Identity/Difference

Immigration policy reform is one of the sites at which state efforts to redefine the logic of identity/difference through which New Zealand has been constituted are taking place. As Doty points out, the "study of immigration and national identity presents us with the opportunity to examine an instance of how boundaries that separate the inside from the outside get constructed, however provisionally" (1996a: 236). States make nations in part through laws governing who may or may not enter a territory, thereby contributing to the reproduction or the transformation of the political community defined by those boundaries. In turn, as these boundaries are redefined, so the identity of the community is rendered more or less secure. The effects of immigration reform in New Zealand, as elsewhere, are registered in increasingly contested understandings of nationhood and in debate over the meaning of national identity.

In common with Australia and other British colonies of white settlement, the New Zealand state until recently pursued a "White

New Zealand" policy (Brawley, 1993, 1995). These policies were originally formulated in response to Chinese immigration at the end of the nineteenth century (Ip, 1995; Palat, 1996a). Between 1881 and 1920, successive governments passed a series of laws placing ever-greater limitations on entry by non-European peoples into New Zealand, eventually producing one of the most restrictive immigration regimes in the world. By the beginning of World War II, 96 percent of non-Māori New Zealanders were of British extraction, a larger percentage than in any other settler colony (Brooking and Rabel, 1995: 34). Well over 50 percent of permanent and long-term arrivals were from the United Kingdom, a trend made possible by the lack of any immigration controls on this source until 1974 (Ongley, 1996: 19–21).

Most of the legal measures to ensure the preservation and reproduction of New Zealand's white and European identity have been aimed at potential immigrants from Asia. Like Australia, New Zealand was constituted and produced at the intersection of Asian labor migration and a British colonial culture (Offer, 1989); in New Zealand, "Chinese and Britons, the earth's two great migrant peoples, jostled together, the white man always top dog" (Kiernan, 1988: 164). Although often overlooked or marginalized in narratives of becoming found in nationalist historiography (e.g., Gordon, 1960; Sinclair, 1980), in a very real sense Asia and the Asian masses have functioned as New Zealand's "constitutive outside" (Mouffe, 1991: 78). The discursive distinction between Europe and Asia has been not external but rather internal to New Zealand identity formation. That distinction was manifested not only through articulations of race and ethnicity, but also in a set of claims about the relative development, technological prowess, and wealth of the European vis-à-vis the Asian (e.g., Adas, 1989). It is in part for this reason that the contemporary rise of East Asia as a site of capital accumulation in the world economy is seemingly invisible to John McKinnon's geography students and yet also causes such anxiety for the New Zealand state: it contradicts the logic of identity/difference through which New Zealand has been constituted.

These "fairly pragmatic" (Hoadley, 1992: 107) immigration policies continued, with some variation, until 1986 (Brawley, 1993; Ongley, 1996). Beginning in the mid-1980s, the composition of New Zealand's immigration changed significantly: Asian immigration grew rapidly, while the proportion coming from "traditional" sources declined, although the absolute number of Asian immigrants remained small (for figures, see Palat, 1996a). The shift in the composition of New Zealand immigration stemmed from the contemporary "rise" of East Asia and the "Asia-Pacific." This meant that growing numbers of would-be immigrants from Taiwan, South Korea, China, Hong Kong, and India, for example—the top five Asian countries of origin for those receiving residence permits in 1994—met the revised criteria for admission (Ongley, 1996; Palat, 1996a). The shift in policy responsible for this new Asian immigration grew out of the neoliberal agenda of successive New Zealand governments after 1984. Within the discourse of competitiveness, the danger is being left behind by other places that have proven more attractive to capital, including human capital, which is articulated as a strategic resource in a world economy where knowledge and skill have allegedly become the chief source of value (e.g., Reich, 1991). Flexible accumulation requires states to adopt immigration policies that measure would-be immigrants not by ethnic, racial, or cultural factors, but only as human capital.

The 1986 *Review of Immigration Policy* explicitly justified the new business immigration policy and the removal of source country preference in terms both of the barrier that such preferences (and the concomitant discrimination against other sources) represented in the development of trading and financial relations with nontraditional countries and of the need to attract entrepreneurial skills and investment capital (Burke, 1986: 15, 19). *Populate or Languish?*, a study undertaken for the New Zealand Business Roundtable (whose members were estimated in 1991 to account for 85 percent of stock-market capitalization (Kelsey, 1995: 75–76) and so can fairly be described as the executive committee of the bourgeoisie), argued that "[a] deregulated economy would greatly benefit from a more elastic supply of workers with skills and entrepreneurial attitudes" (Kasper, 1990: xiv). It therefore called for immigration reform that would "make New Zealand a more attractive location for internationally mobile people, entrepreneurs and capital" (ibid., 54). These "high-quality" immigrants are defined in terms of their possession of investment capital, business and technical skills, and, increasingly—in New Zealand at least—Asian ethnicity and culture. In the face of growing trade relations with East Asia, these latter qualities are seen as strategically useful in fostering closer business relations with that region (e.g., Ip, 1995: 198–99). More generally, "hybridized" or multicultural subjects (Dirlik, 1997: 171)—whether home-grown or in the form of new immigrants—have become a valuable commodity for states and capital as they seek comparative advantage in what is increasingly constructed as a multicultural world economy. According to Prime Minister Mulroney, speaking in 1986 at a conference called "Multiculturalism Means Business," "Canadians who have cultural links to other parts of the globe, who have business contacts elsewhere are of the utmost importance to our trade and investment strategy" (in Mitchell, 1996: 239). Partly in pursuit of such "assets," citizenship is being redefined as a commodity. Again in common with other states, New Zealand now operates an active business immigration policy that enables would-be immigrants to purchase citizenship in return for investment (Ongley, 1996). At the same time, alternative criteria for admission have been tightened to emphasize professional qualifications and work experience. Immigration policy has thus shifted from an emphasis on historical, cultural, and ethnic connections with the dominant European population to considerations of "personal merit" and human and investment capital in determining admission to and residence in New Zealand.

An important objective of immigration policy, according to the 1986 *Review of Immigration Policy*, is "to enrich the multicultural social fabric of New Zealand society" (Burke, 1986: 10). *Multiculturalism* is a contested term in Aotearoa/New Zealand, not least as a result of the past willingness of the state tactically to deploy the language of multiculturalism to defuse and defang Māori claims. Māori make up 13 percent of the population in Aotearoa/New Zealand and, as a result, "indigenous assertions and identities are far more powerfully present" than in the United States, for example (Thomas, 1994: 173). Māori have persistently resisted state efforts to rearticulate New Zealand as multicultural because if Aotearoa/New Zealand is a multicultural place, then Māori have no right to special status as *tangata whenua* ("people of the land"). Theirs becomes merely one culture among many, and they become simply a minority. The state can then "neutralize their claims for justice more effectively" (Walker, 1995: 292). In *Populate or Languish?* (Kasper, 1990), the neoliberal logic of identity for Māori is made explicit. They should not fear becoming a smaller minority, argues Kasper: "They could instead live in a nation of many minorities where the

Māori minority fitted in much better as an equal social group" (ibid., 49). Commenting on this passage, Walker argues that the Treaty of Waitangi was the original immigration policy for Aotearoa/New Zealand, and that although it allowed immigration from Europe, Australia, and Britain, any deviation from those source countries requires consultation by the Crown with their treaty partners, the Māori.[5] The government's neoliberal immigration policy, he says, "must be seen for what it is, a covert strategy to suppress the counter-hegemonic struggle of the Māori by swamping them with outsiders who are not obliged to them by the treaty" (Walker, 1995: 292). Since the 1970s, the state has made a number of concessions to growing Māori activism that begin to open up the possibility of reimagining Aotearoa/New Zealand as a genuinely bicultural place. New Zealand is now officially bilingual, for example, and the Treaty of Waitangi is part of New Zealand law. More recent efforts to articulate New Zealand as a multicultural part of the "Asia-Pacific" thus confront an already existing politics of culture, in the legacies of prior state strategies and projects (mono-, bi-, and multiculturalisms) and Māori projects (biculturalism or Māori sovereignty). This state project must negotiate or attempt to write over narratives of place and belonging that contest the very possibility of multiculturalism.

The neoliberal impulse evident in the new immigration from Asia and its celebration by acolytes such as Kasper not only renders Māori insecure, it also runs headlong into prevailing constructions of New Zealand identity. At stake is the logic of identity and difference through which New Zealanders define who and where they are. Reaction to increased Asian immigration in the 1990s—primarily into Auckland, where the suburb of Howick has been renamed "Chowick" by the locals—has been narrated by international media as the rise of "a new 'yellow peril' " in New Zealand, and traced directly to New Zealand's white and European identity (Chen, 1996). In "Letters to the Editor" columns, face-to-face encounters are reported and reactions to Asian immigration justified. For example:

> Sir,—. . . Sure, the Asians have brought us prosperity but if this Government or any future government continues to use this accelerated method to boost the economy and, by so doing, its own image, it could be we who are assimilated and that is not a price, I am sure, most New Zealanders would wish to pay. We do need immigrants but they should be predominantly from Britain, the country that spawned and developed us in our way of life. ("Letters to the Editor," 1996).

Negative reactions to the new Asian immigration are attributed by some commentators to "cultural parsimony," defined as "a legacy of ethnocentrism . . . which is alive and well and walking the streets, sitting on local school boards, teaching in our classrooms" (McKinnon, 1995: 2). Others have framed them as a sign of New Zealanders' "fundamental unease" and uncertainty about their national identity, an uncertainty deriving both from New Zealand's origins as a British colony and from the contemporary struggles of the Māori for proper recognition as *tangata whenua* (Ip, 1995: 199). A common trope in this framing is that of immaturity: the difficulties that New Zealanders are having in coming to terms with increased immigration, from Asia and elsewhere, reflects the fact that the country is only now "finally and slowly coming of age" (ibid.). Whatever their cause, such reactions are a potential obstacle to the production of the "flexibility" required of neoliberal states in the context of increased capital and human mobility, especially if the state in question also happens to be located in the South Pacific rather than the North Atlantic: "If Asians perceive that their money is welcome, but they themselves, their language and their culture are not, this will detract from the trust which is necessary to develop sound relationships in trade" (Chen, 1994: 2).

Suggested solutions to the problem of "cultural parsimony" include "entertaining Asian children's stories . . . for bedtime," earlier foreign-language training, and curricula "informed by a more open, international spirit" (McKinnon, 1995: 9). Put another way, "we" need new narratives of place and belonging, a new logic of (New Zealand) self and (Asian) other, the better to imagine new modes of subjectivity and to reimagine what it means to be a New Zealander. According to the state, it is only through such a reimagining that "we" can ensure a prosperous future for "our" children. In 1989, then-Minister of Finance David Caygill made clear that the neoliberal vision behind the new immigration policies of the Labour government fundamentally transformed the connection between place and identity. As Bedford sums up the ministerial articulation of government policy: "Mr. Caygill was looking forward to a world inhabited by people who had much more freedom of movement across national boundaries, where economies and their associated labour markets were truly transnational, where people of quite divergent ethnic and cultural backgrounds felt 'comfortable' in many places, not just the ones which they associated with the notion of 'home'" (Bedford, 1996: 350). White and European narratives of place and belonging stand in the way of such a vision. Accordingly, restructuring has been extended from the state to the nation (Kelsey, 1994).

"Asia 2000"

Central to these efforts to rearticulate the relationship between place and identity for New Zealand has been the generation of the government's Asia 2000 initiative. Originally conceived by the deputy prime minister and minister of foreign affairs and trade, Don McKinnon, and the minister for trade negotiations, Philip Burdon, Asia 2000 is the main state vehicle for reimagining what it is to be "New Zealand." Part of the mission of Asia 2000 is literally to convince New Zealanders that they are located not "somewhere in the middle of the Atlantic" but within the Asia-Pacific (e.g., McKinnon, 1993: 35). Government ministers and others now repeatedly link New Zealand's identity to its geographic location rather than to cultural ties with Britain (e.g., D. McKinnon, 1996a: 33). This state initiative has since been moved to the private Asia 2000 Foundation of New Zealand, "an independent grant-making trust" modeled on U.S. foundations such as Ford, Olin, and MacArthur. Located in Wellington, the New Zealand capital, the foundation was launched by Prime Minister Bolger on September 21, 1994. The mission of the foundation, according to its home page (http://www.asia2000.org.nz/index.html), is to "Promote New Zealander's knowledge and understanding of Asian nations," "Build New Zealand's links with Asia," and "Help New Zealanders develop the skills to work with their Asian counterparts and be active and effective partners in the region."

Although only modestly funded—a fact that has prompted some criticism from Asian sources—the foundation has been actively involved in a wide range of grant activities. Original funding from the government was NZ$3 million. In July 1996, this was increased by a further NZ$5 million over the next three years, and supplemented with NZ$1.5 million in contributions from the corporate sector, which was expected increasingly to become a major source of funds. With these monies, the Asia 2000 Foundation, and through it the state and corporate capital—the board of trustees is dominated by leaders of some of the largest corporations in New Zealand—are seeking to reshape New Zealand's relation with Asia on a broad front. Much of that effort goes to producing more and better human capital through language training, and to establishing business, university, and other links with East Asia. There has also been a concerted effort to inform New Zealanders that Asia is not a monolithic place but is in fact made up of a variety of states, cultures, and peoples (e.g., M. McKinnon, 1996; Vasil and Yoon, 1996).

In association with the Institute of Policy Studies, a neoliberal think tank at Victoria University in Wellington, the foundation has been concerned explicitly to renarrate New Zealand's histories. It has commissioned historical studies of Asian immigration into New Zealand and its legacies as part of a program with the overall objective "to promote public understanding of what it means for New Zealand to increase its linkages with the Asia-Pacific Region" (Hawke, 1996: i). Such histories implicate dominant narratives of New Zealand identity directly insofar as they set out to reposition accounts of the Asian other within the overall logic of identity and difference through which New Zealand has been constituted. According to the director of the institute, Gary Hawke, "The principal audience for th[ese] stud[ies] is those who are in a position to influence public opinion in New Zealand, and through them, the public at large" (ibid., ii). This effort is aimed explicitly at transforming identities, and is designed to reeducate New Zealanders about who they are and where they are in the world, and to foster cultural and other forms of exchange with East Asia.

Rewriting History

It is, of course, unsurprising that one of the means through which the rearticulation of New Zealand as a multicultural part of the "Asia-Pacific" and, more broadly, as part of a new world of transnational liberalism is occurring is in the rewriting of "our" histories. It is in part through the production of national histories, with their reliance on assumptions about the unity and necessity of a "self-same, national subject evolving through time" (Duara, 1995: 4), that the contested, contingent, and processual reality of particular nation-states is secured. Projects of national identity are both given expression in and made possible through historiographical conventions that privilege the nation as the master category in relation to which historical narratives are produced. The hegemonic nature of such conventions is reflected in the fact that "Historical consciousness in modern society has been overwhelmingly framed by the nation-state" (ibid., 3). The contemporary rewriting of New Zealand's history remains indebted to the figure of the nation-state, and often amounts to little more than a redefinition of its ethnic content. Thus, we are still in the domain of modernist historical consciousness; these new histories too participate in securing the nation-state—newly competitive and flexible—as the subject of history.

Historiography in New Zealand has been profoundly shaped by the imperial and British origins of the nation-state. Of growing up in the 1950s and 1960s, Claudia Bell recalls that:

> Our "history" was British imperial history. We were kept ignorant about the impact of Pakeha settlement on Māori. In schools we learnt nothing of Māori art, culture or tradition. Our literary references were to British writers. Children's books were about cute little rabbits, Noddy, the Famous Five and Biggles. The body of knowledge transmitted to us at school linked us to our British heritage. In fact, there was no sense of any other. We did not look at anything published by the first New Zealand writers. We did not even know that such literature existed. It seemed that literature, like art and music, could only come from Europe. Indeed, all arts appeared defined by Europe. (C. Bell, 1996: 21–22)

The contemporary reimagining of New Zealand writes against this heritage as "overseas British," and its materialization in narratives that position New Zealand as an exemplary white and European place, and does so in a very specific manner. The growing desire to be "seen as part of Asia" has led to "the first signs of having to engage with the meaning of multiculturalism in New Zealand society. . . . it is the challenges posed by the desire to be economically oriented to Asia that open up the possibilities in terms of multiculturalism in New Zealand" (Kaye Turner, in Mohanram, 1995: 202). The re-articulation of New Zealand as a natural part of the "Asia-Pacific" is essayed in histories that construct New Zealand as "multicultural."

Although the texts produced through collaboration between the Asia 2000 Foundation and the Institute of Policy Studies are self-consciously intended to influence public-opinion makers, they are part of a broader discursive formation through which histories are being rewritten, and thus what it means to be New Zealand is being re-defined. These new and in some respects counterhegemonic histories seek to neutralize concerns about increased immigration from Asia by articulating New Zealand as a multicultural nation of immigrants. That project proceeds through the excavation of local histories of Chinese, Indian, and other nationalities whose presence within has been tacitly denied in hegemonic narratives of New Zealand as white and British. The power authoritatively to narrate New Zealand through state- supported public histories has long lain with the settlers and their descendants. In recent decades, however, there have been growing efforts on the part of a number of previously excluded communities to put forward their histories, either as supplements to or as contestations of the standard narratives of New Zealand. Chinese and Māori historians such as Manying Ip, James Ng, and Ranginui Walker have been especially prominent in this ongoing rewriting of New Zealand, as well as contributing to the debates over neoliberal immigration policy. The contemporary reimagining of New Zealand as a multicultural place thus stems also in part from these other efforts to recover excluded subjects.

An exemplary text is *Immigration and National Identity in New Zealand: One People, Two Peoples, Many Peoples?* (Greif, 1995a) which contains chapters on non-British immigrants—Cambodians, Laotians, Vietnamese, South Asians, Chinese, Jews, Croatians, and Dalmatians—written by authors whose own immigrant identities are also foregrounded in the text, thus materializing the larger argument made in the editor's introduction that New Zealanders *are* and *have always been* multicultural. This retrieval of what had been overlooked subjects and their histories is then linked to the claim that, in the face of East Asia's economic dynamism, they *must be* multicultural or else: "If we reject Asia, our choices are limited, and the economic future is very bleak" (Greif, 1995b: 19). Failure to embrace "that great market of the twenty-first century, Asia" (ibid.,15) is framed as tantamount to opting for a "fortress New Zealand," as "turning the country's back on the outside world. . . . this would mean an end to the Kiwi addiction to the latest mod cons and to modern technology; only the most committed of the counter-culture, alternative lifestylers and survivalists, would want New Zealand to be the Myanmar, Cuba, or North Korea of the lower antipodes" (ibid., 19). Cold War narratives of economic backwardness and U.S. neoliberal narratives of the 1960s and counterculture (Greif is a U.S. immigrant to New Zealand) are thus conjured up to motivate the embrace of a flexible future in Asia. The effect of such narratives is to demonstrate that "we" have in fact always been multicultural—at least in the trivial sense that there have been people from different ethnic and national backgrounds living in the country—and that New Zealand has always been a nation of immigrants, and of immigrants from a variety of places, even if the majority came from Britain.

The renarration of New Zealand as a multicultural nation of immigrants has been extended to include the Māori as well. For instance, according to a government survey of "Asian New Zealanders," "New Zealand is a country of immigration. The entire population is ultimately the consequence of immigration to this country over more than 1,500 years" (New Zealand Now, 1995: 5). Similarly, James Belich's best-selling *Making Peoples: A History of the New Zealanders from Polynesian Settlement to the End of the Nineteenth Century,* opens with paired narratives of "two migrant ships push[ing] through dangerous seas." One of those ships is Viking, the other is Māori: "Both were forebears of the New Zealanders" (Belich, 1996: 13). Belich thus rhetorically equates the Māori discovery of Aotearoa with the Viking discovery of North America. Narrating New Zealand as "a country of immigration" repositions Māori in relation to the land and the state. Although it could be argued that such a narrative valorizes Māori by equating them with the Vikings, it also flattens out and homogenizes time, and thereby establishes a moral equivalence between Māori ("Polynesian immigrants") and others (e.g., "European immigrants," "Asian immigrants"). Such an equation potentially undermines the claims of Māori to special status on the basis of centuries of prior occupation of Aotearoa and to justice arising from the Treaty of Waitangi and the Declaration of Independence.[6] It also tends, despite Belich's recognition of the role of violence "in bulk" in the making of "the New Zealanders" (1996: 450), to obscure or to downplay the moment of power—or, specifically, the disempowerment of the Māori—in the constitution of New Zealand (cf. Kelsey, 1994, 1996; Walker, 1990).

Articulations of New Zealand as a "nation of immigrants" have been common since at least the early 1970s. Only recently, however, has New Zealand identity been articulated in such a way as to position the dominant "Anglo-New Zealand" (the term is Malcolm McKinnon's) population as immigrants, and to foreground the role of the state in enabling and reproducing that identity. In *Immigrants and Citizens: New Zealanders and Asian Immigration in Historical Context* (1996), one of the volumes published under the auspices of the Institute of Policy Studies and the Asia 2000 Foundation, Malcolm McKinnon argues that older versions of this strategy, which typically did not interrogate the identity of the Anglo-New Zealand community as immigrants, effectively reinscribed non-Anglo ethnicity as the mark of difference. Failure to make citizenship rather than ethnic identity with the dominant Pakeha community the sign of belonging stems from New Zealand's origins as a British colony. This argument is supported in McKinnon's text by a reconstruction of the history of New Zealand immigration framed around the history of citizenship, a connection seldom made in New Zealand historiography, and for obvious reasons. As a British colony, citizenship was not a significant mark of national identity prior to independence in 1949 because British subjects were free to enter the colony whenever they chose and to assume residence. Even after independence, citizenship remained of minor consequence until the mid-1970s, when controls were first placed on immigration from Britain (in 1974) and a citizenship act was passed (in 1977) that "abolished the distinction between 'Commonwealth' and 'foreign', effectively substituting for it the distinction between 'New Zealand' and 'foreign'" (ibid., 43). The specific character of the colonial and postimperial relationship between New Zealand and Britain, in other words, reinforced the identity of (New Zealand) state and (ethnically white and British) nation. What is increasingly at stake in anxieties over Asia and Asian immigration, then, is the logic of identity and difference constitutive of New Zealand's postcolonial identity, and the perceived necessity of changing it in the face of new discourses of global competitiveness.

In good problem-solving fashion (Cox, 1996), McKinnon argues that there is a need to find ways of giving "the status New Zealand-born of Asian descent . . . greater salience as a way of shifting the structures which inform thinking on the issue" (M. McKinnon, 1996: 73); that is, identity *as New Zealanders* needs to be foregrounded in such a way that it becomes plain that those who are "New Zealand-born of Asian descent" share with other New Zealanders "something in common" that in turn separates them "from non-New Zealanders, be they British, Australian, Somali or Taiwanese" (ibid., 74). McKinnon is here calling for a reinscription of national identity, but on terms that include rather than exclude non-Anglo New Zealanders. In the face of transnational liberalism, then, the centrality of the nation in the self-definition of "New Zealanders" is to be reinforced.

Similar themes emerge in the other history produced by the Institute of Policy Studies and the Asia 2000 Foundation, *New Zealanders of Asian Origin* (1996), by Raj Vasil and Hong-Key Yoon. With McKinnon, they accept that increased immigration from Asia is inevitable: "Increasing migration of peoples," they claim, "is a worldwide phenomenon. There is an unstoppable movement of people all over the world" (Vasil and Yoon, 1996: 58; see also M. McKinnon, 1996: 2). Moreover, "Continuing internationalization of the New Zealand economy is beginning to create its own demand for a continuing influx of immigrants" and it is in this context that the "Management of ethnic diversity has begun to occupy increasing attention and effort of political rulers and administrators" (Vasil and Yoon, 1996: 59). Concern with problems that stem from the growing internationalization of corporate workforces is a defining feature of much contemporary writing on business and management (Dirlik, 1997). This has led to the development of strategies at the level of the firm through which to manage increased cultural and ethnic diversity, and to bind the loyalty of diverse workforces. What is significant here is the parallel concern evident in Vasil and Yoon's discussion of state strategies in the face of increased immigration from "nontraditional" sources. Articulating this concern in terms of "state building," Vasil and Yoon define the latter as meaning that all citizens are willing "1. to identify themselves fully with the state and have their first and foremost loyalty to it; 2. to obey its laws; and 3. to defend their adopted country and uphold its interests" (1996: 34). What is needed, then, are strategies that enable the state to bind populations marked by increasing ethnic diversity and to mobilize those subjects in pursuit of state interests.[7]

Also in common with McKinnon, Vasil and Yoon locate the origins of the contemporary need for "state building" by the New Zealand state in the 1970s. The necessity of "state building" is traced to shifting relations with the colonizer, Britain, and the "sudden and spectacular awakening" of Māori activism in the 1970s, that is, to those circumstances that Ip, among others, has articulated as evidence of New Zealand's "immaturity" as a nation (ibid., 35;

see also M. McKinnon, 1996: 62; Ip, 1995: 199). Such a representation of the reasons for the contemporary concern with "state building" has significant ideological effects. Specifically, by locating the need for "state building" in the (all too real) anti-Asian sentiments of at least some New Zealanders, attention is displaced from the proximate causes of immigration reform and the turn to Asia in state policy, namely, the election in the 1980s and 1990s of a series of Labour and National governments committed to neoliberal policy reform. The ideological effect, then, is to imply that it is the hybrid nature of New Zealand's postcolonial identity that prompts the necessity of "state building" *rather than* the ongoing restructuring of international capital and the efforts of local capital, operating through the Business Roundtable and the state, to reshape the relationship between the New Zealand space-economy and the world economy. Attention is focused onto the cultural legacies of colonial rule—the problem to which "state building" responds is itself cultural, in other words—and away from a specific set of class strategies that are being pursued through the effort to rearticulate New Zealand as multicultural.

CONCLUSION

The reimagining of New Zealand, I have argued, is part of a state project of capitalist modernity, as the state and capital seek to rework what it means to be New Zealand in ways that facilitate the transition from Fordism to flexible accumulation in the South Pacific. The discourse of transnational liberalism is the new ground upon which state strategies and projects in the capitalist "North," eastern Europe, the former Soviet Union, and the many states under some form of structural adjustment regime in the "South" are being constructed. This discourse also structures the insecurities of communities. It is worth recalling that, immediately prior to the collapse of the state and the emergence of ethnonationalist conflict, Yugoslavia too was being subjected to a rigorous course of structural adjustment (Blackburn, 1993: 102–3). One response of the state to the discourse of transnational liberalism has been to seek to rework conceptions of national identity in ways that facilitate and enable capital accumulation, figured as "competitiveness" and "flexibility." To such ends, the state seeks "to bring together or articulate into a complexly structured instance, a range of political discourses and social practices which are concerned at different sites with the transmission and transformation of power" and to transform that articulation "into a systematic practice of regulation, of rule and norm, of normalization, within society" (Hall, 1985: 93). These state projects are, of course, shaped by the circumstances within which they are pursued. In the face of a perceived need actively to engage with a "dynamic" East Asia and to integrate the New Zealand space-economy into the "Asia-Pacific," for example, state actors have explicitly claimed that identity is malleable—"New Zealand is New Zealand, but our national identity is not frozen at a particular point in our development as a nation" (Bolger, 1992: 23)—and have set out to renarrate New Zealand as flexible, competitive, and multicultural. Similar but distinct strategies—some seeking to rearticulate the nation as multicultural (e.g., Australia, Canada), others not (e.g., China, Malaysia, Singapore)—are being pursued elsewhere. What these state strategies and projects share, however, is a common aim to produce *national* subjects who, in pursuit of their own identity projects, will also further the accumulation function of the state as it is reworked through the discourse of transnational liberalism.

As workforces are internationalized and states and capital seek "high quality" and "hybridized" subjects as assets in pursuit of global competitiveness, so narratives of place and belonging, of self and other, become a potential object of state strategy, to be reworked or not, according to circumstance and need. This is not a new task for the state; through immigration policy and in publicly sponsored narratives of place and belonging, the New Zealand state, in common with others, has long sought to articulate questions of race, ethnicity, and "culture" more broadly in ways that enable government and accumulation. My argument thus implicates the "normalizing power of the state—its control over identity and the interpretation of space" (Shapiro, 1994: 485). It is important, however, not to overestimate state power. Contrary to the heroic, indeed utopian, assumptions evident in some of the pronouncements of New Zealand state actors, identity cannot be manipulated like an interest rate. In response to popular opposition to the new immigration from Asia, the New Zealand state in early 1997 introduced an English-language test, which reduced new entries from that source to a trickle and prompted criticism from states in East Asia. Anxieties have been expressed about both the relatively narrow class basis of the effort to rework New Zealand's identity and the limited extent to which these rearticulations are reaching from the "club to the pub" ("New Zealand's 'Asia Is Our Future' Issue Should Penetrate the Pubs," 1996: 6). The idea that New Zealand's future lies with the Asia-Pacific region is still largely restricted to the "strategic elite," according to Professor Chan Heng Chee, head of Singapore's Institute of Southeast Asian Studies, who visited New Zealand in 1996 as a guest of the Asia 2000 Foundation (in ibid.). She claimed to detect a different view among the majority of New Zealanders—perhaps she had been reading the local newspapers. The articulation of New Zealand as a neoliberal and multicultural place also faces organized contestation: Māori have done so on the basis of an alternative identity politics organized around claims about "culture" (Kelsey, 1996; Pearson, 1996), while groups such as the Campaign Against Foreign Control of Aotearoa have sought to do so through a rearticulation of autonomy and self-determination in the context of a democratized world economy (e.g., Small, 1996). The neoliberal identity project of the state and corporate capital is not the only one on offer to New Zealanders. A crucial question raised by the new politics of culture prompted by the discourse of transnational liberalism is thus the relative ability of social subjects to define the real—as in where New Zealand is, for example, the kind of place it is, and the policies that follow from that site and situation—and to make meaning stick.

Recognition that articulations of New Zealand as part of the "Asia-Pacific" have yet to reach from the "club to the pub" reminds us that the reimagining of New Zealand is very much an elite or top-down strategy. Moreover, it is not accidental that these forms of top-down multiculturalism are addressed primarily to a particular set of class subjects and human capital, those with the resources to make such engagement possible and profitable. From the point of view of the state and capital, it is these subjects that need most actively to engage with East Asia. More generally, it is not necessary that every New Zealander come to see himself or herself as part of the "Asia-Pacific" to the same extent. Certainly, it is likely to be bad for business if—as reported in letters to local newspapers from both recent and not so recent immigrants (e.g., "Letters to the Editor," 1996)—ordinary New Zealanders feel moved by the presence of "Asians" in their local shopping centers to confront those "Asians," insult them, and tell them to go back to where they came from. But it is probably sufficient for the sake of producing a "business climate" conducive to the maintenance and deepening of relations between the New Zealand space-economy and East Asia that people merely refrain from such practices. Reducing their likelihood hardly requires the active embrace of a flexible future in Asia. "Ruling classes have at their disposal a great many . . . techniques of . . . social control, which are a good deal more prosaic and material than persuading their subjects . . . to identify with the destiny of the nation" (Eagleton, 1991: 34). A sense of economic necessity and inevitability, perhaps combined with fear of all the usual, mundane means of social control, not to mention the insecurities and the opportunities that transnational liberalism implies, is just as apt to produce the desired result.

In the face of the dramatic collapse of economies all across East Asia in mid-1997, and the subsequent contraction in tourism from and exports to the region, it remains to be seen how the politics of culture will play out in New Zealand. One thing is certain, however: the sudden financial meltdown in East Asia reveals just how uncertain are the foundations underpinning the millennial dreams of a dynamic "Asia-Pacific" and of a multicultural New Zealand.

NOTES

1. The politics of naming in New Zealand are contentious. Although officially bicultural, the reimagining of identity is still dominated by a British settler culture and its institutions, even as that dominance is increasingly contested by the indigenous people, the Māori, whose name for these islands is Aotearoa. In international policy circles, New Zealand is hailed, not Aotearoa. I will use the term Aotearoa/New Zealand only when referring to Māori contestation of this identity.

2. Stated briefly, *site* refers to how places differ according to local or internal characteristics; *situation* refers to how different places are located within wider sets of relations. I owe this distinction to Eric Sheppard.

3. I define biculturalism and multiculturalism as "representational frameworks of symbols, rules and practices that emerge from written texts or spoken utterances about the politics of ethnicity" (Pearson, 1996: 250). Such a view enables us to recognize the diverse ways in which these frameworks can be articulated with wider sets of social relations and accordingly the different ways in which they may enter into relations of power.

4. Prior to European colonization, the tribes that inhabited Aotearoa had

no collective name. Māori—which meant "normal" or "natural"—is thus both a product of colonization and an administrative term. *Pakeha* is the Māori term for the settlers and their descendants (see Walker, 1990: 297).

5. Signed on February 6, 1840, the Treaty of Waitangi is the document on the basis of which the British declared sovereignty over New Zealand. See the discussion in Walker (1990).

6. Although the state has recently articulated the Treaty of Waitangi as New Zealand's founding document, the claim is contentious. The Declaration of Independence, signed on October 28, 1835, by James Busby, British Resident in New Zealand, and thirty-five chiefs (the Confederation of United Tribes), explicitly recognized New Zealand to be "an Independent State" and declared that "all sovereign power and authority" resided "entirely and exclusively in the hereditary chiefs and heads of tribes in their collective capacity" ("The Declaration of Independence").

7. The explicit model invoked by Yoon and Vasil, who has carried out extensive research there, is Singapore; cf. Ong (1997).

9

Colonizing Cyberspace: "National Security" and the Internet

DIANA SACO

THE STRANGE CASE OF A CODE EXPORTER

In June 1991, cryptographer Philip Zimmermann completed a program called *Pretty Good Privacy* (PGP), a hard-to-crack encryption program that increases computer security by scrambling people's messages. To distribute the program widely, he made it public-domain software and gave it to friends to post on bulletin-board services throughout the United States. One of these friends then redistributed the program by loading it onto domestic computers linked to the Internet (Levy, 1994: 60). Because telephone connections cross borders, however, the Internet is not just a national computer network but a global one. So, "within hours" after his software was posted on the Internet, "people were downloading it all over the country and beyond" (Levy, 1993). Ironically, access to PGP by foreigners brought Zimmermann under criminal investigation. Federal attorneys alleged that the availability of this type of program on the Internet was a violation of "export" restrictions on the distribution of "arms" (Levy, 1994: 60).

The International Traffic in Arms Regulations (ITAR) restricts the export of military equipment to "foreign persons" (U.S. Department of State, 1996). Under the general munitions list in effect in the early 1990s, ITAR designates "cryptographic devices and software (encoding and decoding)" as "Auxiliary Military Equipment" subject to these restrictions. In their attempt to apply ITAR to Zimmermann's case, U.S. attorneys implied that PGP was sensitive, defense-related equipment and that it was exported illegally (Archibald, 1994). This raises two central questions. First, why is the availability of crypto-graphic technology a matter of national security? The quick response is that the U.S. state defines it as such, enacting legislation that constructs it as a technology that, in the wrong hands, threatens national security. Of course, the strategic importance of cryptography for maintaining the secrecy of so-called vital intelligence had long been argued by the state (Bamford, 1982). Its export, moreover, had been restricted since at least the mid-1970s, partly to ensure that U.S. surveillance efforts abroad would not be thwarted by strong (i.e., non-wiretappable) encryption (Schwartau, 1994: 150). In the past, however, cryptography had been a costly, defense-contracted technology that used state-of-the-art mainframe computers to protect sensitive government data and nationwide electronic banking systems. What was unusual about this case was that the exported technology was a program for *personal* computers intended to protect the privacy of "ordinary people and grassroots political organizations" (Zimmermann, 1994b).

What was also new here was the application of ITAR to the Internet. This raises the second question: what constitutes "export" when someone transfers an item not by physically taking it across state borders but by posting it on the Internet? According to Zimmermann's attorney, "Borders are pretty meaningless with the current information networks" (Philip Dubois, in Schofield, 1994). But borders are not meaningless to states. The sovereignty of states depends on a configuration of global space along geopolitical lines, with each state exercising sole authority over its territory. National security, by extension, has rested on the notion that each state must and can protect its sovereign space by regulating the flow of goods and persons across its borders. To the extent that the Internet makes borders meaningless, however, it challenges conventional ways of thinking about space, sovereignty, and security. At a minimum, it has allowed a form of distribution that bypasses customs checkpoints, calling into question the state's capacity to regulate the flow of a different kind of strategic item (digital information) through a new distributional channel (global networks). Zimmermann's case was an initial response. It was also only the tip of the iceberg. State officials and security experts have subsequently given a much broader sense of the new stakes here, for them, in their hyperbolic references to "Information Warfare" and "Cyberwar" (Schwartau, 1994; Waller, 1995). ITAR has been but one way the U.S. state has tried to curb the availability of tools, such as PGP, that undermine its capacity to monitor foreign intelligence. A second way has been to provide an alternate cryptographic technology, for both domestic use and export, that facilitates surveillance. To that end, the Clinton administration—together with the National Security Agency (NSA) and the Federal Bureau of Investigation (FBI)—has promoted the adoption of a new government encryption standard through devices like the Clipper chip: a telephone encryption device with a built-in wiretap mechanism. By trying to make Clipper a standard, U.S. officials have sought to normalize its use and crowd out non-wiretappable alternatives in the process, hoping thereby "to preserve a government capability to conduct electronic surveillance" (White House, 1994a).

As these introductory comments suggest, Zimmermann's case and Clipper open a space for investigating how the state is responding to digital challenges, how it is reimagining itself and its insecurities in the new arena of cyberspace.[1] One possible response, made more often by opponents of regulation, is to welcome the rise of the Internet as providing a new space for global transactions, cooperation, and even senses of citizenship and community (e.g., Rheingold, 1993). Another response, made (significantly) by security advisers in their preliminary assessments of the Internet, is to characterize its "blurring of traditional boundaries" as a threat to state security (RAND, 1996; see also Sullivan, 1996). Along these lines, some officials have begun warning that the extensive computerization of its infrastructure makes the United States "the world's most vulnerable target for information warfare" (former CIA deputy director William Studeman, in Brandt, 1995; see also U.S. Security Policy Board, 1995). By themselves, such concerns might have led officials to support the domestic use of strong encryption, but state surveillance of communication has always been deemed vital to national security. Recently, that notion has expanded to include Internet communication, a form of surveillance that one Pentagon analyst favorably describes as "strategic reconnaissance 'by modem'" (Swett, 1995). The use of strong encryption would make this kind of covert "reconnaissance" more difficult. It is not surprising, then, that the United States has taken a lead in the encryption debate (Hoffman, 1995).[2]

Traditional security studies have paid little attention to how states seek to secure themselves by regulating not just weapons but also certain communications technologies. This oversight is particularly odd for three reasons. First, as just indicated, the United States has tried to curb the use of coded communication by systematically defining cryptographic technology as "munitions." Second, several states have long-established agencies whose sole task is to encode and decode "communications intelligence": in the United States, that role has been filled by the NSA since 1952 (Truman, 1952; see also Bamford, 1982). Third, Internet access by dissidents, such as students in China or Zapatistas in Mexico, has on occasion undermined the state's capacity to control the transnational flow of communication and in ways that it has found threatening (Brandt, 1995; Swett, 1995). It seems, therefore, that a focus on how states seek to regulate cyberspace falls well within the ambit of security studies. Unfortunately, mainstream analysts often deduce national security concerns from exogenous factors (typically, the anarchic structure of the international system) and conclude from this that their focus on *weapons* technology—as the best safeguard within this hostile environment—adequately matches how states understand "military capabilities" and "national security." Although they may acknowledge that security is sometimes affected by technological developments (in "arms"), they do not typically concede that cultural practices shape which technologies are developed and how they are understood. Hence, a significant area of inquiry—how states define their security and insecurity—is foreclosed at the outset.

If, however, "any technology represents a cultural invention" (Escobar, 1994: 211), then even the meaning of "missiles" is open to interpretation (Weldes, this volume; see also Weldes and Saco, 1996: 375–76). Rather than treating such definitions as externally given, I argue that threats are socially constructed according to sets of symbolic practices that are internal to state formation. The process of describing "the threats we face" not only helps to construct those threats; it also brings a particular identity (a "we") into existence, creates interests for that identity, and provides rationales for particular actions. The production of insecurity, in other words, can have both technological and cultural dimensions, and these should be understood as mutually constitutive moments of that process, not as distinct causal factors that can be studied separately.

I use the protean phrase *colonizing cyberspace* to imply both of these dimensions simultaneously. Read as an adjective, *colonizing* modifies *cyberspace* as a kind of active subject: not a passive space to be colonized, but a colonizer in its own right that can overrun human intentions. This sense of "a colonizing cyberspace" emphasizes the technological dimension of (in)security, most evident whenever people speak ambivalently about the technical features of networking. In the extreme, this ambivalence becomes a form of technological determinism, expressed in phrases that characterize the technology as an unstoppable force whose latent potentials *will* give rise to certain practices, despite governmental or individual interventions. Of course, agency does not reside in the technology itself, but rather in the human beings whose practices actualize its potentials. Human agency is implied when *colonizing* is read, alternatively, as a verb form, suggesting an effort by someone to shape, administer, and control cyberspace (e.g., Henry, 1995). That enterprise, moreover, involves knowledge production as much as, if not more than, military or bureaucratic control. The "colonizing *of* cyberspace," in other words, entails some form of cultural imperialism (Tomlinson, 1991): an effort to capture social imaginaries by constructing certain ways of being as legitimate and sensible. Indeed, it is this cultural dimension of (in)security that is exemplified by the U.S. encryption debate—in competing discursive efforts to map the space of cyberspace (e.g., as "superhighway" or as "frontier") and to construct its inhabitants as either "lawless" (and hence, in need of regulation) or "civilized" (and hence, self-restrained). In short, when understood as a verb, *colonizing* describes what each camp in this debate is attempting to do *to* cyberspace: both to territorialize that space and to subjectify its inhabitants in particular ways.

The chapter begins, in the next section, with a brief history of the Internet, highlighting its Cold War origins in U.S. efforts to construct a reliable communications network. Stressing the technological dimension, I argue that these security-motivated innovations in networking had a number of unexpected consequences, not the least of which was the emergence of different cultural constructions of security and insecurity surrounding computer technology. It is to an analysis of these competing cultures, as evident in the U.S. encryption debate, that I turn in the third section. Despite differences, however, arguments surrounding the Clipper chip and Zimmermann's case demonstrate the liberal discourse shared by both sides in this debate. This broader discourse, as I indicate in the fourth section, promotes a free-market ethos and helps to liberalize cyberspace for the rise of a new kind of information capitalism. In the process, other valid security concerns are excluded from discussion to the possible future detriment both of the welfare state and of economically disenfranchised individuals. Because my point of departure for this study of national security and the Internet is the U.S. construction of encryption as "munitions," the analysis in the third and fourth sections focuses on the U.S. encryption debate up to November 1996, when President Clinton signed an order that effectively removed (nonmilitary) encryption from ITAR and thereby decategorized it as a defense article. In lieu of a conclusion, the study ends with a postscript that provides a brief summary of this order and its implications for the (liberal) colonization of cyberspace.

THE TECHNOLOGY OF SECURITY: A HISTORY OF THE INTERNET

The Internet is the outgrowth of an older, state-run computer network established by the U.S. Department of Defense (DoD) in the late 1960s. The ARPAN, as it was called, was based, in part, on the design for a survivable computer communications network: a command-and-control network that could withstand minor damage to the system without interrupting the flow of communication. To heighten the sense that Internet regulation is impossible, some opponents have even claimed that the "Internet was designed to withstand direct nuclear attack" (John Perry Barlow, in Berger, 1995). Although rather overstated, especially in light of what is now known about the devastating effects of nuclear detonations, that claim is not without foundation: a RAND study of the early 1960s had outlined the need for a "robust" computer communications network precisely in terms of withstanding "enemy attack" from the Soviets (Baran, 1990b: 17–18 and 15). Furthermore, the agency where the networking research developed was itself a product of Cold War competition between the superpowers.

In October 1957, the Soviet Union launched Sputnik. U.S. officials were shocked by news of the launch and hustled to finds ways to avoid future "technological surprises" (Norberg and O'Neill, 1992: 33). Among U.S. responses was the 1958 establishment of a new research and development agency within the DoD called the Advanced

Research Projects Agency (ARPA). Later named the Defense Advanced Research Projects Agency (DARPA) to emphasize further its national security mandate, the agency was intended to fund "dual-use" (military and commercial) technological ventures too risky for industry and to provide a forum for defense research on command-and-control issues (ibid., i, 35). Computer research fell under the auspices of a branch of DARPA, established in 1962, called the Information Processing Techniques Office (IPTO). The network project, however, did not begin formally until the late 1960s (ibid., 55). Prior to that, innovations in networking had remained largely conceptual, such as Paul Baran's 1964 RAND report on the concept of *distributed networks*. Baran's (1990a, 1990b) design is worth reviewing at some length because the network that was later implemented by IPTO and that evolved into the Internet was based on essentially the same structural architecture for a survivable network.

Older network designs were based on a system of centralized control. Network sites were connected to each other via a switching station (at the hub of a circuit of sites) that handled all routing functions for the network nodes surrounding it. Even the "decentralized" network design, although it increased the number of switching stations, was nonetheless based on a system of centralized control: sites were still connected via a switching station that, in turn, linked to another switching station that controlled routing for yet another ring of sites (Baran, 1990a: 195). If the centralized network was star-like in its design, with lines of connection rayed out from the switching point to the nodes around it, the decentralized network was more of a constellation of centralized subnetworks (ibid.). Dependence on centralized switching, a feature of both of these older designs, resulted in highly vulnerable systems: in the event of an emergency, such as an "enemy attack" (Baran, 1990b: 15), damage to a switching station could bring down a large portion of the network, if indeed not all of it. The trick therefore was to devise a system that would allow a message to bypass destroyed nodes and find alternate pathways to its destination. The solution was *distributed* networking.

In contrast to the starlike design of centralized systems, the distributed network was based on a weblike design. Each site would link redundantly to several neighboring nodes, each of which could function as a message router (Baran, 1990a: 195). This independent routing depended on yet another innovation, later dubbed "packet switching" (Baran, 1990b: 19). The idea was to segment messages into blocks, combine each message block with delivery information (an address), transmit these "packets" through the weblike network in any direction, and then reassemble the message at its destination (Haring, 1994: 464). If each computer node linked to several others simultaneously and could make its own "smart decision" about which of these other sites to use for sending packets, a message could bypass damaged nodes and reach its destination. Because adding more redundant links would provide nodes with extra routing options, network expansion could further enhance overall performance. This nonhierarchical network design, then, eliminated points of vulnerability, the centralized switching stations, resulting in a very "robust" network that could route around interruptions (Baran, 1990a: 195). Because these networking concepts were radical, expensive, and untested, however, the actual development of a distributed, packet-switching network posed too high an investment risk for the corporate sector.

In the late 1960s, researchers at IPTO became interested in computer networks as a way to facilitate communication and resource sharing among defense researchers at different, remote institutions (Roberts, 1989). They were also convinced that networking technology, once developed, could be transferred to the military to assist it in its command-and-control operations. (This transfer took place in 1984, when a number of nodes connected to the ARPANet were split off into a separate network called MILNet, a secured network restricted to authorized military personnel (Norberg and O'Neill, 1992: 168).) With these goals in mind—and Baran's suggestive work as part of their inspiration (Kleinrock, 1990; Baran, 1990b: 43–47)— IPTO researchers, in 1968, began work on a prototype network. By 1969, the ARPANet was in operation, connecting nodes at four research institutions. The network expanded steadily after that, connecting ten nodes within a year and twenty-four nodes by 1972 (Norberg and O'Neill, 1992: 60).

To connect into the network, potential sites had to be set up to use switching protocols, packet sizes, and transmission bandwidths that the ARPANet could recognize. In time, however, innovations in other types of networks—principally packet radio, another DARPA project—led researchers to investigate the possibilities for *inter*-networking: that is, for communicating across networks with different protocols (Kahn, 1990). In 1974, Vinton Cerf and Robert Kahn (who was, at the time, a program manager for DARPA/IPTO) devised a solution. They proposed connecting different, autonomous networks through *gateways*—nodes that would reformat incompatible data from one network to make it compatible with another—using a set of universal protocols for segmenting, formatting, and routing information (Kahn, 1990; McKenzie and Walden, 1991: 362). The resulting Transmission Control Protocol and Internet Protocol (TCP/IP), as they were called, became standards in 1981. Over the next fourteen months, ARPANet nodes were converted to the new suite of protocols and, by 1983, the *Internet* was in place.

As this brief history indicates, the research and development conducted at DARPA/IPTO proceeded largely by design. But what we know today as the Internet—with its newsgroups, E-mail capabilities, and tens of thousands of networks connected across more than a hundred countries—is the product of a number of unexpected and unintended consequences. As McKenzie and Walden note, "Perhaps the biggest surprise of early ARPANet use was the enthusiastic (even zealous) adoption of electronic mail as the primary medium for scientific and management communication in the DARPA research community, both intersite and intrasite" (1991: 357). This form of relatively immediate and inexpensive communication became so popular that researchers outside defense began demanding access. Academic interest in network communication led the National Science Foundation, in 1986, to create its own network (NSFNet). Operating according to a principle of "universal educational access," the NSF's funding activities helped extend Internet access to college faculty and students in nondefense areas (Krol, 1994: 13). In a short while, the NSFNet took over the ARPANet's role as the backbone of the Internet. The transfer of networking technology to the nondefense community arguably reached its apex in 1990 when the ARPANet, the defense-funded network that had started it all, ceased to exist (Zakon, 1994). And, in what was perhaps the next inevitable transfer (in the context of a liberal society), the NSF completely ceded the public function of Internet backbone to private Internet providers in May 1995 (Miller, 1996: 46; Tony Rutkowski, in Ubois, 1995).

During the 1980s, the state had satisfied itself with subsidizing the maintenance and growth of the Internet by encouraging expanded access, factors, ironically, that helped give rise to an autonomous, even anarchistic, on-line culture (Barlow, 1990; Sterling, 1992). With more and different kinds of users, including businesses, coming on-line, however, the state is now moving in to secure cyberspace against what it regards as illegal abuses, such as hacker break-ins. Given the distributed architecture of the Internet, however, central- ized control over all on-line activity has (thus far) been impossible. In this respect, the Internet is "headless and self-organizing" (Barlow, 1994b). The original, nonhierarchical structure of networking has enabled, and even facilitated, the evolution of the Internet into a kind of "frontier space" that is relatively open and perhaps even lawless. In a rather ironic turn of events, then, what began as a state- run technology intended to enhance security is now regarded as a source of insecurity. As part of its response, the state has begun ex- plicitly extending its security interests into cyberspace: for example, by mapping the Internet in familiar terms as "a space for export," just as earlier explorers mapped the "New World" as "undiscov- ered," the better to claim it. Debates surrounding the Clipper chip and stronger forms of encryption, as I show next, provide a window onto the discourses through which national and personal security are being redefined for cyberspace.

THE CULTURES OF INSECURITY: DECODING THE CRYPTOWAR

Tensions between national security and personal security have been stressed by both sides of the "crypto-war on the electronic frontier" (Levy, 1994). This tension is not a brute fact of the encryption debate, of course, but rather a discursive effect of how it has been constructed—as "war." On one side of this debate are computer civil- liberties groups such as the Electronic Frontier Foundation (EFF) and the Cypherpunks.[3] Championing computer-related rights and, in particular, the individual's right to privacy, these groups support strong encryption and oppose government efforts to implement weaker standards. They are joined by software companies arguing that the state's encryption policy is causing them to lose international sales to foreign competitors unconstrained by similar restrictions.[4] On the other side of the debate are some academic security experts, the Clinton administration, and government agencies such as the FBI and the NSA. This camp places more priority on the increasingly overlapping issues of national security and public safety. Given these concerns, they have advocated wiretappable encryption standards through devices such as the Clipper chip. What is significant, however, and what I will highlight here, is the extent to which both camps frame their competing articulations of security and insecurity through a liberal discourse.

The Clipper Chip versus Pretty Good Privacy

The Clipper chip is actually a microchip for scrambling phone conversations. The reason computer users oppose this telephone encryption device is that the underlying technology can be applied to computers as well. In fact, the NSA, according to one source (Levy, 1994: 50), has already developed a Clipper-like chip, called Capstone, for use in computers. According to their respective designs, when users activate these chips to garble their messages, an internal mechanism simultaneously transmits a signal identifying the chip in use. This signaling device—called, significantly, the Law Enforcement Access Field (ibid.)—directs authorities to the two corresponding wiretap keys needed to decode messages. These two wiretap keys are split and held "in escrow" in two separate locations—at different government agencies, according to the original Clipper proposal (U.S. Department of Justice, 1994). Would-be wiretappers would then have to obtain warrants to retrieve the keys from both "escrow agents" before they could decode Clipper-encrypted messages.[5] This dual-escrow feature, according to advocates, minimizes the risk of illegal and covert wiretaps even by legal authorities: "The key escrow system is a lot like the system used to protect nuclear launch codes (two-person requirement). It's going to be very hard to compromise, because many people and systems must be compromised to get the keys" (Stewart A. Baker, in "Center Stage," 1994). The chip thus "protects privacy" by encrypting conversations and by minimizing illegal wiretaps; at the same time, it aids national security and public safety by maintaining the state's capacity to surveil.

The possibility for greater state surveillance is what worries Clipper opponents. Instead of the breachable "privacy" that key-escrow programs offer, opponents favor the "Pretty Good Privacy" that Zimmermann's program promises and, by all accounts, delivers. PGP is a *split-key* encryption program: a message encoded with one key can be decoded only by using its corresponding partner. The user selects one of these keys as her private key to which only she has access and designates the remaining one as the public key to be distributed to others (hence the more popular name, *public-key* cryptography). Anyone wanting to send a coded message uses the intended recipient's public key for encrypting. At that point, only the recipient can decipher the message because only she possesses the corresponding private key needed to decode the message; even the sender cannot decode it. This split-key system simply requires that people have access to each other's public keys. (Coincidentally, the Internet facilitates the broad distribution of public keys.) In contrast to key-escrow systems, then, public-key cryptosystems are, in fact, more private because the decoding keys are neither shared with senders nor held in escrow by third parties. This last feature is the decisive one for those most concerned with national security and law enforcement. They oppose programs like PGP on the argument that "Widespread use of non-escrowed encryption could irretrievably damage our ability to encourage the use of key escrow encryption, putting at risk law enforcement effectiveness and critical foreign intelligence activities" (McConnell, 1994).

The public-key cryptosystems rest on the liberal public/private dichotomy, reproducing the assumption that "the private" is the domain of the individual. For personal security reasons, individuals share with the public only what pertains to it (i.e., only the public keys). This general mistrust of the public extends as well to the state. Indeed, freedom from a too-intrusive state—typically characterized as Big Government—is a standard of liberal discourse. An "escrow agent," on the other hand, is by definition a trusted and neutral third party who acts as custodian of a valuable item that is the object of arbitration or negotiation involving two interested parties. By extension, the key-escrow cryptosystems favored by state officials draw on another liberal assumption: the pluralist notion that the state can arbitrate between competing interests. In this instance, the two interested parties are "the private person" (including both individuals and corporations) and "the public" (an abstract, collective identity reduced to a set of assumed shared interests in common goods, such as public safety). The state, in turn, is the "neutral arbiter" who can mediate their competing interests, protecting private persons (when appropriate) from public scrutiny and protecting the public from certain kinds of persons (e.g., "criminals" and "terrorists"). Clearly, both sides in this debate reproduce liberal assumptions; they disagree, however, about which aspects of liberalism, in their respective views, should take priority.

Advocating Clipper

The pro-Clipper discourse emphasizes the state's need to assume a mediating role in light of the new technologies:

> Despite its benefits, new communications technology can . . . frustrate lawful government electronic surveillance. Sophisticated encryption can have this effect in the United States. When exported abroad, it can be used to thwart foreign intelligence activities critical to our national interests. In the past, it has been possible to preserve a government capability to conduct electronic surveillance in furtherance of legitimate law enforcement and national security interests, while at the same time protecting the privacy and civil liberties of all citizens. As encryption technology improves, doing so will require new, innovative approaches. (White House, 1994a)

Despite the close connection between "surveillance" and "security" in this discourse, the U.S. state has not (as yet) mandated the use of key-escrow cryptosystems outside state agencies, nor has it outlawed the use of stronger alternatives by citizens. Officials have vowed that comparable key-escrow standards for computers also "would be voluntary" (Al Gore, in *EPIC Alert,* 1994; cf. FBI Director Louis Freeh, in Meeks, 1994).

The state's own liberal discourse partially accounts for this constraint. The voluntary status of Clipper reinforces the liberal assumption that private persons (both individual and corporate) can and should be able to make choices. By making Clipper a choice, moreover, the liberal state appears more neutral on the issue of surveillance than it might otherwise seem if it made key escrow compulsory. Besides protecting individual rights, however, the state must also promote national security and public safety. Therefore, it cannot remain completely neutral on the issue of surveillance. Hence, Clipper cannot be presented as just any choice but the right choice: a point connoted in repeated claims that Clipper strikes a "balance between protection of communications privacy and protection of society" (U.S. Department of Justice, 1994). To advocates, this balance is "reasonable" in that the proposed policy "will reflect all of society's values, not just the single-minded pursuit of total privacy" (Baker, 1994). Encryption, after all, is "a double-edged sword": "It can be used to protect law-abiding citizens, and it can also be used to shield criminal activities, and also activities that could affect the security of this country" (Lynn McNulty, in "Open Sesame," 1994).

The bottom line, for Clipper advocates, is that "There is a trade-off between individual privacy and society's safety from crime. Our society needs to decide where to draw the line" (unnamed "government official," in Markoff, 1993).

Through this broad appeal to "our society," this discourse brings a collective identity into being. It invites us to see ourselves as law-abiding citizens who can become victims of the illicit and terrorist practices of our common enemies: "if encryption technology is made freely available worldwide, it would no doubt be used extensively by terrorists, drug dealers, and other criminals to harm Americans both in the U.S. and abroad" (White House, 1994b). References to encryption-using "terrorists" and "drug dealers" construct a new kind of enemy for the Information Age: computer-literate criminals who can use certain technologies, such as PGP, to conceal their illicit activities. This construct is the "constitutive outside," the "other" that makes possible the collective "we" constructed in this discourse (Mouffe, 1991: 78). Within this framework, Clipper advocates present themselves as being on "our side" in two senses. They support measures that will enhance national security and public safety, and they also claim to sympathize with concerns for protecting privacy: "None of us likes the idea of government intruding willy-nilly on communications that are meant to be private" (Baker, 1994). Even the NSA, according to this discourse, understands and supports domestic encryption: "We have always been in favor of the use of information security technologies by U.S. Businesses to protect their proprietary information" (Michael S. Conn, in Abernathy, 1992).[6] To be sure, because U.S. companies, too, have opposed the state's encryption policy, especially export restrictions, as damaging to their international competitiveness, Clipper advocates have had to engage in some discursive labor to counter these corporate concerns. Responding to this, the NSA has argued that ITAR does not prohibit companies and individuals from exporting cryptography; it simply requires them to submit their products to an "export review process" (ibid.).[7]

Where Zimmermann apparently fell afoul of ITAR was in not submitting PGP to this review process. This has enabled Clipper advocates to construct him in negative terms as naive, disingenuous, and even criminally dangerous: Zimmermann is "playing at this stuff, and when it has real consequences, he wants to deny it. How far do you think you'd get arguing you didn't cause the export of nuclear technology if you sold it in an international airport departure lounge?" (unnamed government source, in J. Schwartz, 1995). This remarkable statement characterizes cryptography not merely as auxiliary munitions, but as an object that is as sensitive and dangerous as nuclear technology. Restricting the export of cryptography, therefore, is as vital to national security as restricting the export of weapons of mass destruction. Because PGP was placed on the Internet, moreover, the statement draws a further parallel between the Internet and "an international airport departure lounge." This parallel serves to construct the Internet as a space for international traffic. By implication, Internet users should be held accountable for what they post (read: "export"). Furthermore, just as people take for granted the need for airport security—especially on international flights, which are commonly understood as favorite targets for both terrorists and smugglers—so, too, should they take for granted the need for security on the Internet, given that it simply is, according to this argument, a space for international traffic.

Although it acknowledges the Internet's blurring of traditional borders, the metaphor of the international airport departure lounge quickly elides this ambiguity in favor of the easy conclusion that the Internet is always, at least, a pre-international space: data placed there *will* go abroad. Such articulations serve to territorialize cyberspace in ways intended to make it safer for states. Once cyberspace is reconfigured in the familiar terms of the domestic/international divide, it can be made to fit the "moral geography" of the modern nation-state system (Shapiro, 1994). This mapping justifies the extension into cyberspace of current norms governing the export of tangible items across geopolitical borders. According to this analogy, then, the transfer of sensitive data on the Internet simply *is* a type of export: it should therefore be regulated. Once the analogy is made, common sense dictates this imperative, opening the way for the projection of existing laws into cyberspace. Hence, the issues raised by Zimmermann's case, according to the U.S. attorney who led the investigation, are "What—if any—policing is to be done on the 'Net? Are we going to throw up our hands and say 'There's no accountability. It's too big to enforce?'" (William P. Keane, in J. Schwartz, 1995).

Although "policing" typically refers to a domestic activity in which states engage, state security analysts have noted that "In cyberspace,

276 · DIANA SACO

the boundaries between nations and private-sector organizations are porous, rendering distinctions between war and crime, and between public and private interests, less meaningful" (RAND, 1996). This ambiguity has opened a space for recasting the concept of policing as an international concern—that is, as an issue that requires the coordinated efforts of states (Nadelmann, 1993). This message can be read as a central point of Clinton's (1995) speech commemorating the fiftieth anniversary of the United Nations. Arguing that "The emergence of the information and technology age has brought us all closer together," Clinton warned that this new closeness broadens the impact of hitherto domestic dangers: "Trouble on the far end of town soon becomes a plague on everyone's house." He thus called on fellow UN members to join the United States "in negotiating and endorsing a declaration on international crime and citizens' safety." Among the initiatives he outlined, moreover, was the need to form "an effective police force partnership" to fight international crime, drug trafficking, terrorism, and the spread of weapons of mass destruction. To the extent that cyberspace is always, already a "pre-international space" vulnerable to illicit uses by both domestic and international criminals, its regulation, according to this collective security discourse, calls for a similar extension and coordination of the policing function of states.

This expanded discourse permits state officials to try trumping domestic concerns by pleading national security concerns, as is evident in the following anecdote of a conversation nonstarter that Clipper opponent John Perry Barlow had with Vice President Al Gore aboard Air Force II: "What [Gore] has apparently been thinking about very hard is cryptography. When I started to open this line of discussion he went all blank and said, 'We have national security interests at stake.' End of discussion" (Barlow, 1994c). Of course, this has not been the end of discussion. As the preceding analysis indicates, Clipper advocates have engaged in a great deal of discursive labor to bring collective identities into being (law-abiding citizens, our society, and even an international police force partnership), to name common enemies (high-tech criminals and terrorists), and to justify the adoption of controversial encryption policies (key escrow as a balanced safeguard against our new threats). These efforts, moreover, have been a direct response to Clipper opponents' own discursive practices.

Opposing Clipper

Computer civil-liberties groups argue that the problems associated with encryption policies are far more complex than just the legal and technical matters of administration, accountability, and enforcement. Even while the Internet is accessible to foreign persons, it is also a domestic space for public conversations among U.S. citizens and for private transactions between them. Because these political and social exchanges are valued and protected in the United States, policing the Internet raises some vexing constitutional issues as well. Of paramount concern is the issue of privacy and its relationship to First Amendment freedoms of speech and association, Fourth Amendment protections against illegal and arbitrary searches and seizures, and Fifth Amendment provisions against self-incrimination (Barlow, 1993a).

Privacy, according to this view, is endangered by the Internet's blurring of the traditional, liberal divide between public and private (cf. Lyon, 1994: 179–98). Even ostensibly private transactions have become more public, because more visible, in cyberspace. Computers have so thoroughly penetrated most spheres of life (particularly, but not exclusively, in advanced societies) that cyberspace overlaps with, and indeed is part of, the physical world. The danger lies in the way a fully digitized society links physical space and cyberspace, making it possible for interested others to track a person's activities in the physical world: "Our transactions and conversations are now more easily traced by the digital trails we leave behind. By following the electronic links we make, one can piece together a depressingly detailed profile of who we are: our health records, phone bills, credit histories, arrest records, and electronic mail all connect our actions and expressions to our physical selves" (Levy, 1993). By concealing our transactions and identities in garbled messages, strong cryptography "presents the possibility of severing these links" (ibid.). It creates the conditions for greater personal security and indeed greater freedom in a fully digitized society, ensuring that no matter how many data banks one's virtual self traverses, each person is "password protected." Hence, privacy and even anonymity are as central to personal security in this discourse as surveillance is to national security in the pro-Clipper discourse.

Opponents view key escrow and export restrictions as state efforts "to establish imperial control over cyberspace" (Barlow, 1994a). Against such efforts, they maintain that the lack of centralized control is precisely what makes cyberspace so positive: "a perfect breeding ground for both outlaws and new ideas about liberty" (Barlow, 1990). Despite these images, however, some Clipper opponents admit that cyberspace, in its current incarnation, is perhaps a bit too unruly: "Sovereignty over this new world is . . . not well defined. Large institutions already lay claim to large fiefdoms, but most of the actual natives are solitary and independent, sometimes to the point of sociopathy" (Barlow and Kapor, 1990). Early on, therefore, in 1990, John Perry Barlow and Mitch Kapor established the Electronic Frontier Foundation in order to "civilize" cyberspace before repressive state precedents could be set:

> [E]xamination of the issues surrounding . . . government actions [i.e., hacker crackdowns] revealed that we were dealing with the symptoms of a much larger malady, the collision between Society and Cyberspace. We have concluded that a cure can lie only in bringing civilization to Cyberspace. Unless a successful effort is made to render that harsh and mysterious terrain suitable for ordinary inhabit[ant]s, friction between the two worlds will worsen. (Ibid.; see also Electronic Frontier Foundation, 1990a, 1990b).

Computer break-ins into proprietary corporate networks—such as the 1989 theft of a portion of Apple Computer programming (Sterling, 1992: 220–21)—had contributed to this friction between society and cyberspace. Although such apparent violations of intellectual property rights seldom resulted in profit losses, they did constitute, at a minimum, a symbolic nose-thumbing by hackers against corporate security efforts. Members of the EFF noted that these threats were often exaggerated by both state officials and the mainstream media, who persistently misunderstood and misrepresented the underground "hacker ethic" (*The Jargon File*, 1994). In the dialectical process by which the media shape social practices, moreover, hackers themselves—typically adolescent, white, middle-class males—further contributed to these exaggerations by adopting the infamous "bad boy" posture associated with them in the media (see Barlow, 1990).

And so, confronted on one side by insolent hackers intent on violating social norms by engaging in the "time-honored adolescent sport of trespassing" (ibid.) and on the other side by state forces willing to trample civil liberties in order to crack down on "the hacker threat," the EFF set itself the task of civilizing cyberspace. Encouraging both individual and corporate computer users to protect themselves (e.g., by using widely available encryption programs) and to respect on-line norms (at least against malicious break-ins) could serve two ends. Self-protection and self-restraint might forestall the need for police-state actions, thereby safeguarding civil liberties, and they might also curb fraudulent incursions into proprietary systems, thereby reinforcing one of a variety of existing social norms that apply to the on-line world as well—albeit, with significant modifications (see Barlow, 1993b). In this respect, a number of individual and corporate security concerns converged in the EFF's civilizing mission.[8] The EFF's mission, like the state's own colonizing project, thus has both subjectifying and territorializing elements. It seeks to educate people about the technology and about on-line norms in order to make them informed, upstanding, and even respectable "cyber-citizens." It also involves a related effort to settle and develop the Electronic Frontier in still more enabling, "user-friendly" ways.[9]

In the early 1990s, the EFF and other opponents of U.S. encryption policy launched a variety of on-line campaigns aimed at discrediting the state's security discourse. Critics of ITAR, for example, designed a "Munition Tshirt" *(sic)* depicting the mathematical source code for the algorithm used in programs such as PGP. Because the source code was reproduced in machine-readable bar code (that is, it could be scanned into a computer and easily converted into a working encryption program), the T-shirt could be classified as export-restricted munitions under then-current ITAR categories. This irony was noted on the T-shirt itself: "WARNING: This shirt is classified as a munition and may not be exported from the United States, or shown to a foreign nation" ("Munition Tshirt," 1995). In addition, on-line images of the T-shirt on U.S. Internet servers were intentionally blurred, as protesters explained, to avoid violating export laws. Such campaigns clearly served to ridicule ITAR restrictions by taking them to their own logical yet absurd conclusions (see also Karn, 1996).

To discredit Clipper, opponents have deployed more sinister images, associating the chip with the cultural image of "Big Brother"—the omnipotent and omnipresent symbol of state surveillance in George Orwell's dystopic novel *1984.* The Clipper chip, they argue, is a device "with Big Brother inside" ("What You Can Do," 1994). The state, as this imagery suggests, is untrustworthy: *it,* and not criminals and terrorists, is the common enemy. The very existence of secret spy agencies such as the NSA—aka "No Such Agency" (Bamford, 1982: 357)—helps to contribute to this lack of trust (Barlow, 1992). Against attempts to present the agency as "expert" in cryptology and therefore best qualified to secure the privacy of citizens, opponents counter by warning that the NSA's expertise in spying is precisely why ordinary citizens should worry: "You don't want to buy a set of car keys from a guy who specializes in stealing cars" (Marc Rotenberg, in Levy, 1994: 70).

Unlike the pro-Clipper discourse—which addresses itself most often to an abstract, collective "we" (as in appeals to "our society")— the anti-Clipper discourse addresses itself most often to a seemingly more concrete and individualistic "you." This difference relates to the competing priorities of each discourse. The former privileges national security and public safety, concerns affecting abstract collectivities. For the latter, however, the key issue is the threat to individual privacy that key escrow and state surveillance more generally engender. In other words, opponents are concerned with issues that affect concrete individuals *as* individuals: me and you. The point is that *you* need to become aware of this encryption issue because it is "Big Government versus Your Privacy" (Aleshire, 1994).

To heighten the sense of the stakes involved, some opponents have articulated these dangers to "your privacy" to a more general concern with threats to democracy. Democracy, they argue, depends on citizens having the ability to assemble in order to affect the course of government, but citizens can exercise this freedom without reprisals only when they can secure their communications from government surveillance:

> There are communications that the government has *no right* to hear— and which private citizens have every right to exclude specifically from government detection. Two examples: first, citizens have the right to conspire (electronically, if they choose) to reform government, because they believe it does not work. Second, they can conspire to remove specific individuals from government, for such reasons, among others, that the government official is believed to be abusing his or her position (e.g., in obtaining illegal wiretaps . . .). If these two kinds of communication cannot be kept from the government under *all*

circumstances—through private encryption means, if necessary—then we do not have a democracy. (White, 1994; emphasis in the original)

The strong claim made here is that democracy simply does not exist wherever governments have the technical wherewithal to monitor any and every conversation. In a similar vein, Zimmermann himself has highlighted the use of PGP "by human rights activists, environmental activists, religious activists, gay activists, and anyone else needing protection from the powerful" (Zimmermann, 1994a; see also Banisar, 1995). Strong cryptography, on this view, protects the privacy and rights especially "of targeted individuals" (Tom Jennings, in Levy, 1993), whereas weak devices such as Clipper, if standardized for domestic use and for export, will threaten democracy and political activism around the world.[10]

Like its pro-Clipper counterpart, then, the discourse of the EFF and other Clipper opponents attempts to effect changes in the way people think about security: specifically, their personal security and the major threats posed to it by computer surveillance technologies in the hands of a too-powerful state. In the process, it, too, addresses a particular identity (private individuals and oppressed groups as targets of surveillance), constructs an enemy (Clipper and the state as Big Brother), and advocates a particular course of action (anonymity through strong encryption as the only source of security in a fully digitized world).

LIBERALISM ON THE ELECTRONIC FRONTIER

As the preceding sections indicate, the Internet, despite its origins as a technology of security, has given rise to competing cultures of insecurity. The issue is not only whether the state can project its sovereign authority into cyberspace given the technical features of networking, but also how the liberal discourse through which the insecurities reimagined by both state and nonstate actors will shape those efforts. To be sure, networking technology—by its distributed, semiautonomous, and global nature—can challenge state authority. If they are willing to adopt more repressive policies, however, states may possess options for controlling local Internet use. The State Council of China, for example, in January 1996, approved a new set of policies requiring citizens to register for Internet access and funneling all incoming international transmissions through state-run gateways (Sullivan, 1996). Such measures clearly will help the Chinese state censor its citizens' access to perhaps most international postings. What this suggests, however, is that states, in their efforts to reassert their authority over cyberspace, may stand a better chance of doing so by regulating on-line debate rather than entering it. This poses a problem for self-styled liberal democracies, which define themselves in terms of universal access, rule by the people, and the free flow of information in an open political process that includes dialogue, debate, and deliberation among citizens and between constituents and their representatives. Liberal states must, at a minimum, seek the consent of computer users for their computer-related policies. It is here that state security concerns may be circumscribed by the personal security concerns of citizens.

Two subsequent developments in U.S. encryption policy support this conclusion. First, given the strong domestic opposition to Clipper, the Clinton administration, in April 1995, established a new, joint defense–civilian board "pledged to accommodate a mix of commercial and federal methods for protecting electronic transactions," a move that some observers characterized as a White House retreat on the Clipper mandate (Constance, 1995). Because the administration continued to support a key-escrow standard, that conclusion seemed premature (Maize, 1995b). Still, in response to privacy concerns about Big Government holding the keys, it did at least drop its initial plan to appoint state agencies as the escrow agents, proposing instead a "commercial escrow" standard that would accept private companies in this role ("Clipper II," 1995). And in an effort to make key-escrow policy more palatable to software exporters, the administration, in May 1996, circulated preliminary plans for what opponents called a "Clipper III" proposal, whereby the state would trade export privileges to software companies in exchange for their agreeing to escrow wiretap keys for their encryption products (Rodger, 1996). To be sure, opponents have rejected these "sons of Clipper," on the same principles that key escrow violates privacy rights and undermines foreign sales (see Center for Democracy and Technology, n.d.); but by attempting to offer compromises, the state has at least shown itself willing (or perhaps forced for reasons of maintaining legitimacy) to address opponents' concerns.

Second, in January 1996, after more than two years of investigation, the U.S. Justice Department announced its decision to drop its case against Philip Zimmermann ("Author Won't Be Prosecuted," 1996). Officials gave no explanation, but, according to one observer, the government wanted to avoid "the public relations nightmare" that Zimmermann's indictment would have caused (Simson Garfinkel, in ibid.). This, too, suggests that the liberal state's power over cyberspace may be circumscribed.

A point seldom acknowledged in the EFF's discourse, however, is that the Electronic Frontier, like its nineteenth-century predecessor, is vulnerable to more than just the state's colonizing efforts. If freedom and anarchy reigned in the frontier of the American West—at least in the social imaginaries of those who projected their hopes there—they did not remain part of its fate for long. As one sympathetic critic of the frontier metaphor observes (Cleaver, 1996), the very adventurers who sought escape from the hardships of urban industrial centers brought existing social frameworks with them and, in particular, notions about private ownership. The projection of property rights into frontier space transformed it into the "cutting edge of capitalist civilization," not its antithesis (Cleaver, 1996). The free and enterprising spirit of the frontier was perfectly compatible with a free-enterprise spirit. The irony is that the very endeavor to sally forth and settle the frontier is what signaled its demise. Whether the Electronic Frontier will meet a similar fate is still an open question. To be sure, the earliest denizens of cyberspace—students, academics, researchers, and educated dropouts—have resisted the commercialization of the Internet: most notably, the arrival of companies willing to violate on-line norms by advertising on the Internet, especially by sending unsolicited mass E-mailings (Elmer-Dewitt, 1994). Even cyberspace veterans, however, are incapable of fully controlling who will gain access to the Internet or how these others will use and transform it. In this respect, the frontier metaphor may fit cyberspace better than most people imagine.

Censorship measures aside, the bulk of the provisions enacted in the Telecommunications Act of 1996 further deregulate the very cable, telephone, and long-distance companies that are making a bid to build what the Clinton administration has dubbed the "Information Superhighway" (Stranahan, 1996). As a result of some of these provisions, particularly those relaxing restrictions on cross-ownership, already large telecommunications corporations can further diversify their services, consolidate their power, and buy up or elbow out smaller competitors. These "deregulatory" measures, combined with the privatization of the Internet, constitute a form of *re*regulation (Barbrook, 1996), following the pattern of what Cleaver (1996) refers to as the "thoroughly modern version of enclosure . . . the expropriation of businesses by businesses." Such trends betray a competitive spirit exemplified and lauded by a new breed of telecom CEO—the "Infobahn Warrior" (Kline, 1994). Rather than opposite visions, then, the paths outlined by the metaphors of the Information Superhighway and the Electronic Frontier tend to converge toward classical liberalism on a new heading: "information capitalism" (White, 1995: 23).

This is not to suggest that Clipper opponents are wrong to invoke the frontier metaphor, especially if, as is evident in their discourse, it evokes resistance to repressive regulations by a Big Brother–like state. But little in the current debate, on either side, reflects a comparable concern with the ways in which capitalist forces too can colonize cyberspace, a trend made more dire by the potentially detrimental effects to tax collection—and, by extension, state-welfare functions—that totally encrypted (and therefore anonymous) electronic financial transfers can have (Munro, 1994). For its part, the EFF's assessment of the Telecommunications Act (Electronic Frontier Foundation, 1996b) criticizes only the censorship provisions and its negative consequences for civil liberties, without commenting at all on the potential, negative effects to universal access that so-called deregulation also may engender (Barbrook, 1996; "Public Interest Issues in the Telecommunications Act of 1996," 1996). This omission is unsurprising in that, elsewhere, both EFF cofounders—in a manner consistent with what critics have identified as the hippie/yuppie mix of their "Californian ideology" (Barbrook and Cameron, 1995)—have applauded deregulation precisely on the classical liberal argument that "Competition does more to keep firms honest than a roomful of regulators" (Kapor, 1993; see also Barlow, 1994c). Perhaps a virulent spread of deregulation from the Internet to other arenas is precisely what Barlow had in mind when he declared: "Mitch and I had always talked about the job of [the] EFF as civilizing the electronic frontier. I think that our job, and your job, increasingly, is going to be frontierizing civilization" (Barlow, 1994c).

The notion of "frontierizing civilization" has not been subject to the same level of critical reflection as the state's security discourse.

The hyperliberalism that notion evokes, however, poses other valid security concerns: for example, restriction of Internet content and access if provision of service comes under the monopolistic control of a handful of megacorporations, or problems of tax evasion and welfare funding if financial transactions become totally anonymous. Evidence exists that officials are worried about these dangers, too (e.g., Mike Nelson, in Munro, 1994), but such concerns have been barely audible amid cloying reminders of the "threats" posed by "high-tech criminals and terrorists." Ultimately, critics are right to reject the latter as exaggerated.

This is not to suggest, however, that the Internet is unproblematic for states. Having developed in a context where physical borders mattered, the state now faces a space without borders: a "virtual" space, with a different kind of physicality, constituted by the movement of bits rather than bodies (Saco, 1998). In this respect, cyberspace is an *anti*geography. It subverts the familiar, comfortable dichotomies of domestic/international and public/private. Private data becomes public because more visible. Similarly, once sensitive data makes its way into the global space of the Internet, it can be stored and redistributed in ways that circumvent domestic laws. Despite Zimmermann's ordeal, for example, PGP is still available on the Internet. Domestic sites merely post "NOT FOR EXPORT" warnings to users outside the United States and then redirect them to non-U.S. servers from which they can safely download the software.

The redundancy and autonomy originally built into networking ("for security reasons") have facilitated these methods for circumventing state law. Because bits can be perfectly reproduced, data archived at one site can be "mirrored" at others without restrictions. Unlike the limited nature of geographic space, moreover, cyberspace is "a peculiar kind of real estate which expands with development" (Barlow, 1992). Hence, as sites proliferate and the technology becomes less costly, network options for bypassing problem nodes also increase: "If you don't like the politics of the system you're on, you can set up your own for the price of a clone and increasingly cheap Internet connection" (Barlow, 1994b). The Internet, in short, deals with local restrictions much like the original ARPANet dealt with damaged nodes: it "routes around" (John Gilmore, in ibid.).

In this context, the state's redefinitions of its security concerns have two significant features, both of which undermine conventional notions of sovereignty. First, new connections between national security and public safety are being articulated. Reflected in these connections is a partial admission that one state, alone, cannot address the threats posed by some of the newer technologies. In the process, the state, traditionally defined in relation to the geopolitical territory it governs, is reimagining itself so as to warrant the application of laws that extend its jurisdiction into the nonterritorial, extrasovereign space of the Internet. The state as target of information warfare characterizes the insecure state in this new context; the state as partner in a collaborative effort to battle international crime offers one future vision of the secure state in a digital environment. A partnership effort to sustain collective jurisdiction over cyberspace, however, may be trumped by new states as they come on line or by older partners as their priorities change (Farber, 1995).

Even assuming that states will be able to coordinate their efforts to redefine security for cyberspace, a second important feature of these redefinitions is that cyberspace also conflates public and private in ways that engender new tensions between national security and personal security. Liberal states, in particular, are facing serious opposition from their own citizens. The U.S. state's solution has been to articulate itself to liberal-pluralist understandings of the state as neutral arbiter. For their part, a number of businesses have questioned the state's capacity to arbitrate computer-related issues without sufficient input from the private sector. Notwithstanding this, some of them have been prepared to make compromises to safeguard their markets and avoid criminal prosecution—for example, CompuServe's temporary, network-wide ban of *alt.sex* newsgroups to avoid violating censorship laws in Germany (Berlin, 1996). The state, too, for its part, cannot as easily dismiss business concerns as idealistic prattle. It has opted instead to enact laws that facilitate corporate efforts to colonize cyberspace.

POSTSCRIPT: 1996 AND AFTER

The state's compromises on privacy issues have not appeased opponents, who have repeatedly rejected all Clipper proposals and have ridiculed ITAR classifications in a variety of on-line campaigns, such as the "Munition Tshirt" (1995). However misinformed such challenges might seem from the state's national security standpoint, their more immediate impact has been to cast doubt on the legitimacy of

ITAR by foregrounding its ridiculous implications: in classifying a T-shirt as "munitions" and in helping to construct a cryptographer (Zimmermann) as "an enemy of the state." What critics have shown quite successfully is that these defense-oriented constructs, proffered by the state as part of its own campaign to colonize cyberspace, strain the limits of common sense. Because the state's campaign is also a discursive one, aimed at securing public consent to state policy, such obviously absurd constructs have not won the day.

Perhaps in partial recognition of this failure, Clinton, on November 15, 1996, signed Executive Order No. 13026 calling for the transfer of nonmilitary encryption products from the United States Munitions List (USML) administered by the State Department under ITAR to the Commerce Control List (CCL) administered by the Commerce Department under the Export Administration Regulations (EAR) ("Executive Order," in White House, 1996a). To help implement this transfer, ITAR was amended, in December 1996, to remove from the USML "all cryptographic items except those specifically designed, developed, configured, adapted, or modified for military applications" (U.S. Department of State, 1996; see also ITAR, 1997). As a result, commercial encryption products have been reclassified from "munitions" to a new category of controlled "Encryption Item" (EI) under the CCL. The administration has characterized this transfer as a "liberalization" of export restrictions (White House, 1996b), a term meant primarily to connote civil liberties. As the preceding analysis suggests, however, this term should be read as well, and more significantly, in classical economic terms: as a softening of export restrictions for the sake of a freer market for the international sales of American cryptographic products. Indeed, as Clinton outlined in the "Memorandum" accompanying the order, his decision was spurred in part "because of the importance to U.S. economic interests of the market for encryption products" (in White House, 1996a).

My point is not, of course, that encryption technology is no longer restricted for national security reasons; on the contrary, the new policy has removed one weakness of the Cold War regulatory regime—the treatment of encryption as "arms"—while shoring up other weaknesses created by the absence of any explicit legislation regarding the Internet. In particular, the new policy implements the administration's concern with national security and public safety by

establishing an interagency board that permits the Departments of
State, Defense, Energy, and Justice and the Arms Control and Disarmament Agency to review export license applications submitted to
the Department of Commerce. In addition, the order explicitly rede-
fines encryption software "technology" (which might be open to
First Amendment safeguards for the free flow of information) as a
"product" subject to greater scrutiny and export control given its
"functional capacity" ("Executive Order," in ibid.): that is, given the
facility with which source codes (programming algorithms) in electronic form can be easily converted into working encryption programs. Furthermore, the accompanying Memorandum directs that
the final regulations to be issued in accordance with the new policy
must establish that the electronic posting of encryption software
onto BBS's and Internet sites "will constitute an export of encryption . . . unless the party making the software available takes precau-
tions adequate to prevent the unauthorized transfer of such code
outside the United States" ("Memorandum," in ibid.). Thus, although
the Zimmermann case has been dropped, the new regulations provide an explicit legal basis for prosecuting similar cases in the future.
Finally, although the administration has slightly backed off its insistence on a key-escrow system, the order reasserts the U.S. state's concern with establishing, at least, "key recovery management infrastructure," by which is meant some mechanism (key-escrow or a
viable alternative) that will ensure intelligence and law enforcement
access to the plaintext version of encrypted communications. In tandem with this last directive, the administration also named a new
"Special Envoy for Cryptography," Ambassador David L. Aaron,
charged with the task of coordinating efforts with other national
governments "to promote the growth of international electronic
commerce and robust, secure global communications in a manner
that protects the public safety and national security" (White House,
1996b). As critics attest, these last two features in particular make
the 1996 policy simply a new version of the same, old policy
program—a point critics have made by dubbing the policy "Clipper
3.1.1" (see center for Democracy and Technology, n.d.).

Certainly, the most significant feature of this policy, from the
standpoint of the preceding analysis, is the decision to cease designating commercial encryption products as defense articles on the

USML. Perhaps because old habits are hard to change, however, the Memorandum directs that if export controls under the new statute prove to be inadequate, the president will retain final authority to determine whether certain products will be "designated or redesignated as defense articles" under ITAR (in White House, 1996a). Notwithstanding this last provision, the move toward classifying commercial encryption products as export-controlled "commodities" rather than "munitions" does recapitulate the state's concern with redefining national security for cyberspace, and in a manner that is structurally consistent with the (economic) liberalization of the Internet. Furthermore, this reclassification articulates national security policy in a way that is discursively more plausible to the variety of computer users who have a stake in this technology and in how it is developed further. In this respect, it demonstrates the (liberal) state's increasing need, in the current context, to take other security concerns into account in the process of articulating its own concerns.

Defining "security" had been the purview of the state for much of the Cold War era, with its focus on military (and primarily nuclear) capabilities. Perhaps because the state held a virtual monopoly on those capabilities and could insulate its technical experts within the defense community, citizens' responses were generally limited to building bomb shelters or demonstrating in peace rallies, neither of which fundamentally challenged the security discourses that had helped to sustain Cold War politics. In the case of digital capabilities, however, most of the experts are outside the defense community, and some, like Zimmermann, are former peace activists (Willis, 1995). Most of the users, moreover, are private citizens, many of whom have different security concerns and are sufficiently well informed to understand the consequences of conducting communications over poorly secured channels. Digital capabilities, in short, are distributed among a wider variety of users, including other sovereign states, privacy-loving individuals, and profit-maximizing corporations, each with different legal understandings, interpretive frameworks, and their own security agendas. Perhaps the most fundamental challenge the state faces in this context, then, is a loss of its exclusive privilege to define "threats" and a comparable decline in the mystique formerly surrounding "national security."

NOTES

Thanks to Lisa Disch, John Mowitt, Michael Shapiro, Edward Kolodziej, Richard Price, Alex Wendt, Jonathan Hill, Naeem Inayatoullah, David Blainey, John Armitage, Elisabeth Binder, and the project participants for their invaluable comments on prior drafts, and to Kevin Corbitt of the University of Minnesota's Charles Babbage Institute (CBI) for data on the history of networking.

1. Coined by Gibson (1984), *cyberspace* refers to the space of all telecommunications, especially via the Internet. Because it has no observable features beyond the images on computer screens, cyberspace is often treated as a constructed "virtual" space in contrast to the "real" physical spaces it simulates. Such dichotomies can be misleading, however, in part because all social space is socially constructed (Lefebvre, 1991; see also Litzinger, this volume). I develop these arguments more thoroughly in my dissertation (Saco, 1998).

2. The United States is not, however, unique in restricting cryptography exports (see John Browning's sidebar, in Levy, 1993). The scant mention of Latin American and African countries in Koops (1996) does suggest, however, that restrictions are more prominent in more computerized societies. Furthermore, the privacy issues framing the U.S. debate may be specific to liberal states. That said, current efforts to globalize networking (Hoffman, 1995; Henry, 1995) will likely make encryption a more salient national security concern, if not also a privacy issue, in many more countries as their networking capabilities develop.

3. A combination of "cyberpunk" (high-tech rebel) and "cipher" (code), *Cypherpunk* refers less to a formal group than to an ethos: "Anyone who decides to spread personal crypto or its gospel is a traveler in the territory of Cypherpunk" (Levy, 1993; see also *The Jargon File,* 1994).

4. Because export restrictions affect both software and hardware and in both computer and telephone products, opposition from the business community has actually included a broader coalition of about fifty software, computer, and telecommunications companies, among them Apple, AT&T, IBM, Lotus, Microsoft, and Sun Microsystems, some of which are also members of the lobby groups Software Publishers Association (SPA) and Business Software Alliance (BSA) (Dinsdale, 1994; Maize, 1995a; U.S. House, 1993b). Despite its opposition, however, AT&T had already begun, by 1994, to integrate the Clipper chip into its line of "secure" telephones (Levy, 1994: 50).

5. Since the Foreign Intelligence Surveillance Act of 1978 (FISA), the NSA, too, has had to obtain wiretap warrants. This restriction, however, pertains only to surveillance within U.S. borders. Applications, moreover, are made to the supersecret Foreign Intelligence Surveillance Court established by FISA (Bamford, 1982: 462–68), which, by 1994, had granted all of the 8,130 applications submitted to it (Brandt, 1995).

COLONIZING CYBERSPACE · 291

6. It is worth noting, however, that this statement conveys only an NSA concern with property, not privacy. In fact, the NSA statements I analyzed mention only the need to protect the security and privacy of *government*, not *personal*, computer systems (Conn, in Abernathy, 1992; McConnell, 1994). The NSA's silence on individual privacy issues is perhaps not surprising given its role as a spy agency.

7. At the behest of software companies and related industries, legislative efforts have been made to relax restrictions and simplify licensing procedures for the export of cryptographic products (see, for example, U.S. House, 1993a, 1993b). Despite some changes, the State Department, throughout the early 1990s, held virtual control through ITAR over encryption exports and often forwarded commercial export requests to the NSA for evaluation given the agency's "technical expertise" in determining whether the export of a particular cryptographic product "could have a negative impact on the national security interests of the United States" ("Declaration of William P. Crowell," Deputy Director of the NSA, taken in *Karn v. U.S. Department of State* [Civ. Act. No. 95-1812 (CRR), D.D.C. 1995], available on-line at URL http://people.qualcomm.com/karn/export/crowell.html, visited November 27, 1998). For a discussion of the more substantial changes made in November 1996, see the Postscript.

8. Perhaps the strongest indication of this convergence is that EFF members include several high-tech CEOs, who also provide the bulk of its funding (Electronic Frontier Foundation, 1995, 1996b; Sterling, 1992: 238).

9. User friendliness is not just about simplicity but about diversity. Initially, network usage was limited to those willing to learn complex operating systems such as Unix. As a consequence, early Internet users were relatively homogeneous (mostly young, educated men), helping give rise to the hacker subculture. But with graphic interfaces and Web hyperlinks, "you don't have to be a Unix hacker to use the Internet anymore—you just point and click" (Rutkowski, in Ubois, 1995: 62). This has led to greater heterogeneity among users and, ironically, to more friction.

10. Although states restrict the export of countersurveillance measures such as strong encryption, critics warn that the export of Western surveillance technologies is unrestrained, "providing invaluable support to military and totalitarian authorities throughout the world" in their efforts "to track the activities of dissidents, human rights activists, journalists, student leaders, minorities, trade union leaders, and political opponents," with often fatal results (Privacy International, 1995). When states concomitantly place export restrictions on cryptography and not on surveillance technologies, the combined effect of these policies is to tip the scales in favor of state surveillance, invariably endangering the lives of political dissenters.

10

Reimagining the State in Post-Mao China

RALPH A. LITZINGER

TOWARD AN ETHNOGRAPHY OF THE POST-MAO STATE

Since the 1980s, there have been a number of attempts to "bring the state back in," to rethink the relationship between the state and the social order it claims to represent and protect (see, for example, Abrams, 1988). Some of this work has shown that theories of the state have a long history in writings about the social (see, for example, Carnoy, 1984; Connolly, 1987, 1991). Other work has aimed to move away from a Cold War conceptual agenda that privileged questions of regime legitimacy, the planning process, state development, and the conflicting interests of actors (see, for example, Escobar, 1995; Verdery, 1996). Michael Taussig (1992) has written forcefully about the imaginary of the "state fetish," the way in which theories of the state have structured experiences of how people live in the space of "society," where social norms, meanings, and identities are believed to be constituted. Much has been written about Michel Foucault's position that the exercise of modern power is not vested in the state and its apparatuses; although Foucault never disputed the claim that there has been the centralization of political power in the form of the modern state, he pointed to other kinds of transformations in power relations, especially those oriented toward individuals and "individualizing technologies of power" (Foucault, 1980b, 1991). In attempts to write ethnographies the state, anthropologists have

293

increasingly come to view the state less as a form of institutional and bureaucratic arrangements for the management and ordering of "society," and more as a space, at once discursive, institutional, and material, where different conceptions of state power, its limits and effects, are interpreted and engaged (see, for example, Gupta, 1995; Mbembe, 1992).

This essay explores the reimagining of state and society in post-Mao China, as these imaginings impinge on questions of security and insecurity in ethnic minority politics. There has been important work in the China field examining the nature of state and society relations during the Maoist period and under Deng Xiaoping's reforms (see, for example, Shue, 1988; Siu, 1989a, 1989b; Walder, 1986). Other work has focused on the legacies of socialism under Deng's modernization campaign, exploring the particular conditions of the Chinese Communist Party's attempt to bring about an effective socialist transformation of Chinese society and the consciousness of its people (see, for example, Dirlik and Meisner, 1989). More recently, scholars have pointed to how many young Chinese are taking refuge from party ideology by "seeking entertainment" *(zhaole)* in discos and fancy restaurants (see Schell, 1995). Zha Jianying (1995) has pointed to the contemporary fascination with popular culture, soap operas, and tabloid gossip, with its stunning absence of national memory. Ironically, the party has been fully complicit in this tide of mass forgetting, ever fearful that critical interpretations of the past (whether this past be the Maoist regime or the Tiananmen incident in 1989) will undermine its authority, its self-inscribed identity as the agent of China's march toward progress. Given these changes, how do we now think the Chinese state? How does the state continue to be the preeminent provider of security? How does it make itself visible as a force in everyday social life? How does it safeguard its identity as the central bearer of the power and sovereignty of the people (Connolly, 1991; Saco, this volume)?

To explore these questions, this essay examines debates about "traditional culture" among ethnic minority scholars in the late 1980s and early 1990s. This was a period when many minority intellectuals were eagerly responding to Deng Xiaoping's charge to "seek truth from facts" and discard Mao's dictum to "take class struggle as the key link" (Litzinger, 1998). Specifically, I examine the resurgence of Yao popular ritual under Deng Xiaoping's reforms, drawing on fieldwork in the Yao mountains *(Da Yao Shan)* in Jinxiu County in Guangxi province.[1] The Yao are one of China's officially recognized ethnic minorities *(shaoshu minzu)*; the group is composed of some 1.5 million people, spread across the provinces of south and southwest China. The term *Yao* has been around since the Tang dynasty, used as a way of naming conglomerations of upland "tribal" peoples (Lemoine and Chiao Chien, 1991). The Yao were known historically as stubborn mountain recluses, often rejecting the claims of the imperial center that participation in tax and corvée labor systems constituted a form of cultural enlightenment. It was not until the Chinese Communist Party completed its massive historical and ethnological identification *(minzu shibie)* project in the 1950s that the Yao were written into the official memory of the Chinese nation (see Litzinger, 1995). Since at least the late 1940s, Yao popular ritual has been treated by the state as a "remnant" of presocialist "feudal" structures and as a source of local political authority for religious specialists.

Most analyses of popular ritual in post-Mao China have aimed to assess the effectiveness of practices of revolution and modernization in remaking local society (Shue, 1988; Madsen, 1989). Helen Siu (1989a, 1989b) has argued that the contemporary worship of ancestors, the celebration of community and temple festivals, the training of new priests, sorcerers, and shamans, are not simply about the resurgence of cultural practices that survived the "encounter" with the Maoist state. What we are seeing today are "new reconstitutions" of tradition, built on the cultural fragments that remain after decades of state intervention in local affairs, a gradual but unrelenting process in which the social bases for popular rituals and their political functions were effectively destroyed. Building on Siu's work, this essay argues that the "return" of Yao ritual practices must be understood within the context of a reform politics that has been seeking to return to everyday life some sense of normalcy, social order, and everyday routine (see Pemberton, 1994). Whereas the Maoist regime marked ritual practice as a lingering fragment of a feudal social order that always potentially threatened the socialist transformation of society, the post-Mao regime has implored scholars, intellectuals, government and party officials, as well as village ritual specialists to discover the useful and productive possibilities of religious thought and ritual practice. My project in this essay is to show that the intensive study and selective promotion of Yao ritual practice provides a window into ongoing debates and struggles over how state security is to be

defined and achieved in post-Mao China. What are the points of convergence between discourses of cultural recovery and the search for
new political technologies aimed to ensure social and political order?
How can we think about the "return" of ritual in post-Mao China
without romanticizing ritual, or the local, or the ethnic minority as
subjects of resistance?[2] What might this "return" tells us about how
state power and the social are being reimagined in post-Mao China?[3]

My discussion is organized in the following way. I begin by highlighting some of the ways in which the Yao, and the places and regions in which they live, have been defined as instances of the "backward" and the "remote." My somewhat extended discussion of the
various fields of discourse in which the Yao have been officially
named is intended to show how different "sites" of knowledge production, including fieldwork encounters, reconstructions of local bureaucracies, and images of state power in public culture, must be
central to the study of the state (see Gupta, 1995: 375). I then turn to
a discussion of Yao ritual, paying attention less to the formal properties and codes of these rituals, and more to how the reform regime's
"civilized village campaign" has aimed to control the meanings of
these rituals. These rituals are treated by some as exotic remnants of
past social orders, by others as instances of a local knowledge that
are themselves exemplars of the civilized *(wenming)*. The construct
of "civility," as we shall see, is heavily implicated in the post-Mao refashioning of productive, able bodies (Anagnost, 1992, 1994a). The
problematic I trace here, then, is not simply one of bringing the state
back in, but how one begins to understand the linkages between
imaginings of "traditional" ritual practices and the politics of state
security and insecurity in post-Mao China.

POST-MAO THEORIES OF HISTORICAL LAG AND CULTURAL LACK

*To become a socialist-modern, civil citizen is to overcome the conditions of
one's predicament of cultural lack.*

*To modernize Yao society we need to break through the condition of Yao
self-isolation in the mountains, and we must cast off all outmoded concepts
and customs. It is necessary to heighten the cultural quality of the Yao, to
develop educational undertakings in order to cultivate a new generation of
Yao people.*
—INTERVIEW WITH A PARTY SECRETARY IN JINXIU VILLAGE, GUANGXI

Since the early 1980s, Yao ritual specialists, scholars, party cadre, and
peasants have promoted, albeit in strikingly different ways, ritual

practices suppressed during the Maoist period. At issue in these cultural practices of recovery are struggles over how to define community security and insecurity, order and disorder, autonomy and subjection in a period in which the Chinese Communist Party claims to
be removing itself from the control of everyday social life (see Anagnost, 1992). In the course of my research, I was struck by how my
research consultants often spoke of Yao society *(Yaozu shehui)* as a
categorical space that could be documented, known, and, perhaps
most important, managed, transformed, and modernized.[4] Much of
my research had been arranged by Yao ethnologists who were eager
to impress on me the resilience and durability of Yao culture in the
face of three decades of party development projects and political
campaigns. For many Yao ethnologists, trained at state-run nationalities institutes and now permitted to undertake "research investigations" *(yanjiu diaocha)* for the first time in more than thirty years,
the rearticulation of a Yao cultural space depended on the delineation of a series of boundaries and borders, epistemological, historical, and ethnic. Yao culture, for example, was often represented by
ritual practices that had been passed on through the centuries and
that could be understood through proper guidance and instruction
by ritual specialists. This culture was also defined in opposition to the
beliefs, practices, languages, and sensibilities of other ethnic groups,
the northern Chinese, the Cantonese, and other officially recognized
ethnic minorities such as the Zhuang and the Miao. Historically, Yao
culture was seen to have its origins in the ancient past, traceable to
a mythical progenitor whose offspring took root on the southern
shores of the Dongting Lake in present-day Hunan Province (Huang
Yu and Huang Fangping, 1990).

Yao culture has also been presented within the dominant narrative of the Chinese modern nation-state. This narrative treats the nation as a subject of history that will, through the guiding wisdom of
the party-state, overcome the stifling traditions of the past. Since the
consciousness-raising practices of Chinese Communist Party activists
who first entered Yao regions in the mid-1940s, since the building of
the first "modern" schools and the introduction of newspapers and
party study booklets in the early 1950s, many Yao cultural practices
have been officially subsumed under the category of "feudal superstitions" *(fengjian mixin)*. This category marks those modes of thinking and behavior that keep the populace from realizing its destiny in
history. In short, since the late 1940s, the Yao social world has been

marked as a bounded space that could be defined ideologically and ultimately transformed. The modernization of regions defined by the party-state as remote and underdeveloped *(luohou pianpi)* has depended heavily on the dissemination of new conceptions of just what "local" social worlds signified to rural residents and to the emergent nation that had now turned its gaze upon the ethnic margins.

The post-Mao Yao subject—if one can indeed speak of a singular, unified subject—is thus confronted with a certain double bind: embraced for its colorful contribution to a multiethnic nation-state and yet repeatedly marked as a "problem." The constitutive force of this act of naming is perhaps best captured in Althusser's (1971) notion of interpellation, in which subject-formation is based on the reprimand, an act of censorship that does not merely repress or control the subject, but also enables its judicial and social formation. "In the reprimand the subject not only receives recognition, but attains as well a certain order of social existence, in being transformed from an outer region of indifferent, questionable, or impossible being to the discursive or social domain of the subject" (Butler, 1993: 121). The key point here is that subject constitution is accomplished through a "hailing," an ideological function in which the subject is called upon, singled out, identified, and named, as a uniquely valuable actor in a social or political formation. Such a focus on how identities are formed through practices of naming and recognition enables us to see that the ethnic minority in China is not merely "one of China's forty millions," as June Dreyer (1976) put it. The ethnic minority is a legal fiction, emerging into national visibility through the classificatory act of a state identification project. This project, first carried out in the 1950s, resulted in the official construction of fifty-six national minorities. What is sometimes overlooked is how the "identification" practice has been sustained on other fronts, usually through ideological campaigns and administrative languages that have cast ethnic minorities in idioms of threat, deficiency, and problem. It is through the performative act of naming that the ethnic subject continues to be identified as a site for post-Mao ideological work.

The configuration of Yao social realities through idioms of remoteness, cultural lag, and historical paralysis was often presented to me as part of a scientific vocabulary necessary for Yao scholars, intellectuals, and party cadre in their work of figuring out the "correct" relationship between the "traditional" and the "modern." In an era where "truth is now sought from facts" (as opposed to the blind dogma of Maoist slogans and theories of the revolutionary subject), this containment of difference has afforded a certain degree of theoretical certainty, where cultural practices are fixed as either retarding or enhancing the creation of socialist-modern subjects. This discourse gets circulated in everyday speech, becoming part of everyday lived reality. The language of the remote and the backward appears, for example, when Yao farmers reflect upon extant agricultural methods and call for technical and managerial assistance to increase productivity; when Yao ritual specialists talk about how their craft today differs from what it was in the past, how past rituals were too extravagant *(shechi)* and wasteful of valuable resources; when older Yao women discuss embroidery patterns and how the making of "traditional costumes" demanded too much time and took away from the development of other needed areas of expertise for women; and when peasants point out to visiting research teams how the culture and customs of one local group (or "ethnic subgroup," *minzu zhixi)* are qualitatively different, indeed inferior, to those of another.

As with other, mostly rural populations in China, ethnic minorities are said to be the repositories of cultural practices that have long histories of development and transformation (Litzinger, 1995). As in previous periods of socialist mobilization, these cultural practices continue to be treated as though they might disrupt the power of the reform state to set the terms of post-Mao discourse on order and development; that is, these practices continue to be marked as a threat to the security of the state. Yao ritual, for example, has been marked since the 1950s as an object of official scorn and an area for ideological transformation. By the time of the Great Leap Forward in the late 1950s, most Yao ritual specialists were forbidden to train novices; during the Cultural Revolution (1967–76), Yao ritual texts, many copies of which were first hand copied in the 1800s, were confiscated and subsequently burned by Red Guards in public rituals aimed at crushing all forms of reactionary thinking. Through all of these campaigns, Yao ritual was repeatedly constructed as a "remnant" *(canji).* This term is derived from Lewis Henry Morgan's eighteenth-century theory of social evolutionism and Friedrich Engels's subsequent reworking in *The Origin of the Family, Private Property, and the State* (see McKhann, 1994). It works to fix cultural practices in stages of historical progression and thus always invokes the sense of a vestige or a trace of the past that persists into the present; Chinese state socialism has always been aimed in large part at eradicating, or at the very least controlling and managing, these unwanted remnants of the past. In the post-Mao period, the remnant continues to be a significant discursive figure, though it has now been incorporated into a less politicized reading of traditional culture as a sign of the nation's depth and strength. Official readings of Yao ritual now aim to reconstitute it as a sign of the larger domain of "Yao traditional culture," a culture said to embody and signify the boundaries of the Yao minority.

This politics of naming and surveillance stems in part from the popular resurgence of Yao ritual activities in many villages, such as the recruitment and training of Taoist ritual specialists (*shigong* and *daogong*), community "cleansing" rituals *(jiao)*, ordination rites *(dujie)*, and elaborate weddings and funerals. These practices are not only monitored by local officials, but villagers themselves are required to ensure that the practices do not violate the tenets of the "civilized village campaign" *(wenming cun yundong)*, a countrywide ideological project the party-state has used to get villagers to practice forms of "self-rule." Instituted in many Yao villages in the mid-1980s, this campaign should be understood as a pedagogical practice that aims to remedy deficiencies in the populace. As outlined in the tenets of the campaign, these deficiencies refer to the "wasteful extravagances" *(shechi)* of popular ritual; peasant tendencies to account for the material conditions of life through "religious superstitions"; fear and disdain for modern education and schools; excessive drinking and gambling; "irrational" desires for "excess" offspring; even certain forestry and agricultural practices (one of the first projects of the party in Yao regions in the 1950s was to get them to "settle down," to end the roaming life of swidden cultivators). Monthly villagewide study meetings are held to determine which households should be publicly granted a plaque commemorating them as a "civilized household" *(wenming hu)*.

There are several initial points to be drawn from the way in which Yao ritual has been linked in practice to the implementation of the civilized village campaign, a linkage I will explore in greater detail later on. The first is that the "reconstitution" of Yao ritual practice reveals how the "return of the traditional" is both closely monitored by new technologies of state power and situated within larger discursive fields of categorization and signification. Yao ritual is not simply a stable and bounded world of meaning refracting or responding to the workings of power; it is one space among many where constructions of state power and the social world this power aims to contain and manage are produced. The resurgence of Yao ritual is constantly monitored by local officials, constantly subjected to frameworks that draw boundaries between the modern and the traditional, superstition and religion, domestic and community practice; the representation of ritual is seemingly always trapped in such logics of displacement (see Anagnost, 1994b). Yao ritual is also represented through constructions of a political temporality, of how Maoist radicalism misrepresented and misunderstood the importance of ritual to Yao modes of social order and identity. Thus, a post-Mao Yao identity has been constructed in part by drawing attention to that which it ultimately desires to transcend—the feudal past, the excesses of radical Maoism—haunting signs of fragmentation, disorder, and irrationality.

A second point about Yao ritual concerns the specificity of the ethnic minority context. In both the Maoist era and the reform period, the Chinese state has encouraged the expression of ethnic markers such as language, dress, and religious practice. Signs of ethnic minority difference have historically provided a space of radical cultural otherness, a space that could perhaps be left alone by the state because the exotic, while tantalizing, was not fully perceived as a threat. Yao ritual, though certainly displayed in all of its theatrical otherness at major state functions throughout the 1950s and 1960s, has long been marked as a threat to socialist mobilization at the local level. Under the reforms, Yao priests, with their colorful robes, fantastic dances, and bizarre magical accoutrements, have been appropriated as symbols of Chinese national and cultural diversity, mostly by way of the photograph and videotape. But it would be a mistake to read Yao ritual only in terms of its incorporation into economies of exotic consumption. As with the return of ritual practice in other areas of the country, Yao ritual practices must be understood in the context of a reform crisis over questions of national stability and disorder. Ann Anagnost (ibid., 233) has suggested that many urbanites read reports about popular ritual with a "quasi-pornographic" fascination, as if these rituals were separated from the reader in both space and time. My concern here is with how these rituals are read and interpreted in local communities, how they are intimately tied to local histories of political categorization and suppression. Ritual returns not simply as a nostalgic re-creation of an internal otherness; it is more complexly tied to reform-era discourses on state security and insecurity and the promotion of localized cultural practices as new technologies of social control.

CONTAINING YAO RITUAL

Chinese Communist Party documents from the 1950s reveal an acute concern about the social position of Taoist priests in Yao social life at the time of the communist victory (Huang Yu and Li Weixin, 1983). It is evident from these documents and from my interviews in Jinxiu that the social and political moorings of this ritual practice were targeted for removal. The uprooting occurred in all the familiar ways: the party, beginning in the 1950s, established an entirely new organizational system, eradicated the once extant system of Yao headman *(shipai touren)*, and slowly, through processes of recruitment and indoctrination, incorporated local leaders and promising youth into the administrative structure of the state apparatus. Many of the Taoist priests with whom I studied came to be employed, at one time or another, in the local government; three of the five priests I came to know well were party members. The authority these priests once commanded was not eradicated but rather appropriated and reincorporated into the party's system of governance; they retained their positions of authority yet spoke to their communities now with a new language. Many of these priests-cum-party members devised, through the years, strategies for coping with the demands of the revolutionary state's successive political campaigns. As they put it, they participated enthusiastically in their jobs, but also learned tactics for survival, especially the importance of manufacturing the desired attitude and expression *(biaoxian)* of a given campaign. Others, however, fared less well. For example, in the 1950s, those who protested the dismantling of temples and the indiscriminate cutting of trees (seen as the abodes of local spirits) were publicly criticized in a large struggle meeting; their stubborn clinging to "feudal superstitions" was even arbitrarily linked to "bad class" backgrounds. I know of one Taoist priest, so ostracized in the 1950s and 1960s for his family's pre-1949 landholdings and his own defense of his ritual status, that he later forced his daughter to change her surname so she, untouched by his bad class background, could enter a school in Guilin in the early 1970s.

There is a very real sense, then, that the post-1949 state has been successful not only at transforming the social, economic, and ritual practices that sustained the social position of local leaders, but also at infusing into local consciousness new modes of political authority, community, history, and personhood. And yet, what struck me in the course of my research was how the reconstitution of these rituals, their visibility once again in public and domestic spaces, was generating interest—among Chinese ethnologists, foreign anthropologists, national and international tourists, as well as local villagers—in how these rituals were enacted and what they meant before they were politically banished from the social landscape. The reconstitution of these rituals has led many of my research consultants to engage in critical readings of the very "traditional" social worlds the party-state has long sought to control and transform. Their reflections did not merely reproduce the official practice to reduce these "traditional" rituals to embodiments of China's "rich and varied" ethnic landscape. Rather, they seemed to be about the imaginative rehabitation of a social landscape marked by haunting absences (see Stewart, 1988), but also about how the party, given its mistakes in the past, could again protect and speak for the interests of local communities. These reflections do not reveal a popular, autonomous Yao voice. They rather reveal, I want to suggest, that the state's assiduous focus on practices it hopes either to contain or one day to dispel from the social landscape establishes new forms of meaning, new strategies of self-identification, and new processes of negotiation over state attempts to manage and transform everyday life. The "socialist modernization" of Yao ritual, then, does not mark the space where the state meets society. It marks the space for critical debates for the reimagining of the relationship of the party to the masses; of how Maoist-era campaigns differ from the developmental projects of the present; and finally, of the conditions under which the reform state can continue to speak for, protect, and secure the interests of the ethnic minority subject.

Aside from the noisy *(renao)* weddings and funerals that always command public attention, the ordination rite *(dujie)* for a young Yao boy is one of the most popular of Yao rituals (Zhang Youjun,

1986; Huang Yu and Huang Fangping, 1990). This is a kind of rite of passage carried out when a boy is between the ages of ten and fifteen. Here the young initiate is introduced to the Taoist pantheon and acquires spirit soldiers to assist him in his future ritual practice; several weeks (usually long evenings) are required in preparation as he memorizes Taoist texts, fasts, abstains from eating meat, and lives on little sleep. This ritual practice was strictly prohibited during the Cultural Revolution. In the five years between 1987 and 1992 in the four villages surrounding the town of Jinxiu, only two boys went through the *dujie,* though in other regions of the county these ordination rites are more common and are organized somewhat differently. Some of the priests, older women, and local researchers complain of the simplicity and inauthenticity of these reconstructed initiation rites. But, for many, none of this really matters, for there is an excitement that the rituals can even be enacted again.

Local party and government bureaus are actively involved in the study and promotion of these rituals. This interest stems in part from curiosity with the spectacular nature of these activities, for many have never witnessed them before. Moreover, official discourse on this rite, as I indicated earlier, defines it as a remnant of a past historical stage, one that suspiciously lingers on, possessing a kind of power to disrupt the present quest for modernization. Thus, curiosity is intertwined with a kind of monitoring function: there are known limits on when these rituals can take place, how much money should be spent, how long they should last, and so on. Photographs, videos, interviews, tape recordings are all used in the documentation process. For those cadre assigned to study these cultural practices, there is a sense of urgency in this collection of data. A party member from the Jinxiu cultural artifacts center explained to me the importance of getting down every word the Taoist masters uttered, for soon the opportunity to document these cultural traditions would be lost. When I asked him about the initiates that had been ordained in recent years, he laughed and said, "of course they read and chant the *daojing,* but they now have so little time, and besides, there is so little demand."

This comment reflects a popular sentiment that the Yao mountains are today an already radically transformed place. But what it overlooks is how the remaking of these ritual practices provides an interpretive space for talk and reflection on the history of the state's attempt to eradicate these practices. During the Chinese New Year in 1991, a *dujie* rite was performed in a village in the near vicinity of the town of Jinxiu. This was a staged enactment for a camera crew and research team from another city in China. The performance was organized in conjunction with the county government. A group of Taoist priests who had worked on a "real" *dujie* several years prior in another village were called together. The visiting research team paid for the necessary materials, purchased the chickens to be sacrificed, the bamboo and other supplies needed to erect the ritual platform, and each of the priests was paid a small commission for his time. It was a festive affair for the entire village.

After several days of clearing out the front common room of a villager's house, waiting for the auspicious day, and assembling the ritual platform where the scroll paintings of the Three Pure Ones and other Taoist gods would hang, the ritual began. For several hours the *shigong* and *daogong* performed from memory and by consulting hand-copied versions of Taoist texts an assortment of dances, prayers, and incantations. The initial movements are all geared toward informing the Taoist hierarchy of the purpose of the rite, and preparing the gods to meet the new initiate. All present agreed that although this young boy of eight had not studied the necessary Taoist texts and had not fasted, the performance could still be considered a genuine *dujie* rite; he would, when all was done, have a place in the world of the Taoist bureaucracy. The young boy clearly had no idea what was going on, and in fact his selection was quite arbitrary: he was hanging around and seemed interested enough. A moment of hesitation occurred, however, when he was brought into the room by an older cousin dressed in one of the People's Liberation Army (PLA) uniforms available for sale in any of the local markets, a PLA hat atop his head, the red star of the party affixed just above the bill. Something was askew.

The conversation that immediately ensued is worth relating. One of the organizers of the performance was concerned that because the body of the young boy would not immediately be cloaked in the Taoist robes, the uniform would show up in the video and photographs. This, it was argued, just would not look right. People nodded, evidently aware of the irony, but also aware they were treading upon dangerous ground. Someone else, one of the members of the small orchestra, argued that this did not matter, for these were the clothes he wore daily. Following this, members of the priestly entourage, a local official, and several older women observing the proceedings huddled together and consulted in low whispers. Sitting on the other side of the room and being a guest in the house, I did not dare pry into what was being said. After about five minutes, the silence and anticipation subsided: it was announced that of course the young boy could wear the PLA uniform.

Although this was not declared publicly at the time, I was later told of what had been decided. Having the boy change out of the uniform would be too much of an ordeal, not worth the hassle of worrying about whether the documentation of this traditional rite was tainted by something so obviously not of the "traditional." Besides, it was reasoned, why should the PLA and the party not be represented in a documentary on the rich and colorful traditions of the Yao people? Just look at everything the party had done for these villages under the reforms: local markets were thriving, households controlled the surplus of their harvests, people were employed and making money, new houses were being built, roads were being paved, tourists were flocking to the area, and people once again had freedom of religion. Moments later, the young boy was led in procession around the ritual platform, priests dancing and chanting around him. A long Taoist robe and the cap of the Taoist master were brought out. Within moments the PLA uniform was gone from view, enshrouded now in something more than a sign of the traditional: the very sign of a practice once ravaged by the campaigns of the Maoist state.

But is it just the destructiveness of the Red Guards and the Maoist state that was brought to visibility here? Days later, in discussing this episode with friends, I learned something about how state discourse on traditional culture is sometimes perceived. It was pointed out that it was local Yao (mostly older women) who argued that the PLA uniform should remain on the boy. This then led to a discussion about "the problem" of Yao traditional culture, how it should be represented in these staged enactments, and its place in a modernizing China. The party, I was told, had it wrong. Traditional culture and modernization were not opposed at all. What the party and so many scholars of the Yao failed to realize is that Yao traditional cultural practices always emphasized the importance of maintaining social order, of good relations with neighbors and outsiders, of respect for

REIMAGINING THE STATE IN POST-MAO CHINA · 307

authority and an awareness of one's social position. It had only been in the last thirty years, since the Guomindang entered the region and then later with the mistakes of the ultraleftists, that the Yao social order has been totally disrupted. This speaker argued that outsiders with little knowledge of and respect for Yao traditions had wreaked havoc on the Yao. During the Cultural Revolution, Yao engravings on the beams above front doors, scroll paintings, and traditional customized furniture had all been removed from households and burned in the central square of Jinxiu town. During the Great Leap Forward, the towering trees the Yao remember so dearly were cut down and their wide trunks yanked from the ground. People from different villages were indiscriminately housed together, Zhuang mixed with Yao, one Yao "subgroup" mixed with the next. People were forcibly moved from their homes, made to live with strangers with whom they had no relations, so their house could be occupied as a temporary headquarters for a production team. As for the mixing of a PLA uniform with a Taoist robe: as my friend reasoned, why, after all, should the Yao be bothered by such a thing? The PLA had long been a part of everyday life in these villages. The assertion that the PLA uniform should be removed from a representation of a Yao ritual was absurd. It was the television crew and a local official (a Yao himself) who were most concerned with representing a "traditional" Yao rite without the presence of the state, symbolized by the PLA uniform.

On the one hand, this speaker's commentary seems to reaffirm the way in which the reform state defines itself against the Maoist past. It also resonates with the way in which the post-Mao state is stressing the functional attributes of traditional culture, especially those practices that seem to maintain social order and reinforce relations of authority. This functionalist reading has clearly displaced previous class-based readings. What it seems we are seeing in this post-Mao discourse is both the influx of Euro-American anthropological theories of ritual and reproduction (a point I will return to in the conclusion) and a restoration of Confucian discourses on ritual and authority (Dirlik, 1995). But this is not entirely correct, if we are to think of social order as a social fact, one given collective representation through ritual and other social practices. Moreover, it is not simply that post-Mao China is characterized by a contested moral order, so that calls for conformity fall on suspicious ears. Social order is itself an effect of power, not simply returned and managed by an enlightened reform-era party-state. It is an object of discourse and thus invariably opened up for critical engagement by social actors. This is why the reform period is never beyond reproach, as many see clearly the party's inability to act as an exemplar, or to contain the forces it has unleashed. As my friend put it, the party encourages everyone to get rich, yet disparities in opportunity and income are fueling all kinds of jealousies, creating an environment of intense competition and behind the scenes maneuvering. The party rants on about everyone becoming civilized *(wenming)*, yet the party itself, with its corruption, frequent meetings, and elaborate feasts, is hardly a symbol of the frugal, an important attribute of the civilized. And the party dares to reprimand those who spend too much money on ritual practices, weddings, and funerals. The point here is not that the reform state has been able to convince people that social order is in their own interest, but that the very question of social order, how it is achieved, and who is to control and manage it is itself an effect of power (Yang, 1988).

On the other hand, this speaker questions the value of any representation of ritual practice that bears no mark of the history of post-1949 China, of how the party once actively infiltrated these practices and is now remaking them (and many others) based on the aims of the reform regime. Thus, while we see a reaffirmation of the post-Mao discourse on the importance of maintaining social order, we also see a perspective that works against the allochronic logics of the modernist narrative. It critically engages the attempt to represent these "traditional" cultural practices as if they belong to remote places and times. Asserted in their place is a popular sentiment that the Yao can adapt their traditions to the demands and exigencies of the moment. It asserts that the claims to culture, civilization, and modernity do not rest solely within the imaginings of the state. By calling into question the state's claim to embody the modern, these kinds of critical reflections expose the state's discursive construction of the traditional as a site opposed to the modern. Moreover, they question the "cleansing" of all signs of the history of the People's Republic of China in these reconstructions. The irony is played out. State power, disappeared, reemerges as a force that once again is seen, as with the Guomindang and Maoist states, as imposing its will on communities without a full grasp of local realities. For many Yao, their traditions emerge not as the other of modernity but as a some-what different cultural force.

THE DISCOURSE OF SOCIAL MORALITY

In post-Mao China, then, Yao ritual is both marked as an instance of the ethnic traditional and subjected to a politics of surveillance. There is also evidence of a discourse on the importance of Yao social morality to post-Mao China's socialist modernization effort. In my conversations and interviews with Yao scholars, party officials, and Taoist specialists, many stressed the importance of returning a sense of social morality to everyday village life. I found myself dismayed— in large part because I had been trained in an academic moment in which ritual practices such as this were often romanced as potential sites of resistance—that ritual practices once marginalized under Maoism were now being treated as potentially contributing to the rationalized social order the post-Mao regime was seeking. Many of my research consultants argued that, if properly managed, certain ritual practices may in fact complement the party's project of return-ing some semblance of order and regulated routine to everyday life.

I also found a haunting convergence between the focus on Yao ritual and the ideological content and disciplinary procedures of the post-Mao party's civilized village campaign. Yao social morality *(Yaozu shehui daode)* was thus identified as an object to be studied, known, and represented. Constructed as a mode of ethnic conscious-ness and everyday decent behavior, Yao social morality was grounded in Yao ritual life and constructed as integral both to the civilized vil-lage campaign and to debates on the quality of the Yao as an ethnic people. I found myself observing the discursive construction and ap-propriation of local ethnic knowledges to serve the political will of the reform state. Many with whom I worked argued for the moral fortitude of local folk customs, modes of social interaction, and everyday habits. They strongly rejected the imputation of these prac-tices to the category of "feudal superstition."

In publications on Yao culture and society, one indeed finds an almost repetitious fixation on the customs of Yao social morality (Song, 1991). The fascination with everyday practices believed to in-culcate a sense of social morality, and thus presumably ensure social order, is clearly the result of the post-Mao leadership's rethinking of the relationship between state power and local cultural knowledge.

In fact, the leadership is not only responding to the imperatives of the current modernization drive, but is also having a conversation with the past. The study of social morality among the "common folk" of China has a long intellectual and political history, for questions of morality have been intricately linked to questions of education and political indoctrination. In the 1920s, for example, during the heyday of the folklore movement led by such intellectuals as Zhou Zuoren, there was a movement to study the maxims, proverbs, and folktales of the common people. It was thought that these oral and collective practices of transmitting knowledge, however rustic and irrational, served to both cultivate the individual and bind the local community to a common national vision (see Hung Chang-tai, 1985). Folklore studies in 1920s China represented a certain ambivalent move away from strongly Confucian statist views that moral learning and political thought had to be drilled into the uncultured peasant. Mao Zedong, as well, was acutely aware of the didactic power of "folk wisdom" to both inspire moral cultivation and incite revolutionary action.

In the current period, the entire Yao studies industry in China seems to be organized around the idea that Yao traditional culture, often conceived as epistemological domains essentially premodern, can serve state projects of ensuring social order and raising the cultural quality of the Yao. The discourse on Yao social morality is thus integral to the "return" of Yao ritual and other practices seen as part of the corpus of Yao tradition. Yao social morality is identified by three basic rules of conduct. Yao scholars in particular state that the maintenance of these rules is essential to the successful negotiation of power structures, of which the Yao evidently recognize two: first, the power structure of the spirit world and in particular the hierarchies of the Taoist pantheon; second, the power structures needed for everyday government. Not surprisingly, post-Mao writings on Yao social morality focus in on the rules for conduct in the maintenance of everyday social order. The first concerns a strong sense of abiding by the rules of tradition *(chuangtong xing)*, which, in this context, refers to respect for and awareness of one's place in everyday social hierarchies. The second concerns an emphasis on good relations and cooperation with neighbors, and a cultural emphasis on hospitality and openness to outsiders traveling in the mountains. This cultural attribute is also said to be evidenced in the Yao custom of adopting children from other ethnic groups, and a belief that Yao ethnicity is not inherited but practiced through correct behavior. The third and final feature concerns the importance the Yao place on praise and condemnation in everyday social disciplining. Yao social morality is said to reveal a dialectic between social discipline and social reproduction.

It is noteworthy that a positive discourse on Yao social morality is largely absent from party work-team documents and ethnological investigative reports written in the 1950s. When I inquired about this discrepancy, it was pointed out that the question of Yao morality was largely ignored by party officials in the 1950s because of the emphasis then on locating Yao practices that revealed an inclination for revolutionary agency. In the immediate post-1949 period, Yao morality was interpreted with extreme ambivalence, constructed as excessively conservative, a form of feudal consciousness that retarded the building of a modern socialist nation. But the making of a revolutionary subject has now been displaced by an overriding concern for stability, order, and the establishment of peaceful relations between ethnic groups and social classes. The traditional customs and practices that habituate a sense of social responsibility and morality are now being embraced for their functional contribution to the post-Mao social and political order (Litzinger, 1998).

The significance of Yao ritual to the making of good citizens cannot be understood without first considering the importance the reform state is now placing on the everyday monitoring of social order, a surveillance function returned to the masses themselves. The civilized village campaign is one of the fundamental ways in which the post-Mao party state continues, even after its so-called retreat from the everyday control of production (reproduction is an entirely different issue, of course), to engage in ideological work in everyday life (see Anagnost, 1992; Dirlik, 1982). The campaign's tenets or "compacts" *(xiangyue)* stipulate a set of ideal behaviors that all villagers are required to follow. They cover everything from interactions between spouses, to public behavior (spitting, yelling, fighting are all discouraged), to payment of taxes under the household production system, and, perhaps most important, to regulating births and the use of birth-control methods. Adherence to the tenets is monitored through political meetings composed of members of the village households, an official from the county's party office, and the village head.

During these meetings, which can last anywhere from several hours to several evenings, villagers enter into a discussion about the behavior of every member of the household. These meetings are sometimes very lighthearted and playful, sometimes very serious and troubling. During the household meetings, comparisons are made to other villagers' behavior and how the village committees interpreted and handled them. When the discussions have ended, and each household has been scrutinized for its adherence to the code for civility, a public village ceremony is held in which each household is awarded a red plaque to hang over the threshold of the house. In conjunction with a party leadership that claims to have returned to the masses some governing power, the villagers have conferred on themselves the status of being "civilized" *(wenming)*.

The display of this plaque indicates that the household has demonstrated its love of country by showing its adherence to the tenets of the village compact. The object is for a majority of the households to receive public recognition so that the entire village can be given the status of being a "civilized village" *(wenming cun)*. Households yet to receive this public recognition are identified as having some outstanding problem *(hai mei chuli de wenti)*. In most cases, the problem concerned adherence to the family planning project; perhaps a couple had exceeded its birth ratio and hidden a pregnancy, or had admitted a certain difficulty in using birth-control techniques. In this case, another committee, centered in the county hospital, is sent to consult and educate the household members on the importance of family planning. Other common transgressions are strained relations between spouses, public displays of anger or fighting, or conflicts between other members of the household. Frequently, there are intravillage skirmishes over assigned responsibilities in collective labor, such as reforestation work. There are also instances of drunken and disorderly behavior, but these are usually handled by family members and never enter into discussion at the village meetings. Finally, references to civilized behavior are constantly made in everyday sociality. If a couple is fighting, someone will yell out that they are not being civilized *(bu wenming)*. Even young children who avoid their homework and sneak down to the town's video game parlor are scolded for not manifesting behavior that becomes someone of a civilized family. Likewise, households

that do not encourage their children to attend school can be subjected to the scrutiny of village committees.

The focus on social morality and the regulation of behavior therefore represents a quite conscious party effort to intervene in everyday social practice. What really surprised me in my work on these
campaigns, however, is that there seemed to be a certain consensus
that the campaign did not constitute a form of "ideological work"
(sixiang gongzuo), at least not in the sense of how this political concept was defined and applied during the Maoist period. Moreover,
most local officials and villagers did not see the project as a correc-
tive intervention in a socially disordered moment of the reforms.
Rather, they saw it as an educational practice that returned to everyday life a form of traditional moral discourse, in which villagers determine and settle among themselves rules for social conduct and
punishments for minor transgressions. It was perceived as a form of
democratic socialism that both spoke against the abuse of power
under Maoism and recognized the usefulness of a "traditional"
mode of regulating social life. The campaign was popular because,
as with other ideological projects aimed at educating the masses, it
sought to raise the villagers' consciousness, to prepare them for development, for the eventual influx of capital and investment that
would one day come to these "isolated" hills. Civilizing the local social world, then, was to raise the cultural quality of the people, to re-
mold them as a subject that would be able to participate more fully
in the modernization of Yao society and all of China.

CONCLUSION: THE SPECTER OF STATE POWER

What does all of this tell us about the power of the post-Mao state to
both create and limit the terrain for the imagining of state and society, identity, and community? I have argued that a discourse on a
"traditional" Yao social morality has been made possible by the
post-Mao regime's focus on issues of social order, good relations between the party and the masses, and social harmony between different ethnic groups. A Foucauldian reading would point not to the
power of the state to define reality, but to how power has become diffused and disseminated in localized, everyday practices of social regulation. Surely, it is hard not to see here a gradual fusing of a discourse
on the need for civilized behavior into a local practice, which has, in

effect, rendered invisible the origins of the discourse, and which has, in turn, reconstituted the state's authority at the local level.

I want to push the analysis further, however, and ask about the relationship between a civilizing project for the love of the country and the invocation of a "traditional" Yao morality. Rather than assume an organic unity between "the seal of the symbol and the wax of the recipient" (Taussig, 1992: 54), we should inquire into the slippages, the gaps that occur between a discourse and its reception, between the political will of the reform regime and the recovery of "traditional" cultural practices. It seems to me that many of the Yao with whom I worked were turning the discourse on social morality back upon the state, claiming that the party had lost the ability, and the moral voice, to set the terms of social interaction and community relations (Siu, 1989b). As I have attempted to detail, various Yao practices and knowledges were pointed to as a way of returning some semblance of normalcy, routine, and order to everyday village life. To be sure, all of this plays nicely into the hands of the reform regime, as it attempts to promote forms of local government in which villagers take an active role. Yet, there is a certain danger in these interpretations of the power of traditional orders; for such discourses, in looking back to a period of stability before modern projects of developing the Yao hills in the name of the Chinese nation, unsettle the official histories that the Yao were once "liberated" from feudal exploitation. These localized renderings of histories of development disrupt the construction of the Maoist period as the reform era's other, unsettling the attempt to fix the Maoist period as a site of unrestrained political excess and the reform period as a moment of settled tranquillity. Many Yao indeed recognize and embrace the reform state's claim to be embarking on a new mode of local government, one respectful of the democratic impulses of the masses and of local ethnic traditions. But their active participation in new forms of local governance also destabilizes the party-state, forcing it, in effect, constantly to construct itself as fundamentally different from previous regimes of power. This challenges the reform regime's claim that civilizing power resides elsewhere, in other places, held and distributed by powerful outsiders that speak in the name of development and the truths of modernity (Escobar, 1995). The post-Mao party-state is thus forced to present itself as something other than a spectacle, a haunting force of transformation and disorder.

The state is not the only ghostly force in everyday life. Yao rituals are also haunting remnants both of the traditional order and of the history of state projects to eradicate and transform these rituals. Yao rituals have thus "returned" to post-Mao China in the context of two discursive spaces. First, they have been singled out as objects of official policy and ethnic scholarship. The study of Yao ritual is buttressed by institutional structures at the local, national, and international levels; research projects are formulated within a tradition-modernization framework and research institutes vie for limited funds to collect knowledge about local practices in order to promote development projects. Second, their return is part of the increased popularization of religious belief and ritual practice across rural and urban China (Madsen, 1989). They are popular in terms of their wide appeal for villagers, tourists, government officials, and academics; in terms of their constitution as objects of knowledge in international arenas of scholarship; in terms of cross-border movements of Yao peoples making contacts with their Yao "brothers and sisters" across the globe; and in terms of the way they are defined as potentially disruptive of China's modernization agenda. One of my research consultants told me that he hoped that one day the Yao mountains would become a kind of museum: on display would be the colorful cultural diversity of the many Yao "subgroups"; Yao women would be adorned in ethnic garb; Yao actors would perform the dances and sing the songs of this great minority nationality. Tourism would develop; scholars would descend upon the county; this remote place would be freed from its poverty and backwardness. This vision of a local future tied to larger fields of power betrays just how popular, how desired, Yao ritual Taoism and other markers of the traditional and the ethnic have become. It also reveals how the return of Yao ritual is not easily positioned in some fixed relationship between struggle and power, state and society *within China*; it must be understood as well in terms of how it is situated in relation to larger global spaces of culture and capital flows (Schein, 1996).

I began this essay with the observation that the Chinese Communist Party has long relied on the language of crisis to constitute its authority, to safeguard its identity as the central bearer of the power and sovereignty of the people. The rhetoric of security and insecurity, of social order and disorder, of productivity and counterproductivity is often seen as residing within the control of the state. I have attempted here to treat this language as a discourse, one diffused throughout the social landscape, one that has structured both an everyday feeling of urgency and, in the case of the Yao elite with whom I worked, mobilized an active participation in the study and promotion of "traditional" practices (see Litzinger, 1998). Yet, I have also tried to explicate how the return of Yao ritual, the discourse on social morality, and the almost obsessive concern with questions of social order produces an array of responses: critical commentaries on state power, nostalgic renderings of the past, images of landscapes haunted by absences. This is why I have drawn attention to such a minor disruption over the presence of a PLA uniform on the body of a Yao Taoist initiate. The question of whether an ostensible sign of state power should be allowed to intermingle with a "traditional" ritual activity reveals how these staged rituals are a contested interpretive ground. A local official sees a PLA uniform as contaminating the purity of the representation as a sign of the traditional; a Yao, also an official in the local government, argues that the two should be allowed to mix, for to present the situation in any other way is to misrepresent the history of the area. Both perspectives reveal an engagement with the constructed nature of these rituals as representations. The party has always placed great emphasis on the dissemination of powerfully appealing images, languages, and slogans to mobilize the masses. It has also learned, perhaps most readily during the worst years of the Cultural Revolution, but also again during the 1989 occupation of Tiananmen (Perry, 1992), that these signifying practices can be turned against it. It is perhaps time that discussions of state security and insecurity attend to the contested nature of the state as an imaginary construct—a construct that does not simply legitimate the state's authority, but that also enables alternative uses, other ways of understanding social and political realities, other ways of reenchanting the world (Taussig, 1992: 54; Foster, 1983).

I conclude this essay, then, with the image of the young boy being led around a ritual platform paid for by a government television station. One day this documentary may be broadcast to millions of viewers across China. The circulation of these images will, in turn, fuel national and even international interest in the cultural traditions of the Yao people. Yet, local struggles will continue. Many of the Yao with whom I have worked have learned that the voicing of different conceptions of history and culture is to invite further confinement to other worlds, other times. The imagining of distant sources of moral and political authority, of calling upon spirit soldiers to protect local communities when the party itself claims this protective function, is also to recall a not too distant time when state power was exercised in the most destructive of fashions. As Yao confront the claim that their cultural practices impede the socialist modern agenda, it is important to attend to how their stories of a transformed past constitute a critical reading of the disruptions that have occurred in their own lives. These critiques are rarely turned into oppositional movements; it would be illusory to view them as somehow threatening the security of the reform regime. What they do is question the way in which the reform regime is invested in constructing itself as a qualitatively different regime, one that has transcended the mistakes of past regimes; they thus draw attention to the arbitrary, discursively constructed boundaries between the pre-1949 period, Maoist socialism, and the reform present. This is not to deny the far-reaching cultural, economic, social changes that have occurred in China since the 1940s. It is rather to remind ourselves that the fixing of these historical boundaries has been central to how the reform regime projects itself to the world, at once inviting foreign capital investment *and* creating desires for the traditional, the authentic, for social spaces cleansed of any sign of political contest.

NOTES

1. The Yao mountains to which I refer are located in the southern province of Guangxi, some eighty kilometers from the thriving tourist center of Guilin, now known globally for its magnificent scenery. In the 1950s, the Yao mountains were administratively renamed the Jinxiu Yao Autonomous County. "Autonomous" *(zizhi)* here refers to the fact that the Yao people compose the majority of the county's population, and to the somewhat disputable claim that most local officials are themselves members of the Yao nationality. No counties, prefectures, or provinces are autonomous in the sense that they possess a constitutional right to secede from the nation.

2. Akhil Gupta has noted the astonishing lack of attention on the state in ethnographic work. He attributes this to a fieldwork methodology that has privileged face-to-face contact and spatial proximity between the anthropologist and the informant (Gupta, 1995: 375). Cultural anthropology has long

attempted to look beyond the state to the realm of the social, or what is often termed in anthropological parlance "the local." The embrace of the local has, in turn, impelled many anthropologists to seek out and privilege so-called native or indigenous "voices," spaces of difference believed to reveal other, usually non-Euro-American, epistemological domains. Recent interventions in what might be called a postcolonial anthropology have rendered problematic any easy congruence between the local and the native; it is increasingly difficult to see cultures and societies as self-contained functional units of knowledge (Appadurai, 1986b; Gupta and Ferguson, 1992; Narayan, 1993: 671).

3. See Anagnost (1994b) and Schein (1992) for similar approaches to the post-Mao state. See Perry's (1994) discussion of a host of problems with state and society paradigms in the field of Chinese studies. Mayfair Yang (1994) has written provocatively about her own involvement in the construction of state power through a culture of fear in 1980s urban China. For a more general approach, see Timothy Mitchell's (1991b: 78) discussion of state and society paradigms in the social sciences.

4. I use the term *research consultants* in place of the standard term *informants* in order to highlight the collaborative nature of my research with Yao scholars, intellectuals, county government and party officials, and local tourist guides, some of whom invited me to join them in their research projects. My own research was originally conceived as a study of how these "agents" of the state, some of whom were both long-standing members of the Chinese Communist Party and ordained priests in the Yao Taoist specialty, were involved in the study and promotion of Yao ritual practice in the post-Mao period. Funding for this project was provided by the Committee for Scholarly Communication with the People's Republic of China and a Fulbright-Hays dissertation grant. In China, I was graciously hosted by the Central Nationalities Institute in Beijing.

11

Missing the End of the Cold War in International Security

HUGH GUSTERSON

This chapter explores representations of superpower relations by American international security studies specialists in the journal *International Security* in the years and months immediately before the end of the Cold War—an event that was largely unexpected, and certainly unpredicted, in mainstream international security circles.[1] Indeed, it is fair to say that readers who relied on the journal *International Security* alone for their understanding of world politics would have been taken more or less completely by surprise by the end of the Cold War in the fall of 1989.[2] In the words of two prominent international relations scholars, "measured by its own standards, the profession's performance was embarrassing. There was little or no debate about the underlying causes of systemic change, the possibility that the Cold War could be peacefully resolved, or the likely consequences of the Soviet Union's visible decline.... Practitioners remained insensitive to the change after it was well underway" (Lebow and Risse-Kappen, 1995: 2).

Unlike most of the essays in this volume, which focus on the actions and statements of political leaders, or on deeply embedded and dispersed communitarian or national discourses, this piece explores the specialized discursive world of a group of security studies intellectuals—a small epistemic community mediating the worlds of government and academia that has constructed an influential expert discourse on security issues (Cohn, 1987; Herken, 1985; Kaplan,

1983). Although I attend its seminars and interact with its members as part of my normal academic routine, I have not undertaken a formal anthropological study of this community. What follows is a constructivist reading of one of the community's key journals informed by my collegial knowledge of this community, by my training as an anthropologist specializing in security issues, and by my personal biography as an antinuclear activist turned academic.

SECURITY STUDIES

Security studies developed in the kind of hybrid, interstitial intellectual space the historian of science Peter Galison (1997) has referred to as a "trading zone." Located on the borderlands between more established fields, intellectual trading zones are developed by people from different disciplinary backgrounds who nonetheless share a set of thematic interests around which they interact from their different disciplinary vantage points. Classic contemporary examples of such trading zones would include chaos theory and cosmology in the physical sciences and cultural studies in the humanities. Galison argues that, faced with a need to communicate in the absence of a shared disciplinary vocabulary, the inhabitants of trading zones develop "pidgins" and "creoles" that evolve into mature discourses as the interstitial zones develop into recognized, institutionalized fields.

Security studies developed in an intellectual trading zone peopled by academics, military officers, think-tank staffers, weapons scientists, and government officials discussing security issues in an intellectual vocabulary drawn eclectically from physics, political science, history, and economics. Practiced in an archipelago of political-science departments, think tanks, national laboratory adjunct centers, university arms-control centers,[3] and in the mazeways of the Pentagon, security studies had by the early 1980s achieved mature stability in terms of its basic vocabulary and concepts and its institutional infrastructure. Two leading practitioners of security studies, surveying the field in 1988, saw it as global in scope but focused principally on U.S.-Soviet relations, especially on the nuclear relationship between the superpowers and on the balance of power in Europe—issues largely discussed in the field from an American, or at least Western, vantage point (Nye and Lynn-Jones, 1988). We might add that, because the core inter-disciplinary dialogue in security studies in the 1980s was between political scientists and physical scientists, the epistemology of security studies was deeply positivist, and its vocabulary was inflected by the idioms of physics (the international system was full of "forces," "vacuums," and "balances") and economics (targets were "lucrative," alliances were "bargains," and nuclear attacks had "payoff matrices"). Participants in security studies included self-identified liberals and conservatives.

My first entry into the orbit of security studies was as an antinuclear activist of European origin working for the Nuclear Freeze Campaign in the United States in the early and mid-1980s. At this time, the U.S. peace movement was campaigning for an end to the nuclear arms race as a prelude to a more complete, if vaguely formulated, restructuring of the relationship between the superpowers (Forsberg, 1982, 1984; McCrea and Markle, 1989; Solo, 1988; Waller, 1987). Meanwhile, the European peace movement, influenced particularly by the visionary British historian and intellectual E. P. Thompson, was less focused on arms-control proposals, arguing instead that it was time to dismantle the Cold War itself and to move beyond a mode of civilization Thompson dubbed "exterminist." At a time when the governments of the Western alliance were arguing that it would be a sign of weakness to forgo new deployments of nuclear weapons, the European peace movement saw the rejection of new U.S. nuclear weapons slated for deployment in Europe in the 1980s as a vital first step in the direction of ending the arms race, transcending the Cold War, and demilitarizing Western society (New Left Review, 1982; Thompson, 1982, 1985; Thompson and Smith, 1981, 1986).

As I moved from the antinuclear movement to the academy in the mid-1980s, deciding to focus my graduate study on the political culture of nuclear weapons, I became more familiar with, and frustrated by, the field of academic security studies. Where the antinuclear movement was exploring scenarios to reverse the arms race and transform the Cold War system of antagonistic blocs, such possibilities were off the agenda in mainstream security studies.[4] The dominant discourse in security studies seemed to me, even in its liberal versions, to broadly legitimate the status quo, evincing an ahistorical and conservative (with a small "c") aversion to discussions of fundamental political change. This manifested itself in a predilection for "technostrategic discourse" (Cohn, 1987) and game theory as the preferred way of discussing nuclear weapons; in an unquestioned

assumption that the relationship between the United States and the
Soviet Union would be one of insurmountable rivalry that could
at best be carefully managed; and in an insistence, influenced by
(neo)realism in academic international relations theory, that the international sphere was to some degree anarchic and that there were
therefore limits to the scope of agreements and cooperation that
could be negotiated.[5]

By the late 1980s, in the waning years of the Cold War, security
studies, although it was full of energetic debates about new weapons
systems and international relations theories, had for this reader an
increasingly "ancien régime" quality.[6] Its practitioners, persisting in
their search for the alchemical formulas of strategic stability, insisted
in the face of mass movements to end the arms race and Mikhail
Gorbachev's calls for "new thinking" that it was naive to think that
the Cold War or the arms race could be transcended. For example,
Albert Carnesale and Richard Haass, a Democrat and a Republican
at Harvard's Kennedy School of Government, concluded in 1987 in
their collaborative evaluation of the scope of arms control that
"what emerges above all is the modesty of what arms control has
wrought. . . . Proponents and critics, liberals and conservatives,
hawks and doves—all seem to exaggerate the potential and actual
impact of arms control" (Carnesale and Haass, 1987: 355). At about
the same time, Stanley Hoffman, a member of the field's liberal wing,
concluded in the midst of Gorbachev's reforms: "The very nature of
international reality rules it [disarmament] out. . . . They [security
studies specialists] see the contest between Washington and Moscow . . . [and] they believe that it . . . cannot be transcended . . . because it is the very essence of international politics that the two
biggest actors must be rivals, that the growth of the power of one
must cause fear in the other" (Hoffman, 1986: 5). Comments such
as these made many of those in the peace movement who followed
academic security studies decide that it was part of the problem, not
the solution.

In this chapter, writing as an antinuclear activist turned constructivist academic, I explore the literature on U.S.-Soviet relations in
the journal *International Security* in the three years immediately preceding the end of the Cold War to see how it functioned to sustain
views such as Hoffman's. Focusing on the treatment in *International*

Security of two crucial themes—the nuclear arms race and the implications of Gorbachev's reforms—I examine the ways in which authors in the journal constructed a discursive world within which the indefinite continuation of the Cold War was plausibly presumed and what we would in retrospect narrate as signs of the impending end of the Cold War were rendered dubious or invisible.

Marcus (this volume) asks how we can exploit fissures in the master discourse of security studies in order to deconstruct it and allow new discourses to emerge. Surely, the end of the Cold War, unpredicted in mainstream security studies circles, presents us with a large fissure to probe. In this context, it is tempting, especially given the emphasis on positivist modes of argumentation, deterministic analysis, and predictive accuracy within mainstream security studies, to play security studies specialists at their own epistemological game and to portray the 1980s as a giant science experiment whose outcome the security studies specialists ought to have predicted the way we expect astronomers to predict comets. This would, however, be to fall back into a variant of the very discourse I am critiquing. If at times I seem to be making a positivist argument of this kind, it is only in an occasional spirit of irony—temporarily borrowing another's discourse in order to shake it apart from within. My mode of argument here, then, in accordance with Marcus's admonition to exploit fissures in the master discourse, is to expose the gaps and weaknesses in empiricist security studies at the end of the Cold War by means of a constructivist argument that nevertheless highlights the fact that mainstream security studies failed in its own positivist terms.

The final years of the Cold War were, in retrospect, marked by great historical fluidity and contradiction. In such circumstances, we should expect from analysts a complex grasp of possibilities rather than the precise prediction of events so emphasized by positivist traditions of policy analysis. It is the essence of the kind of constructivist approach taken here to argue not for inevitable patterns of events, but for the decisive importance of human agency and understanding in shaping history and for the plausibility of multiple representations of the world—in other words, for a certain contingency and openness in the path of history and in its interpretation. Thus, all the essays in this volume, arguing against the grain of positivism, make the point, in different ways, that international affairs are sufficiently ambiguous that they can be plausibly constructed in multiple ways by political analysts and actors. This is not just an academic exercise but an attempt to ground the argument that, at key junctures in history, important state actors might have behaved differently than they did. Thus Weldes (this volume) and Milliken (this volume) argue that we have retroactively reified as self-evident security crises two events (the invasion of Korea in 1950 and the stationing of nuclear missiles in Cuba in 1962) that need not have been so. In a complementary but converse way, I show here that the international system of the 1980s was sufficiently susceptible to multiple constructions that it was quite possible for America's most prestigious international security specialists to fail to see a "crisis" (the end of the Cold War) that did in fact materialize.[7] Ken Booth (1995: 333–34), speaking of the final years of the Cold War, has said that we cannot "say that the story we heard from the professors did not contain elements of reality, only that the story we did *not* hear also contained elements of reality." Thus, the problem with the dominant discourse in security studies in the 1980s was not that its construction of the international system was wrong—it was in fact perfectly plausible—but that it so marginalized discussion of competing constructions.

In the end, the telling failure here is not that the international security studies community did not predict what actually happened, but that they were to a striking degree unable to even entertain the possibility of its happening.[8] In the words of Richard Ned Lebow and Thomas Risse-Kappen, "political scientists and their theories failed not only to anticipate any of the dramatic events of the last several years but also to recognize the possibility that such changes could take place" (Lebow and Risse-Kappen, 1995: 1). What interests me here about the dominant discourse in security studies, then, is not a failure in prediction that, within the framework of conventional social science, would be mortally discrediting, but a failure in vision that suggests a massive blind spot in the discourse. The unpredicted end of the Cold War then becomes important as a symptom that helps diagnose that blind spot.

INTERNATIONAL SECURITY

Rather than analyze the entire international security studies literature since the mid-1980s, this essay focuses for purposes of parsimony and coherence on one segment of the broader discourse community, following the evolution of debate in the journal *International Security*. In the 1980s and 1990s, this journal served as a salon for an international security elite straddling the worlds of academia and policy. It was chosen for analysis here because of the stature of many of its contributors[9] and because, unlike other journals in the field such as *International Organization, International Studies Quarterly*, and *World Politics*, it mixes theoretical and policy-oriented articles in such a way as to create a discussion where the theoretical and policy issues entailed in security studies are densely interwoven with one another. In the 1980s, *International Security* provided a forum for debates about such matters as the Reagan defense buildup, the Strategic Defense Initiative (SDI), the case for and against the B-2 bomber, the feasibility of nuclear war-fighting strategies, the balance of conventional forces in Europe, the prospects for peace in the Middle East, and the dynamics of the U.S. relationship with Japan and other allies. *International Security* has also provided a consistent forum for theoretical debates about, for example, the merits of neoliberal institutionalism, the contested relationship between democracy and international peace, and the stability of different kinds of alliance structures in the international system.

International Security was founded in the mid-1970s by a young group of scholars in the Cambridge area. Reacting against the style of established journals in the field, such as *Foreign Policy*, the editors of *International Security* wanted a journal that would feature rigorous, well-footnoted, refereed articles on policy-relevant issues rather than "ex cathedra" pronouncements on policy issues by leading figures. *International Security* soon developed a unique identity as a journal that dealt with policy issues in a more scholarly way than did other journals in the field, even though it did not only publish articles by academics.

Edited at Harvard and published by MIT Press, *International Security* and its editorial board have a strong Cambridge and East Coast establishment tilt. The board has included Harvard University's Joseph Nye and Ashton Carter (both of whom served in the first Clinton administration), and Albert Carnesale (an arms-control negotiator for the Carter administration who went on to become provost of Harvard, then president of UCLA). The editorial board has also included Herb York and Michael May, two former directors of the nuclear weapons laboratory in Livermore, California; Thomas

Schelling, one of the originators of game theory in security studies; Brent Scowcroft, the general whose commission helped push forward the MX missile; Richard Betts of the Brookings Institute; and such acclaimed masters of international relations and deterrence theory as Alexander George, John Mearsheimer, Barry Posen, Robert Jervis, Stanley Hoffman, and Lawrence Freedman. Under the guidance of people such as these, *International Security* provides a forum where academics, think-tank analysts, government officials, and would-be government officials can come together to debate security issues. In these debates, the contributors to *International Security* have by no means spoken with one voice, and some have used the journal as a platform from which to attack major U.S. weapons programs such as SDI, the MX missile, and the B-2 bomber. Still, discourse within the journal has functioned within certain parameters, and it is to the definition of these parameters that I now turn.

THE INTERNATIONAL SECURITY DISCOURSE COMMUNITY

Commitments to particular constructions of the world crystallize within discourse communities.[10] Members of discourse communities are bound together both by shared allegiance to explicitly formulated propositions about the world (that the existence of nuclear weapons makes the international system more stable, for example) and by common consumption of aspects of discourse that exist on the edge of awareness (figures of speech that identify nuclear weapons with male virility or international relations theory with the solidity of Newtonian physics, for example). Michel Foucault (1980b) points out that discourses inevitably draw boundaries around themselves by celebrating certain kinds of statements while excommunicating others, which then take on the status of what he calls "subjugated knowledges." (Thus, in the defense community in the 1980s, for example, one could not have continued to belong to that community if one said that nuclear weapons were immoral and that the United States should unilaterally disarm.)

Foucault also pointed out that discourses do not meld people into community by enforcing complete agreement or conformity. On the contrary, discourses thrive on debate and controversy—this is how they elaborate themselves—but in ways that are channeled and contained. Foucault (1980a) argued that discourses construct community and reality most subtly and effectively by means of what he called "incitement to discourse"—by channeling disagreements into certain frameworks within which the act of disagreement obscures actors' shared allegiance to deeper structures of thought that contain their disagreements. Thus, in the act of debating, members of a discourse community unthinkingly reproduce the categories, taken for granted, that make disagreement possible. As an example, in the discursive world of security studies in the 1980s, actors were incited by the Reagan administration's SDI proposal to a discourse on the feasibility of strategic defense in which, although the debate was never consensually resolved, the conduct of the debate reinforced axiomatic beliefs in the defense community that stationary land-based multiple-warhead missiles were destabilizing, that game theoretic models of nuclear "exchanges" were an important tool in discussing the pros and cons of defenses, and that the abolition of nuclear weapons by treaty was not feasible. As I will show, a debate on the abolition of ballistic missiles that took place in the pages of *International Security* in the final years of the Cold War similarly reinforced certain foundational precepts of strategic discourse, even as participants in the debate disagreed about the best path forward in terms of strategic weapons deployments.

Finally, as Donna Haraway (1990, 1991) has argued, academic discourses consist of more than systems of facts, beliefs, and propositions. Academic discourses become compelling in part because they implicitly embody, often at the edge of awareness, narratives to which listeners are drawn. Haraway argues with reference to the science of primatology that primatologists, in constructing laws of primate behavior, implicitly told stories about primate gender, sexuality, and violence that had human resonance in an era of patriarchy, capitalism, and colonialism and that primatology should be seen as an epic-displaced narrative of humanity, not just as a set of observational claims about primates. In a similar vein, I have argued elsewhere (Gusterson, 1991) that the dominant discourse in security studies embodied a "Cold War narrative" in which drama and meaning derived from an unending, but constantly shifting, clash between two global empires, and from the repeated introduction of new technological possibilities and threats into the story line. Despite efforts on the part of the antinuclear movement to substitute different stories (ending either in global extinction or transcendence of the arms race), this story remained compelling in the pages of *International Security* to the very end of the Cold War, as I will now show.

MISSING THE END OF THE COLD WAR I: NUCLEAR WEAPONS

In the last three years of the Cold War, *International Security* published twenty articles on nuclear weapons issues. Although many of these discussed some quite dramatic reconfigurations of the superpower arsenals—abolishing ballistic missiles, scrapping the B-2 bomber, 50 percent cuts in weapons, and deploying SDI—not one discussed the possibility that the arms race, let alone the Cold War, might end. In fact, all more or less explicitly assumed that it would continue, whatever the fate of individual weapons systems.

In a winter 1986–87 article, for example, Blechman and Utgoff discussed future spending projections for SDI. Assuming that the U.S. defense budget would continue to rise and deploying various graphic curves to plot this, their low projection was for a 54 percent increase in defense spending by 2010 and their high projection was for a 100 percent increase—both enough to pay for an SDI system. They discussed whether this should be paid for by an 11 percent increase in income tax or, more probably, by a mix of tax increases, cuts in social programs, and deficit spending. At only one point in the article did they ask whether the relationship between the United States and the Soviet Union might fundamentally shift in the next fifteen years: "Deployment of strategic defenses conceivably could lead to a breakthrough in relations with the Soviet Union and far-reaching arms control agreements—perhaps specifying a transition to a defense-dominated strategic regime involving much smaller forces, as well as reductions in forces in Europe" (Blechman and Utgoff, 1986–87: 63). Here, the only transformation in U.S.-Soviet relations the authors could imagine was presented as a consequence of breakthroughs in weapons technologies, not politics.

In the summer of 1987, incited by Gorbachev's suggestion at Reykjavik the previous year that both superpowers abolish ballistic missiles, *International Security* published four articles on ballistic missile abolition. Richard Perle (1987) argued that a world without ballistic missiles would be a world in which Soviet superiority in strategic bombers and conventional forces would become more important unless the United States continued to develop SDI and modernize its remaining nuclear forces.[11] Leon Sloss argued that the abolition of ballistic missiles would save the most money for the Soviets, who would "almost certainly" invest it in modernizing other nuclear weapons; he worried that it would also lead to "a relaxation in U.S. defense efforts based on the belief that tensions with the Soviet Union had declined" (Sloss, 1987: 187). Thomas Schelling favored the abolition of land-based intercontinental ballistic missiles (ICBMs), but warned that "in years to come" U.S. submarines might become vulnerable to a Soviet attack and that the United States should therefore phase out submarine-launched ballistic missiles (SLBMs) in favor of cruise missiles "over the next decade or two" (1987). Randall Forsberg, the furthest to the left of the contributors, argued that the abolition of ballistic missiles was of peripheral importance as long as the United States continued to rely on the threat of nuclear war to protect its allies in Europe and Asia, recommending a switch from extended to existential deterrence.[12]

The following summer, in 1988, a little over one year before the end of the Cold War, *International Security* published an article by Michael May, George Bing, and John Steinbruner on the possible consequences of 50 percent cuts in the superpower arsenals. They concluded that 50 percent cuts were quite safe because they would have little effect on either casualty rates in a nuclear war or strategic stability. If cuts went deeper, they did worry about the "reaction of the major U.S. allies to a situation where the U.S. would no longer be so obviously the military and strategically dominant partner. National considerations might come to receive more priority relative to alliance considerations than they do now. Such an effect would not be expected in the case of the Soviet Union and the Warsaw pact" (May, Bing, and Steinbruner, 1988: 132–33). The last sentence, as it turned out, got the course of events over the next decade exactly back to front.

Two issues later, *International Security* sponsored a debate on the possible abolition of sea-launched cruise missiles (SLCMs). Henry Mustin (1988–89) and Linton Brooks (1988–89) both argued that the Interm (INF) Treaty of 1987 had weakened the credibility of American nuclear threats by removing one rung (land-based intermediate missiles) of the escalatory ladder, and that SLCMs were vital in replacing the missing rung. Rose Gottemoeller (1988–89) and Theodore Postol (1988–89), on the other hand, argued that it would be better to restrict SLCMs now before—as they surely would otherwise—the Soviets perfected them over the next decade.

Finally, in the fall of 1989, *International Security* published three articles on stealth technologies, especially the B-2 bomber. Of the three, I will discuss only Michael Brown's.[13] In the very season that saw the end of the Cold War, fall 1989, just as the Soviets were initiating their second unilateral moratorium on nuclear testing in a decade, Brown argued: "Given that the Soviet Union began to deploy accurate ICBMs approximately ten years after the United States did so, it is not unreasonable to assume that the Soviet Union will deploy highly accurate SLBMs by the end of the 1990s, roughly ten years after the D-5 [missile on the Trident II submarine] comes on line" (Brown, 1989: 10). Worrying about a future crisis in which the Soviets might launch a disarming first strike against a United States reliant mainly on stationary ICBMs and unscrambled bombers for its deterrent, he called for the United States to scrap the B-2 bomber and the MX missile and to invest substantial resources in a "large Trident [submarine] force" and a new mobile land-based single-warhead ICBM.

If this panoramic overview of three years' articles gives some sense of the scope and depth of the assumption that the Cold War would continue, we need to look in more detail at a particular debate in order to analyze the particular discursive mechanisms that anchored this presumption and made it real. These discursive mechanisms, and the power of the ontological assumption that the arms race and the Cold War would continue indefinitely, are nicely dramatized by a debate on ICBM "modernization" that took place in the pages of *International Security* in 1987–88.

There are two ways to frame the context of this debate, one in terms of a slowly shifting calculus of military hardware capabilities, the other in terms of a rapidly evolving drama of political change. In the minds of most defense intellectuals, the context for this debate consisted only of the shifting nuclear hardware capabilities of the two superpowers. Because both countries had learned to MIRV[14] their missiles and greatly increase their accuracy in the 1970s, it had become possible (in the abstract world of strategic theory at least) that one side could use its multiwarhead missiles to knock out the land-based missile force of its opponent in a preemptive bolt from the blue. The Carter administration had proposed to close this "window of vulnerability" by deploying a new ICBM, the MX, that would routinely circulate between shelters on thousands of miles of railway in Utah and Nevada, in an elaborate nuclear shell game. This plan collapsed in the face of political opposition, especially in Utah and Nevada, where the MX was to be based (Glass, 1993). In 1983, the Scowcroft Commission, appointed to resolve the ICBM problem, proposed a two-track plan: deploying fifty "rail-garrison" MX missiles in such a way that they could be dispersed rapidly by train in the event of a crisis, and also building a new small intercontinental ballistic missile (SICBM) that would have only one warhead and would, therefore, be a less "lucrative" target for Soviet ICBMs than the ten-warhead MX. The Scowcroft Commission's solution generated as much controversy as it resolved, however, and defense intellectuals were still arguing over the wisdom of its recommendations at the time of the *International Security* debates in 1987.

The other way one might contextualize this debate on ICBM modernization is to embed it in the rapidly unfolding drama of U.S.-Soviet relations in the years of perestroika. Gorbachev had ascended to power as the Soviet general secretary in March 1985 and, by 1987, had made substantial progress in implementing his policies of glasnost and perestroika and in reshaping Soviet foreign policy. In August 1985, in what he declared was a bid to end the nuclear arms race completely, he had unilaterally suspended Soviet nuclear testing, and he maintained this moratorium for eighteen months despite continued U.S. nuclear testing. At Reykjavik in 1986, Gorbachev had proposed not only a ban on SDI, but also the complete elimination of all ballistic missiles and, eventually, the complete elimination of all nuclear weapons of all kinds. In 1987, he accepted the INF Treaty, even though its terms were widely seen as more advantageous to the United States than to the Soviet Union. At the same time, Gorbachev was articulating new ideas of mutual security and, with respect to conventional weapons, defensive defense—the reconfiguration of military forces in such a way that they would be appropriate for defense but not offense. By the summer of 1987, he had made substantial reforms in Soviet domestic politics as well, including the relaxation of the state's central control of economic enterprise and the abolition of the Communist Party's monopoly in politics. This monopoly had been the keystone of Soviet politics since Lenin.

It is striking that, in no less than seven different articles on ICBM modernization in *International Security,* none of the political changes summarized in the preceding paragraph are explored or even mentioned—with the exception of one author (Ruina, 1987: 102), who does briefly mention in his final paragraph that "the Soviets under Gorbachev seem readier than ever to be accommodating and to agree to acceptable limits on nuclear arms."[15] Only one author, the same one, questioned whether the United States needed a new ICBM at all. The context in which the U.S. ICBM force is situated in these articles is not the political relationship between the superpowers but the interlocking configuration of their nuclear hardware.[16] In other words, the narrative that underlies these analysts' articles is one that brackets and freezes politics while finding its dynamism in the evolution of technology.

Attention to Soviet politics and even to arms-control proposals and agreements might have produced a perception of diminishing threat, but the focus on hardware did not. Thus, Donald Hicks (1987: 174), for example, despite the Soviet testing moratorium, the INF Treaty, and the internal reforms, concluded unambiguously that the Soviet threat was increasing: "although the Soviet threat has continued to increase, the strength of the U.S. bomber and submarine legs of the strategic triad is sound and improving."

It is characteristic of recent security studies discourse to marginalize possible intentions of adversaries and to privilege instead analysis of their technical capabilities and worst-case scenarios for their employment. Thus, John Toomay (1987: 194–95) argues:

> Our approach emphasizes Soviet potential capability rather than intent, because intent is qualitative and transitory. . . . We are not satisfied to make the probability of a Soviet attack low; we must make that probability vanishingly small. . . . No matter that these attacks [scenarios for Soviet preemptive attacks on U.S. ICBMs] are complex and stylized, requiring an order of precision not likely within Soviet capability, because even low likelihoods are too high.

This analytic convention of assuming the worst and focusing only on hardware capabilities enacts a bias toward the status quo and ensures that an adversary's policy changes or emergent transformations in the structural relationship between the superpowers will lie largely outside even the peripheral vision of the analyst. It also focuses the analyst's intellectual energy on elaborate hyperreal scenarios of how nuclear wars might be fought rather than scenarios (which, in the end, turned out to be more realistic) of how the Cold War might be ended. Only a year before the end of the Cold War, Barry Fridling and John Harvey published an article in which they anguished over the possibility that a rail-garrison MX missile force might not be able to disperse quickly enough to avoid obliteration by a Soviet first strike. They also worried that the dispersal of MX missiles by rail might be sabotaged by "covert Soviet agents in train control facilities scattered throughout the nation" who might have secretly installed weight sensors on railroad tracks or hidden transmitters on the missile trains themselves (Fridling and Harvey, 1988–89: 134).

With the benefit of hindsight, from the other side of the great divide constituted by the end of the Cold War, it is easy to mock such scenarios as paranoid and unreal. However, they made eminent sense within the frame of reference of a discourse—technostrategic discourse—that took it as given that the arms race was a fact of life and would continue indefinitely. This assumption of an indefinite arms race was, as is so often the case with the most powerful structuring assumptions in any discourse, rarely articulated explicitly, but its functioning can clearly be seen in the discourse nonetheless. It is present, for example, in Barry Fridling and John Harvey's (1988–89: 140) concern that the MX "does not provide a hedge against future vulnerability of submarines" and in their recommendation that "increased funds for ICBM basing research and development (R&D) need to be appropriated at the earliest opportunity in order to provide the next administration with feasible alternatives for Peacekeeper or alternate approaches to retaining the viability of ICBMs" (ibid., 114). The assumption is more explicit in Toomay (1987: 201):

> After 35 years of successful deterrence, is our vigilance waning? Are we becoming complacent? Have we lost interest in the details? . . . Perhaps we should remind ourselves that the men and women in our strategic forces have been faithfully adhering to a discipline of technical and operational standards, requiring a monastic dedication—every hour of every day for ten thousand days; that we have sunk billions into every facet of the nuclear umbrella, keeping it intact; and that our deterrence posture is a bulwark of strength throughout the free world.

We even find the assumption of an indefinite arms race in the most liberal of the seven articles: Jack Ruina (1987: 189) writes that "there is some possibility that, in the future, new technologies might threaten a second leg of the triad," and that "if the political climate either deteriorates badly so that strategic force enhancement is in order, or improves substantially so that there is a real interest in deep reductions, a new and different strategic weapons system may be needed with characteristics we cannot now specify" (ibid., 192). While arguing that no new ICBM needed to be deployed at all and criticizing "conflict scenarios that are truly surrealistic and depend upon assumptions of perverse and suicidal reasoning by the adversary," Ruina (ibid., 187–88) does not articulate the possibility that the arms race might completely end or that freezing ICBM deployments might be a means of bringing it to an end. Instead, he can only cast his argument as an appeal for deferral in the face of the shifting dynamics of an endless superpower competition. This is a perfect example of what Foucault meant by "incitement to discourse."

MISSING THE END OF THE COLD WAR II: SOVIET REFORM

In the two years preceding the end of the Cold War, the only authors in *International Security* who came anywhere close to sensing what was about to happen were three Soviet specialists: Jack Snyder, Stephen Meyer, and Mark Kramer. It is significant that, while the nuclear strategists and international relations grand theorists were continuing about their business as usual, it was Soviet specialists—more attuned to domestic politics and well aware of the transformative scope of Gorbachev's reforms—who caught glimpses of the potential transformation of an entire order, though they could not discern the shape of this transformation to come. It is also no coincidence that the titles of two of their three articles end with question marks: in all three articles there is a pervasive tone of disorientation and uncertainty. In Stephen Meyer's (1988: 132) words, "Gorbachev's effort to recast Soviet military doctrine has created a great deal of confusion and uncertainty in what was a very stable policy environment."

Snyder, Meyer, and Kramer all take Gorbachev's reforms seriously and, unlike the nuclear specialists who discount statements about intentions and focus solely on hardware, they pay considerable attention to Soviet doctrinal discussions and statements. Thus, Meyer (1988: 125) says, "I reject immediately the argument that the ongoing doctrinal dialogue in the Soviet Union is mere propaganda," and Snyder (1987–88: 120), highlighting the unprecedented scope of Gorbachev's initiatives, says:

Even Khrushchev understood that superficial concessions could de-mobilize the West, buying time and preparing the ground for a strat-egy of offensive detente. But the articulation of the correlation of forces theory by Khrushchev and Brezhnev clearly signaled their in-tentions from the outset of their detente diplomacy. There is nothing analogous to the correlation of forces theory in Gorbachev's strategic arguments. On the contrary, he insists that this kind of a one-way ap-proach to security constitutes a "world of illusions."

Snyder and Meyer both agree that Gorbachev, faced with the need to divert resources from the military sector to economic develop-ment, had established an alliance with the intelligentsia against the military-industrial complex and was aiming for a profound restruc-turing of Soviet society. "Gorbachev is aiming for nothing less than smashing the power of the entrenched Stalinist interest groups. . . . The military-industrial complex, old-style ideologues, and autarkic industrial interests are in eclipse. Civilian defense intellectuals, re-formist ideologues, and supporters of liberalized trade policies among the intelligentsia are gaining influence and trying to force changes" (Snyder, 1987–88: 109–10). Snyder and Meyer also agree in taking "new thinking" seriously and believing that Gorbachev genuinely aimed to move toward a relationship with the United States based on mutual security.

When it came to taking the next step, however, and proposing ex-plicitly that the Cold War might end, Snyder, Meyer, and Kramer squinted into the darkness and drew back at the last moment. Read-ing these articles, one has a strong sense of authors stumbling in unknown terrain, wrestling with the unthinkable. All three recall Khrushchev's failure, a generation earlier, to make his liberalization of the Soviet Union enduring and self-sustaining. The narrative of Khrushchev's failure haunts their attempts to make sense of Gor-bachev's reformism so that, perceiving Gorbachev through the lens of this failure, they worried that the reforms of the 1980s were, like those of the Khrushchev era, a prelude to a backlash and to a re-intensification of Cold War.

Snyder (1987–88: 93) begins his article by elliptically circling the unthinkable: "Many Americans have long believed that Soviet ex-pansionism stems from pathological domestic institutions, and that the expansionist impulse will diminish only when those institutions undergo a fundamental change. The Gorbachev revolution in Soviet domestic and foreign policy has raised the question of whether that

time is close at hand." Later in the article, drawing back a little, Snyder sets limits on the opening he created with these words. One way
he sets limits is to say that, if the reforms do succeed, then Gorbachev will be able "to seek structural changes in Soviet military
posture that would stabilize the military competition" (ibid., 116–17).
In other words, the Cold War would be scaled back but not closed
down. The second way Snyder sets limits on the degree of change to
be expected is by articulating limiting circumstances that would
bring about a domestic backlash and a reintensification of Cold War.
Thus, he says that the reformers might well be defeated in a situation
where "SDI was being deployed, Eastern Europe was asserting its
autonomy, and Soviet clients were losing their counter-insurgency
wars in Afghanistan, Angola, and Ethiopia" (ibid., 128). As it turned
out, of course, this is almost exactly the course that history took, but
the reform process intensified and the Cold War ended.[17]

Stephen Meyer's argument follows a similar trajectory. Opening
with a similarly expansive gesture, he says in his first paragraph:
"some of the ideas being articulated are doctrinally and ideologically
revolutionary in the context of Soviet security policy. Indeed, the ongoing doctrinal dialogue, if carried to its logical extreme, could imply
even greater changes in Soviet military policy than those associated
with Khrushchev's doctrinal initiatives of the late 1950s and early
1960s" (Meyer, 1988: 124). In his conclusion, however, Meyer says:

> Should they [the reforms] spawn new problems, then more tradi-
> tional elements in the leadership would have an opening to attack the
> full spectrum of new political thinking—including new thinking on
> security. The turmoil in Azerbaijan during 1987–88 is one case in
> point. Equally ominous—and perhaps more directly connected with
> external security—would be another burst of political self-assertion,
> tinged with anti-Soviet behavior, in Eastern Europe. Powerful mem-
> bers of the Politburo seeking to contain the power and authority of
> the general secretary could use such events to create a consensus
> against the new political thinking. (Ibid., 156–57)

Meyer concludes by adding that "looking beyond Gorbachev, there
is no reason to expect that future general secretaries—or other members of the Politburo—will be 'new thinkers'" (ibid., 157).

Mark Kramer, writing for an issue of *International Security* that
was on the newsstands after the Berlin Wall came down, was equally

concerned that events in Eastern Europe would cause a crackdown and equally perplexed by Gorbachev's policies. After all, it was an axiom in security studies in the 1980s that, as one international relations theorist paraphrased it, "hegemons are expected to make every possible effort to retain their principal sphere of influence" (Lebow, 1995: 35). Although noting that "the precise limits of the Soviet Union's willingness to accept internal change in Eastern Europe are still unclear," Kramer is confident that those limits excluded the possibility of what in fact did eventually happen:

> [A] major problem with Gorbachev's approach is that it may eventually result in such ambiguity about the limits of Soviet tolerance that East bloc countries will be overwhelmingly tempted to test those limits. Already an impression has spread in Eastern Europe that the "threshold" needed to provoke Soviet military intervention has been raised so high that almost anything short of a renunciation of socialism or withdrawal from the Warsaw Pact is now feasible. (Kramer, 1989–90: 26)

Although all three authors took Gorbachev's reforms seriously and were well aware that they held out the possibility of fundamentally transforming Soviet society, none of them could finally countenance the possibility that, as eventually transpired, the Soviet Union could allow Eastern Europe to go free, and, although all three are careful to eschew predictions of the future in favor of menus of scenarios, none of them speculated that the Cold War could end. If this was unthinkable for the nuclear specialists discussed earlier because of their decontextualized reduction of the arms race to a matter of technical rationality, it was unthinkable to the Soviet specialists, one suspects, for a different reason: not because they could not think politically, but because the Cold War was the containing structure within which they had learned to constitute the Soviet Union as an object of study, the context within which they had learned their analytic reflexes. Without the Cold War, the Soviet Union would no longer exist as the familiar object of their expertise. It would become another country—as indeed it did.

A NEW SECURITY STUDIES?

Ken Booth (1995: 329) has asked the rhetorical question: "If academic international relations theory could not adequately describe,

338 · HUGH GUSTERSON

explain or predict such a turning point in history [as the end of the Cold War], should it not be discarded as another of the failed projects buried by the Wall?" I hoped in the early 1990s that practitioners of conventional security studies would be chastened by their spectacular failure to foresee the end of the Cold War and that this failure would trigger an internal critique of the dominant discourse and the efflorescence of new discourses.[18] To what degree did this happen in the pages of *International Security*?

In the winter of 1992–93, *International Security* did publish a major critique of the prevailing wisdom in security studies—John Lewis Gaddis's article "International Relations Theory and the End of the Cold War." This article used the unexpected end of the Cold War as a battering ram against the dominant discourse in security studies and international relations theory, particularly its traditional focus on positivism and prediction. Gaddis (1992–93: 5–6) opened his article by saying:

> Historians, political scientists, economists, psychologists, and even mathematicians have claimed the power to detect patterns in the behavior of nations and the individuals who lead them; an awareness of these, they have assured us, will better equip statesmen—and states— to deal with the uncertainties that lie ahead.
>
> The end of the Cold War provides an unusual opportunity to test these claims. That event was of such importance that no approach to the study of international relations claiming both foresight and competence should have failed to see it coming. None actually did so, though, and that fact ought to raise questions about the methods we have developed for trying to understand world politics.

Gaddis attacked the dominant international security studies paradigm on three grounds. First, he attacked the very notion of deterministic predictability that anchors international relations theory's aspirations to become a Newtonian science of international affairs. Second, he criticized the denial of learning, agency, and human will central to the dominant international security studies paradigm, taking issue with the presumption that humans are like molecules that repetitively obey grand laws of motion. Third, he attacked the common privileging of structure over process in security studies and its fundamental presumption that, like the basic laws of physics, the laws of the international system remain static and do not evolve over time.

Gaddis's view has not been unopposed, however, and there have been attempts to recuperate the rupture opened by the unexpected end of the Cold War, particularly by (neo)realists in security studies.[19] The first of these, published before Gaddis's article, was John Mearsheimer's controversial "Back to the Future: Instability in Europe after the Cold War." Mearsheimer begins by stating that "the world can be used as a laboratory to decide which theories best explain world politics" (1990: 9) and asking which theory in security studies has proved most reliable in understanding the past so that we can use the same theory to orient our expectations and behavior in the future. One might expect neorealism to fare poorly in such a contest, given the neorealists' failure to foresee the end of the Cold War, but Mearsheimer ignores this issue. Picking his test case carefully, he takes as his acid test not the ability of a theory to explain the end of the Cold War but its ability to account for the "long peace" of the Cold War itself.[20] He argues that neorealism, which took it as a core axiom that bipolar systems are more stable than multipolar ones, was best able to explain this abnormally long period of stability and is therefore the most reliable theory to guide our actions in the future.[21] Mearsheimer then argues that, far from being a cause for celebration, the end of the Cold War is a dangerous development that, by introducing multipolarity, threatens to make Europe war-prone again unless a strong Germany emerges as a balancing power within Europe. Warning of the danger that Europe will be revisited by war, he concludes by advocating "managed nuclear proliferation" to Germany as a way of creating a new strategic stability anchored by nuclear deterrence within Europe.

A second realist article, Kenneth Waltz's "The Emerging Structure of International Politics" (1993), follows a broadly similar strategy of ignoring security studies' failure to foresee the end of the Cold War, and insisting that, the peaceful end of the Cold War notwithstanding, the international system remains anarchic and (neo)realism remains the best theory for understanding it. Slyly treating the end of the Cold War as if it were anticipated all along, he says: "in a 1964 essay, I predicted that bipolarity would last through the century. On the brow of the next millennium, we must prepare to bid bipolarity adieu and begin to live without its stark simplicities and comforting symmetry" (ibid., 44). After making the case that (neo)realism perfectly explained the superpowers' behavior throughout the Cold War, he goes on to argue that the Cold War ended because the underlying structure of the international system itself changed. He concludes, like Mearsheimer, by warning that the new multipolar order will be less stable than the old one.[22]

A third realist article, this one explicitly rebutting Gaddis's stinging attack on international relations theory, is William Wohlforth's (1994–95) "Realism and the End of the Cold War." Where Mearsheimer and Waltz avoid the topic of this chapter—the failure of international relations specialists to foresee the end of the Cold War—Wohlforth confronts it head-on. Wohlforth opens his article by saying, "a central question faces students and practitioners of international politics. Do the rapid decline and comparatively peaceful collapse of the Soviet state, and with it the entire postwar international order, discredit the realist approach?" (ibid., 91). His answer: "A thoroughly realist explanation of the Cold War's end and the relatively peaceful nature of the Soviet Union's decline that relies entirely on the propositions of pre-1989 theory is in many ways superior to rich explanations based on other theoretical traditions" (ibid., 92).

Wohlforth argues that the realist failure to foresee the end of the Cold War is in fact unproblematic for two reasons. First, realists never said the end of the Cold War was impossible: "No particular finding about the Cold War's end will suffice to falsify an entire research program, such as realism. For a single series of events to constitute a critical test of a theory, it must not only be inconsistent with the theory but be unambiguously ruled out by it" (ibid., 95). Second, realists made few predictions anyway: "Such criticisms miss Waltz's main contention: that a theory of international politics cannot predict state behavior or explain international change. Waltz and his followers often employed the theory to discuss Cold War statecraft, but its core predictions are only two: balances will form; and bipolar systems are less war-prone than multipolar ones" (ibid., 101–2). Wohlforth argues that, in retrospect, the peaceful end of the Cold War makes sense within the framework of realism because "declining challengers" (such as the Soviet Union in the 1980s) behave differently from "declining hegemons," being less likely to respond to their decline by launching preventive war. He concludes that, "although it appeared to require an intellectual revolution in Moscow, a policy of careful appeasement and retrenchment is a historically common response to relative decline. The Roman, Byzantine, and

Venetian empires attempted such strategies when they confronted the dilemma of decline" (ibid., 115).

CONCLUSION

As Richard Ned Lebow and Thomas Risse-Kappen have written, in the 1980s "most theorists and policy analysts assumed that bipolarity and its associated Soviet-American rivalry would endure for the foreseeable future. In the unlikely event of a system transformation, the catalyst for it would be superpower war" (Lebow and Risse-Kappen, 1995: 1). As I have sketched out here, many security studies specialists have refused to be chastened by the fact that their assumptions were so spectacularly contradicted by events. Lebow and Risse-Kappen report that, at the conference that generated their edited volume, one prominent international relations theorist argued that the end of the Cold War proved nothing because it was only a single "data point." Meanwhile, Wohlforth argues that realism was not discredited by the end of the Cold War because it never explicitly ruled out the possibility that the Cold War might end. This leads one to wonder, with Lebow, whether it is "impossible for realists to predict much of anything before the fact but all too easy for them to explain anything once it has occurred" (Lebow, 1995: 36). If the unforeseen end of the Cold War does not discredit the theories and assumptions of this variant of realism, what would have, or what might yet? Would a U.S.-Soviet nuclear war have been seen as discrediting their theories? Would fifty years of stable multilateralism now? Or bandwagoning in the new Europe? Or could ex post facto explanations be found for all of these phenomena too?

Finally, the dominant discourse in security studies reminds this writer of the famous case of Azande witchcraft in the anthropological literature (see Evans-Pritchard, 1937). Among the Azande of Africa, witchcraft was a system for explaining the provenance of misfortune: if something bad happened, it was a witch's fault, and magic had to be used to fend off the witchcraft. The anthropologist Edward Evans-Pritchard found that witchcraft theories could never be empirically falsified because the system always contained plausible explanations for its own failure to predict events or cure ills (this particular witch doctor was incompetent, the witch's magic was stronger than the curer's, the ritual had been enacted improperly, etc.). The dominant discourse in security studies bears an uncanny resemblance

342 · HUGH GUSTERSON

to witchcraft among the Azande in that, although its practitioners boast about their predictive successes, there is apparently no kind of event that would enable one to falsify the discourse. It is a discourse that gives interpretive meaning to events but cannot be tested by them. Whether the Cold War continued or ended, security studies could account for it. Whether the Cold War ended violently or peacefully, security studies had an explanation for it. Whether the Soviets attempted to repress the East Europeans or gave them their freedom as the Cold War ended, security studies could explain it. If war breaks out in the post–Cold War international system, it will prove the realist presumption of anarchy; and if war does not break out, it will demonstrate the functioning of the balance of power or will be a lull before the next war. As E. P. Thompson (1982: 10–11), the most incisive of the Cold War's critics, wrote: "the practitioners [of Cold War discourse] are trapped within the enclosed circularity of their own self-validating logic. Every conclusion is entailed within the theory's premises, although a finely wrought filigree of logic may be spun between one and the other." In such a situation, as Thomas Kuhn argued long ago, the way to change people's minds may not be to argue with old paradigms but to build new ones.

NOTES

My thanks to Stanford University's Center for International Security and Arms Control for inviting me to present an early version of the chapter, and to Noam Chomsky, Lynn Eden, Peter Katzenstein, Steve Miller, Robert Latham, Stephanie Platz, Scott Sagan, and Steve Van Evera for their thoughtful responses to earlier drafts. Thanks also go to Roberta Brawer for showing me the relevance of the "trading zone" literature.

1. The field discussed in this chapter goes by a number of names, each with its own nuance. These names include "security studies," "strategic studies," "international relations," and "peace and conflict studies." I call the field "international security studies" following the usage of Nye and Lynn-Jones (1988).

2. One could make the case (as Cynthia Enloe has pointed out) for many endings of the Cold War (cf. Booth, 1997: 85). In putting the end of the Cold War in the fall of 1989, I am following the dominant convention, which ties the end of the Cold War to the fall of the Berlin Wall in November 1989.

3. It is a hallmark of the kind of knowledge developed in trading zones that it is as likely to be elaborated in adjunct centers at universities or free-standing institutes (the Sante Fe Institute being the classic example) as institutionalized in university departments.

4. Many mainstream security studies specialists, defending their failure to foresee the end of the Cold War, have told me that the end of the Cold War was an extraordinary event that no one predicted. This depends what one means by "predict." By the mid-1980s, many in the peace movement, without putting their money on a specific date, argued that the end of the Cold War was a possibility to work toward (New Left Review, 1982; Thompson, 1982).

5. See Cohn (1987) and Gusterson (1993) for an elaboration of these criticisms. On a more philosophical note, security studies was also almost entirely untouched by the critiques of positivism and eruptions of critical theory that were turning neighboring fields of knowledge upside down in the 1980s, producing the reflexive and feminist turns in anthropology, deconstruction in literary studies, social constructivism in science studies, and the view from below in history. Since the late 1980s, however, security studies has changed, opening itself to new voices (anthropologists, for example) and to new issues (ethnic conflict, environmental security, etc.).

6. For a systematic critique of security studies in the 1980s as an "ancien régime" worldview, written by a self-described "fallen realist," see Booth (1997).

7. The argument here is, of course, broadly Kuhnian: that successful theoretical paradigms work to render certain kinds of anomalous patterns invisible (Kuhn, 1962). Seen in this light, international security specialists in the 1980s were like those gifted medieval astronomers who were more interested in elaborating the considerable successes of the Ptolemaic paradigm than in attending to a few observations that did not fit comfortably within it.

8. My argument here is strongly indebted to Starn (1992). Starn asks how it was that Andeanists in anthropology were so taken by surprise by the eruption of the Maoist Sendero Luminoso and of civil war in Peru in the 1980s. He finds the answer primarily in a common trope in anthropological writing of peasants as isolated bearers of unchanging traditions, arguing that this intellectual predisposition obstructed anthropologists from seeing the degree to which, despite colorful folkloric costumes, these peasants had been absorbed into global capitalist society. I would argue that there is an isomorphism between one kind of anthropology's nostalgic emphasis on the unchanging traditionalism of peasant life and one kind of security studies' focus on enduring anarchy and military rivalry as defining features of the international system.

9. Contributors have included theorists such as Hedley Bull, Kenneth Waltz, John Mearsheimer, Stephen Walt, and Robert Keohane and practitioners such as Robert McNamara and McGeorge Bundy.

10. Examples of analyses of discourse communities include Foucault (1973, 1979, 1980a); Lutz and Collins (1993); Said (1979). Analyses of the discourse of Western defense communities include Chilton (1985); Cohn (1987); Der Derian and Shapiro (1989); Edwards (1996); Gusterson (1991, 1996); Manoff (1989); Taylor (1992).

11. Perle's claim that the Soviets led in strategic bombers would not have been accepted by most defense analysts. In the same issue of the journal, for example, Sloss (1987: 194–95) says that the Soviets were behind the United States in strategic bombers.

12. In a situation of extended deterrence, the U.S. nuclear umbrella is extended over allies. In a situation of existential deterrence, nuclear weapons exist only to deter the use of nuclear weapons against one's own country.

13. The others are Lepingwell (1989) and Welch (1989).

14. *MIRV* stands for "multiple independently targetable reentry vehicles." A MIRVed missile bears several warheads, each capable of hitting a separate preprogrammed target. Thus, one MX missile could, in theory at least, knock out ten different targets.

15. The other articles are Chayes (1987); Dougherty (1987); Fridling and Harvey (1988–89); Hicks (1987); Lodal (1987); and Toomay (1987).

16. These articles also slight the importance of U.S. domestic politics. The Carter administration's plans for deployment of the MX had collapsed in the face of grassroots and congressional political opposition, and the eruption of a massive antinuclear movement in the United States in the early 1980s was complicating the Reagan administration's search for an alternative deployment plan (Glass, 1993). The authors refer only obliquely to such phenomena, however. Toomay (1987: 193), for example, refers to "political, economic, and social issues which create cross-currents in the decision-making process."

17. As Steven Miller (personal communication) points out, there was, on the other hand, a coup attempt in the Soviet Union when it became clear that the Soviet empire was collapsing.

18. For a broader discussion of the implications of the end of the Cold War for security studies, especially for international relations theory, see Booth (1995); Halliday (1995); Hogan (1992); and Lebow and Risse-Kappen (1995).

19. Besides the articles discussed here, *International Security* also published a cluster of articles attacking neoliberal institutionalism and democratic peace theory and arguing for the continuing importance of anarchy as the defining feature of the international system. See Layne (1994), Mearsheimer (1994–95), and Spiro (1994), for example.

20. We might note here that, in Ken Booth's words, "we talk about peace (as in 'We've had peace since 1945') in such a way that peace can only mean the 'absence of world war.' This is a bizarre conception . . . when it cloaks well over 20 million violent deaths" (Booth, 1995: 334).

21. Mearsheimer's argument is, throughout, played out with a deck stacked in favor of neorealism. He claims to demonstrate that the underlying features of the international system have not changed by testing two rival theories, one of which (neoliberalism) assumes evolution in the international system while the other (neorealism) assumes constancy. He then tests the rival theories in terms of their ability to predict past behavior in the system. Thus, the conclusion (that the anarchy of the state system persists) is smuggled into the method.

22. In a prediction that may come back to haunt him, Waltz also—pointing out that "balance-of-power theory leads one to expect that states, if they are free to do so, will flock to the weaker side"—predicts the decay of NATO and the Western alliance as European states move to balance American power (Waltz, 1993: 74–75).

In/Security and the Politics
of Disciplinarity

JOHN MOWITT

PARADIGMS LOST

This essay has essentially two purposes. First, it draws on the North American reception of the work of Michel Foucault in order to establish how questions of security and questions of disciplinarity intertwine. Second, it rereads Foucault's discussion of security in order to nuance and further complicate the relation between security and the history of states. Needless to say, these purposes have significant implications for each other. Precisely to the extent that security and discipline pressure and illuminate each other, they both frustrate and challenge our thinking about states. Are they like disciplines? Are disciplines like states? Do both states and disciplines share a history in which security is at stake? If so, what might that tell us about security itself? To frame a response to such questions, it will be necessary not simply to sketch something like a geopolitical history of disciplines, but also to draw on Foucault's presentation of security in order to contest the terms of such a history. Thus, at the end of the day, it will be my purpose to argue that the effort to theorize in-security cannot avoid the way insecurity has registered itself in the precincts of disciplinary reason. This means, of course, that the debate over security can no longer be securely located within those fields that have traditionally presided over it, and further, that this is a good thing.

In the North American music industry, the artist formerly known as Prince is often characterized as a "crossover artist." This designation refers to the fact that his music is consumed by audiences whose taste cultures typically do not overlap. If I begin here, it is because I want to suggest that Foucault was something of a "crossover theorist"; that is, Foucault's work—which from its very inception worked the seam between history and philosophy—attracted readers from disciplines that shared little until these very readers began to confer with one another about their enigmatically shared attraction. It has been argued—usually by those aware of his French reputation—that, initially, this was detrimental to the U.S. reception of Foucault. Not only was the cultural and political context of his work missing, but Foucault ended up being affiliated with figures (such as R. D. Laing, Thomas Szaz, and David Cooper) with whom he actually shared very little. Today, of course, virtually all of his major works are available in English and they have become consequential for many who otherwise care little about "radical psychiatry." Nevertheless, he remains an embattled and controversial figure (especially in the social sciences), and it is this that merits scrutiny. In drawing on the figure of the "crossover theorist," I aim to emphasize chiefly two things as this piece unfolds: first, that Foucault's work prepared its own interdisciplinary reception by exhibiting a radically interdisciplinary logic; and second, that an important impact of his reception (and for now I will continue to overstate his centrality) has been its role in fostering what I would characterize as a crisis of interdisciplinarity. Because it will be my contention that this crisis is linked—in a manner yet to be specified—to the "end of the Cold War," it is through a consideration of this crisis that my effort to situate disciplines within a geopolitical framework will find its bearings.

It strikes me that today interdisciplinary research, under way for quite some time but that of late has acquired the status of a "buzzword," is haunted by a paradox, namely, the more rigorously interdisciplinary research has been pursued, the more it has tended to lose its identity—the more, in effect, those involved in the interdisciplinary initiative are certain only about what it is not. To be sure, this state of affairs registers the general crisis of "accountability" that has convulsed postsecondary education throughout North America. But beyond that, interdisciplinarians of various stripes have indeed felt pressured of late to state more carefully what constitutes the intellectual advantage of their approach.

Time was when disciplines such as English and psychology were seen not only as the opposite of, but as opposed to, interdisciplinary research. However, that was before scholars began to excavate juridical, philosophical, mathematical, and sociological elements (to name just a few) buried within the foundations of such disciplines. Conversely, one can also recall when sociology, ethnic studies, or women's studies—all quintessentially interdisciplinary endeavors— were conceived as shaking the very foundations of disciplinary power. But that too was before scholars realized how seductive disciplinary legitimation could be made in an institutional context driven by the sort of "professionalism" that arises when economic scarcity comes to dominate the concerns of educators and taxpayers alike. In effect, what we have learned is that being interdisciplinary is very hard to do. Although some have concluded that this reveals the fundamental limitation of the entire interdisciplinary initiative, others—among whom I include myself—have seized upon the difficulties that arise in interdisciplinary research as occasions for reexamining what such research is all about, as well as restating its comparative advantages.

I will unpack this point by appealing to the work of Thomas Kuhn. Written almost exclusively during the heyday of the Cold War (not to mention the so-called space race and the Cuban missile crisis), Kuhn's work sought to establish the historicity of scientific knowledge, a point that the "science wars" have again rendered controversial. Although reluctant to embrace the "epistemological anarchy" of his colleague Paul Feyerabend, Kuhn nevertheless was concerned to explain how sciences, as it were, changed their minds. At the core of his explanation stood the concept of a paradigm, that is, a way of representing what counted as knowledge within (and, I will argue, among) specific sciences. Predictably, history entered science for Kuhn through the portal of the puzzle; that is, the sciences developed as researchers attempted to mobilize paradigms to solve the puzzles deemed worthy by those very paradigms. Typically, puzzles arose as paradigms attempted—with varying results—to account for the data they were understood to explain. When paradigms failed to explain puzzles, they became ripe for historical displacement. To use his own famous example, the Ptolemaic cosmology had trouble explaining, among other things, the so-called retrograde motion of the planets, and as a consequence, its geocentric paradigm was eventually decisively eclipsed by the Copernican paradigm of heliocentrism. Same planets, different worlds.

At the time (Kuhn's text, *The Structure of Scientific Revolutions*, appeared in 1962), this view produced a storm of controversy; the specter of politicized science often seemed to haunt the rhetoric of Kuhn's less charitable detractors. In retrospect, this is nothing short of astonishing, for clearly the notion of history affirmed by Kuhn lacked any expressly insurgent or otherwise political character. In fact, Kuhn's view—the subtleties provoked by the conundrum of quantum theory notwithstanding—failed to accomplish two politically important things. First, it never radicalized its historical critique of knowledge; that is, though it was prepared to insist that abysses separated one paradigm from another, it could not countenance the possibility that a world might arise in which the very notion of solving puzzles might become unintelligible. Some sort of retrospective rational construction was always going to be possible. Second, Kuhn's view addressed itself to the dynamics of interdisciplinarity only insofar as it understood them as an emanation of the logic of puzzle solving; that is (for the moment I will simply bracket the matter of the difference between a science and a discipline), disciplines interacted only to seek out conceptual resources for more adept puzzle solving, much as a stymied commuter might turn to a fellow traveler for help with 24 Down. Obviously, these matters are related even as the limits they exemplify occur at different levels of philosophical abstraction. And quite apart from what they represent as criticisms of Kuhn's project, such limits invite us to recognize that, to some degree, the interdisciplinarity Kuhn allows "to go without saying" is one founded on the logic of puzzle solving. This is the paradigm of interdisciplinarity that is now in crisis.

In fact, the interdisciplinary crisis in which we find ourselves today is not one defined by the disciplinary cooperation that arises around the activity of puzzle solving. Instead, what one encounters are disciplines reorganizing, not around puzzles-to-be-solved, but around questions-to-be-posed. Significantly, these are haunting questions; which is to say, these are questions that stand out because, although they are persistent, they verge on being impossible to pose. Moreover, these questions are crucial because they highlight precisely what reigning disciplinary paradigms render unintelligible. Due to the very unruliness of contemporary interdisciplinarity, these questions arise among or amid disciplines rather than within them, prompting members of affected disciplines to gather at their shared boundaries in order to participate in the labor of collective self-examination. To characterize the situation succinctly but inaccurately, we have met the enemy and it is us, or, put less whimsically, puzzle solving has itself become the puzzle. In fact, it may well be insoluble, and therein lies our in/security. Jean-François Lyotard has characterized the world where puzzle solving is being eclipsed by experimentation (rather than consensus formation) as the postmodern condition. This may not be the right word; it is, however, the right world.

For Kuhn, disciplines developed and interacted in order to solve puzzles that had arisen, usually within otherwise autonomous disciplines, but around data about which there was some consensus. The very possibility of a puzzle depended on such data. However, as any casual observer of the debate over creationism knows, there is today profound (even if mistaken) cultural doubt about whether such data (for example, a fossil record consistent with the demands of Darwinism) exists. In the absense of the very bone of contention, spirit is spooked by the glare of its own illumination. Though the problem of security may well have been the furthest thing from Jacques Lacan's mind, he was clearly on to something when, in 1948, he argued that knowledge itself was a paranoid structure (Lacan, 1977: 16–17). This is especially true—and here it would make sense to situate Lacan's intervention not just within the history of French psychoanalysis, but within the postwar political history of France (he does, after all, invoke *la guerre froide* in his account of paranoia)—when basic research, even in those fields where data more readily grounds consensus, is swept up into the struggle to achieve "preparedness." Under such circumstances, not only are certain puzzles deemed more urgent than others, but a certain premium comes to be placed on the epistemology of puzzle solving. Those sciences and disciplines committed to such an epistemology—for lack of a better term, I will call it positivism—benefit from this premium by assuming the social significance of "real" knowledge, that is, knowledge that really helps a particular nation-state produce an account of the real that does not interfere with, and may even facilitate, its perceived need to secure, maintain, and defend its sovereignty.

In his provocative genealogy of the field of comparative literature, Edward Said has drawn attention to the way the National Defense Education Act of 1958—by stressing the importance of foreign-
language preparedness in the context of a general preoccupation with
national security—produced an intimate and ultimately compromising link between academic disciplines and the interests of the state
(Said, 1994: 47). This suggests that there is considerably more than
"simply" a metaphoric relation between the labor of securing a disciplinary paradigm (that is, one capable of spawning not just relevant puzzles, but the very relevance of puzzle solving) and the labor
of securing the territorial interests of the state. Without in any overt
way casting his lot with the Kennedy administration, Kuhn nevertheless participated in the labor of securing the territorial interests of
the United States by demonstrating how paradigmatically regulated
puzzle solving allowed knowledge to become more secure, that is,
less likely to be caught off guard when the world of puzzles, quanta,
and nuclear warheads threatened to come to an end. Not only did
science have a history, but our science had a future. In refusing to
radicalize the historicization of scientific knowledge, Kuhn rendered
the end of the world unthinkable, in effect, survivable. He also assured the eventual irrelevancy of his project; for, as I have said, we
are now haunted not by the data our paradigms cannot assimilate,
but by the suspicion that our puzzles themselves are trying to kill us.
Just to invoke a convenient, but loaded, example, there is no "away"
where the results of nuclear testing can be thrown anymore. It would
seem, then, that we need desperately to figure out how to pose the
right questions, or neither states nor disciplines will be secure from
the answers with which we have armed ourselves.

SICK QUESTIONS

If I link Foucault so intimately to this crisis, it is because his work
virtually enacts the border crossings that have come to define it. Initially read by literary scholars competent in the French language and
essentially dismissed by Anglo-American philosophy, Foucault has
come to be read quite widely, and has, in effect, given those precincts
within the humanities that concern themselves with matters of critical
theory and methodology a heretofore unheard-of purchase within
the social sciences. In fact, I would characterize the presence of my
essay in this volume as a sign of this very state of affairs.

But beyond that, Foucault has—and this is perhaps most visible in *Discipline and Punish* (1979)—articulated a trenchant critique of the link between institutions such as prisons, the social sciences (notably subfields such as criminology), and disciplinary power. Thus, quite apart from the way his work effects a rich interdisciplinary dialogue, there is the matter of how his texts render the disciplinary mediation of knowledge so palpable. This quality of the work has had very particular repercussions within the social sciences, where disciples (members of disciplines) have long been haunted by the potentially oxymoronic character of both its name and its project. Foucault "crosses over" not by shuttling back and forth between two clearly bounded constituencies, but by being read and valued by scholars who no longer know precisely where they stand: Are they in one field as opposed to another? Are they satisfied that they know what they know? My point is not, of course, that Foucault has in some sense precipitated the crisis of interdisciplinarity, but rather that his work, and the fate inscribed in its reception history outside Europe, are symptoms of this crisis in the making. He thus acquires a certain heuristic privilege in the context of a study devoted, as this one is, to representing the crisis of interdisciplinarity at once thematically and structurally. The theme of insecurity is therefore hardly accidental.

Although, as I have indicated, I want to examine Foucault's discussion of security in some detail, there is an aspect of the role I am ascribing to Foucault in the crisis of interdisciplinarity and security that warrants further elaboration. When asked to characterize, or respond to, his own reception, Foucault often emphasized how, much like the body of the regicide pulled apart at the beginning of *Discipline and Punish,* his work was routinely twisted into alignment either with the left or the right. As he put it:

> There have been Marxists who said I was a danger to Western democracy—that has been written; there was a socialist who wrote that the thinker who resembled me most closely was Adolf Hitler in *Mein Kampf.* I have been considered by liberals as a technocrat, an agent of the Gaullist government; I have been considered by people on the right, Gaullists or otherwise, as a dangerous left-wing anarchist; there was an American professor who asked why a crypto-Marxist like me, manifestly a KGB agent, was invited to American universities, and so on. (In Rabinow, 1984: 376)

Perhaps Foucault had forgotten (the list would otherwise appear to be comprehensive) that when he addressed the "Schizo-Culture" conference at Columbia University in 1975, he was interrupted by a member of the audience who boisterously denounced him as a CIA agent. Although Foucault himself has not—to my knowledge—made this point, it is striking that the perplexity he stirred was consistently managed by appealing to the organizing political dichotomies of the Cold War period. I agree with those who insist that one ought to make every effort to declare himself or herself (and Foucault certainly went out of his way to erase some of the more hackneyed distinctions between communism and capitalism), but it is worth considering—as Said clearly has—how the geopolitical frame of intelligibility enabled by the Cold War circulated in discourses that had little ostensively to do with policy debate. And, it is no doubt crucial here to emphasize the uniquely enigmatic role played by France (particularly, but not exclusively, under de Gaulle) within the context of NATO. I emphasize this because the paranoid calculations that greeted every gesture toward independent decision making made by France (calculations that were not, for that reason alone, unwarranted) would seem to have reappeared in the frenzy of speculation that surrounded "French theory" during the sixties and seventies. Although in Foucault's case this may have had as much to do with his identity as a queer as with anything else (and the trope of the easily compromised homosexual traitor resonates deeply in Cold War rhetoric), it is clear that his reluctance to declare himself openly was read within a context where such reluctance was immediately regarded as cause for suspicion (Edelman, 1993).

Observations such as these begin to indicate just how careful one must be in indexing the crisis of interdisciplinarity symptomatized in Foucault to the end of the Cold War; for, clearly, the crossing over that he both stimulated and embodied was in place well before 1988—a point that invites us to consider that the disciplinary realization of this end may have been under way for some time. It may also mean, of course, that what the end of the Cold War is supposed to have meant, it has not meant. In effect, the end is still not near. To sort through such matters intelligently will require that we address the problem of security—specifically as it appears in Foucault— directly. This will allow us then to confront squarely the disciplinary dispersion of the security problematic.

Foucault elaborated his approach to the problem of security in the context of his analysis of "biopower," an analysis first broached—in his published work—in the closing pages of *The History of Sexuality,* volume 1 (1980a). This work, which fulfilled the promises made in his inaugural lecture, was followed by a series of courses, the summaries of which are now available in a volume titled, aptly, *Résumés des cours 1970–1982* (Foucault, 1989). The courses of particular relevance are the one from 1975–76, "Society Must Be Defended"; the one of 1977–78, "Security, Territory, and Population"; the one of 1978–79, "The Birth of Biopolitics"; and the one of 1979–80, "On the Government of the Living." Although a few papers emerged from this work—"The Dangerous Individual," "Politics and Reason," and "Governmentality" (all three now anthologized in English translation)—the concerns driving it were left, as it were, dangling by Foucault's decision to bring *The History of Sexuality* as close to conclusion as possible. Because Colin Gordon, Peter Miller, and Graham Burchell have undertaken an excavation of this material, I will not repeat their labor of love here. Instead, let me turn directly to those moments of Foucault's arguments that bear directly on the matters at hand.

One of the striking things about *The History of Sexuality* (volume 1) is that it makes virtually no reference whatsoever to what had been one of the central organizing categories of *Discipline and Punish,* namely, discipline, and this in spite of the fact that only a year separates their publication. Elsewhere, I have argued that concern over the very possibility of resistance played a significant role in this analytic strategy (Mowitt, 1996). It is as though discipline, or perhaps "disciplinary power" more generally, came to be regarded as at once too narrow (that is, only socially effective through very particular sorts of disciplinary institutions: prisons, hospitals, schools, etc.) and too compromising an example of power's nonjuridical, or "productive," character to warrant further elaboration. As a result, Foucault begins his articulation of the apparatus of sexuality by appealing to the category of "population" (demonstrably more inclusive than "prisoners," "patients," or "students"), which he politicizes through his invocation of biopower. In the immediate context of his discussion of sexuality, biopower enables him to sketch the difference between a monarch's ability to administer death and the state's ability to administer life. Thus, population, as a designator

organized by this difference, becomes the object of different administrative strategies, and, in fact, comes into being as the result of the
articulation and deployment of these very strategies. Biopower is,
then, both the exercising of state power on life and the production of
a form of life that supports the state.

In the lectures from the late 1970s, biopower is fleshed out in the
context of a consideration of the "art of governing." Specifically, in
"Security, Territory, and Population," Foucault argues that as statesmen began to approach government as a matter not of securing the
consent of the governed, but of securing the lives of the population,
they had ever more frequent recourse to the techniques of policing as
a way to surveil and manage the body politic. I hasten to add here, as
does Foucault, that policing does not refer primarily to the "thin
blue line," but rather to the rich repository of practices gathered together under the German category of *Polizeiwissenschaft*. Drawing
on a variety of sources, but centrally J. G. Von Justi's *Elements of
Police,* Foucault clarifies that policing meant "at once an art of government and a method for the analysis of a population living on a
territory" (Kritzman, 1988: 83). Noting that Von Justi was sensitive
to the paradox here between extending the power of the state while
tending to the happiness of its subjects, Foucault emphasizes that
policing was sharply distinguished from politics, which was understood to bear exclusively upon the state's external confrontations
with other states. Although we are no doubt inclined to be suspicious of such distinctions, it is important to recognize how otherwise
comprehensive policing was. Virtually everything from the administration of territory to the moral conduct of individuals fell within its
purview. Clearly, we are dealing here with an ordering of bodies in
space that extends far beyond the reach of disciplinary power—an
extension that, apart from its other analytic virtues, also makes it
easier to see how power, in the form of policing, is involved in producing, rather than simply negating, the conditions of life.

In a conversation with Robert Bono from this period titled "Social Security," Foucault does two things that merit our attention in
the present context. First, he clearly links the administrative bureaucracy of the welfare state to policing, thus making the art of governing and the act of securing the territory on which a population lives
synonymous. The police are thus first and foremost "security forces."
Second, in concentrating on the "perverse effects" of social security

(namely, the production of dependency and the solicitation of abuse), he implicitly reinscribes Von Justi's distinction between the intrinsic and extrinsic theaters of policing, or, in effect, between policing and politics. This is remarkable because much of what is gained here as insight into the micropolitics of security is nearly sacrificed to an insistent, if not even stubborn, localism where the question of "the political" is indefinitely deferred. Even if we grant that the effort to pin Foucault down within the austere binaries of Cold War politics is wrongheaded, we still want to know whether, for example, he conceives of the state as emerging from the regulated dispersion of civil society just as discipline emerged from the chaos of techniques and practices that fueled its subsequent ordering of them. Or, to put the matter more provocatively, is the concept of a police state simply a pleonasm, and if not, precisely why not?

These are questions for which Foucault never provided answers, and those hoping to find answers here will unfortunately be disappointed because I am in no position to provide them either. Instead, I will deploy Foucault's discussion of security in order to underscore a distinctly disciplinary aspect of the "end of the Cold War," namely, the tendency among those whose disciplinary paradigms were comparatively well served by the governmentality of the Cold War to interpret its "end" as a shift in the very nature of state security—in effect, as a new puzzle to solve. Under such circumstances, the crisis of interdiscipinarity itself invites precisely the sort of policing that typically remains obscured by accounts of security that constitute it as essentially an aspect of the national question. In saying this, I am, of course, nuancing my earlier suggestion that in Foucault's work from the mid-1970s security effectively sublates discipline. In fact, security provides Foucault with a framework within which to depict how the state—as an embodiment of territorial interest—might actually be placed on a continuum with disciplinary institutions such as prisons and schools. Now, however, what this relation allowed one to see about discipline (its implication in the social logic of security) must be supplemented from the opposite angle by considering what it allows one to see about security, especially as an object of disciplinary knowledge.

At the risk, then, of repeating a gesture Foucault was often rebuked for, namely, erasing and then reinscribing breaks, I will broach the relevant issues here simply by drawing attention to the fact that his discussion of security and biopower undermines the centrality given to the "end of the Cold War." The idea that preoccupations with security in the context of everyday life acquire urgency in the wake of the Cold War would appear to ignore precisely what is stressed in Foucault, namely, the concerted elaboration of policing, not simply within civil society, but as the very texture of what Jacques Donzelot has called "the social" (Donzelot, 1984).

Because Foucault situates the advent of security, understood as the projection of biopower through policing, in the nineteenth century and traces its development up through the late twentieth, any effort to specify the consequences of the "end of the Cold War" would have to be done with this broader framework in mind. What might result is a thesis such as the following: the discourse of the Cold War (and, for the sake of convenience, I will concentrate on the United States), promulgated everywhere from *The Manchurian Candidate* or *Invasion of the Body Snatchers* to the various resolutions of the UN Security Council, produced a frame of intelligibility within which, among other things, life itself could be fused to the interests, if not the very existence, of the state. If, as Freud argued in his analysis of Daniel Paul Schreber (an appellate court judge in Austria), paranoia and hypochondria are indissociably linked, then given this fusion of life and the state, national immunization programs and civil defense drills ought to be seen as the expressions of a policing, a securing of identitites, that is explicitly coordinated with a politics. The U.S. "war against polio" was not therefore simply a catachresis, nor was it just a patriotic "holdover" from World War II. Instead, it was a formulation that gave symptomatic expression to the strategic link between the state's capacity for international violence and domestic practices of social welfare.

Thus, with the breakup of the Soviet Union and the disintegration of the Warsaw Pact, the paranoid construction that legitimated the U.S. state's international posture lost the principle of its coherence. As a result, what becomes starkly visible, on such a reading, is the policing that addressed and incited the very social ills that the state was then positioned to heal. In the absence of an internationally legitimated state to secure national identity against some enabling other (for example, the "Red menace"), the management of health, which, necessarily, bred low-level insecurities (hence the link drawn by Freud between paranoia and hypochondria), gives way to a broad anxiety about life itself. And, although it is certainly true that new enabling others have been floated since 1988—international terrorists, Saddam Hussein, militant Islam, and so on—the obsessive foci of public discussion in the United States are the new "plagues" of AIDS, computer viruses, drugs, and domestic violence (everything from child and spousal abuse to militias). In effect, generalized hypochondria emerges to supplement a failing paranoid fantasy, which is not in any way to suggest that those afflicted with mortal illness have "made themselves" sick. On the contrary. It does mean, however, that in constructing the etiology of illness (whether psychosomatic or not), a tendency to explain everything in conspiratorial terms, even "real" causes of "real" diseases, comes to characterize public discourse about such matters. As both Republicans and Democrats in the United States maneuver to dismantle the welfare state, it is clear that—quite apart from the significant economic agenda operating here (and one must acknowledge the presence in this equation of the interests of capitalism itself)—many no longer see the state as either interested in or capable of securing the life of society itself. It is as though in the absence of an official other to revile and plot against, the state is exposed as at once insidious and inept, and for that very reason quite dangerous to its own citizens. Thus, the "end of the Cold War" represents not a decisive break with the logic of security, but a realignment that throws into relief problems and sites of contestation that earlier had been less accessible, that is, intelligible. In this sense, Foucault's reluctance to articulate the relation between policing and politics might well be seen as an anticipation of the very transformation wrought by the Cold War.

Assuming that Foucault might indeed offer such an account of the significance of the "end of the Cold War," does it not then make sense that his project has come to play such a vexed role in the crisis of interdisciplinarity? Why? Well, if—as I have argued—it is in relation to his work (though certainly not his alone) that readers from diverse fields have come to challenge the validity and utility of puzzle solving as a way to grasp the growth of knowledge, and if puzzle solving was vital to securing disciplinary and scientific authority in the context of the Cold War, then either the "end of the Cold War" must be denied (producing the cumbersome burden of an alternative account) or it must be converted into a new puzzle to be solved. One way to do this, of course, is to characterize this end as radically affecting some object of scholarly scrutiny, say, security. By the same token, those whose work might complicate such a gesture, say, by producing an account of security that makes it difficult to use the "end of the Cold War" to open up the intranational and domestic scene, become problematical figures. In this respect, the crisis of interdisciplinarity assumes its proper place on the list of plagues besetting the national community now that the "Red menace" has been vanquished. In fact, one might even argue that the struggle to manage this crisis (for example, calls for greater public accountability of education tax dollars, the confinement of the crisis to rogue disciplines such as cultural studies, etc.) is one of the chief means by which the Cold War will be made to survive its own end. Foucault, unlike other frontline critical theorists, had the misfortune of actually addressing himself to matters of security, and it is perhaps for this reason that his contribution to this general situation remains distinctive. However, this is an incidental matter. The question we need to ask is: how are we to foster the circumstances under which the questions haunting those concerned with matters of security might be posed?

Because a full reply to such a query would require the transformation of the conditions of academic knowledge production, it obviously cannot be made here. Nevertheless, if it makes sense to link the interests of those concerned to limit the fallout of the crisis of interdisciplinarity with those concerned to salvage puzzle solving, then perhaps one way to foster the circumstances called for earlier would be to displace the debate over security. This would mean intensifying the crisis of interdisciplinarity, that is, extending and deepening the questioning that defines it so as to credentialize the speculations of those who may know less about foreign policy than they do about policing, whether the latter manifests itself in the form of a TV ratings system or in the activities of their neighbors. The questions these "experts" might pose are irrelevant to broad matters of security only if security belongs to those whose reflections about it have actually influenced national policy formation. I am not sure anyone believes that this group is asking the right questions anymore. From a perspective such as this, "crossover theorists" have a certain advantage in that they thrive where irrelevance is capable of being given a political meaning. Does this imply that nothing is irrelevant? No, it implies only that there is no relevance without policing, without discipline, without security. If the unposable questions are to be posed, they will have to be uttered in a context where a crisis interrupts the reticulation of policing and the like. Were it not for the fact that security experts are themselves experts in insecurity, it would make sense to characterize this context as one where "crossover theorists" and insecurity experts meet. For this reason, it may be best simply to observe that the insecurities that security secures itself against may actually be muffled by the "screaming across the sky." Obviously, other listening devices will have to be attempted if other questions are to be heard.

Bibliography

Abd al-Jabbar, Falih. 1991. "The Gulf War and Ideology: The Double-Edged Sword of Islam." In Haim Bresheeth and Nira Yuval-Davis, eds., *The Gulf War and the New World Order.* London: Zed Books. 211–17.

Abdel-Malek, Amouar. 1968. *Egypt: Military Society.* New York: Random House.

Abdelnasser, Walid M. 1994. *The Islamic Movement in Egypt: Perceptions of International Relations 1967–1981.* New York: Kegan Paul International.

Abel, Elie. 1966. *The Missile Crisis.* Philadelphia: J. P. Lippincott Company.

Abernathy, Joe. 1992 (June 24). "*Houston Chronicle* Interview: The NSA Papers." [WWW document] URL http://www.quadralay.com/www/Crypt/NSA/letter.html (visited May 18, 1995).

Abrams, Phillip. 1982. *Historical Sociology.* Somerset: Open Books.

———. 1988. "Notes on the Difficulty of Studying the State." *Journal of Historical Sociology* 1(1): 58–89.

Abu-Lughod, Lila. 1991. "Writing against Culture." In Richard G. Fox, ed., *Recapturing Anthropology: Working in the Present.* Santa Fe, N.Mex.: School of American Research Press. 137–62.

Abu-Rabi, Ibrahim M. 1996. *Intellectual Origins of the Islamic Resurgence in the Modern Arab World.* Albany: State University of New York Press.

Acheson, Dean. 1969. *Present at the Creation: My Years in the State Department.* New York: W. W. Norton.

Acuna, Rodolfo. 1988. *Occupied America: A History of Chicanos.* 3d ed. New York: HarperCollins.

Adas, Michael. 1989. *Machines as the Measure of Men: Science, Technology and Ideologies of Western Dominance.* Ithaca, N.Y.: Cornell University Press.

Agnew, John, and Stuart Corbridge. 1995. *Mastering Space: Hegemony, Territory and International Political Economy.* London: Routledge.

Ahmed, Feroz. 1984. "The Late Ottoman Empire." In Marian Kent, ed., *The Great Powers and the End of the Ottoman Empire.* London: Allen and Unwin. 5–30.

Alavi, Hamza. 1972. "The State in Post-Colonial Societies: Pakistan and Bangladesh." *New Left Review* 74: 59–87.

al-Azmeh, Aziz. 1995. "Nationalism and the Arabs." *Arab Studies Quarterly* 17(2): 1–17.

Aleshire, Keith. 1994. "Big Government versus Your Privacy." *ComputerUser* (Minneapolis) (July): 32.

Alker, Hayward R., and Thomas J. Biersteker. 1984. "The Dialectics of World Order: Notes for a Future Anthropologist of International Savoir Faire." *International Studies Quarterly* 28(2): 121–42.

Alker, Hayward R., and David Sylvan. 1986. "Political Discourse Analysis." Unpublished manuscript.

Allied Military Government of Venezia Giulia. 1947. *A Political History of Zone A of Venezia Giulia under Allied Military Government (12 June 1945 to 10 February 1947).*

Allison, Graham T. 1971. *Essence of Decision: Explaining the Cuban Missile Crisis.* Boston: Little Brown and Company.

Allison, Roy. 1988. *The Soviet Union and the Strategy of Non-Alignment in the Third World.* Cambridge: Cambridge University Press.

Alonso, Ana María. 1994. "The Politics of Space, Time, and Substance: State Formation, Nationalism, and Ethnicity." *Annual Review of Anthropology* 23: 379–405.

Alsop, Stuart, and Charles Bartlett. 1962. "In Times of Crisis." *Saturday Evening Post* 235 (December 8), 16–20.

Althusser, Louis. 1971. "Ideology and the Ideological State Apparatuses (Notes Toward an Investigation)." In *Lenin and Philosophy and Other Essays,* translated by B. Brewster. London: New Left Books. 127–86.

Anagnost, Ann. 1992. "Socialist Ethics and the Legal System." In Jeffrey N. Wasserstrom and Elizabeth J. Perry, eds., *Popular Protest and Political Culture in Modern China: Learning from 1989.* Boulder, Colo.: Westview Press. 177–205.

———. 1994a. "The Politicized Body." In Angela Zito and Tani Barlow, eds., *Body, Subject, and Power in China.* Chicago: University of Chicago Press. 131–56.

———. 1994b. "The Politics of Ritual Displacement." In Charles F. Keyes,

Laurel Kendall, and Helen Hardacre, eds., *Asian Visions of Authority: Religion and the Modern States of East and Southeast Asia*. Honolulu: University of Hawaii Press. 221–54.

Anaya, Rudolfo A., and Francisco Lomeli, eds. 1989. *Aztlan: Essays on the Chicano Homeland*. Albuquerque: Academia/El Norte Publications.

Anderson, Benedict. 1991. *Imagined Communities: Reflections on the Origins and Spread of Nationalism*. Rev. ed., London: Verso.

Anderson, M. S. 1966. *The Eastern Question: 1774–1923*. New York: St. Martin's Press.

Appadorai, A. 1982. "Non-Alignment: Some Important Issues." In K. P. Misra, ed., *Non-Alignment: Frontiers and Dynamics*. New Delhi: Vikas Publishing House. 3–11.

Appadorai, A., and M. S. Rajan. 1985. *India's Foreign Policy and Relations*. New Delhi: South Asian Publishers.

Appadurai, Arjun, 1986a. "Introduction: Commodities and the Politics of Value." In Arjun Appadurai, ed., *The Social Life of Things: Commodities in Cultural Perspective*. New York: Cambridge University Press. 3–63.

———. 1986b. "Theory in Anthropology: Center and Periphery." *Comparative Studies in Society and History* 28(1): 356–61.

———. 1991. "Global Ethnoscapes: Notes and Queries for a Transnational Anthropology." In R. J. Fox, ed., *Recapturing Anthropology: Working in the Present*. Santa Fe, N.Mex.: School of American Research Press. 191–210.

———. 1993. "Patriotism and Its Futures." *Public Culture* 5(3): 411–29.

———. 1996. *Modernity at Large: Cultural Dimensions of Globalization*. Minneapolis: University of Minnesota Press.

Archibald, Dale. 1994. "Opinion—Telecommunications: The New Frontier." *Computer Buyer's Resource* (Minneapolis) (March), 5, 24.

Asad, Talal. 1991. "Afterword: From the History of Colonial Anthropology to the Anthropology of Western Hegemony." In George Stocking Jr., ed., *Colonial Situations: Essays on the Contextualization of Ethnographic Knowledge*. Madison: University of Wisconsin Press. 314–24.

———, ed. 1973. *Anthropology and the Colonial Encounter*. New York: Humanities Press.

Ashley, Richard K. 1984. "The Poverty of Neorealism." *International Organization*. 38(2): 225–86.

———. 1989. "Imposing International Purpose: Notes on a Problematic of Governance." In Ernst-Otto Czempiel and James Rosenau, eds., *Global Change and Theoretical Challenge: Approaches to World Politics for the 1990s*. New York: Lexington Books. 251–90.

"Asian News Gathering." 1995. *Asia 2000 Foundation of New Zealand* 4: 4–5.

"Asian Studies Workshop." 1994. *Asia 2000 Foundation of New Zealand* 1: 7.

Atkins, G. Pope. 1989. *Latin America in the International Political System.* Boulder, Colo.: Westview Press.

"Author Won't Be Prosecuted." 1996 (January 11). [On-line search query] The Associated Press On-line News Service, URL http://professional. infoseek.com/ (Wire Services search) (visited January 18, 1996).

Ayoob, Mohammed. 1983–84. "Security in the Third World: The Worm about to Turn." *International Affairs* 60(1): 41–51.

———. 1993. "Unraveling the Concept: 'National Security' in the Third World." In Baghat Korany, Paul Noble, and Rex Brynen, eds., *The Many Faces of National Security in the Arab World.* New York: St. Martin's Press. 31–55.

———. 1995. *The Third World Security Predicament: State Making, Regional Conflict, and the International System.* Boulder, Colo.: Lynne Rienner.

Baker, Russell. 1959. "Eisenhower Holds Popularity Lead—But Indians Warmly Recall Informality Displayed by Khrushchev on Tour." *New York Times,* December 11, 16.

Baker, Stewart A. 1994. "Don't Worry, Be Happy: Why Clipper Is Good for You." *Wired* 2.06. [Text file] Wired Ventures, Ltd., URL http://www.eff. org/pub/Privacy/Clipper/clipper_good_nsa.article (visited May 18, 1995).

Ballinger, Pamela. 1996. " 'Istriani d.o.c.': Silences and Presences in the Construction of Exodus, the Istrian Esodo." In Maja Povrzanovic and Renata Jambresic Kirin, eds., *War, Exile and Everyday Life.* Zagreb: Institute of Ethnology and Folklore Research. 117–32.

Bamford, James. 1982. *The Puzzle Palace: A Report on America's Most Secret Agency.* New York: Penguin Books.

Banerjee, Sanjoy. 1994. "National Identity and Foreign Policy." In N. Choudhry and S. Mansur, eds., *Indian Economy and Polity, 1966–1991: The Indira-Rajiv Years.* Boulder, Colo.: Westview Press.

Banisar, David. 1995 (October). "Bug Off! A Primer for Human Rights Groups on Wiretapping." [WWW document] URL http://www.privacy. org/pi/reports/bug_off.html (visited January 20, 1996).

Baran, Paul. 1990a. "Packet Switching." [Photocopy] Attachment 3 of transcript of interview by Judy O'Neill, March 5, in "Role of DARPA/IPTO in the Development of Computer Science Oral History Collection." Minneapolis: Charles Babbage Institute, University of Minnesota. Originally published in John C. McDonald, ed., *Fundamentals of Digital Switching.* 2d ed. Plenum Publishing, 1990. 193–235.

———. 1990b. Transcript of interview by Judy O'Neill, March 5, in "Role of DARPA/IPTO in the Development of Computer Science Oral History Collection." Minneapolis: Charles Babbage Institute, University of Minnesota.

Barbrook, Richard. 1996 (March 30). "Hypermedia Freedom: Deregulation or Reregulation?" [Text file] URL http://mediafilter.org/ZK/Conf/Conf_Email/March.30.1996.21.25.57 (visited May 31, 1996).

Barbrook, Richard, and Andy Cameron. 1995. "The Californian Ideology." [WWW document] URL http://www.wmin.ac.uk/media/HRC/ci/calif5. html (visited January 26, 1997).

Barlow, John Perry. 1990 (June 8). "Crime and Puzzlement." [Text file] FTP spies.com/Library/Cyber/barlow.txt (visited May 21, 1995).

———. 1992. "Decrypting the Puzzle Palace." Communications of the ACM, July. [Text file] URL http://www.eff.org/pub/Privacy/decrypting_puzzle.palace (visited May 18, 1995).

———. 1993a. "A Plain Text on Crypto Policy." EFFector Online 6(1), September 17. [On-line serial] URL http://www.eff.org/pub/EFF/Newsletters/EFFector/effector6.01 (visited May 18, 1995).

———. 1993b (December). "Selling Wine without Bottles: The Economy of Mind on the Global Net." [Text file] URL http://www.eff.org/pub/Intellectual_property/idea_economy.article (visited May 31, 1996).

———. 1994a. "Jackboots on the Infobahn." Wired 2.04: 40, 44, 46–48.

———. 1994b. "Jack In, Young Pioneer!" [WWW document] URL http://www.eff.org/pub/Publications/John_Perry_Barlow/HTML/jack_in_young_pioneer.html (visited January 29, 1996).

———. 1994c (January 17). "Stopping the Information Railroad." Keynote address to the USENIX Conference, San Francisco. [Text file] URL http://www.eff.org/pub/GII_NII/info_railroad_usenix_barlow_eff.speech (visited May 31, 1996).

Barlow, John Perry, and Mitchell Kapor. 1990. "Across the Electronic Frontier." [Text file] URL http://www.eff.org/pub/EFF/electronic_frontier.eff (visited May 18, 1995).

Barnett, Michael. 1992. Confronting the Costs of War: Military Power, State, and Society in Egypt and Israel. Princeton, N.J.: Princeton University Press.

Barrera, Mario. 1988. Beyond Aztlan: Ethnic Autonomy in Comparative Perspective. New York: Praeger.

Barthes, Roland. 1972. Mythologies. New York: Hill and Wang.

Beck, Ulrich. 1992. Risk Society: Towards a New Modernity. London: Sage Publications.

Bedford, Richard. 1996. "International Migration and National Identity."

In Richard Le Heron and Eric Pawson, eds., *Changing Places: New Zealand in the Nineties.* Auckland: Longman Paul. 350–60.

Belich, James. 1996. *Making Peoples: A History of the New Zealanders from Polynesian Settlement to the End of the Nineteenth Century.* Auckland: Allen Lane, Penguin Press.

Bell, Avril. 1996. "'We're Just New Zealanders': Pakeha Identity Politics." In Paul Spoonley, David Pearson, and Cluny Macpherson, eds., *Nga Patai: Racism and Ethnic Relations in Aotearoa/New Zealand,* Palmerston North, New Zealand: Dunmore Press. 144–58.

Bell, Claudia. 1996. *Inventing New Zealand: Everyday Myths of Pakeha Identity.* Auckland: Penguin Books.

Benton, Ted. 1977. *Philosophical Foundations of the Three Sociologies.* London: Routledge and Kegan Paul.

Berg, Lawrence D., and Robin A. Kearns. 1996. "Naming as Norming: 'Race', Gender, and the Identity Politics of Naming Places in Aotearoa/New Zealand." *Environment and Planning D: Society and Space* 14(1): 99–122.

Berger, Bob. 1995. "The Circuit Rider." *NetGuide* (September): 30–32.

Berlin, Eric. 1996 (April 16). "CompuServe Bows to Germany." [WWW document] URL http://www.minfod.com/CurrentTrends/article2.html (visited May 3, 1996).

Bernstein, Barton J. 1976. "The Week We Almost Went to War." *Bulletin of the Atomic Scientists* 32: 13–21.

———. 1979. "Bombers, Inspections, and the No Invasion Pledge: Kennedy and Ending the Missile Crisis." *Foreign Service Journal* 56(7): 8–12.

———. 1980. "The Cuban Missile Crisis: Trading the Jupiters in Turkey?" *Political Science Quarterly* 95: 97–125.

Bernstein, Richard J. 1978. *The Restructuring of Social and Political Theory.* Philadelphia: University of Pennsylvania Press.

———. 1983. *Beyond Objectivism and Relativism: Science, Hermeneutics, Praxis.* Philadelphia: University of Pennsylvania Press.

Besteman, Catherine. 1997. "Violent Politics and the Politics of Violence: The Dissolution of the Somali Nation-State." *American Ethnologist* 23(3): 579–96.

Biersteker, Thomas, and Cynthia Weber. 1996. *State Sovereignty as Social Construct.* Cambridge: Cambridge University Press.

"Billy the Bully." 1996. *Times of India* (New Delhi), March 5, 10.

"BJP Is Opposed to Ties with US at Cost of Self-Respect." 1995. *Hindustan Times* (New Delhi), October 31, 12.

Blackburn, Robin. 1993. "The Break-Up of Yugoslavia and the Fate of Bosnia." *New Left Review* 199: 100–119.

Blaney, David L. 1992. "Equal Sovereignty and an African Statehood:

Tragic Elements in the African Agenda in World Affairs." In Martha L. Cottam and Chih-Yu Shih, eds., *Contending Dramas: A Cognitive Approach to Post-War International Organization.* New York: Praeger. 211–26.

Blechman, Barry, and Victor Utgoff. 1986–87. "The Macroeconomics of Strategic Defenses." *International Security* 11(3): 33–70.

Blight, James G., and David A. Welch. 1990. *On the Brink: Americans and Soviets Reexamine the Cuban Missile Crisis.* 2d ed. New York: Noonday Press.

Blight, James G., Joseph S. Nye, and David A. Welch. 1987. "The Cuban Missile Crisis Revisited." *Foreign Affairs* 66(1): 170–88.

Boas, Franz. 1925. *Contributions to the Ethnology of the Kwakiutl.* New York: Columbia University Press.

Bodine, John. 1968. "A Tri-Ethnic Trap: The Spanish Americans in Taos." In June Helm, ed., *Spanish-Speaking People in the United States* (Proceedings of the 1968 American Ethnological Society). Seattle: American Ethnological Society.

Bogneri, Marcello. 1993. *Il culto di Dante a Pola nell'ultimo secolo.* Trieste: Unione degli Istriani.

Bolger, James. 1992. "New Zealand and Asia." Address at Massey University, Palmerston North, New Zealand, August 19. *Ministry of External Relations and Trade Record* 1(3): 20–24.

———. 1994. "New Zealand and the Asia-Pacific Region." Address to the New Zealand Institute of International Affairs, Wellington, November 9. *Ministry of Foreign Affairs and Trade Record* 3(6): 20–24.

Booth, Ken. 1995. "Dare Not to Know: International Relations Theory versus the Future." In Ken Booth and Steve Smith, eds., *International Relations Theory Today.* State College: Pennsylvania State University Press. 328–50.

———. 1997. "Security and Self: Reflections of a Fallen Realist." In Keith Krause and Michael C. Williams, eds., *Critical Security Studies: Concepts and Cases.* Minneapolis: University of Minnesota Press. 83–120.

Borneman, John. 1992. *Belonging in the Two Berlins: Kin, State, Nation.* Cambridge: Cambridge University Press.

———. 1995. "American Anthropology as Foreign Policy." *American Anthropologist* 97(4): 663–72.

———. 1997. *Settling Accounts: Violence, Justice and Accountability in Post-Socialist Europe.* Princeton, N.J.: Princeton University Press.

Bostdorff, Denise M. 1994. *The Presidency and the Rhetoric of Foreign Crisis.* Columbia: University of South Carolina Press.

Boutros-Ghali, Boutros. 1995. "Democracy: A Newly Recognized Imperative." *Global Governance* 1(1): 3–12.

Bowman, Alfred Connor. 1982. *Zones of Strain: A Memoir of the Early Cold War.* Stanford, Calif.: Hoover Institution Press.

Bowman, Glenn. 1995. "Terror, Pain and the Impossibility of Community." Paper presented at the conference "War, Exile, and Everyday Life," Zagreb, March.

Boyarin, Jonathan. 1994. *Remapping Memory: The Politics of Timespace.* Minneapolis: University of Minnesota Press.

Boyer, Paul. 1985. *By the Bomb's Early Light: American Thought and Culture at the Dawn of the Atomic Age.* New York: Pantheon Books.

Brands, H. W. 1990. *India and the United States: Never the Twain.* Boston: Twayne Publishers.

Brandt, Daniel. 1995 (November 3). "Infowar and Disinformation: From the Pentagon to the Net." [WWW document] URL http://com.primenet.com/callme/news/infowar.html (visited, April 30, 1996).

Brawley, Sean. 1993. " 'No "White Policy" in NZ': Fact and Fiction in New Zealand's Asian Immigration Record, 1946–1978." *New Zealand Journal of History* 27(1): 16–36.

———. 1995. *The White Peril: Foreign Relations and Asian Immigration to Australasia and North America, 1919–1978.* Sydney: University of New South Wales Press.

Brecher, Michael, Jonathan Wilkenfeld, and Sheila Moser. 1988. *Crises in the Twentieth Century.* Vol. 1, *Handbook of International Crises.* Oxford: Pergamon Press.

Breckenridge, Carol A., and Peter van der Veer, eds. 1993. *Orientalism and the Postcolonial Predicament: Perspectives on South Asia.* Philadelphia: University of Pennsylvania Press.

Briggs, Charles L., and John R. Van Ness, eds. 1987. *Land, Water, and Culture: New Perspectives on Hispanic Land Grants.* Albuquerque: University of New Mexico Press.

British Documents on the End of Empire. Series A, vol. 2. London: Her Majesty's Stationary Office.

Broad, William. 1992. *Teller's War: The Top-Secret Story behind the Star Wars Deception.* New York: Simon and Schuster.

Brooking, Tom, and Roberto Rabel. 1995. "Neither British Nor Polynesian: A Brief History of New Zealand's Other Immigrants." In Stuart William Greif, ed., *Immigration and National Identity in New Zealand: One People, Two Peoples, Many Peoples?* Palmerston North, New Zealand: Dunmore Press 23–49.

Brooks, Linton. 1988–89. "Nuclear SLCMs Add to Deterrence and Security." *International Security* 13(3): 169–74.

Brown, Michael. 1989. "The U.S. Manned Bomber and Strategic Deterrence in the 1990s." *International Security* 14(2): 5–46.

Bryant, B. 1995. *Environmental Justice: Issues, Policies, and Solutions.* Washington, D.C.: Island Press.

Brzezinski, Zbigniew. 1962. "Cuba in Soviet Strategy." *New Republic,* November 3, 7–8.

Bulganin, N. A. 1956a. Report on trip to India, Burma, and Afghanistan by N. A. Bulganin, Chairman of the U.S.S.R. Council of Ministers (*Pravda and Izvestia,* December 30, 1955, 1–2, condensed text). Reproduced in "Supreme Soviet: Bulganin's Report on Asia Trip," *Current Digest of the Soviet Press,* vol. 7, no. 51 (February 1), 13–17.

———. 1956b. Speech by N. A. Bulganin to the Indian Parliament (*Pravda and Izvestia,* November 22, 1955, 1–2, condensed text). Reproduced in "Bulganin and Khrushchev Visit Asia—I," *Current Digest of the Soviet Press,* vol. 7, no. 47 (January 4), 3–5.

Bull, Hedley. 1984. "The Revolt against the West." In Hedley Bull and Adam Watson, eds., *The Expansion of International Society,* New York: Oxford University Press. 217–28.

Bullard, R. D. ed. 1993. *Confronting Environmental Racism: Voices from the Grassroots.* Boston: South End Press.

Bundy, McGeorge. 1988. *Danger and Survival: Choices about the Bomb in the First Fifty Years.* New York: Random House.

Burgat, François, and William Dowell. 1993. *The Islamic Movement in North Africa.* Austin: University of Texas Press.

Burke, K. 1972. *Dramatism and Development.* Barre, Mass.: Clark University Press.

Burke, Kerry. 1986. *Review of Immigration Policy.* Wellington: Government Printer.

Butler, Judith. 1993. "Gender Is Burning: Questions of Appropriation and Subversion." *Bodies That Matter: On the Discursive Limits of 'Sex.'"* New York and London: Routledge. 121–42.

Buzan, Barry. 1991. *People, States, Fear: An Agenda for International Security Studies in the Post–Cold War Era.* 2d ed. Boulder, Colo.: Lynne Rienner.

Campbell, David. 1992. *Writing Security: United States Foreign Policy and the Politics of Identity.* Rev. ed. 1998. Minneapolis: University of Minnesota Press.

———. 1993. *Politics without Principle: Sovereignty, Ethics, and Narratives of the Gulf War.* Boulder, Colo.: Lynne Rienner.

———. 1994. "Foreign Policy and Identity: Japanese 'Other'/American 'Self.'" In Stephen J. Rosow, Naeem Inayatullah, and Mark Rupert, eds., *The Global Economy as Political Space.* Boulder, Colo.: Lynne Rienner. 147–69.

Carmichael, Virginia. 1993. *Framing History: The Rosenberg Story and the Cold War.* Minneapolis: University of Minnesota Press.

Carnesale, Albert, and Richard Haass. 1987. "Conclusions: Weighing the Evidence." In Albert Carnesale and Richard Haass, eds., *Superpower Arms Control: Setting the Record Straight.* Cambridge, Mass.: Ballinger. 329–55.

Carnoy, Martin. 1984. *The State and Political Theory.* Princeton, N.J.: Princeton University Press.

Carter, Dale. 1988. *The Final Frontier: The Rise and Fall of the American Rocket State.* London: Verso.

Castoriadis, Cornelius. 1987. *The Imaginary Institution of Society.* Translated by Kathleen Blamey. Cambridge: MIT Press.

Castro, Fidel. 1992. "Transcript of Fidel Castro's Remarks at the Havana Conference on the Cuban Missile Crisis," January 11. Foreign Broadcast Information Service. Reprinted in Laurence Change and Peter Kornbluh, eds., *The Cuban Missile Crisis, 1962: A National Security Archives Documents Reader.* New York: New Press, 1992. 330–45.

Center for Democracy and Technology. N.d. "A History of Clinton Administration Encryption Policy Initiatives." [WWW document] URL http://www.cdt.org/crypto/admin/initiatives.html (visited 1998, November 28).

"Center Stage." 1994 (May 26). On-line Question-and-Answer Session with Stewart A. Baker. *America Online, Inc.* (AOL) [on-line commercial service] (Filename: AUD0526.LOG).

Chakrabarty, Dipesh. 1992. "Postcoloniality and the Artifice of History: Who Speaks for 'Indian' Pasts?" *Representations* 37: 1–26.

Chandra, Bipan. 1993. *Essays on Indian Nationalism.* New Delhi: Har-Anand Publications.

Chatterjee, Partha. 1986. *Nationalist Thought and the Colonial World: A Derivative Discourse?* London: Zed Press. Reprint, Minneapolis: University of Minnesota Press, 1988.

———. 1993. *The Nation and Its Fragments.* Princeton, N.J.: Princeton University Press.

Chatterjee, Partha, and Gyan Pandey, eds. 1992. *Subaltern Studies.* Vol. 7. Delhi: Oxford University Press.

Chavez, John R. 1984. *The Lost Land: The Chicano Image of the Southwest.* Albuquerque: University of New Mexico Press.

Chayes, Abram. 1962. "The Legal Case for U.S. Action in Cuba." Address at Harvard Law School, November 3. *Department of State Bulletin,* November 19. 763–65.

Chayes, Antonia Handler. 1987. "Managing the Politics of Mobility." *International Security* 12(2): 154–62.

Chen, Elaine. 1996. "A New 'Yellow Peril' for New Zealand?" *sinorama* 21(10). [WWW document] URL http://sinanet.com/bay/sinorama/1096/article1/english/1.htm1 (visited February 9, 1997).

Chen, Mai. 1994. "New Zealand's Future in Asia: Facing Up to the Hard Issues." *Asia 2000 Foundation of New Zealand* 1: 3.

Chengappa, Raj. 1996. "Interview with I. K. Gujral." *India Today*, June 30, 39.

Chilton, Paul, ed. 1985. *Language and the Nuclear Arms Debate: Nukespeak Today.* London: Frances Pinter.

Choueiri, Youssef M. 1994. *Islamic Fundamentalism.* Boston: Twayne Publishers.

Churchill, Ward. 1993. *Struggle for the Land: Indigenous Resistance to Genocide, Ecocide, and Expropriation in Contemporary North America.* Monroe, Maine: Common Courage Press.

Clark, Helen. 1995. "New Zealand and Asia: The Need for a More Mature Approach." *New Zealand International Review* 20(4): 2–5.

Cleaver, Harry. 1996 (February 18). "The 'Space' of Cyberspace: Body Politics, Frontiers and Enclosures." [WWW document] URL http://www.lawyernet.com/members/jimfesq/wca/22/SPACEOFCYBERSPACE.html (visited May 28, 1996).

Cleveland, William L. 1994. *A History of the Modern Middle East.* Boulder, Colo.: Westview Press.

Clifford, James. 1988. *The Predicament of Culture: Twentieth-Century Ethnography, Literature, and Art.* Cambridge: Harvard University Press.

Clifford, James, and George E. Marcus, eds. 1986. *Writing Culture: The Poetics and Politics of Ethnography.* Berkeley: University of California Press.

Clinton, William J. 1995 (October 22). Remarks to the United Nations General Assembly on the Occasion of the United Nations' Fiftieth Anniversary, New York. [Text file] URL gopher://gopher.undp.org:5000/00/other/95_10/951022162715.txt (visited January 14, 1996).

"Clipper II: Don't Trip over the Dogs and Ponies." 1995. *VTW BillWatch* 17, September 7. [WWW document] URL http://www.isse.gmu.edu/students/pfarrell/nist/vtwover.html (visited January 20, 1996).

Cohen, Felix. 1941. *Handbook of Federal Indian Law.* Washington D.C.: U.S. Government Printing Office.

Cohn, Carol. 1987. "Sex and Death in the Rational World of Defense Intellectuals." *Signs* 12(4): 687–718.

Collier, Jane. 1997. "The Waxing and Waning of 'Subfields' in North American Sociocultural Anthropology." In Akhil Gupta and James Ferguson, eds., *Anthropological Locations: Boundaries and Grounds of a Field Science.* Berkeley: University of California Press.

Colummi, Cristiana, Liliana Ferrari, Gianni Nassisi, and Germano Trani, eds. 1980. *Storia di un esodo, Istria 1945–1956.* Trieste: Istituto Regionale per la Storia del Movimento di Liberazione nel Friuli Venezia Giulia.

Comaroff, John L., and Paul C. Stern, eds. 1995. *Perspectives on Nationalism and War.* Amsterdam: Gordon and Breach.

Committee for the Defense of the Italian Character of Trieste and Istria. 1953. *Trieste: November 1953: Facts and Documents.* Trieste.

Congressional Register. 1945. Washington, D.C.: U.S. Governmental Printing Office.

Connolly, William E. 1987. *Politics and Ambiguity.* Madison: University of Wisconsin Press.

———. 1991. *Identity\Difference: Democratic Negotiations of Political Paradox.* Ithaca, N.Y.: Cornell University Press.

Constance, Paul. 1995 (August 25). "White House Retreats on Clipper Mandate: New Board Promises Encryption Options." *Government Computer News.* [WWW document] Cahners Publishing Company, URL http://www.cahners.com/gcn/GCNNEWS/082195/SI-PMO.HTM (visited January 17, 1996).

Cooper, Kenneth J. 1996. "India's Move to Block Test Ban Pact in U.N. Is Popular at Home." *Washington Post,* August 23, A24.

Corber, Robert J. 1993. *In the Name of National Security: Hitchcock, Homophobia, and the Political Construction of Gender in Postwar America.* Durham, N.C.: Duke University Press.

Coronil, Fernando, and Julie Skurski. 1991. "Dismembering and Remembering the Nation: The Semantics of Political Violence in Venezuela." *Comparative Studies in History and Society.* 33(2): 288–337.

Costigliola, Frank. 1995. "Kennedy, the European Allies, and the Failure to Consult." *Political Science Quarterly* 110(1): 105–23.

Cox, Geoffrey. 1977. *The Race for Trieste.* London: William Kimber.

Cox, Robert W. 1986. "Social Forces, States, and World Orders: Beyond International Relations Theory." In Robert O. Keohane, ed., *Neorealism and Its Critics.* New York: Columbia University Press. 204–54.

Cox, Robert W., with Timothy J. Sinclair. 1996. *Approaches to World Order.* Cambridge: Cambridge University Press.

Crawford, Beverly, and Ronnie Lipschutz. 1994. "Discourses of War: Security and the Case of Yugoslavia." YCISS Occasional Paper (27).

Cumings, Bruce. 1992a. "Rimspeak; or, The Discourse of the 'Pacific Rim.'" In Arif Dirlik, ed., *What Is in a Rim? Critical Perspectives on the Pacific Region Idea.* Boulder, Colo.: Westview Press. 29–47.

———. 1992b. "The Wicked Witch of the West Is Dead. Long Live the Wicked Witch of the East." In Michael J. Hogan, ed., *The End of the*

Cold War: Its Meanings and Implications. Cambridge: Cambridge University Press. 87–101.

Dalby, Simon. 1990. *Creating the Second Cold War.* London: Pinter Publishers.

———. 1992. "Security, Modernity, Ecology: The Dilemmas of Post–Cold War Security Discourse." *Alternatives* 17(1): 95–134.

Daniel, Valentine. 1996. *Charred Lullabies: Chapters in an Anthropology of Violence.* Princeton, N.J.: Princeton University Press.

Darby, Phillip, and A. J. Paolini. 1994. "Bridging International Relations and Postcolonialism." *Alternatives* 19(3): 371–98.

Davies, Bronwyn, and Rom Harré. 1990. "Positioning: The Discursive Production of Selves." *Journal for the Theory of Social Behavior* 20(1): 43–63.

Dawn, C. Ernest. 1988. "The Formation of Pan-Arab Ideology in the Interwar Years." *International Journal of Middle East Studies* 20(1): 67–91.

Debeljuh, Loredana Bogliun. 1993. "Comments on Istria." *Vita Italiana* 2: 20–25.

———. 1994. "L'Istria e l'idea Jugoslava," *Panorama,* April 15, 11.

"The Declaration of Independence." [WWW document] URL http://www. wcc.govt.nz/poneke/tow/independ.txt (visited April 16, 1997).

DeGrazia, Victoria. 1981. *The Culture of Consent: Mass Organization of Leisure in Fascist Italy.* Cambridge: Cambridge University Press.

Deighton, Ann. 1993. *The Impossible Peace: Britain, the Division of Germany and the Origins of the Cold War.* Oxford: Clarendon Press.

Dekmejian, R. Hrair. 1995. *Islam in Revolution: Fundamentalism in the Arab World.* Syracuse, N.Y.: Syracuse University Press.

del Castillo, Richard Griswold. 1990. *The Treaty of Guadalupe Hidalgo: A Legacy of Conflict.* Norman: University of Oklahoma Press.

de los Angeles Torres, Maria. 1995. "Beyond the Rupture: Reconciling Our Enemies, Reconciling Our Selves." In Ruth Behar, ed., *Bridges to Cuba/ Puentas a Cuba.* Ann Arbor: University of Michigan Press. 25–43.

Denich, Bette. 1994. "Dismembering Yugoslavia: Nationalist Ideologies and the Symbolic Revival of Genocide." *American Ethnologist* 21(2): 367–90.

Der Derian, James, and Michael Shapiro, eds. 1989. *International/ Intertextual Relations: Postmodern Readings of World Politics.* Lexington, Mass.: Lexington Books.

Derrida, Jacques. 1974. *Of Grammatology.* Baltimore: Johns Hopkins University Press.

Deutsch, Karl. 1953. *Nationalism and Social Communication: An Inquiry into the Foundations of Nationality.* Cambridge: MIT Press; and New York: John Wiley and Sons.

Devlin, John. 1991. "The Baath Party: Rise and Metamorphosis." *American Historical Review* 96(5): 1396–1407.

Dinsdale, Andrew P. 1994. "Issue Management in a Networked World: The Case of 'Clipper.'" *Computer-Mediated Communication Magazine* 1(5) (September 1). [WWW document] URL http://sunsite.unc.edu/cmc/mag/1994/sep/issue.html (visited March 5, 1996).

Dirks, Nicholas B. 1996. "Is Vice Versa? Historical Anthropology and Anthropological History." in Terrence J. McDonald, ed., *The Historical Turn in the Human Sciences*. Ann Arbor: University of Michigan Press. 17–51.

Dirks, Nicholas B., Geoff Eley, and Sherry Ortner, eds. 1994. *Culture/Power/History: A Reader in Contemporary Social Theory*. Princeton, N.J.: Princeton University Press.

Dirlik, Arif. 1982. "Spiritual Solutions to Material Problems: The 'Socialist Ethics and Courtesy Month' in China." *South Atlantic Quarterly* 81(4): 359–75.

———. 1992. "The Asia-Pacific Idea: Reality and Representation in the Invention of a Regional Structure." *Journal of World History* 3(1): 55–79.

———. 1994. *After the Revolution: Waking to Global Capitalism*. Hanover, Nebr.: Wesleyan University Press.

———. 1995. "Confucius in the Borderlands: Global Capitalism and the Reinvention of Confucianism." *Boundary 2* 22(3): 229–74.

———. 1997. *The Postcolonial Aura: Third World Criticism in the Age of Global Capitalism*. Boulder, Colo.: Westview Press.

Dirlik, Arif, and Maurice Meisner, eds. 1989. *Marxism and the Chinese Experience: Issues in Contemporary Chinese Socialism*. Armonk, N.Y.: M. E. Sharpe.

Divine, Robert A. 1971. *The Cuban Missile Crisis*. Chicago: Quadrangle Books.

Documents on British Policy Overseas. Series 1, vols. 1–4; series 2, vols. 2 and 4. London: Her Majesty's Stationary Office.

Donohue, John. 1983. "Islam and the Search for Arab Identity." in John Esposito, ed., *Voices of Resurgent Islam*. New York: Oxford University Press. 48–65.

Donohue, John, and John Esposito. 1982. *Islam in Transition: Muslim Perspectives*. New York: Oxford University Press.

Donzelot, Jacques. 1984. *L'Invention du social*. Paris: Fayard.

Dorticós, Osvaldo Torrado. 1962. Address to the United Nations General Assembly, October 8, 1962. *Plenary Meetings*, vol. 2, October 5 to November 20. 369–76.

Doty, Roxanne Lynn. 1993. "Foreign Policy as Social Construction: A Post-

Positivist Analysis of U.S. Counterinsurgency Policy in the Philippines."
International Studies Quarterly 37(3): 297–320.

———. 1996a. "Immigration and National Identity: Constructing the Nation." *Review of International Studies* 22(3): 235–55.

———. 1996b. *Imperial Encounters: The Politics of Representation in North-South Relations.* Minneapolis: University of Minnesota Press.

Dougherty, Russell E. 1987. "The Value of ICBM Modernization." *International Security* 12(2): 163–72.

Drainville, André. 1995. "Of Social Spaces, Citizenship, and the Nature of Power in the World Economy." *Alternatives* 20: 51–79.

Dreyer, June. 1976. *China's Forty Millions: Minority Nationalities and National Integration in the People's Republic of China.* Cambridge: Harvard University Press.

Drinnon, Richard. 1990. *Facing West: The Metaphysics of Indian Hating and Empire Building.* New York: Schocken Books.

Duara, Prasenjit. 1995. *Rescuing History from the Nation: Questioning Narratives of Modern China.* Chicago: University of Chicago Press.

Dutt, V. P. 1984. *India's Foreign Policy.* New Delhi: Vikas Publishing House.

Eagleton, Terry. 1991. *Ideology: An Introduction.* London: Verso.

Ebright, Malcolm. 1994. *Land Grants and Lawsuits in Northern New Mexico.* Albuquerque: University of New Mexico Press.

"The Economists' Debate on Their Shortcomings and Tasks." 1949. *Current Digest of the Soviet Press,* vol. 1, no. 11 (April 12), 3–23.

Edelman, Lee. 1993. "Tearooms and Sympathy, or, the Epistemology of the Water Closet." In Henry Abelove, Michèle Aina Barale, and David M. Halperin, eds., *The Lesbian and Gay Studies Reader.* New York: Routledge. 553–74.

Edelman, Murray. 1988. *Constructing the Political Spectacle.* Chicago: University of Chicago Press.

Edwards, Paul. 1996. *The Closed World: Computers and the Politics of Discourse in Cold War America.* Cambridge: MIT Press.

Eichstaedt, Peter H. 1994. *If You Poison Us: Uranium and Native Americas.* Santa Fe, N.Mex.: Red Crane Books.

Eisenhower, Dwight D. 1945. "National Strength Is a Necessity." Address to the American Legion National Commanders, Chicago, November 20. In *Vital Speeches of the Day,* December 1. 108–10.

———. 1959a. "Security in the Free World." Radio-TV address to the nation, March 16. In *Documents on American Foreign Relations, 1959.* New York: Harper and Brothers, for the Council on Foreign Relations, 1960. 24–34.

———. 1959b. "Talk in Parliament." Texts of the Eisenhower speeches to

India's Parliament and at Delhi University, *New York Times,* December 11, 15.

Electronic Frontier Foundation (EFF). 1990a. Mission Statement. [Text file] URL http://www.eff.org/pub/EFF/mission.eff (visited May 18, 1995).

———. 1990b (July 10). "New Foundation Established to Encourage Computer-Based Communications Policies." [Text file] URL http://www.eff.org/pub/EFF/Historical/eff-founded.announce (visited May 18, 1995).

———. 1995 (August 3). "EFF Online Business Community Sponsors." [WWW document] URL http://www.eff.org/sponsors/sponsors.html (visited May 31, 1996).

———. 1996a. (February 1). "Your Constitutional Rights Have Been Sacrificed for Political Expediency: EFF Statement on 1996 Telecommunications Regulation Bill." [Text file] URL http://www.eff.org/pub/Alerts/cda_020296_eff.statement (visited May 31, 1996).

———. 1996b (March 13). "EFF Board, Staff and Volunteers—Biographical Information." [Text file] URL http://www.eff.org/pub/EFF/bios.eff (visited May 31, 1996).

Elmer-Dewitt, Philip. 1994. "Battle for the Soul of the Internet." *Time* 144(4) (July 25): 50–56.

EPIC Alert. 1994. Vol. 1, no. 4, July 21. [On-line serial] FTP cpsr.org/cpsr/alert/EPIC_Alert_1.04 (visited May 18, 1995).

Eriksen, Thomas Hylland, and Iver B. Neumann. 1993. "International Relations as a Cultural System: An Agenda for Research." *Cooperation and Conflict* 28(3): 233–64.

Escobar, Arturo. 1994. "Welcome to Cyberia: Notes on the Anthropology of Cyberculture." *Current Anthropology* 35(3): 211–31.

———. 1995. *Encountering Development: The Making and Unmaking of the Third World.* Princeton, N.J.: Princeton University Press.

Esposito, John. 1991. *Islam and Politics.* 3d ed. Syracuse, N.Y.: Syracuse University Press.

Etzold, Thomas H., and John Lewis Gaddis, eds. 1978. *Containment: Documents on American Policy and Strategy, 1945–1950.* New York: Columbia University Press.

Evans-Pritchard, Edward Evan. 1937. *Witchcraft, Oracles and Magic among the Azande.* Oxford: Oxford University Press.

———. 1940. *The Nuer: A Description of Modes of Livelihood and Political Institutions of a Nilotic People.* Oxford: Clarendon Press.

Evans-Pritchard, Edward Evan, and Meyer Fortes. 1958. *African Political Systems.* London: Oxford University Press.

Export Institute of New Zealand. 1996. *Export Outlook News,* March. [WWW document] URL http://www.nzwwa.com/business/ex-importers/export/news_march96/index.htm (visited June 26, 1997).

Farber, David. 1995. "Living in the Global Information Infrastructure: Some Concerns." *Computer-Mediated Communication Magazine* 2(4) (April 1). [WWW document] URL http://sunsite.unc.edu/cmc/mag/1995/apr/farber.html (visited March 5, 1996).

Fay, Brian. 1975. *Social Theory and Political Practice.* London: George Allen and Unwin.

Feierman, Steven. 1990. *Peasant Intellectuals: Anthropology and History in Tanzania.* Madison: University of Wisconsin Press.

Feldman, Allen. 1991. *Formations of Violence: The Narrative of the Body and Political Terror in Northern Ireland.* Chicago: University of Chicago Press.

Foerstel, Lenora, and Angela Gilliam. 1992. *Confronting the Margaret Mead Legacy: Scholarship, Empire and the South Pacific.* Philadelphia: Temple University Press.

"The Foreign Devil." 1995. *Business World* (New Delhi), August 23–September 5, 38–48.

Forrest, Suzanne. 1989. *The Preservation of the Village: New Mexico's Hispanics and the New Deal.* Albuquerque: University of New Mexico Press.

Forsberg, Randall. 1982. "A Bilateral Nuclear Weapons Freeze." *Scientific American* 247(5): 52–61.

———. 1984. "The Freeze and Beyond: Confining the Military to Defense as a Route to Disarmament." *World Policy Journal* 1(2): 285–318.

———. 1987. "Abolishing Ballistic Missiles." *International Security* 12(1): 190–96.

Foster, Hal. 1983. *The Anti-Aesthetic: Essays on Postmodern Culture.* Port Townsend, Wash.: Bay Press.

Foucault, Michel. 1973. *The Order of Things: An Archaeology of the Human Sciences.* New York: Vintage Books.

———. 1979. *Discipline and Punish: The Birth of the Prison.* Translated by Alan Sheridan. New York: Vintage Books.

———. 1980a. *The History of Sexuality.* Vol. 1, An Introduction. New York: Vintage Books.

———. 1980b. *Power/Knowledge.* New York: Pantheon Books.

———. 1989. *Résumés des cours 1970–1982.* Paris: Julliard.

———. 1991. "Governmentality." In Graham Burchell, Colin Gordon, and Peter Miller, eds., *The Foucault Effect: Studies in Governmentality.* Chicago: University of Chicago Press. 87–104.

Frankel, Boris. 1997. "Beyond Labourism and Socialism: How the Australian Labour Party Developed the Model of 'New Labour.'" *New Left Review* 221: 3–33.

Fridling, Barry, and John Harvey. 1988–89. "On the Wrong Track? An

Assessment of MX Rail Garrison Basing." *International Security* 13(3): 113–41.

Friedman, Jonathan. 1994. *Cultural Identity and Global Process*. London: Sage Publications.

Fromkin, David. 1989. *A Peace to End All Peace: The Fall of the Ottoman Empire and the Creation of the Middle East*. New York: Avon Books.

Gaddis, John Lewis. 1982. *Strategies of Containment: A Critical Appraisal of Postwar American National Security Policy*. New York: Oxford University Press.

———. 1992–93. "International Relations Theory and the End of the Cold War." *International Security* 17(3): 5–58.

Galison, Peter. 1997. *Image and Logic: A Material Culture of Microphysics*. Chicago: University of Chicago Press.

"Gandhi as a 'Reactionary Utopian.'" 1949. *Current Digest of the Soviet Press*, vol. 1, no. 37 (October 11), 3–7.

García, Cristina. 1992. *Dreaming in Cuban*. New York: Ballantine Books.

Gardner, Richard. 1970. *¡Grito! Reis Tijerina and the New Mexico Land Grant War of 1967*. New York: Harper Colophon Books.

Garthoff, Raymond L. 1987. *Reflections on the Cuban Missile Crisis*. Washington, D.C.: Brookings Institute.

Geertz, Clifford. 1973. *The Interpretation of Cultures: Selected Essays*. New York: Basic Books.

George, Jim. 1994. *Discourses of Global Politics: A Critical (Re)Introduction to International Relations*. Boulder, Colo.: Lynne Rienner.

Gerges, Fawaz A. 1994. *The Superpowers and the Middle East: Regional and International Politics, 1955–1967*. Boulder, Colo.: Westview Press.

Gershoni, Israel, and James P. Jankowski. 1995. *Redefining the Egyptian Nation, 1930–1945*. Cambridge: Cambridge University Press.

Gibson, Phillip. 1996. "Right Place, Right Time—Our Future with Asia." *Issues,* Bell Gully Biddle Weir Newsletter, November 13. [WWW document] URL http://www.bgbw.co.nz/publish/issues9602.htm (visited February 5, 1997).

Gibson, William. 1984. *Neuromancer*. New York: Ace Books.

Giuricin, Gianni. 1993. *Se questa è liberazione*. Trieste: Italo Svevo.

Glass, Matthew. 1993. *Citizens against the MX: Public Languages in the Nuclear Age*. Urbana: University of Illinois Press.

Goldstein, Judith, and Robert O. Keohane, eds. 1993. *Ideas and Foreign Policy: Beliefs, Institutions, and Political Change*. Ithaca, N.Y.: Cornell University Press.

Gong, Gerrit. 1984. *The Standard of "Civilization" in International Society*. Oxford: Clarendon Press.

Gopal, S. 1984. *Jawaharlal Nehru: A Biography*. Vol. 3. Cambridge: Harvard University Press.

Gordon, Bernard K. 1960. *New Zealand Becomes a Pacific Power*. Chicago: University of Chicago Press.

Gottemoeller, Rose. 1988–89. "Finding Solutions to SLCM Arms Control Problems." *International Security* 13(3): 175–83.

"Govt. Considering Legal Option on Polls in Kashmir: U.S. Harbouring 'Evil Designs' in J & K: Chavan." 1995. *The Hindu*, December 5, 1.

Gow, James. 1992. *Legitimacy and the Military: The Yugoslav Crisis*. London: Pinter.

Gramsci, Antonio. 1971. *Selections from the Prison Notebooks*. Edited and translated by Quintin Hoare and Geoffrey Nowell Smith. New York: International Publishers.

Greenblatt, Stephen. 1991. *Marvelous Possessions: The Wonder of the New World*. Chicago: University of Chicago Press.

Greif, Stuart William, ed. 1995a. *Immigration and National Identity in New Zealand: One People, Two Peoples, Many Peoples?* Palmerston North, New Zealand: Dunmore Press.

———. 1995b. "Introduction. The Interweaving Themes of New Zealand Immigration." In Stuart William Greif, ed., *Immigration and National Identity in New Zealand: One People, Two Peoples, Many Peoples?* Palmerston North, New Zealand: Dunmore Press. 7–20.

Grinde, Donald, and Bruce Johansen. 1995. *Ecocide of Native America: Environmental Destruction of Indian Lands and Peoples*. Santa Fe, N.Mex.: Clear Light Books.

Gromyko, Anatoliia. 1971. "The Caribbean Crisis, Part I: The U.S. Government's Preparation of the Caribbean Crisis," and "The Caribbean Crisis, Part II: Diplomatic Efforts by the U.S.S.R. to Eliminate the Crisis." Reprinted in Ronald R. Pope, ed., *Soviet Views of the Cuban Missile Crisis*. Washington, D.C.: University Press of America, 1982. 161–226.

Grovogui, Siba N'Zatioula. 1996. *Sovereigns, Quasi Sovereigns, and Africans*. Minneapolis: University of Minnesota Press.

Gupta, Akhil. 1992. "The Song of the Nonaligned World: Transnational Identities and the Reinscription of Space in Late Capitalism." *Cultural Anthropology* 7(1): 63–79.

———. 1995. "Blurred Boundaries: The Discourse of Corruption, the Culture of Politics, and the Imagined State." *American Ethnologist* 22(2): 375–402.

Gupta, Akhil, and James Ferguson. 1992. "Beyond 'Culture': Space, Identity, and the Politics of Difference." *Cultural Anthropology* 7(1): 6–23.

———. 1997a. *Anthropological Locations: Boundaries and Grounds of a Field Science*. Berkeley: University of California Press.

———. 1997b. *Culture, Power, Place: Explorations in Critical Anthropology*. Durham, N.C.: Duke University Press.

Gupta, Shekar. 1994. "Indo-US Relations: Enter the Heavyweights." *India Today* (New Delhi) (October 31): 48–51.

Gupta, Surendra K. 1988. *Stalin's Policy Towards India 1946–1953*. New Delhi: South Asian Publishers.

Gusterson, Hugh. 1991. "Endless Escalation: The Cold War as Postmodern Narrative." *Tikkun* 6(5): 45–92.

———. 1993. "Realism and the International Order after the Cold War." *Social Research* 60(2): 279–300.

———. 1995. "NIF-ty Exercise Machine." *Bulletin of the Atomic Scientists* (September–October): 22–26.

———. 1996. *Nuclear Rites: A Weapons Laboratory at the End of the Cold War*. Berkeley: University of California Press.

Haas, Peter M., ed. 1992. "Knowledge, Power, and International Policy Coordination." Special issue of *International Organization* 46(1).

Haddad, Yvonne Y. 1980. "The Arab-Israeli Wars, Nasserism and Islamic Identity." In John Esposito, ed., *Islam and Development: Religion and Sociopolitical Change*. Syracuse, N.Y.: Syracuse University Press. 106–30.

———. 1992. "Islamists and the 'Problem of Israel': The 1967 Awakening." *Middle East Journal* 46(2): 266–85.

———. 1996. "Islamist Perceptions of U.S. Policy in the Middle East." In David W. Lesch, ed., *The Middle East and the United States: A Historical and Political Reassessment*. Boulder, Colo.: Westview Press. 419–37.

Halbwachs, Maurice. 1992. *On Collective Memory*. Translated by Lewis Coser. Chicago: University of Chicago Press.

Hale, Charles. 1994. *Resistance and Contradiction: Miskitu Indians and the Nicaraguan State, 1894–1987*. Stanford, Calif.: Stanford University Press.

Hall, Stuart. 1985. "Signification, Representation, Ideology: Althusser and the Post-Structuralist Debates." *Critical Studies in Mass Communication* 2(2): 91–114.

———. 1986. "The Problem of Ideology—Marxism without Guarantees." *Journal of Communication Inquiry* 10(2): 28–44.

———. 1988. "The Toad in the Garden: Thatcherism among the Theorists." In Cary Nelson and Lawrence Grossberg, eds., *Marxism and the Interpretation of Culture*. Urbana: University of Illinois Press. 35–73.

———. 1996. "When Was 'the Postcolonial'? Thinking at the Limit." In Iain Chambers and Lidia Curti, eds., *The Post-Colonial Question: Common Skies, Divided Horizons*. London: Routledge. 242–60.

Halliday, Fred. 1995. "The End of the Cold War and International Relations: Some Analytic and Theoretical Conclusions." In Ken Booth and

Steve Smith, eds., *International Relations Theory Today,* State College: Pennsylvania State University Press. 38–61.

Hannerz, Ulf. 1989. "Notes on the Global Ecumene." *Public Culture* 1(2): 66–75.

Hanson, Randel D. 1994. "Enduring Prospects for Radioactive Reservations: The Monitored Retrievable Storage Plan, the Department of Energy, and American Indians." Paper delivered at the American Studies Association Annual Meeting, Nashville, Tennessee, October 27–30.

———. 1997. "Dependent Sovereignty: American Indians, Nuclear Waste, and the New World Order." In George Marcus, ed., *Corporate Futures.* Chicago: University of Chicago Press.

Haraway, Donna. 1988. "Situated Knowledges: The Science Question in Feminism and the Privilege of Partial Perspective." *Feminist Studies* 14(3): 575–99.

———. 1990. *Primate Visions: Gender, Race, and Nature in the World of Modern Science.* New York: Routledge.

———. 1991. *Simians, Cyborgs and Women: The Reinvention of Nature.* New York: Routledge.

Haring, Donald R. 1994. "Internetworking with Transmission Control Protocol/Internet Protocol." In Fritz E. Froelich et al., eds., *The Encyclopedia of Telecommunications.* Vol. 9. New York: Marcel Dekker. 459–90.

Harries, Owen. 1993. "The Collapse of 'the West': The Separation of Europe and America." *Foreign Affairs* 72(4): 41–53.

Hawke, Gary. 1996. "Foreword." In Malcolm McKinnon, *Immigrants and Citizens: New Zealanders and Asian Immigration in Historical Context.* Wellington: Institute of Policy Studies. i–ii.

Hayden, Robert. 1994. "Recounting the Dead: The Rediscovery and Redefinition of Wartime Massacres in Late- and Post-Communist Yugoslavia." In Rubie Watson, ed., *Memory, History and Opposition under State Socialism.* Santa Fe, NMex.: School of American Research Press. 167–84.

"The Heart of India." 1959. *New York Times,* December 10, 38.

Henry, Shannon. 1995. "Colonizing the Internet." *Washington Technology Online,* November 23. [WWW document] URL http://www.wtonline. com/wtonline/issues/1995_NOVEMBER_23/cover/cover1.html_5129-6 (visited May 3, 1996).

Herken, Gregg. 1985. *Counsels of War.* New York: Alfred A. Knopf.

Herman, Edward S., and Noam Chomsky. 1989. *Manufacturing Consent: The Political Economy of the Mass Media.* New York: Pantheon Books.

Hermann, Charles F., ed. 1972. *International Crises: Insights from Behavioral Research.* New York: Free Press.

Herz, John. 1951. *Political Realism and Political Idealism: A Study in Theories and Realities.* Chicago: University of Chicago Press.

Herzfeld, Michael. 1993. *The Social Production of Indifference: Exploring the Symbolic Roots of Western Bureaucracy.* Chicago: University of Chicago Press.

Heuser, Beatrice. 1989. *Western "Containment" Policies in the Cold War: The Yugoslav Case, 1948–53.* London: Routledge.

Hicks, Donald. 1987. "ICBM Modernization: Consider the Alternatives." *International Security* 12(2): 173–81.

Hoadley, Steve. 1992. *The New Zealand Foreign Affairs Handbook.* 2d ed. Auckland: Oxford University Press.

Hobsbawm, Eric, and Terence Ranger, eds. 1983. *The Invention of Tradition.* New York: Cambridge University Press.

Hoffman, Lance J. 1995. "Encryption Policy for the Global Information Infrastructure." Invited Keynote Address to the Eleventh International Conference on Information Security, May 9–12, Capetown, South Africa. [WWW document] URL http://www.seas.gwu.edu/seas/instctsp/DOCS/PAPERS/ictsp-95-01.html (visited April 30, 1996).

Hoffman, Stanley. 1977. "An American Social Science: International Relations." *Daedalus* 106(3): 41–60.

———. 1986. "On the Political Psychology of Peace and War: A Critique and an Agenda." *Political Psychology* 7(1): 1–21.

Hogan, Michael J., ed. 1992. *The End of the Cold War: Its Meaning and Implications.* New York: Cambridge University Press.

Horsman, Reginald. 1981. *Race and Manifest Destiny: The Origins of American Racial Anglo Saxonism.* Cambridge: Harvard University Press.

Hourani, Albert. 1983. *Arabic Thought in the Liberal Age, 1798–1939.* Cambridge: Cambridge University Press.

Hovsepian, Nubar. 1995. "Competing Identities in the Arab World." *Journal of International Affairs* 49(1): 1–24.

Huang Yu and Huang Fangping. 1990. *Yaozu* (The Yao nationality). Beijing: Renmin Chubanshe.

Huang Yu and Li Weixin. 1983. *Guangxi Yaozu shehui lishi diaocha* (Investigation of the social history of the Guangxi Yao). Nanning: Guangxi Minzu Chubanshe.

Huat, Chua Beng. 1996. "Culturalisation of Economy and Politics in Singapore." In Richard Robison, ed., *Pathways to Asia: The Politics of Engagement.* St. Leonards, NSW: Allen and Unwin. 87–107.

Hung Chang-tai. 1985. *Going to the People: Chinese Intellectuals and Folk Literature, 1918–1937.* Cambridge: Harvard University Press.

Hunt, Michael. 1987. *Ideology and U.S. Foreign Policy.* New Haven: Yale University Press.

Huntington, Samuel. 1993. "The Clash of Civilizations." *Foreign Affairs* 72(3): 22–49.

International Physicians for the Prevention of Nuclear War and the Institute for Energy and Environmental Research (IPPNW and IEER). 1991. *Radioactive Heaven and Earth: The Health and Environmental Effects of Nuclear Weapons Testing in, on, and above the Earth.* New York: Apex Press.

———. 1992. *Plutonium: Deadly Gold of the Nuclear Age.* Cambridge, Mass.: International Physicians Press.

"The International Traffic in Arms Regulations" (ITAR). 1992. *Code of Federal Regulations (CFR),* Title 22 (Foreign Relations), chapter 1 (Department of State), Parts 120–30 (Subchapter M: International Traffic in Arms Regulations). [WWW document] URL http://www.epic.org/crypto/export_controls/itar.html (visited November 28, 1998).

———. 1997. *Code of Federal Regulations (CFR),* Title 22 (Foreign Relations), chapter 1 (Department of State), Parts 120–30 (Subchapter M: International Traffic in Arms Regulations). [WWW document] URL http://www.fas.org/spp/starwars/offdocs/itar/index.html (visited November 19, 1998).

Ip, Manying. 1995. "Chinese New Zealanders. Old Settlers and New Immigrants." In Stuart William Greif, ed., *Immigration and National Identity in New Zealand: One People, Two Peoples, Many Peoples?* Palmerston North, New Zealand: Dunmore Press. 161–99.

Islamoglu-Inan, Huri, ed. 1987. *The Ottoman Empire and the World Economy.* Cambridge: Cambridge University Press.

Jackson, Robert H. 1990. *Quasi-States: Sovereignty, International Relations and the Third World.* Cambridge: Cambridge University Press.

Jaimes, M. Annette, ed. 1992. *The State of Native America: Genocide, Colonization, and Resistance.* Boston: South End Press.

Janis, Irving L. 1983. *Groupthink: Psychological Studies of Policy Decisions and Fiascos.* 2d ed. Boston: Houghton Mifflin.

The Jargon File. 1994 (May 10). Version 2.9.12 [Computer program]. FTP ftp.std.com/obi/Nerd.Humor/webster/jargon.

Jensen, Kenneth M., ed. 1993. *Origins of the Cold War: The Novikov, Kennan and Roberts "Long Telegrams" of 1946.* Washington, D.C.: United States Institute of Peace.

Jervis, Robert. 1978. "Cooperation under the Security Dilemma." *World Politics* 30(2): 167–214.

Job, Brian. 1992. "The Insecurity Dilemma: National, Regime and State Securities in the Third World." In Brian Job, ed., *The Insecurity Dilemma: National Security of Third World States.* Boulder, Colo.: Lynne Rienner. 11–36.

Johnston, Alistair Iain. 1995. "Thinking about Strategic Culture." *International Security* 19(4): 32–64.

Kahn, Robert E. 1990. Electronic transcript of interview by Judy O'Neill, April 24, in "Role of DARPA/IPTO in the Development of Computer Science Oral History Collection." Minneapolis: Charles Babbage Institute, University of Minnesota.

Kamiya, Matake. 1995. " 'Asia Fever'—No More Than Cupboard Love?" *Asia 2000 Foundation of New Zealand* 3: 3.

Kaplan, Fred. 1983. *Wizards of Armageddon*. New York: Simon and Schuster.

Kapor, Mitchell. 1993. "Where Is the Digital Highway Really Heading? The Case for a Jeffersonian Information Policy." *Wired*, 1.3. [Text file] URL http://www.eff.org/pub/GII_NII/nii_kapor_eff_wired.article (visited May 31, 1996).

Kapur, Harish. 1972. *The Soviet Union and the Emerging Nations: A Case Study of Soviet Policy Towards India*. London: Michael Joseph.

Kardelj, Edvard. 1953. *Trieste and Yugoslav-Italian Relations*. New York: Yugoslav Information Center.

Karmi, Ghada. 1991. "Saddam's Support." *Marxism Today* 23(4): 26–27.

Karn, Phil. 1996 (December 26). "Karn v. US Department of State— The Applied Cryptography Case." [WWW document] URL http://www. qualcomm.com/people/pkarn/export/index.html (visited January 14, 1996).

Karpat, Kemal H. 1996. "The Ottoman Rule in Europe from the Perspective of 1994." In Vojtech Mastny and R. Craig Norton, eds., *Turkey between East and West: New Challenges for a Rising Regional Power*. Boulder, Colo.: Westview Press. 1–44.

Kasper, Wolfgang. 1990. *Populate or Languish? Rethinking New Zealand's Immigration Policy*. Wellington: New Zealand Business Roundtable.

Katyal, K. K. 1995. "U.S. Embassy Denies Chavan's Charge." *The Hindu*, December 6, 1.

Katzenstein, Peter, ed. 1996. *The Culture of National Security: Identity and Norms in World Politics*. New York: Columbia University Press.

Kaviraj, Sudipta. 1992. "The Imaginary Institution of India." In Partha Chatterjee and Gyan Pandey, eds., *Subaltern Studies*, vol. 7. Delhi: Oxford University Press. 1–39.

Kelsey, Jane. 1994. "Restructuring the Nation: The Decline of the Colonial Nation-State and Competing Nationalisms in Aotearoa/New Zealand." In Peter Fitzpatrick, ed., *Nationalism, Racism and the Rule of Law*. Aldershot: Dartmouth Publishing Company. 177–94.

———. 1995. *Economic Fundamentalism*. London: Pluto Press.

———. 1996. "From Flagpoles to Pine Trees: Tino Rangatiratanga and

Treaty Policy Today." In Paul Spoonley, David Pearson, and Cluny Macpherson, eds., *Nga Patai: Racism and Ethnic Relations in Aotearoa/ New Zealand*. Palmerston North, New Zealand: Dunmore Press. 177–201.

Kennan, George F. 1946. Moscow Embassy Telegram 511 ("The Long Telegram"), February 22. Reprinted in Thomas H. Etzold and John Lewis Gaddis, eds., *Containment: Documents on American Policy and Strategy, 1945–1950*. New York: Columbia University Press, 1978. 152–55.

Kennedy, John F. 1961a. "Address before the American Society of Newspaper Editors," April 20. In *Public Papers of the Presidents, John F. Kennedy, 1961*. Washington, D.C.: U.S. Government Printing Office, 1962. 304–6.

———. 1961b. "Address in New York before the General Assembly of the United Nations," September 25. In *Public Papers of the Presidents, John F. Kennedy, 1961*. Washington, D.C.: U.S. Government Printing Office, 1962. 618–26.

———. 1961c. "Address to the Thirty-Ninth Annual Convention of the National Association of Broadcasters," May 8. In *Public Papers of the Presidents, John F. Kennedy, 1961*. Washington, D.C.: U.S. Government Printing Office, 1962. 367–70.

———. 1961d. "Special Message to Congress on Urgent National Needs," May 25. In *Public Papers of the Presidents, John F. Kennedy, 1961*. Washington, D.C.: U.S. Government Printing Office, 1962. 396–406.

———. 1962a. "Kennedy's Cuba Statement," September 4. *New York Times*, September 5, 2.

———. 1962b. "Transcript of the President's News Conference on Foreign and Domestic Matters," September 13. *New York Times*, September 14, 12.

———. 1962c. "The U.S. Response to the Soviet Military Buildup in Cuba." Report to the American People, October 22. Department of State Publication 7449, Inter-American Series 80. Washington, D.C.: U.S. Government Printing Office, 1962.

Kennedy, Robert F. 1971. *Thirteen Days: A Memoir of the Cuban Missile Crisis*. New York: W. W. Norton.

Keohane, Robert O. 1988. "International Institutions: Two Approaches." *International Studies Quarterly* 32(4): 379–96.

Keohane, Robert O., and Lisa Martin. 1995. "The Promise of Institutionalist Theory." *International Security* 20(1): 39–52.

Khalidi, Rashid. 1991. "Arab Nationalism: Historical Problems in the Literature." *American Historical Review* 96(5): 1363–73.

Khalidi, Rashid, Lisa Anderson, Mohammed Muslih, and Reeva Simon, eds.

1991. *The Origins of Arab Nationalism.* New York: Columbia University Press.

Khalil, Muhammad. 1962. *The Arab States and the Arab League: A Documentary Record.* Vol. 2, *International Affairs.* Beirut: Khayats.

Khouri, Philip. 1991. "Continuity and Change in Syrian Political Life: The Nineteenth and Twentieth Centuries." *American Historical Review* 96(5): 1374–95.

Khrushchev, Nikita. 1956a. Speech by N. S. Khrushchev at citywide meeting in Bangalore, November 26, 1955 (*Pravda*, November 28, 1955, 1; *Izvestia*, November 29, 1955, condensed text). Reproduced in "Bulganin and Khrushchev Visit Asia—II," *Current Digest of the Soviet Press*, vol. 7, no. 48 (January 11), 5–6.

———. 1956b. Speech by N. S. Khrushchev at Indian-Soviet Society Reception in Bombay, November 24, 1955 (*Pravda* and *Izvestia*, November 26, 1955, 1–2, condensed text). Reproduced in "Bulganin and Khrushchev Visit Asia—II," *Current Digest of the Soviet Press*, vol. 7, no. 48 (January 11), 3–4.

———. 1956c. Speech by N. S. Khrushchev at Mandalay Airport, Burma (*Pravda*, December 6, 1955, 1; *Izvestia*, December 7, 1955, 3, condensed text). Reproduced in "Bulganin and Khrushchev Visit Asia—III," *Current Digest of the Soviet Press*, vol. 7, no. 49 (January 18), 6.

———. 1956d. Speech by N. S. Khrushchev on his visit to Bhakra-Nangal on November 22, 1955 (by special TASS correspondent. *Pravda* and *Izvestia*, November 23, 1955, 1, condensed text). Reproduced in "Bulganin and Khrushchev Visit Asia—I," *Current Digest of the Soviet Press*, vol. 7, no. 47 (January 4), 9.

———. 1956e. Speech by N. S. Khrushchev on trip to India, Burma, and Afghanistan, (*Pravda* and *Izvestia*, December 30, 1955, 3–5, condensed text). Reproduced in "Supreme Soviet: Khrushchev's Report on Asia Trip," *Current Digest of the Soviet Press*, vol. 7, no. 52 (February 8), 14–20.

———. 1956f. Speech by N. S. Khrushchev to the Indian Parliament (*Pravda* and *Izvestia*, November 22, 1955, 2, condensed text). Reproduced in "Bulganin and Khrushchev Visit Asia—I," *Current Digest of the Soviet Press*, vol. 7, no. 47 (January 4), 5–7.

———. 1961. "Transcript of Khrushchev's News Conference on U.S. Plane and Other Issues." *New York Times*, July 13, 6.

———. 1970. *Khrushchev Remembers.* With an introduction, commentary and notes by Edward Crankshaw, translated and edited by Strobe Talbot. New York: Bantam Books.

Kiernan, Victor, 1988. *The Lords of Human Kind: Black Man, Yellow Man, and White Man in an Age of Empire.* London: Cresset Library.

Kim, Gye-Dong. 1993. *Foreign Intervention in Korea*. Aldershot: Dartmouth Publishing Company.

Klare, Michael. 1995. *Rogue States and Nuclear Outlaws: America's Search for a New Foreign Policy*. New York: Hill and Wang.

Klein, Bradley. 1994. *Strategic Studies and World Order*. Cambridge: Cambridge University Press.

Kleinrock, Leonard. 1990. Electronic transcript of interview by Judy O'Neill, April 3, in "Role of DARPA/IPTO in the Development of Computer Science Oral History Collection." Minneapolis: Charles Babbage Institute, University of Minnesota.

Kline, David. 1994. "Infobahn Warrior." *Wired* 2.07: 86–90, 130–31.

Kolko, Gabriel. 1980. *Confronting the Third World: United States Foreign Policy, 1945–1980*. New York: Pantheon Books.

Koops, Bert-Jaap. 1996 (January 12). "Crypto Law Survey." [WWW document] URL http://cwis.kub.nl/~frw/people/koops/lawsurvy.htm (visited April 30, 1996).

Korany, Bahgat, Paul Noble, and Rex Brynen, eds., 1993. *The Many Faces of National Security in the Arab World*. New York: St. Martin's Press.

Kramer, Mark. 1989–90. "Beyond the Brezhnev Doctrine: A New Era in Soviet-East European Relations?" *International Relations* 14(3): 25–67.

Kratochwil, Friedrich. 1993. "The Embarrassment of Changes: Neo-Realism as the Science of Realpolitik without Politics." *Review of International Studies* 19(1): 63–80.

Krause, Keith, and Michael Williams. 1996. "Broadening the Agenda of Security Studies: Politics and Methods." *Mershon International Studies Review* 40(2): 229–54.

Krause, Keith, and Michael Williams, eds. 1997. *Critical Security Studies: Concepts and Cases*. Minneapolis: University of Minnesota Press.

Kreisberg, Paul H. 1985. "India after Indira." *Foreign Affairs* 63(4): 873–91.

Krippendorf, Ekkehart. 1987. "The Dominance of American Approaches in International Relations." *Millennium* 16(2): 207–14.

Krishna, Gopal. 1984. "India and the International Order: Retreat from Idealism." In Hedley Bull and Adam Watson, eds, *The Expansion of International Society*. Oxford: Clarendon Press. 269–87.

Krishna, Sankaran. 1993. "The Importance of Being Ironic: A Postcolonial View on Critical International Relations Theory." *Alternatives* 18: 385–417.

———. 1994. "Inscribing the Nation: Nehru and the Politics of Identity in India." In Stephen Rosow, Naeem Inayatullah, and Mark Rupert, eds., *The Global Economy as Political Space*. Boulder, Colo.: Lynne Rienner. 189–202.

———. 1996. "Cartographic Anxiety: Mapping the Body Politic in India."

In Michael J. Shapiro and Hayward R. Alker, eds., *Challenging Boundaries: Global Flows, Territorial Identities*. Minneapolis: University of Minnesota Press. 193–214.

Kritzman, Lawrence, ed. 1988. *Politics, Philosophy, Culture: Interviews and Other Writings*. New York: Routledge.

Krol, Ed. 1994. *The Whole Internet: User's Guide and Catalog*. 2d ed. Sebastopol, Calif.: O'Reilly and Associates.

Kuhn, Thomas. 1962. *The Structure of Scientific Revolutions*. Chicago: University of Chicago Press.

Kuletz, Valerie. 1998. *The Tainted Desert: Environmental Ruin in the American West*. New York: Routledge Press.

Kunhi Krishnan, T. V. 1974. *The Unfriendly Friends: India and America*. New Delhi: Indian Book Company.

Kux, Dennis. 1992. *India and the United States: Estranged Democracies 1941–1991*. Washington D.C.: National Defense University Press.

Lacan, Jacques. 1977. *Écrits: A Selection*. Translated by Alan Sheridan. New York: W. W. Norton.

Laclau, Ernesto. 1977. *Politics and Ideology in Marxist Theory*. London: Verso.

Laclau, Ernesto, and Chantal Mouffe. 1987. "Post-Marxism without Apologies." *New Left Review* 166: 79–106.

LaDuke, Winona, and Ward Churchill. 1985. "Native America: The Political Economy of Radioactive Colonialism." *Journal of Ethnic Studies* 13(3): 107–32.

Laffey, Mark, and Himadeep Muppidi. 1993. "The Social Construction of Identity and Interest in Postcolonial States: Foreign Policies of India and New Zealand." Paper presented at the Annual Meeting of the International Studies Association, Acapulco, March 23–27.

Lansford, Robert R., Larry D. Adcock, Lucille M. Gentry, and Shaul Ben David. 1995. *The Economic Impact of the Department of Energy on the State of New Mexico, Fiscal Year 1994*. Albuquerque: U.S. Department of Energy, in cooperation with New Mexico State University.

Lapid, Yosef, and Friedrich Kratochwil, eds. 1996. *The Return of Culture and Identity in IR Theory*. Boulder, Colo.: Lynne Rienner.

Larner, Wendy, and Paul Spoonley. 1995. "Post-Colonial Politics in Aotearoa/ New Zealand." In Daiva Stasiulis and Nira Yuval-Davis, eds., *Unsettling Settler Societies: Articulations of Gender, Race, Ethnicity and Class*. London: Sage Publications. 39–64.

Lasswell, Harold D. 1953 [1935]. "Nations and Classes: The Symbols of Identification." In Bernard Berelson and Morris Janowitz, eds., *Reader in Public Opinion and Communication*, enlarged edition. New York: Free Press of Glencoe. 28–42.

Latham, Robert. 1995. "Thinking about Security after the Cold War." *International Studies Notes* 20(3): 9–16.

"Launching of Asia 2000." 1994. *Asia 2000 Foundation of New Zealand* 1: 2–3.

Layne, Christopher. 1994. "Kant or Cant: The Myth of the Democratic Peace." *International Security* 19(2): 5–49.

Lebow, Richard Ned. 1995. "The Long Peace, the End of the Cold War, and the Failure of Realism." In Richard Ned Lebow and Thomas Risse-Kappen, eds., *International Relations Theory and the End of the Cold War.* New York: Columbia University Press. 23–56.

Lebow, Richard Ned, and Thomas Risse-Kappen, eds. 1995. *International Relations Theory and the End of the Cold War.* New York: Columbia University Press.

Lefebvre, Henri. 1991. *The Production of Space.* Translated by Donald Nicholson-Smith. Oxford: Blackwell Publishers.

Leffler, Melvin. 1992. *A Preponderance of Power: National Security, the Truman Administration, and the Cold War.* Stanford, Calif.: Stanford University Press.

Lemoine, Jacques, and Chiao Chien. 1991. *The Yao of South China: Recent International Studies.* Paris: Pangu, Éditions de l'A.F.E.Y.

Lepingwell, John. 1989. "Soviet Strategic Air Defense and the Stealth Challenge." *International Security* 14(2): 64–100.

"Letters to the Editor." 1996. *New Zealand Herald,* April 13, 6.

Levy, Steven. 1993. "Crypto Rebels: Pretty Good Revolution." *Wired* 1.2. [Text file] Wired Ventures, Ltd., URL http://www.eff.org/pub/Privacy/crypto_rebels.article (visited May 18, 1995).

———. 1994. "The Battle of the Clipper Chip." *New York Times Magazine,* June 12, 44–51, 60, 70.

Lewis, Bernard. 1990. "The Roots of Muslim Rage." *Atlantic Monthly* 266(3) (September): 47–63.

Lewontin R. C., Ira Katznelson, Laura Nader, and Noam Chomsky, eds. 1997. *The Cold War and the University: Toward an Intellectual History of the Post–Cold War Years.* New York: New Press.

Limaye, Satu P. 1993. *U.S.—Indian Relations: The Pursuit of Accommodation.* Boulder, Colo.: Westview Press.

Lincoln, Bruce. 1989. *Discourse and the Construction of Society: Comparative Studies of Myth, Ritual, and Classification.* New York: Oxford University Press.

Lipietz, Alain. 1992. *Towards a New Economic Order: Postfordism, Ecology and Democracy.* New York: Oxford University Press.

Lipschutz, Ronnie, ed. 1995. *On Security.* New York: Columbia University Press.

Litzinger, Ralph. 1995. "Making Histories: Contending Conceptions of the Yao Past." In Stevan Harrell, ed., *Cultural Encounters on China's Ethnic Frontiers.* Seattle: University of Washington Press. 117–39.

———. 1998. "Memory Work: Reconstituting the Ethnic in Post-Mao China." *Cultural Anthropology* 13(2): 224–55.

Lodal, Jan. 1987. "SICBM Yes, HML NO." *International Security* 12(2): 182–86.

Los Alamos National Laboratory. 1995. *Institutional Plan, FY 1996–2001.* Los Alamos, N.Mex.: Los Alamos National Laboratory.

Lundestad, Geir. 1989. "Moralism, Presentism, Exceptionalism, Provincialism, and Other Extravagances in American Writings on the Early Cold War Years." *Diplomatic History* 13(4): 527–45.

Lutz, Catherine, and Jane Collins. 1993. *Reading National Geographic.* Chicago: University of Chicago Press.

Lyon, David. 1994. *The Electronic Eye: The Rise of Surveillance Society.* Minneapolis: University of Minnesota Press.

Macaulay, Thomas. 1995. "Minute on Indian Education." Excerpted in Bill Ashcroft, Gareth Griffiths, and Helen Tiffin, eds., *The Post-Colonial Studies Reader.* London: Routledge. 428–30.

McClintock, Anne. 1992. "The Angel of Progress: Pitfalls of the Term 'Post-Colonialism.'" *Social Text* 31/32: 84–98.

McConnell, John M. 1994 (July 8). "NSA Letter to Sen. Hollings." *EFFector Online* 7(12), July 22. [On-line serial] URL http://www.eff.org/pub/EFF/Newsletters/EFFector/HTML/effect07.12.html#nsaletter (visited February 12, 1998).

McCrea, Frances, and Gerald Markle. 1989. *Minutes to Midnight: Nuclear Weapons Protest in America.* Newbury Park, Calif.: Sage.

McKenzie, Alexander A., and David C. Walden. 1991. "ARPANET, the Defense Data Network, and Internet." In Fritz E. Froelich et al., eds., *The Encyclopedia of Telecommunications.* Vol. 1. New York: Marcel Dekker. 341–76.

McKhann, Charles F. 1994. "The Naxi and the Nationalities Question." In Stevan Harrell, ed., *Cultural Encounters on China's Ethnic Frontiers.* Seattle: University of Washington Press. 39–62.

"McKinnon Blasts NZ Press." 1995. *Asia 2000 Foundation of New Zealand* 3: 5.

McKinnon, Don. 1993. "Foreign Policy Making—50 Years on." Speech to the Otago Foreign Policy School, Otago University, May 14. *Ministry of External Relations and Trade Record* 1(11): 30–37.

———. 1996a. "The National Government's Foreign Policy Open and Internationally Engaged." Speech to the Dunedin Institute of International Affairs, Dunedin, September 19. *New Zealand Executive*

Government Speech Archive. [WWW document] http://www.executive. govt.nz/93-96/minister/dpm/dps1909.htm (visited Feburary 5).

———. 1996b. "New Zealand's Relations with Asia: A Vision for the Future." Speech to the Joint New Zealand/Indonesia and Australia/Indonesia Business Councils, Jakarta, July 2. *Ministry of External Relations and Trade Record* 5(2): 32–35.

McKinnon, John. 1995. "Countering Cultural Parsimoniousness." *Asia 2000 Foundation of New Zealand* 2: 3, 9.

McKinnon, Malcolm. 1996. *Immigrants and Citizens: New Zealanders and Asian Immigration in Historical Context.* Wellington: Institute of Policy Studies.

McMahon, Robert J. 1994. *The Cold War on the Periphery: The United States, India and Pakistan.* New York: Columbia University Press.

Madsen, Richard. 1989. "Foreword." In Donald E. MacInnis, ed., *Religion in China Today: Policy and Practice.* Maryknoll, N.Y.: Orbis Books.

Maize, Kennedy. 1995a (August 14). "Lobbying Picks Up on Encryption Policy." [On-line search query] Newsbytes News Network, URL http://professional.infoseek.com/(Wire Services search) (visited January 18, 1996).

———. 1995b (September 6). "Industry Slams Govt's Encryption Export Plan." [On-line search query] Newsbytes News Network, URL http://professional.infoseek.com/(Wire Services search) (visited January 18, 1996).

Majeski, Stephen J., and David J. Sylvan. 1991. "Modeling Theories of Constitutive Relations in Politics." Paper presented at the Twenty-Fifth World Congress of the International Political Science Association, Buenos Aires, July 21–25.

Malhotra, Inder. 1995. "Mind Your Business: The US Will Do Itself a Good Turn by Leaving Indo-Iranian Relations Alone." *Sunday* (Calcutta), December 24–30, 10.

Malinowski, Bronislaw. 1961. *Argonauts of the Western Pacific: An Account of Native Enterprise and Adventure in the Archipelagos of Melanesian New Guinea.* New York: E. P. Dutton.

Malkki, Liisa. 1995. *Purity and Exile: Violence, Memory and National Cosmology among Hutu Refugees in Tanzania.* Chicago: University of Chicago Press.

———. 1996. "Speechless Emissaries: Refugees, Humanitarianism, and Dehistoricization." *Cultural Anthropology* 11(3): 1–28.

Manoff, Robert. 1989. "Modes of War and Modes of Address: The Text of SDI." *Journal of Communication* 39(1): 59–83.

Mansingh, Surjit. 1984. *India's Search for Power: Indira Gandhi's Foreign Policy 1966–1982.* New Delhi: Sage Publications.

Marcus, George E. 1992. "A Broad(er)side to the Canon, Being a Partial Account of a Year of Travel among Textual Communities in the Realm of Humanities Centers, and Including a Collection of Artificial Curiousities." In George E. Marcus, ed., *Rereading Cultural Anthropology.* Durham, N.C.: Duke University Press. 103–23.

———. 1994a. "After the Critique of Ethnography: Faith, Hope, and Charity, but the Greatest of These Is Charity." In Robert Borofsky, ed., *Assessing Cultural Anthropology.* New York: McGraw-Hill. 40–54.

———. 1994b. "On Ideologies of Reflexivity in Contemporary Efforts to Remake the Human Sciences." *Poetics Today* 15(3): 383–404.

———. 1995a. "Ethnography in/of the World System: The Emergence of Multi-Sited Ethnography." *Annual Review of Anthropology* 24: 95–117.

———, ed. 1995b. *Technoscientific Imaginaries: Conversations, Profiles, and Memoirs. Late Editions 2, Cultural Studies for the End of the Century.* Chicago: University of Chicago Press.

Marcus, George E., and Dick Cushman. 1982. "Ethnographies as Texts." *Annual Review of Anthropology* 11: 25–69.

Marcus, George E., and Michael Fischer. 1986. *Anthropology as Cultural Critique: An Experimental Moment in the Human Sciences.* Chicago: University of Chicago Press.

Mardin, Serif. 1962. *The Genesis of Young Ottoman Thought: A Study in the Modernization of Turkish Political Ideas.* Princeton, N.J.: Princeton University Press.

Markoff, John. 1993. "Electronics Plan Aims to Balance Government Access with Privacy." *New York Times,* April 16. [Text file], in Clipper Introduction (compilation), URL http://www.eff.org/pub/Privacy/Clipper/clipper.intro (visited May 18, 1995).

May, Lary, ed. 1989. *Recasting America: Culture and Politics in the Age of Cold War.* Chicago: University of Chicago Press.

May, Michael, George Bing, and John Steinbruner. 1988. "Strategic Arsenals after START." *International Security* 13(1): 90–133.

Mbembe, Achille. 1992. "The Banality of Power and the Aesthetics of Vulgarity in the Postcolony." *Public Culture* 4(2): 1–30.

Mearsheimer, John. 1990. "Back to the Future: Instability in Europe after the Cold War." *International Security* 15(1): 5–56.

———. 1994–95. "The False Promise of International Institutions." *International Security* 19(3): 5–49.

Meeks, Brock. 1994 (October 20). "*CyberWire Dispatch*: Jacking in from the 'Sooner or Later' Port." [WWW document] URL http://cyberwerks.com:70/oh/cyberwire/cwd/ cwd.94.10.20.html (visited April 6, 1995).

Meinig, D. W. 1993. *The Shaping of America: A Geographical Perspective on 500 Years of History.* Vol. 2. New Haven: Yale University Press.

Menon, K. P. S. 1963. *The Flying Troika.* Bombay: Oxford University Press.

Meyer, Gail E. 1980. *Egypt and the United States: The Formative Years.* Rutherford, N.J.: Farleigh Dickinson University Press.

Meyer, Steven. 1988. "The Sources and Prospects of Gorbachev's New Political Thinking on Security." *International Security* 13(2): 124–63.

Miller, Steven E. 1996. *Civilizing Cyberspace: Policy, Power, and the Information Superhighway.* New York: ACM Press.

Milliken, Jennifer, and David Sylvan. 1996. "Soft Bodies, Hard Targets and Chic Theories: U.S. Bombing Policy in Indochina." *Millennium* 25(2): 321–59.

Mintz, Sidney. 1985. *Sweetness and Power: The Place of Sugar in Modern History.* New York: Viking Press.

Mitchell, Katharyne. 1996. "In Whose Interest? Transnational Capital and the Production of Multiculturalism in Canada." In Rob Wilson and Wimal Dissanayake, eds., *Global/Local: Cultural Production and the Transnational Imaginary.* Durham, N.C.: Duke University Press. 219–51.

Mitchell, Timothy. 1991a. *Colonising Egypt.* 2d ed., Berkeley: University of California Press.

———. 1991b. "The Limits of the State: Beyond Statist Approaches and Their Critics." *American Political Science Review* 85(1): 77–96.

Mittelman, James H., ed. 1996. *Globalization: Critical Reflections.* Boulder, Colo.: Lynne Rienner.

Mohanram, Radhika. 1995. "Biculturalism, Postcolonialism, and Identity Politics in New Zealand: An Interview with Anna Yeatman and Kaye Turner." In Gita Rajan and Radhika Mohanram, eds., *Postcolonial Discourse and Changing Cultural Contests: Theory and Criticism.* Westport, Conn.: Greenwood Press. 189–203.

"Monroe Doctrine Guards West." 1961. *New York Times,* July 13, 3.

Moore-Gilbert, Bart. 1997. *Postcolonial Theory: Contexts, Practices and Politics.* New York: Verso.

Morgenthau, Hans J. 1962. "Negotiations or War?" *New Republic,* November 3, 9.

———. 1978. *Politics among Nations: The Struggle for Power and Peace.* 5th rev. ed. New York: Alfred A. Knopf.

Mouffe, Chantal. 1991. "Democratic Citizenship and the Political Community." In Miami (Ohio) Theory Collective, eds., *Community at Loose Ends.* Minneapolis: University of Minnesota Press. 70–82.

Mowitt, John. 1992. *Text: The Genealogy of an Antidisciplinary Object.* Durham, N.C., and London: Duke University Press.

———. 1996. "Queer Resistance: Michel Foucault and Samuel Beckett's 'The Unnamable.'" *Symploke* 4(1–2): 135–52.

"Munition Tshirt." 1995. [WWW document] West El Paso Information

Network, URL http://colossus.net/wepinsto/wsft_f/wspp_f/wsppts.html (visited January 14, 1996).

Munro, Neil. 1994. "Of Taxes, Taps, and 'Total Encryption.'" *Washington Technology Online,* November 24. [WWW document] URL http://www.wtonline.com/wtonline/issues/1994_NOVEMBER_24/gen_news/gen_news1.html__5129-6 (visited May 3, 1996).

Muppidi, Himadeep. 1995. "The Indian State, Its Brother, the Brother's Ally and the Ally's Other: The Security Dilemma of a Postcolonial State." Manuscript.

Mustin, Henry. 1988–89. "The Sea-Launched Cruise Missile: More Than a Bargaining Chip." *International Security* 13(3): 184–90.

Nadelmann, Ethan. 1993. *Cops across Borders: The Internationalization of U.S. Criminal Law Enforcement.* University Park: Pennsylvania State University Press.

Nader, Laura. 1997. "The Phantom Factor: The Effect of the Cold War on Anthropology." In Noam Chomsky et al., eds., *The Cold War and the University: Toward an Intellectual History of the Post–Cold War Years.* New York: New Press. 107–46.

Nagengast, Carole. 1994. "Violence, Terror, and the Crisis of the State." *Annual Review of Anthropology* 23: 109–36.

Nandy, Ashis. 1983. *The Intimate Enemy: Loss and Recovery of Self under Colonialism.* Delhi: Oxford University Press.

Naqvi, Jawed. 1995. "India Woos Iran, US Frowns." *India West* (California), April 21, 1.

Narayan, Kirin. 1993. "How Native Is a 'Native' Anthropologist?" *American Anthropologist* 95(3): 671–86.

Narula, Sunil. 1995. "Indo-U.S. Ties: A Diplomatic Dichotomy." *Outlook* 1(11) (New Delhi). (December 20): 27–30.

Nathan, James A. 1975. "The Missile Crisis: His Finest Hour Now." *World Politics* 27(2): 256–81.

———, ed. 1992. *The Cuban Missile Crisis Revisited.* New York: St. Martin's Press.

Nathanson, Charles E. 1988. "The Social Construction of the Soviet Threat: A Study in the Politics of Representation." *Alternatives* 13(4): 443–83.

Nehru, Jawarhalal. 1961. *India's Foreign Policy: Selected Speeches, September 1946–April 1961.* New Delhi: Publications Division, Government of India.

New Left Review, ed. 1982. *Exterminism and Cold War.* London: Verso.

New Zealand Now. 1995. *Asian New Zealanders.* Wellington: Statistics New Zealand.

"New Zealand's 'Asia Is Our Future' Issue Should Penetrate the Pubs." 1996. *Asia 2000 Foundation of New Zealand* 7: 6.

Nietschman, Bernard, and William Le Bon. 1987. "Nuclear Weapons States and Fourth World Nations." *Cultural Survival Quarterly* 11(4): 5–7.

Ninkovich, Frank. 1994. *Modernity and Power: A History of the Domino Theory in the Twentieth Century*. Chicago: University of Chicago Press.

Niva, Steve. 1991. "The Battle Is Joined." In Phyllis Bennis and Michel Moushabeck, eds., *Beyond the Storm: A Gulf Crisis Reader*. New York: Olive Branch Press. 55–71.

Norberg, Arthur L., and Judy E. O'Neill. 1992. "A History of the Information Processing Techniques Office of the Defense Advanced Research Projects Agency." With contributions by Kerry J. Freedman. Minneapolis: Charles Babbage Institute, University of Minnesota.

Nordstrom, Carolyn. 1992. "The Dirty War: Civilian Experience of Conflict in Mozambique and Sri Lanka." In Kumar Rupesinghe, ed., *Internal Conflict and Governance*. New York: St. Martin's Press. 27–43.

Nordstrom, Carolyn, and JoAnn Martin, eds. 1992. *The Paths to Domination, Resistance, Terror*. Berkeley: University of California Press.

Nordstrom, Carolyn, and Antonius C. G. M. Robben, eds. 1995. *Fieldwork under Fire: Contemporary Studies of Violence and Survival*. Berkeley: University of California Press.

Nostrand, Richard L. 1992. *The Hispano Homeland*. Norman: University of Oklahoma Press.

Novak, Bogdan C. 1970. *Trieste, 1941–1954: The Ethnic, Political and Ideological Struggle*. Chicago: University of Chicago Press.

Nye, Joseph S., Jr., and Sean M. Lynn-Jones. 1988. "International Security Studies: A Report on a Conference on the State of the Field." *International Security* 12(4): 5–27.

"October 27, 1962: Transcripts of the Meeting of the ExComm." 1987–88. Transcribed by McGeorge Bundy, edited by James Blight. *International Security* 12(3): 30–92.

Offe, Claus. 1984. *Contradictions of the Welfare State*. John Keane, ed. London: Hutchinson.

Offer, Avner. 1989. *The First World War: An Agrarian Interpretation*. Oxford: Clarendon Press.

Ong, Aihwa. 1997. "Chinese Modernities: Narratives of Nation and of Capitalism." In Aihwa Ong and Donald Nonini, eds., *Ungrounded Empires: The Cultural Politics of Modern Chinese Transnationalism*. New York: Routledge. 171–202.

Ong, Aihwa, and Donald Nonini, eds. 1997. *Ungrounded Empires: The Cultural Politics of Modern Chinese Transnationalism*. New York: Routledge.

Ongley, Patrick. 1996. "Immigration, Employment and Ethnic Relations." In Paul Spoonley, David Pearson, and Cluny Macpherson, eds., *Nga*

Patai: Racism and Ethnic Relations in Aotearoa/New Zealand. Palmerston North, New Zealand: Dunmore Press. 13–34.

"Open Sesame." 1994 (April 7). Transcript of the *MacNeil/Lehrer News-Hour,* Public Broadcasting System. [Text file] URL http://www.eff.org/pub/Privacy/macneil-lehrer_crypto.transcript (visited May 18, 1995).

Ortiz, Alfonso. 1969. *The Tewa World: Space, Time Being and Becoming in a Pueblo Society.* Chicago: University of Chicago Press.

Ortiz, Roxanne Dunbar. 1980. *Roots of Resistance: Land Tenure in New Mexico, 1680–1980.* Los Angeles: Chicano Studies Research Center and American Indian Studies Center, UCLA.

Ó Tuathail, Gearóid. 1996. *Critical Geopolitics: The Politics of Writing Global Space.* Minneapolis: University of Minnesota Press.

Ó Tuathail, Gearóid, and John Agnew. 1992. "Geopolitics and Discourse: Practical Geopolitical Reasoning and American Foreign Policy." *Political Geography* 11(2): 190–204.

Owen, Roger. 1981. *The Middle East in the World Economy 1800–1914.* New York: Methuen.

Palat, Ravi Arvind. 1996a. "Curries, Chopsticks and Kiwis: Asian Migration to Aotearoa/New Zealand." In Paul Spoonley, David Pearson, and Cluny Macpherson, eds., *Nga Patai: Racism and Ethnic Relations in Aotearoa/New Zealand.* Palmerston North, New Zealand: Dunmore Press. 35–54.

———. 1996b. "Pacific Century: Myth or Reality?" *Theory and Society* 25: 303–47.

Passerini, Luisa. 1979. "Work, Ideology and Consensus under Italian Fascism." *History Workshop* 8: 82–108.

———. 1987. *Fascism in Popular Memory: The Cultural Experience of the Turin Working Class.* Translated by Robert Lumley and Jude Bloomfield. Cambridge: Cambridge University Press.

Paterson, Thomas G. 1989. *Meeting the Communist Threat: Truman to Reagan.* New York: Oxford University Press.

Patterson, David. 1992. *The Shriek of Silence: A Phenomenology of the Holocaust.* Lexington: University Press of Kentucky.

Pearson, David. 1996. "Crossing Ethnic Thresholds: Multiculturalisms in Comparative Perspective." In Paul Spoonley, David Pearson, and Cluny Macpherson, eds., *Nga Patai: Racism and Ethnic Relations in Aotearoa/New Zealand.* Palmerston North, New Zealand: Dunmore Press. 247–66.

Pemberton, John. 1994. *On The Subject of "Java."* Ithaca, N.Y.: Cornell University Press.

Peretz, Don. 1966. "Israel and the Arab Nations." In Jack H. Thompson and Robert D. Reischauer, eds., *Modernization of the Arab World.* New York: D. Van Nostrand. 166–77.

Perle, Richard. 1987. "Reykjavik as a Watershed in U.S.-Soviet Arms Control." *International Security* 12(1): 175–78.

Perry, Elizabeth. 1992. "Introduction: Chinese Political Culture Revisited." In Jeffrey Wasserstrom and Elizabeth Perry, eds., *Popular Protest and Political Culture in Modern China*. Boulder, Colo.: Westview Press. 1–13.

———. 1994. "Trends in the Study of Chinese Politics: State-Society Relations." *China Quarterly* 139 (September): 704–13.

Peteet, Julie. 1994. "Male Gender and Rituals of Resistance in the Palestinian Intifada: A Cultural Politics of Violence." *American Ethnologist* 21(1): 31–49.

(Il) Piccolo. February 1995–June 1996.

Piscatori, James. 1990. "The West in Arab Foreign Policy." In Robert O'Neill and R. J. Vincent, eds., *The West and the Third World: Essays in Honor of J. D. B. Miller*. New York: St. Martin's Press. 129–52.

———. 1991. "Religion and Realpolitik: Islamic Responses to the Gulf War." In James Piscatori, ed., *Islamic Fundamentalisms and the Gulf Crisis*. Chicago: The Fundamentalisms Project, American Academy of Arts and Sciences. 1–27.

Pope, Ronald, R., ed. 1982. *Soviet Views of the Cuban Missile Crisis*. Washington, D.C.: University Press of America.

Porath, Yehoshua. 1986. *In Search of Arab Unity*. London: Frank Cass.

Posen, Barry. 1993. "The Security Dilemma and Ethnic Conflict." *Survival* 35(1): 27–47.

Postol, Theodore. 1988–89. "Banning Nuclear SLCMs: It Would Be Nice if We Could." *International Security* 13(3): 191–202.

Prakash, Gyan, 1992a. "Can the Subaltern Ride? A Reply to O'Hanlon and Washbrook." *Comparative Studies in Society and History* 34(l): 168–84.

———. 1992b. "Postcolonial Criticism and Indian Historiography." *Social Text* 31/32(10) (nos. 2 and 3): 8–19.

———, ed. 1995. *After Colonialism: Imperial Histories and Postcolonial Displacements*. Princeton, N.J.: Princeton University Press.

Pred, Allan, and Michael John Watts. 1992. *Reworking Modernity: Capitalisms and Symbolic Discontent*. New Brunswick, N.J.: Rutgers University Press.

Privacy International. 1995 (November). Summary of "Big Brother Incorporated: A Report on the International Trade in Surveillance Technology and Its Links to the Arms Industry." [WWW document] URL http://www.privacy.org/pi/reports/big_bro/ (visited January 20, 1996).

"Protests Greet Raphael." 1994. *Asian Recorder,* vol. 40, no. 17 (April 23–29), 23903; New Delhi: Ashish Printers.

"Public Interest Issues in the Telecommunications Act of 1996." 1996 (February). [Text file] Benton Foundation, URL http://cdinet.com/cgi-bin/ lite/Benton/Goingon/telecom-post.html (visited May 31, 1996).

Pulido, Laura. 1996. *Environmentalism and Economic Justice: Two Chicano Struggles in the Southwest.* Tucson: University of Arizona Press.

Rabel, Roberto G. 1988. *Between East and West: Trieste, the United States and the Cold War, 1941–1954.* Durham, N.C.: Duke University Press.

Rabinow, Paul. 1977. *Reflections on Fieldwork in Morocco.* Berkeley: University of California Press.

———, ed. 1984. *The Foucault Reader.* New York: Pantheon Books.

Rafael, Vicente L. 1994. "The Cultures of Areas Studies in the United States." *Social Text* 41: 91–111.

RAND. 1996 (March 5). "Strategic War . . . in Cyberspace." [WWW document] URL http://www.rand.org/publications/RB/RB7106/RB7106.html (visited May 3, 1996).

Reich, Robert. 1991. *The Work of Nations: Preparing Ourselves for Twenty-First Century Capitalism.* New York: Alfred A. Knopf.

Remnek, Richard B. 1975. *Soviet Scholars and Soviet Foreign Policy: A Case Study in Soviet Policy Towards India.* Durham, N.C.: Carolina Academic Press.

Rheingold, Howard. 1993. *Virtual Communities: Homesteading on the Electronic Frontier.* Reading, Mass.: Addison-Wesley.

Rhodes, Richard. 1986. *The Making of the Atomic Bomb.* New York: Simon and Schuster.

———. 1995. *Dark Sun: The Making of the Hydrogen Bomb.* New York: Simon and Schuster.

Richardson, James L. 1988. "Crisis Management: A Critical Appraisal." In Gilbert R. Winham, ed., *New Issues in International Crisis Management.* Boulder, Colo.: Westview Press. 13–36.

Rieff, David. 1995. *Slaughterhouse.* New York: Simon and Schuster.

———. 1996. "The Institution That Saw No Evil." *New Republic,* February 12, 19–24.

Ringmar, Erik. 1996. "On the Ontological Status of the State." *European Journal of International Relations.* 2(4): 439–66.

Roberts, Lawrence G. 1989. Electronic transcript of interview by Arthur L. Norberg, April 4, in "Role of DARPA/IPTO in the Development of Computer Science Oral History Collection." Minneapolis: Charles Babbage Institute, University of Minnesota.

Robinson, James A. 1972. "Crisis: An Appraisal of Concepts and Theories." In Charles F. Hermann, ed., *International Crises: Insights from Behavioral Research.* New York: Free Press. 20–35.

Rodger, Will. 1996 (May 18). "White House Reviving Clipper Wiretap Plan."

[WWW document] Interactive Enterprises, LLC, URL http://www.zdnet. com/intweek/daily/960518y.html (visited May 21, 1996).

Romero, Hilario. 1995. "Los Alamos, D.C.: Growing Up under a Cloud of Secrecy." *Race, Poverty, and the Environment.* 5(3 and 4): 9–10.

Rose, Leo. 1990. "India's Foreign Relations: Reassessing Basic Policies." In Marshall M. Bouton and Philip Oldenburg, eds., *India Briefing: 1990.* Boulder, Colo.: Westview Press. 51–75.

Rosenbaum, Robert J. 1981. *Mexicano Resistance in the Southwest: "The Sacred Right of Self-Preservation."* Austin: University of Texas Press.

Rosenthal, Debra. 1990. *At the Heart of the Bomb: The Dangerous Allure of Weapons Work.* New York: Addison-Wesley.

Rothman, Hal K. 1992. *On Rims and Ridges: The Los Alamos Area since 1880.* Lincoln: University of Nebraska Press.

Roy, Olivier. 1994. *The Failure of Political Islam.* Cambridge: Harvard University Press.

Rubinstein, Robert, and Mary Foster, eds. 1988. *The Social Dynamics of Peace and Conflict: Culture in International Society.* Boulder, Colo.: Westview Press.

———. 1989. *Peace and War: Cross-Cultural Perspectives.* New Brunswick, N.J.: Transaction.

Ruggie, John. 1993. "Territoriality and Beyond: Problematizing Modernity in International Relations." *International Organization* 47(1): 139–74.

Ruina, Jack. 1987. "More Is Not Better." *International Security* 12(2): 187–92.

Rupert, Mark. 1997. "Globalization and the Reconstruction of Common Sense in the U.S." In Stephen Gill and James Mittelman, eds., *Innovation and Transformation in International Studies.* Cambridge: Cambridge University Press. 138–52.

Rusk, Dean. 1962. "American Republics Act to Halt Soviet Threat to Hemisphere." Statement to the Council of the Organization of American States, October 23. *Department of State Bulletin,* November 12, 720–23.

Ryan, Henry Butterfield. 1982. *The Vision of Anglo-America: The US-UK Alliance and the Emerging Cold War, 1943–1946.* Cambridge: Cambridge University Press.

Saco, Diana. 1998. "Cyberspace and Democracy: Spaces and Bodies in the Age of the Internet," Ph.D. dissertation, University of Minnesota.

Said, Edward W. 1979. *Orientalism.* New York: Random House.

———. 1994. *Culture and Imperialism.* New York: Vintage Books.

Sando, Joe S. 1992. *Pueblo Nations: Eight Centuries of Pueblo Indian History.* Santa Fe, N.Mex.: Clear Light Publishers.

Sayyid, Bobby. 1994. "Sign o' Times: Kaffirs and Infidels Fighting the Ninth

Crusade." In Ernesto Laclau, ed., *The Making of Political Identities.* New York: Verso. 264–86.

Schaffer, Howard. 1993. *Chester Bowles: New Dealer in the Cold War.* London: Harvard University Press.

Schein, Louisa. 1992. "Reconfiguring the Dominant: Multidimensionality in the Manufacture of the Miao." Paper presented at the Ninety-First Annual Meeting of the American Anthropological Association, San Francisco, December 2–6.

————. 1996. "The Other Goes to Market: The State, the Nation, and Unruliness in Contemporary China." *Identities* 2(3): 197–222.

Schell, Orville. 1995. "China—The End of an Era." *Nation,* July 17–24, 84–98.

Schelling, Thomas. 1987. "Abolition of Ballistic Missiles." *International Security* 12(1): 179–83.

Schlesinger, Arthur M. 1965. *A Thousand Days: John F. Kennedy in the White House.* Boston: Houghton Mifflin.

————. 1973. *The Imperial Presidency.* Boston: Houghton Mifflin.

Schofield, John. 1994. "Pretty Good Phil: The Story of Philip Zimmermann, Author of Pretty Good Privacy." *Keep Out* 1(1) (August–September). [On-line serial/compressed], available on *CompuServe* [on-line commercial server] (Go NCSA/ Infosecurity Forum/Library 3: News/Case Studies/ Filename: KPOUT1.ZIP).

Schwartau, Winn. 1994. *Information Warfare: Chaos on the Electronic Superhighway.* New York: Thunder's Mouth Press.

Schwartz, John. 1995. "Privacy Program: An On-Line Weapon? Inventor May Face Indictment for Encryption Software Sent Abroad." *Washington Post,* April 3, final edition, sec. A, 1. [Text file] available on *CompuServe* [on-line commercial service] (Go Newspaper Archives/*Washington Post*).

Schwartz, Stephan I., ed. 1995. " 'Four Trillion Dollars and Counting': The Nuclear Weapons Cost Study Project Committee, the Brookings Institution." *Bulletin of the Atomic Scientists* (November–December): 32–52.

Seale, Patrick. 1986. *The Struggle for Syria: A Study of Post-War Arab Politics, 1945–1958.* New Haven: Yale University Press.

Seddon, David. 1991. "Politics and the Gulf Crisis: Government and Popular Responses in the Maghreb." In Haim Bresheeth and Nira Yuval-Davis, eds., *The Gulf War and the New World Order.* London: Zed Books. 104–16.

Seeger, Joseph C. 1995. "Crisis Research: The State of the Field." *International Studies Notes* 20(3): 17–22.

Shapiro, Michael J. 1988. "The Construction of the Central American Other: The Case of 'Guatemala.' " In *The Politics of Representation: Writing*

Practices in Biography, Photography, and Policy Analysis. Madison: University of Wisconsin Press. 89–123.

———. 1994. "Moral Geographies and the Ethics of Post-Sovereignty." *Public Culture* 6(3): 479–502.

———. 1997. *Violent Cartographies: Mapping Cultures of War.* Minneapolis: University of Minnesota Press.

Shapiro, Michael J., and Hayward R. Alker, eds. 1996. *Challenging Boundaries: Global Flows, Territorial Identities.* Minneapolis: University of Minnesota Press.

Sharabi, Hisham. 1970. *Arab Intellectuals and the West: The Formative Years, 1875–1914.* Baltimore: Johns Hopkins University Press.

Shohat, Ella. 1992. "Notes on the 'Post-Colonial.'" *Social Text* 31/32: 99–113.

Shue, Vivian. 1988. *The Reach of the State: Sketches of the Chinese Body Politic.* Stanford, Calif.: Stanford University Press.

Simmons, Marc. 1979. "History of the Pueblos since 1821." In Alfonso Ortiz, ed., *Handbook of North American Indians,* vol. 9, *Southwest.* Washington, D.C.: Smithsonian Institution.

Sinclair, Keith. 1980. *A History of New Zealand.* Revised and enlarged edition. Harmondsworth, Middlesex: Penguin Books.

Singh, Anita Inder. 1993. *The Limits of British Influence: South Asia and the Anglo-American Relationship, 1947–56.* New York: St. Martin's Press.

Siu, Helen. 1989a. *Agents and Victims in South China: Accomplices in Rural Revolution.* New Haven: Yale University Press.

———. 1989b. "Recycling Rituals: Politics and Popular Culture in Contemporary Rural China." In Perry Link, Richard Madsen, and Paul G. Pickowicz, eds., *Unofficial China: Popular Culture and Thought in the People's Republic of China.* Boulder, Colo.: Westview Press. 121–37.

Sloss, Leon. 1987. "A World without Ballistic Missiles." *International Security* 12(1): 184–89.

Sluga, Glenda. 1994. "Trieste: Ethnicity and the Cold War, 1945–54." *Journal of Contemporary History* 29: 285–303.

Small, Dennis. 1996. *The Cost of Free Trade: Aotearoa/New Zealand at Risk.* Christchurch: Campaign Against Foreign Control of Aotearoa.

Smith, Paul. 1997. *Millennial Dreams: Contemporary Culture and Capital in the North.* London: Verso.

Snyder, Glenn. 1990. "Alliance Theory: A Neorealist First Cut." *Journal of International Affairs.* 44(1): 103–23.

Snyder, Jack. 1987–88. "The Gorbachev Revolution: A Waning of Soviet Expansionism?" *International Security* 12(3): 93–131.

Soguk, Nevzat. 1996. "Transnational/Transborder Bodies: Resistance, Accommodation, and Exile in Refugee and Migration Movements on the U.S.-Mexican Border." In Michael J. Shapiro and Hayward R. Alker, eds., *Challenging Boundaries: Global Flows, Territorial Identities.* Minneapolis: University of Minnesota Press. 285–325.

Solo, Pam. 1988. *From Protest to Policy: Beyond the Freeze to Common Security.* Cambridge, Mass.: Ballinger.

Song Enzhang. 1991. "The Family System and Its Ethos among the Yunnan Yao." In Jacques Lemoine and Chiao Chien, eds., *The Yao of South China: Recent International Studies.* Paris: Pangu, Éditions de l'A.F.E.Y. 229–47.

Sorenson, Theodore. 1965. *Kennedy.* New York: Harper and Row.

Spanier, John. 1973. *American Foreign Policy since World War II.* New York: Praeger.

Spiro, David. 1994. "The Insignificance of the Liberal Peace." *International Security* 19(2): 50–86.

Spivak, Gayatri Chakravorty. 1987. *In Other Worlds: Essays in Cultural Politics.* New York: Methuen.

Spurr, David. 1993. *The Rhetoric of Empire: Colonial Discourse in Journalism, Travel Writing and Imperial Administration.* Durham, N.C.: Duke University Press.

Starn, Orin. 1992. "Missing the Revolution: Anthropologists and the War in Peru." In George Marcus, ed., *Rereading Cultural Anthropology.* Durham, N.C.: Duke University Press. 152–80.

Steel, Ronald. 1969. "End Game." *New York Review of Books,* March 13, 15–22.

Steering Committee of the Joint Evaluation of Emergency Assistance to Rwanda. 1996. *Joint Evaluation of Emergency Assistance to Rwanda, book 2, Early Warning and Conflict Management.* In *The International Response to Conflict and Genocide: Lessons from the Rwanda Experience.* 5 vols. Copenhagen: Steering Committee of the Joint Evaluation of Emergency Assistance to Rwanda (March).

Stephanson, Anders. 1995. *Manifest Destiny: American Expansionism and the Empire of Right.* New York: Hill and Wang.

Sterling, Bruce. 1992. *The Hacker Crackdown: Law and Disorder on the Electronic Frontier.* New York: Bantam.

Stevenson, Adlai. 1962. "U.N. Security Council Hears U.S. Charges of Soviet Military Buildup in Cuba." Speech to the United Nations Security Council, October 23. *Department of State Bulletin,* November 12, 723–34.

Stewart, Kathleen. 1988. "Nostalgia—A Polemic." *Cultural Anthropology* 3(3): 227–41.

Stoffle, Richard, and Michael J. Evans. 1988. "American Indians and Nuclear Waste Storage: The Debate at Yucca Mountain, Nevada." *Policy Studies Journal* 16(4): 751–67.

Stone, I. F. 1966. "The Brink." *New York Review of Books,* April, 4, 12–16.

Stranahan, Paul. 1996 (April 24). "Telecommunications Act of 1996." [WWW document] Jones International, Ltd., URL http://www.digitalcentury.com/encyclo/update/telcom1.html (visited May 31, 1996).

Sullivan, Erin. 1996 (March 26). "Regulation of Internet Access in China." [WWW document] URL http://www.ta.doc.gov/aptp/china/NETREG.HTM (visited May 3, 1996).

Swett, Charles. 1995 (July 17). "Strategic Assessment: The Internet." Paper prepared for the Office of the Assistant Secretary of Defense for Special Operations and Low-Intensity Conflict (Policy Planning). [WWW document] URL http://www.fas.org/cp/swett.html (visited May 30, 1996).

Sylvester, Christine. 1994. *Feminist Theory and International Relations in a Postmodern Era.* Cambridge: Cambridge University Press.

Taussig, Michael. 1992. *The Nervous System.* New York and London: Routledge.

Taylor, Bryan C. 1992. "The Politics of the Nuclear Text: Reading Robert Oppenheimer's Letters and Recollections." *Quarterly Journal of Speech* 78: 429–49.

Taylor, Peter. 1990. *Britain and the Cold War: 1945 as Geopolitical Transition.* London: Pinter Publishers.

"Text of U.N.-Cuban Notes." 1962. October 27. *New York Times,* October 28, 31.

Textor, Robert, ed. 1991. *The Peace Dividend as Cultural Concept.* Special issue of *Human Peace* 9(1–3).

Thakur, Ramesh, and Carlyle Thayer. 1992. *Soviet Relations with India and Vietnam.* New York: St. Martin's Press.

Thomas, Nicholas. 1994. *Colonialism's Culture: Anthropology, Travel and Government.* Princeton, N.J.: Princeton University Press.

Thomas, Raju G. C. 1993. *South Asian Security in the 1990s: Adelphi Paper 278.* London: International Institute for Strategic Studies.

Thompson, E. P. 1982. *Beyond the Cold War: A New Approach to the Arms Race and Nuclear Annihilation.* New York: Pantheon Books.

———. 1985. *The Heavy Dancers: Writings on War, Past and Future.* New York: Pantheon Books.

Thompson, E. P., and Dan Smith, eds. 1981. *Protest and Survive.* New York: Monthly Review Press.

———. 1986. *Prospectus for a Habitable Planet.* London: Penguin.

Thompson, Robert Smith. 1992. *The Missiles of October: The Declassified Story of John F. Kennedy and the Cuban Missile Crisis.* New York: Simon and Schuster.

Thornton, Thomas Perry. 1988. "India's Foreign Relations: Problems along the Borders." In Marshall M. Bouton and Philip Oldenburg, eds., *India Briefing: 1988.* Boulder, Colo.: Westview Press. 57–83.

Thorson, Stuart, and Donald Sylvan. 1982. "Counterfactuals and the Cuban Missile Crisis." *International Studies Quarterly* 26(4): 539–71.

Tilly, Charles. 1985. "War Making and State Making as Organized Crime." In Peter B. Evans, Dietrich Rueschemeyer, and Theda Skocpol, eds., *Bringing the State Back In.* Cambridge: Cambridge University Press. 169–91.

Todorov, Tzvetan. 1982. *The Conquest of America: The Question of the Other.* Translated by Richard Howard. New York: Harper and Row.

Tomlinson, John. 1991. *Cultural Imperialism: A Critical Introduction.* Baltimore: Johns Hopkins University Press.

Toomay, John. 1987. "Strategic Forces Rationale—A Lost Discipline?" *International Security* 12(2): 193–202.

Treaty on the Non-Proliferation of Nuclear Weapons. 1968. July 1, 21 U.S.T. 483, T.I.A.S. 6839, 729 U.N.T.S. 161.

"Triumph in Asia." 1959. *New York Times,* December 13, 1E.

Trouillot, Michel-Rolph. 1995. *Silencing the Past: Power and the Production of History.* Boston: Beacon Press.

True, Jacqui. 1996. "'Fit Citizens for the British Empire?': Class-ifying Racial and Gendered Subjects in 'Godzone' (New Zealand)." In Brackette F. Williams, ed., *Women Out of Place: The Gender of Agency and the Race of Nationality.* New York: Routledge. 103–28.

Truman, Harry S. 1945. "Special Message to the Congress Recommending the Establishment of a Department of National Defense," December 19. In *Public Papers of the Presidents, Harry S. Truman, 1945.* Washington, D.C.: U.S. Government Printing Office, 1961. 546–60.

———. 1947. "Special Message to the Congress on the Marshall Plan," December 19. In *Public Papers of the Presidents, Harry S. Truman, 1947.* Washington, D.C.: U.S. Government Printing Office, 1963. 515–29.

———. 1950. "Radio and Television Report to the American People on the Situation in Korea," September 1. *Public Papers of the Presidents, Harry S. Truman, 1950.* Washington, D.C.: U.S. Government Printing Office, 1965. 609–14.

———. 1952 (October 24). Memorandum to Secretaries of State and Defense establishing the National Security Agency. [Text file] FTP cpsr.org/cpsr/privacy/crypto/nsa_charter.txt (visited May 18, 1995).

———. 1956. *Memoirs.* 2 vols. Garden City, N.Y.: Doubleday.

Turner, Paul, and David Pitt. 1989. *The Anthropology of War and Peace: Perspectives on the Nuclear Age.* South Hadley, Mass.: Begin and Garvey.

Ubois, Jeff. 1995. "Ruling Class." Interview with the Executive Director of the Internet Society. *Internet World* (January): 60–65.

Unger, Leonard, and Kristina Segulja. 1990. *The Trieste Negotiations.* Washington, D.C.: Foreign Policy Institute, Paul H. Nitze School of Advanced International Studies, no. 16.

United Nations Security Council. 1994a. *Security Council Resolution Renewing the Mandate of UNOSOM II until 30 September 1994.* S/Res/923, May 31.

———. 1994b. *Statement on the Conditions for the Deployment and Renewal of Peacekeeping Operations.* S/PRST/1994/22, May 3.

U.S. Department of Energy. 1995a. *Closing the Circle on the Splitting of the Atom: The Environmental Legacy of Nuclear Weapon Production in the United States and What the DOE Is Doing about It* (DOE, Office of Environmental Management).Washington, D.C.: U.S. Government Printing Office.

———. 1995b. *Dual Axis Radiographic Hydrodynamic Test Facility: Final Environmental Impact Statement.* 2 vols. (DOE/EIS-0228). Washington D.C.: U.S. Government Printing Office.

———. 1995c. *Estimating the Cold War Mortgage* (FDOE/EM-0232). Washington, D.C.: U.S. Government Printing Office.

———. Secretary of Energy Advisory Board Task Force. 1995. *Alternative Futures for the Department of Energy National Laboratories* ("The Galvin Report"). Washington, D.C.: Department of Energy.

U.S. Department of Justice. 1994 (February 4). "Attorney General Makes Key Escrow Encryption Announcements." [Text file] FTP cpsr.org/cpsr/privacy/crypto/clipper/reno_key_escrow_announcement_feb_94.txt (visited May 18, 1995).

U.S. Department of State. 1961. "Forces of Change in Latin America." Department of State Publication 7157, Inter-American Series 64. Washington, D.C.: U.S. Government Printing Office.

———. 1969. *Foreign Relations of the United States, Diplomatic Papers, 1945.* Vol. 6, *The British Commonwealth; The Far East.* Washington, D.C.: U.S. Government Printing Office.

———. 1972a. *Foreign Relations of the United States, 1947.* Vol. 3, *The British Commonwealth.* Washington, D.C.: U.S. Government Printing Office.

———. 1972b. *Foreign Relations of the United States, 1947.* Vol. 6, *The Far East.* Washington, D.C.: U.S. Government Printing Office.

———. 1973. *Foreign Relations of the United States, 1947.* Vol. 1, *General; The United Nations.* Washington, D.C.: U.S. Government Printing Office.

———. 1974. *Foreign Relations of the United States, 1948.* Vol. 3, *Western Europe.* Washington, D.C.: U.S. Government Printing Office.

———. 1975. *Foreign Relations of the United States, 1948.* Vol. 5, *The Near East, South Asia, and Africa.* Washington, D.C.: U.S. Government Printing Office.

———. 1976a. *Foreign Relations of the United States, 1950*. Vol. 2, *The United Nations; the Western Hemisphere*. Washington, D.C.: U.S. Government Printing Office.

———. 1976b. *Foreign Relations of the United States, 1950*. Vol. 7, *Korea*. Washington, D.C.: U.S. Government Printing Office.

———. 1977a. *Foreign Relations of the United States, 1950*. Vol. 1, *National Security Affairs; Foreign Economic Policy*. Washington, D.C.: U.S. Government Printing Office.

———. 1977b. *Foreign Relations of the United States, 1951*. Vol. 6, *Asia and the Pacific*. Washington, D.C.: U.S. Government Printing Office.

———. 1983. *Foreign Relations of the United States, 1952–54*. Vol. 11, *Africa and South Asia*. Washington, D.C.: U.S. Government Printing Office.

———. 1987. *Foreign Relations of the United States, 1955–57*. Vol. 8, *South Asia*. Washington, D.C.: U.S. Government Printing Office.

———. 1994. *Foreign Relations of the United States, 1961–63*. Vol. 13, *West Europe and Canada*. Washington, D.C.: U.S. Government Printing Office.

———. 1996 (December 30). Amendments to the International Traffic in Arms Regulations, *Federal Register*, 61(251), 61 FR 68633. [Text file] URL http://www.cdt.org/crypto/clipper311/961230_itar.txt (visited November 28, 1998).

———. Bureau of Public Affairs. 1962. "Developments in the Cuban Situation." *Foreign Affairs Outlines*, Department of State Publication 7454, Inter-American Series 81. Washington, D.C.: U.S. Government Printing Office, October.

U.S. General Accounting Office. 1995. "Department of Energy: National Laboratories Need Clearer Missions and Better Management, Report to the Secretary of Energy" (GAO/RCED-95-10). Washington, D.C.: U.S. Government Printing Office.

U.S. House. 1993a. Legislation to Amend the Export Administration Act of 1979. 103d Cong., 1st sess., HR 3627. *Congressional Record* 139 (November 24). [Text file] URL http://www.eff.org/pub/Privacy/ITAR_export/cantwell_hr3627.bill (visited May 18, 1995).

———. 1993b. Remarks by Representative Maria Cantwell (Democrat, Washington) on Legislation to Amend the Export Administration Act of 1979 (HR 3627). 103d Cong., 1st sess. *Congressional Record* 139 (November 24). [Text file] URL http://www.eff.org/pub/Privacy/ITAR_export/cantwell_hr3627.summary (visited May 18, 1995).

U.S. National Security Council. 1948. NSC 7, "The Position of the United States with Respect to Soviet-Directed World Communism," March 30. Reprinted in Thomas H. Etzold and John Lewis Gaddis, eds., *Contain-*

ment: Documents on America Policy and Strategy, 1945–1950. New York: Columbia University Press, 1978. 164–69.

———. 1950. NSC 68, "United States Objectives and Programs for National Security," April 14. Reprinted in Thomas H. Etzold and John Lewis Gaddis, eds., *Containment: Documents on America Policy and Strategy, 1945–1950.* New York: Columbia University Press, 1978. 385–442.

"U.S. Questions Kashmir Accession." 1993. *Asian Recorder,* volume 39, no. 47 (November 19–25): 23554–55; New Delhi: Ashish Printers.

U.S. Security Policy Board. 1995 (December). "White Paper on Information Infrastructure Assurance." [WWW document] URL http://www.fas.org/sgp/whitepap.html (visited May 30, 1996).

U.S. Senate. Committee on Foreign Relations. 1984. *United States Security Interests in South Asia: (Pakistan—India).* Staff Report, April. Washington, D.C.: U.S. Government Printing Office.

Utvik, Bjorn Olav. 1995. "Filling the Vacant Throne of Nasser: The Economic Discourse of Egypt's Islamist Opposition." *Arab Studies Quarterly* 17(4): 29–54.

Vasil, Raj, and Hong-Key Yoon. 1996. *New Zealanders of Asian Origin.* Wellington: Institute of Policy Studies.

Verdery, Katherine. 1991. *Nationalist Ideology under Socialism: Identity and Cultural Politics in Ceausescu's Romania.* Berkeley: University of California Press.

———. 1996. *What Was Socialism, What Comes Next?* Princeton, N.J.: Princeton University Press.

Visweswaran, Kamala. 1994. *Fictions of Feminist Ethnography.* Minneapolis: University of Minnesota Press.

Walder, Andrew. 1986. *Communist Neo-Traditionalism: Work and Authority in Chinese Industry.* Berkeley: University of California Press.

Walker, Ranginui. 1990. *Ka Whawhai Tonu Matou: Struggle without End.* Auckland: Penguin Books.

———. 1995. "Immigration Policy and the Political Economy of New Zealand." In Stuart William Greif, ed., *Immigration and National Identity in New Zealand: One People, Two Peoples, Many Peoples?* Palmerston North, New Zealand: Dunmore Press. 282–302.

Walker, R. B. J. 1984. "World Politics and Western Reason: Universalism, Pluralism, Hegemony." In R. B. J. Walker, ed., *Culture, Ideology and World Order.* Boulder, Colo.: Westview Press. 182–216.

Waller, Douglas C. 1987. *Congress and the Nuclear Freeze: An Inside Look at the Politics of a Mass Movement.* Amherst: University of Massachusetts Press.

———. 1995. "Onward Cyber Soldiers." *Time* 146(8) (August 21): 38–44.

Walt, Stephen M. 1987. *The Origins of Alliances*. Princeton, N.J.: Princeton University Press.

———. 1991. "The Renaissance of Security Studies." *International Studies Quarterly* 35(2): 211–39.

Waltz, Kenneth. 1979. *Theory of International Politics*. Reading, Mass.: Addison-Wesley.

———. 1993. "The Emerging Structure of International Politics." *International Security* 18(2): 44–79.

Weber, Cynthia. 1995. *Simulating Sovereignty: Intervention, the State, and Symbolic Exchange*. Cambridge: Cambridge University Press.

Weber, Max. 1962. "Theodicy, Salvation, and Rebirth." In Max Weber, *Sociology of Religion*, translated by Ephraim Fischoff. Boston: Beacon Press. 138–50.

Weigle, Marta, ed. 1975. *Hispanic Villages of Northern New Mexico: A Reprint of Volume II of the 1935 Tewa Basin Study, with Supplementary Materials*. Santa Fe, N.Mex.: The Lightning Tree.

Welch, David A., and James G. Blight. 1987–88. "The Eleventh Hour of the Cuban Missile Crisis: An Introduction to the ExComm Transcripts." *International Security* 12(3): 5–92.

Welch, Jasper. 1989. "Assessing the Value of Stealthy Aircraft and Cruise Missiles." *International Security* 14(2): 47–63.

Weldes, Jutta. 1993. "Constructing National Interests: The Logic of U.S. National Security in the Post-War Era." Ph.D. dissertation, University of Minnesota.

———. 1996. "Constructing National Interests." *European Journal of International Relations* 2(3): 275–318.

———. 1999. *Constructing National Interests: The United States and the Cuban Missile Crisis*. Minneapolis: University of Minnesota Press.

Weldes, Jutta, and Diana Saco. 1996. "Making State Action Possible: The U.S. and the Discursive Construction of 'the Cuban Problem,' 1960–1994." *Millennium* 25(2): 361–95.

Wendt, Alex. 1987. "The Agent-Structure Problem in International Relations Theory." *International Organization* 41(3): 335–70.

———. 1992. "Anarchy Is What States Make of It: The Social Construction of Power Politics." *International Organization* 46(2): 391–425.

"What You Can Do." 1994. *Wired* 2.04: 48–49.

White, Keith. 1995. "The Killer App: *Wired* Magazine, Voice of the Corporate Revolution." *The Baffler* 6: 23–28.

White, Richard. 1994 (March 17). "An Invitation to a Debate: Encryption on the Electronic Frontier." [Text file] available on *CompuServe* [on-line commercial service] (Go NCSA/Infosecurity Forum/Library 6: Encryption/ Filename: ENCRYPT).

White House. 1994a (February 4). "Fact Sheet: Public Encryption Management." [Text file] URL http://www.eff.org/pub/Privacy/Clipper/wh_clipper.factsheet (visited May 18, 1995).

———. 1994b (February 4). Statement of the Press Secretary announcing adoption of the Clipper Standard. [Text file] URL http://www.eff.org/pub/Privacy/Clipper/wh_press_secy.statement (visited May 18, 1995).

———. 1996a. "Text of President Clinton's Executive Order [and Related Documents] Implementing Clipper 3.1.1." [WWW document] URL http://www.cdt.org/crypto/clipper311/clipper311exo.html (visited November 30, 1998).

———. 1996b. "Vice President Announces Special Envoy for Cryptography." [WWW document] URL http://www.cdt.org/crypto/clipper311/961115_WH_pr.html (visited November 28, 1998).

"White House Tapes and Minutes of the Cuban Missile Crisis: ExComm Meetings October 1962." 1985. *International Security* 10(1): 164–203.

Williams, Michael C. 1992. "Rethinking the 'Logic' of Deterrence." *Alternatives* 17: 67–93.

Williams, Raymond. 1983. *Keywords*. London: Fontana.

Willis, Kim. 1995. "Best B.E.T.: Arms and the Man?" *USA Today,* November 13, final edition, sec. LIFE, 01D. [Text file] available on *CompuServe* [on-line commercial service] (Go *USA Today* Archives).

Wohlforth, William. 1994–95. "Realism and the End of the Cold War." *International Security* 19(3): 9–129.

Wolf, Eric. 1982. *Europe and the People without History*. Berkeley: University of California Press.

"World Competitiveness On-Line: New Zealand." 1997. International Institute for Management Development [WWW document] URL: http://www.imd.ch/wcy/profiles/nz/html (visited June 12, 1997).

Wright, Quincy. 1942. *A Study of War*. Chicago: University of Chicago Press.

Yanagisako, Sylvia, and Carol Delaney. 1995. *Naturalizing Power: Essays in Feminist Cultural Analysis*. New York: Routledge.

Yang, Mayfair. 1988. "The Modernity of Power in the Chinese Socialist Order." *Cultural Anthropology* 3(4): 408–27.

———. 1994. *Gifts, Favors, and Banquets: The Art of Social Relationships in China*. Ithaca, N.Y.: Cornell University Press.

Yeatman, Anna. 1994. "State and Community." In Andrew Sharp, ed., *Leap into the Dark: The Changing Role of the State in New Zealand since 1984*. Auckland: Auckland University Press. 206–24.

Zabusky, Stacia. 1995. *Launching Europe: An Ethnography of the European Cooperation in Space Science*. Princeton, N.J.: Princeton University Press.

Zakon, Robert Hobbes. 1994. "Hobbes' Internet Timeline v1.3." [WWW document] URL http://tig.com/IBC/Timeline.html (visited April 6, 1995).

Zerriffi, Hisham, and Arjun Makhijani. 1996. "The Stewardship Smokescreen." *Bulletin of Atomic Scientists* (September–October): 22–28.

Zha Jianying. 1995. *China Pop: How Soap Operas, Tabloids, and Bestsellers Are Transforming a Culture.* New York: New Press.

Zhang Youjun. 1986. *Yaozu zhongjiao lunji* (Collected articles on Yao religion). Nanning: Guangxi Yaozu Yanjiuxuehui.

Zimmermann, Philip. 1994a. Foreword to *Protect Your Privacy: The PGP User's Guide* by William Stallings. Reprinted in *Computer Underground Digest* 6(100), November 27. [Text file] URl http://venus.soci.niu.edu/~cudigest/CUDS6/cud6.100 (visited May 21, 1998).

———. 1994b. "PGP User's Guide Volume I: Essential Topics." Version 2.6. [Text file/compressed] URL http://www.eff.org/pub/Net_info/Tools/Crypto/PGP/pgp26doc.zip (visited January 29, 1996).

Contributors

PAMELA BALLINGER is assistant professor of sociology and anthropology at Bowdoin College. She has published articles on Italian fascism, repressed memory, and the Istrian exodus.

MICHAEL N. BARNETT is professor of political science at the University of Wisconsin-Madison. He is the author of *Confronting the Costs of War: Military Power, State, and Society in Egypt and Israel*; *Dialogues in Arab Politics: Negotiations in Regional Order*; and articles on international relations theory, Middle Eastern politics, and the United Nations.

RAYMOND DUVALL is Morse-Alumni Distinguished Teaching Professor of Political Science, and associate director of the Interdisciplinary Center for the Study of Global Change, at the University of Minnesota. His current research focuses on the constitution of authority in discourses of a global economy. His articles have been published in *International Organization, American Political Science Review, International Studies Quarterly, Journal of Conflict Resolution,* and other journals and edited volumes.

HUGH GUSTERSON is associate professor of anthropology and science studies at the Massachusetts Institute of Technology. He is the author of *Nuclear Rites: A Nuclear Weapons Laboratory at the*

413

End of the Cold War, and he writes on the culture of Russian and American nuclear weapons scientists and antinuclear activists, on militarism in popular culture, and on theoretical issues in security studies.

MARK LAFFEY is lecturer in international politics, Department of Political Studies, School of Oriental and African Studies, University of London.

RALPH A. LITZINGER is assistant professor of cultural anthropology at Duke University. His research addresses ethnic minority politics in the context of Chinese socialist and postsocialist nationalism. His book *Writing the Margins: Minority Politics in China at the Cold War's End* is forthcoming.

GEORGE MARCUS is professor and chair of anthropology at Rice University. During the 1980s, he was involved in the critiques of anthropology and the reinvention of critical ethnography through books like *Writing Culture,* which he edited with James Clifford. He assesses the legacies and current possibilities of these critiques in his recent book *Ethnography through Thick and Thin.*

JOSEPH MASCO is a cultural anthropologist who has published essays on gift exchange, colonialism, and the politics of ethnographic representation in *Comparative Studies of Society and History* and *American Anthropologist.* He is currently completing a book that examines how the end of the Cold War has affected concepts of security, experiences of national belonging, and cross-cultural politics around Los Alamos National Laboratory in New Mexico.

JENNIFER MILLIKEN is assistant professor at the Graduate Institute of International Studies in Geneva, Switzerland. She has published discourse studies of U.S. Cold War policy and U.S. intervention in Vietnam, and has researched the Korean War for a book on the social construction of state action. Her current research interest is on the topic "Intervention for Statemaking: The West in Postcolonial State Formation."

JOHN MOWITT teaches in the departments of cultural studies and comparative literature and of English at the University of Minnesota. He has published widely on critical theory and cultural politics. Recently, he completed a second book, *Percussion: Drumming, Beating, Striking.*

HIMADEEP MUPPIDI is an assistant professor in the Institute for Global Studies at the University of Minnesota. He was a visiting assistant professor of political science at the University of Wisconsin-Madison. His dissertation examines the social construction of competitive economic restructuring in the global economy.

STEVE NIVA is a doctoral candidate in political science at Columbia University, a member of the board of the Middle East Research and Information Project (MERIP), and a visiting assistant professor of international relations at Clark University. His dissertation examines the impact of contending constructions of state sovereignty on the Middle East state system during decolonization, including pan-Arabist and Islamist constructions of sovereign authority and international order.

DIANA SACO completed her Ph.D. in political science from the University of Minnesota in 1998. She has published in the *European Journal of International Relations, Millennium* (with Jutta Weldes), and in an edited collection on masculinity and the media. Her forthcoming book explores the democratic possibilities of the Internet from the standpoint of the mediated social spaces produced by people in their online interactions with each other.

JUTTA WELDES is lecturer in international relations at the University of Bristol. Her recent research has focused on U.S. foreign policy, U.S. relations with Cuba, and the role of popular culture in legitimizing U.S. foreign policy. She is the author of *Constructing National Interests: The United States and the Cuban Missile Crisis* (Minnesota, 1999), and has published in the *European Journal of International Relations, Mershon International Studies Review, Millennium,* and *Theory and Society.*

Index

Aaron, David L., 288
Abdulhamid II, Sultan, 155
Acheson, Dean, 103, 104, 109
Advanced Research Projects Agency (ARPA), 266–267
Aflaq, Michel, 159
agency, 18–19, 265, 323
Ahmed, Feroz, 156
al-Afghani, Jamal al-Din, 155
al-Asad, Hafiz, 167
al-Banna, Hassan, 160, 168
Alger, Horatio, 243
Allied Military Government of Venezia Giulia (AMG), 64, 74, 75, 76
Allison, Graham, 36
al-Tahtawi, Rafiʻ, 154
Althusser, Louis, 298
Anagnost, Ann, 301
Andeanism, 6
Anderson, Benedict, 59
anthropology, 6, 7; as global Cold War project, 227; and identification of difference, 226; and

methodology, 7–8; and the state, 5, 6–8, 23
anticolonial insecurities, 149
anticolonialism: and identity, 135; in Indian security imaginary, 128, 136; in Soviet Union and India, 142; in United States and India, 121, 122, 140–142
antinuclear movement, 213, 327; and LANL, 222, 223; and plutonium economy, 222–224; and post-Cold War insecurity, 224; and U.S. government secrecy, 222–223
Aotearoa, 246, 247, 253; defined, 259 n. 1
Appadurai, Arjun, 8
appeasement narrative, 103–104
Arab-Israeli war of 1973, 165
Arab League, 162
Arab National Congress, 158
arms race, 328; as ontological assumption, 330, 332, 333–334
ARPANet, 268, 269, 285

Yao, 301; and representation, 14; as reproduced in crises, 53–55; and security imaginary, 124–125. *See also* difference

identity, collective: bureaucratic, 179–180; and encryption debate, 274, 276; formation of, 91, 94, 115; and intervention, 91

Ikhwan al-Muslimin, 159, 160. *See also* Muslim Brotherhood

immigration policy: and identity, 238; and New Zealand identity, 243–249

imperialism: of Soviet Union in Korea, 97, 114; and state system, 152; of United States in Caribbean crisis, 38; of United States in Korea, 98, 104; of United States in Philippines, 99–100; Western, 99, 155, 156

India: as hailed by United States in Korean War, 105–109; independence of, 122, 127, 129, 130, 138–139; relations with Soviet Union, 121–123; relations with United States, 121–123; security imaginary as postcolonial, 120; and Soviet security imaginary, 133–142; United States as threat to, 120; and U.S. security imaginary, 133–142

indifference: and bureaucracy, 185–193; defined, 185–186; sources of, 185–186

Indo-Pak Wars, 122, 123

information capitalism, 266, 284

Information Processing Techniques Office (IPTO), 267, 268, 269

insecurity: collective, 93, 95; and construction of state, 14–15; culture of in UN, 199–200; decentered approach to, 225–226;

defined in security studies, 9–10; and disciplines, 347–348, 352; as discursive construction, 92; geoeconomic, 236; indigenous in New Mexico, 213–218; and interacting security imaginaries, 142–145; naturalization of, 20–21; for New Zealand state and capital, 235, 239; as object of analysis, 10; and production of identity, 10; regional in Middle East, 148–150; and representation, 14; and security imaginaries, 120; as social and cultural production, 10–13; technology dimension, 265; theorization of, 347

Institute of Policy Studies, 250, 251, 254, 255

interdisciplinarity: as conversation, 2, 24–25; crisis of, 348, 350–351, 357; 360–361; and disciplinary power, 349; and end of Cold War, 348; as exchange, 21–22; and Foucault, 348; paradox of, 348–349

Interim (INF) Treaty (1987), 329, 331, 332

international community, 95; and indifference, 185; as moral order, 196; redefined after Cold War, 189–190; and Rwandan genocide, 184, 193–199; and Security Council, 193–199; and UN as bureaucracy, 187–188

International Monetary Fund (IMF), 233, 236

international organizations, politics of, 200

international relations, 2, 3–5, 17, 23; and crises, 56; and end of Cold War, 337–338; and explanation

UN Charter, 188
United Nations Department of
Peacekeeping Operations
(DPKO), 175, 180–181
United Nations High Commission
for Refugees (UNHCR), 201
United Nations Operation in
Rwanda (UNAMIR), 173,
180–182, 183, 195
United Nations Secretariat,
180–182; defined, 202 n. 1; and
genocide, 184; and international
community defined, 189; and
policy toward Rwanda, 197;
and Security Council, 181; and
UN interests, 200–201
United Nations Security Council,
105, 106, 112; and criteria for
peacekeeping, 191–193; defined,
202 n. 1; and genocide in
Rwanda, 184, 193–199; and
international community defined, 189; and intervention in
Rwanda, 182, 197–199; and
language of genocide, 198; and
peacekeeping, 173; and peacekeeping in Rwanda, 174,
180–183; as representative of
international community, 194;
and UN interests, 200–201
United States: criticism of UN inaction in Rwanda, 183; national
interest, 179, 193–194; policy
on peacekeeping in Rwanda,
174; relations with India,
119–120; and role of Security
Council in Rwanda, 195; security imaginary of, 133–142
U.S. Declaration of Independence,
205
U.S. Department of Defense (DOD),
266

U.S. Department of Energy,
312–214, 216, 222, 224; and
LANL, 210; and nuclear waste
storage, 216, 225
United States Justice Department,
282–283
U.S. Mission to the United Nations,
173
United States of Mexico, 205
U.S.–Soviet relations: as focus of security studies, 320; and ICBM
modernization, 331; in International Security, 322–323, 328
U.S. state identity: and credibility,
47–48; and Cuban missile crisis,
41, 48–56; and freedom, 43–44;
and leadership, 42–44; as masculinist, 42, 46, 48, 50; as reenacted in Cuban missile crisis,
53–54; and strength and will,
46; and the West, 116
Utgoff, Victor, 328

Valdevit, Giampaolo, 78
Varga, Eugene, 139
Vasil, Raj, 255
Von Justi, J. G., 356, 357

Walden, David, 269
Walker, Ranginui, 247, 252
Walt, Stephen, 56, 149
Waltz, Kenneth, 339–340
Waste Isolation Pilot Plant, 206
Watts, Michael John, 234
Weber, Cynthia, 95–96
Weber, Max, 186
West, the, 92, 122; and colonial
encounter in Middle East,
149–152; as democratic,
100–101; and Islamic revival-
ism, 166; as a social construc-
tion, 15, 114–115; as superior,

99–100; and threat to Ottoman
Empire, 153–156
Western Hemisphere, 43, 48, 49
White New Zealand policy, 243–244
White Sands Missile Range, 206
Williams, Michael, 4
Williams, Raymond, 1
Wilson, Woodrow, 73
Wohlforth, Wolfgang, 340, 341
World Bank, 236

Xiaoping, Deng, 294

Yanagisako, Sylvia, 5
Yao: and Chinese cultural diversity,
301; and Chinese state narratives, 297–302; and civilized
village campaign, 300, 309,
311–313; culture of, 297;
defined, 295; and discourse of
social morality, 309–313, 314;
popular ritual of, 295; and resurgence of popular ritual, 300,

303–309, 315; as traditional,
298–299; and politics of surveil-
lance, 309
Yoon, Hong-Key, 255
York, Herbert, 325
Young Ottomans, 155
Young Turks, 155, 156
Yugoslavia, breakup of, 65; and
Korean war, 107; and occupa-
tion of Trieste, 70; and struc-
tural adjustment, 256; war in
former, 82, 88, 115
Yugoslav-Soviet split, 75

Zabusky, Stacia, 201
Zhakov, E. M., 139
Zigante, Denis, 77
Zimmerman, Philip, 261, 271, 281,
285, 287, 289; and legal case,
263, 265–266, 274–275; legal
case dropped, 282–283, 288
Zuoren, Zhou, 310